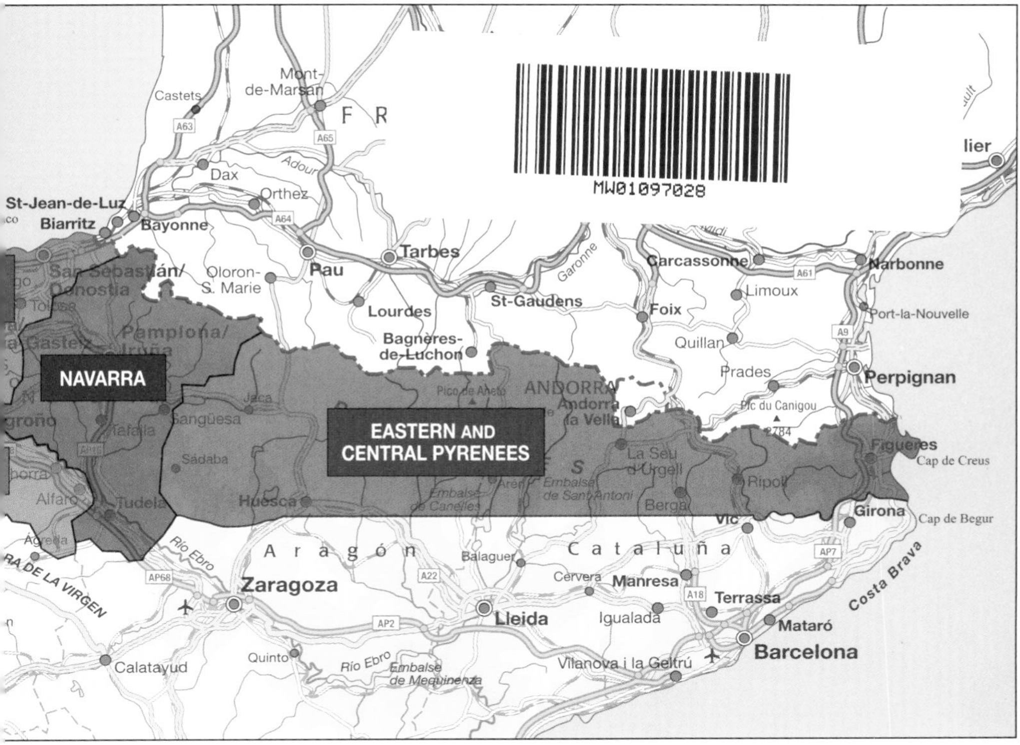

NAVARRA
EASTERN AND CENTRAL PYRENEES
St-Jean-de-Luz
Biarritz
Bayonne
Castets
Mont-de-Marsan
Dax
Orthez
Adour
Pau
Tarbes
Oloron-S. Marie
Lourdes
Bagnères-de-Luchon
St-Gaudens
Garonne
Carcassonne
Narbonne
Limoux
Foix
Quillan
Port-la-Nouvelle
Prades
Perpignan
Pic du Canigou
2784
Pico de Aneto
ANDORRA
Andorra la Vella
La Seu d'Urgell
Ripoll
Figueres
Cap de Creus
Berga
Girona
Cap de Begur
Vic
San Sebastián/Donostia
Pamplona/Iruña
Jaca
Sangüesa
Tafalla
Sádaba
Alfaro
Tudela
Huesca
Agreda
Aragón
Cataluña
Balaguer
Río Ebro
Zaragoza
Lleida
Cervera
Manresa
Terrassa
Igualada
Mataró
Barcelona
Costa Brava
Embalse de Canelles
Embalse de Sant Antoni
Calatayud
Quinto
Río Ebro
Embalse de Mequinenza
Vilanova i la Geltrú
A63
A65
A64
A61
A9
AP68
A22
AP2
A18
AP7

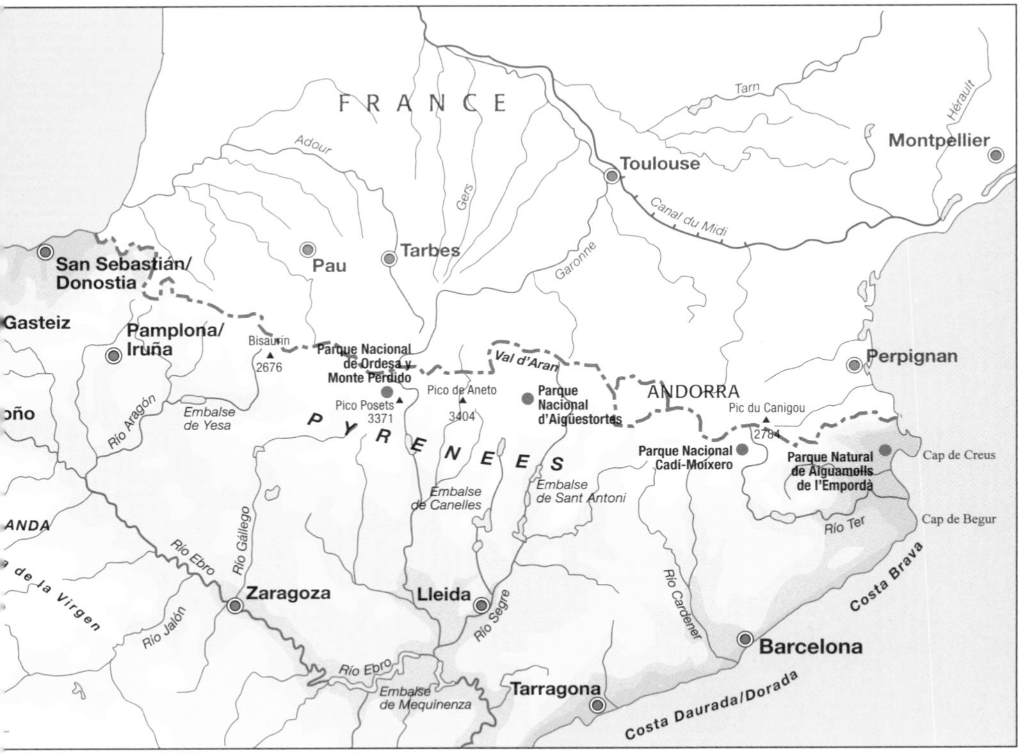

FRANCE
Adour
Tarn
Hérault
Montpellier
Toulouse
Canal du Midi
Gers
Garonne
Pau
Tarbes
San Sebastián/Donostia
Gasteiz
Pamplona/Iruña
Bisaurin
2676
Parque Nacional de Ordesa y Monte Perdido
Pico Posets
3371
Pico de Aneto
3404
Val d'Aran
Parque Nacional d'Aigüestortes
ANDORRA
Pic du Canigou
2784
Perpignan
Parque Nacional Cadí-Moixero
Parque Natural de Aiguamolls de l'Empordà
Cap de Creus
Cap de Begur
PYRENEES
Río Aragón
Embalse de Yesa
Embalse de Canelles
Embalse de Sant Antoni
Río Ter
Río Gállego
Río Ebro
Río Cardener
Costa Brava
Zaragoza
Lleida
Río Segre
Barcelona
Río Jalón
Río Ebro
Embalse de Mequinenza
Tarragona
Costa Daurada/Dorada

INSIGHT GUIDES

# NORTHERN SPAIN

# PLAN & BOOK
# YOUR TAILOR-MADE TRIP

## TAILOR-MADE TRIPS & UNIQUE EXPERIENCES CREATED BY LOCAL TRAVEL EXPERTS AT INSIGHTGUIDES.COM/HOLIDAYS

Insight Guides has been inspiring travellers with high-quality travel content for over 45 years. As well as our popular guidebooks, we now offer the opportunity to book tailor-made private trips completely personalised to your needs and interests. By connecting with one of our local experts, you will directly benefit from their expertise and local know-how, helping you create memories that will last a lifetime.

## HOW INSIGHTGUIDES.COM/HOLIDAYS WORKS

**STEP 1**

Pick your dream destination and submit an enquiry, or modify an existing itinerary if you prefer.

**STEP 2**

Fill in a short form, sharing details of your travel plans and preferences with a local expert.

**STEP 3**

Your local expert will create your personalised itinerary, which you can amend until you are completely satisfied.

**STEP 4**

Book securely online. Pack your bags and enjoy your holiday! Your local expert will be available to answer questions during your trip.

# CONTENTS

## Introduction



## History & Features



## Places

## Travel Tips

### TRANSPORT



### A – Z



### ANGUAGE



### FURTHER READING



## Maps



### LEGEND

Insight on
Photo Story

# THE BEST OF NORTHERN SPAIN: TOP ATTRACTIONS

△ **Bilbao and the Guggenheim Museum**. Frank Gehry's futuristic, titanium-covered art gallery commands the riverside in the exciting Basque city of Bilbao, which has made a reputation for itself as a vibrant centre for art, culture – and good living. See page 180.

▽ **San Sebastian**. A wide beach extending around a perfect horseshoe bay with a castle at one end, a funfair at the other and an island in the middle make this Spain's most stately resort. See page 187.

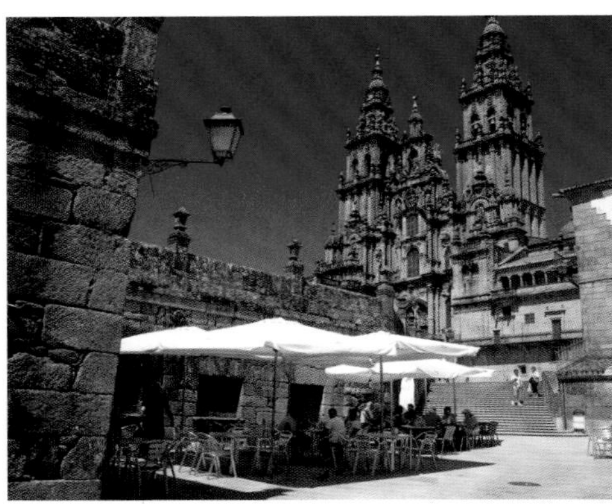

△ **Santiago de Compostela**. Every year, thousands of pilgrims walk across northern Spain to this magnificent city. The city-centre, a harmonious cluster of historic buildings gathered around the Baroque facade of the cathedral, never disappoints. See page 255.

△ **Picos de Europa**. These attractive mountains
easily accessible on a day-trip from the north
They offer a variety of dramatic scenery
walk through, and a wealth of butterf
wildflowers to discover. See page 21

△ **Santillana del Mar**. As if preserved in time, Santillana is the perfect, well-to-do medieval town and has been called "the prettiest place in Spain". A great place to stroll and take in the atmosphere. See page 202.

▷ **Pre-Romanesque churches of Asturias**. Exquisite early churches dot the ancient green landscapes of Asturias. They developed their singular characteristics apart from other architectural traditions and each is a gem worth visiting in its own right. See page 222.

◁ **Sanfermines Fiesta, Pamplona**. The fiesta lover's fiesta is internationally famous for its early morning run of bulls mingled with humans through the narrow streets: an adrenalin rush just watching it from behind a barricade. See page 156.

**edral**. The first of Spain's great Gothic of the power of the Castilian kings. It r-shaped vaulting and holds the ng hero, El Cid. See page 235.

△ **Ordesa National Park and the Pyrenees**. Spectacular hikes and elusive wildlife lure hikers and climbers to this high-altitude national park that crosses the border into France. The scenery is magnificent even if you don't feel energetic. See page 149.

▽ **San Juan de la Peña monastery**. Built under a dramatic rock overhang in a remote location in the hills, this ancient Romanesque monastery is said for a time to have been one of the custodians of the Holy Grail. See page 150.

# THE BEST OF NORTHERN SPAIN: EDITOR'S CHOICE

## MOST BEAUTIFUL TOWNS AND VILLAGES

**Covarrubias**. This pretty town is a delightful cluster of half-timbered houses around a handsome church on the banks of the Río Arlanza. See page 241.

**Laguardia**. Rioja wine-making is the main trade of this medieval town on top of a hill enclosed by ramparts and gateways. See page 194.

**Besalú**. Important in the middle ages, this town has preserved a medieval nucleus together with a synagogue and a picturesque bridge. See page 140.

**Alquézar**. A well-restored medieval hill town in Aragon's wild Sierra de Guara, organised around an 11th-century collegiate church. See page 152.

**Anciles**. A delightful renovated village of stone mansions and narrow streets at the end of a winding lane from Benasque. See page 148.

*The picturesque hill town of Alquézar.*

*Besalú's medieval bridge.*

## BEST CASTLES

**Olite**. A fantasy castle of fairy-tale spires built by Carlos the Noble in the 15th century, with Mudéjar decorations inside. See page 161.

**Loarre**. This Romanesque fortress stands on a superb vantage point in the foothills of the Pyrenees and looks over the lowlands of Aragón. See page 152.

**Javier (Xavier)**. The birthplace of Saint Francis Xavier, the patron saint of Navarre is a pleasing fusion of three buildings, including a church. See page 166.

**Monterrei**. This palace-fortress complex stands on a hill overlooking the Támega and is one of the best-preserved fortresses in Galicia. See page 261.

*Castle of Loarre.*

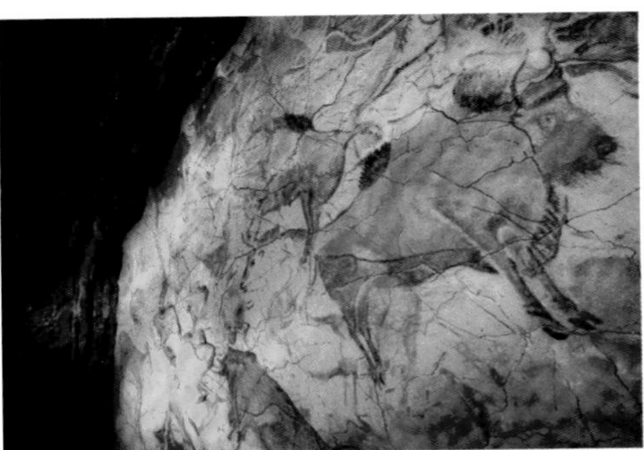

*Replica of the Cave of Altamira.*

## BEST CAVES

**Altamira**. The authentic "Sistine Chapel of Stone Age Art" can only be visited with luck, but the on-site museum contains a convincing replica. See page 203.

**Tito Bustillo**. Numbers of visitors are restricted to see the dozen marvellous prehistoric paintings here, which date from 40,000 years ago. See page 229.

**Valporquero**. This extensive limestone cavern in northern León has many chambers with beautiful stalactite and stalagmite formations that are sensitively illuminated. See page 248.

**Covadonga**. A shrine to the Virgin Mary has been built in this cavern on the edge of the Picos de Europa. See page 214.

**Zugarramurdi**. In olden days witches used to gather in this immense cavern in light woodland in Navarra, close to the French border. See page 164.

## BEST COASTAL RESORTS

**Cadaqués**. An attractive whitewashed, flower-decked town on the northern part of the Costa Brava on the Mediterranean, associated with the artist Salvador Dalí. See page 139.

**Castro Urdiales**. A prominent Gothic church and the remains of a Templar castle stand by the attractive harbour filled with fishing boats. See page 209.

**Hondarribia**. A historic Basque town at the mouth of the Bidasoa river, connected by ferry to its opposite number, Hendaye in France. See page 190.

**Costa Verde**. The "Green Coast" of Asturias has several pretty harbour and beach towns, including Luarca and Cudillero. See page 226.

*Santo Domingo de Silos monastery.*

## BEST CHURCHES AND MONASTERIES

**Valle de Boí**. This secluded valley in the Catalan Pyrenees has a stunning collection of Romanesque churches each distinguished by a tall bell tower. See page 147.

**Santo Domingo de Silos**. The monks' regular Gregorian plainsong chanting is a highlight of this elegant working monastery, which is also a centre for Mozarabic studies. See page 242.

**Monasterio de Suso**. This curious, ancient cave church was carved out of the rock in Romanesque and Mozarabic style. See page 174.

**Panteon de los Reyes, León**. An extraordinary collection of brilliant 12th-century murals, showing religious scenes and medieval daily life, decorates this Romanesque chamber. See page 247.

**León Catedral**. Renowned for its extraordinary stained glass, this cathedral is illuminated by 125 large windows, the oldest dating from the 13th century. See page 246.

*The pretty coastal town of Cudillero.*

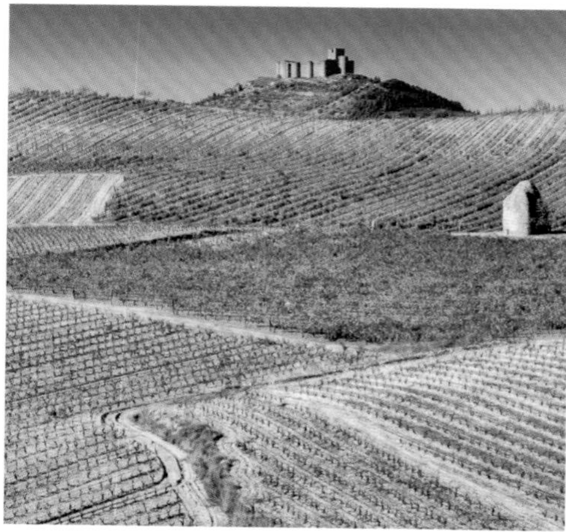

*Vineyards in autumn, La Rioja.*

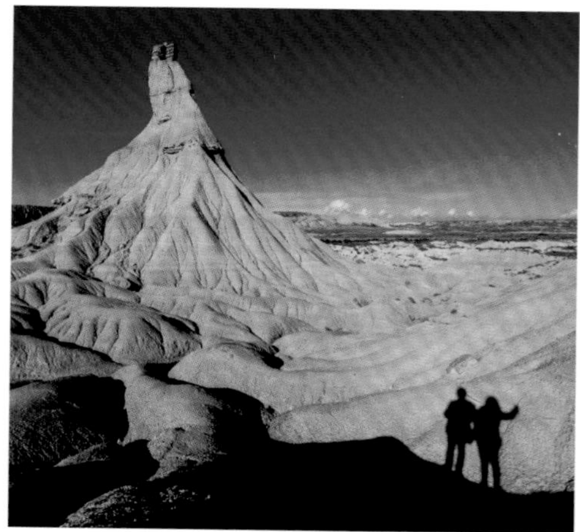

*Las Bardenas Reales, Navarra.*

## BEST WINE REGIONS

**Empordà**. Producers in this wine region in the north of Catalonia have marked out a route for visitors to follow. See page 71.

**La Rioja**. Spain's wine region par excellence is geared up for wine touring. Some of the more prestigious producers have invested in stunning architecture. See page 171.

**Rías Baixas**. The heavily indented Atlantic coastline of Galicia is not only a scenic treat but also produces fine white wines. See page 269.

**Txakoli**. This lesser-known light white wine is produced by vineyards on the Basque coast and best sampled in the town of Getaria. See page 186.

## BEST LANDSCAPES

**Parc Nacional d'Aigüestortes**. The lakes, woods and waterfalls of this mountain national park are home to golden eagles, otters and other wildlife. See page 145.

**Bardenas Reales**. When the road gives out you find yourself in a desert, with astonishing, eroded rock formations all around. See page 162.

**Cies islands**. To enjoy the wild seascapes of this Atlantic archipelago-cum-national park you have to take a boat trip from Vigo or Baiona. See page 266.

**Río Sil gorges, Galicia**. There are a great many scenic gorges all across northern Spain and this is one of the longest and finest. See page 261.

*Estany Negre, Parc Nacional d'Aïguestortes.*

## BEST MUSEUMS

**Mining Museum, El Entrego**. Asturias's industrial heritage is explained in this repurposed coal mine where the hard life of the miner is recreated. See page 229.

**Museum of Evolution, Burgos**. The human story from the earliest times is explored in this museum related to the revolutionary excavations in the Sierra de Atapuerca. See page 237.

**Cider Museum**. Cider is the preferred drink in much of the north and here you can discover the secrets of its elaboration. See page 229.

**Teatre-Museu Dalí (Figueres)**. The eccentric, surrealist artist Salvador Dalí is responsible for this uniquely theatrical museum of the absurd, which amuses and bemuses in equal measure. See page 140.

*The Mae West room at the Teatre-Museu Dalí.*

*San Sebastián is famous for its pintxos.*

## BEST CITIES FOR TAPAS

**San Sebastián**. Famous for its ranks of bar-top tapas, here known as *pintxos*. One good street to start with is Calle 21 de Agosto. See page 187.

**Logroño**. The capital of Riojan wine is supposed to have Spain's greatest concentration of tapas bars. Try especially Calle del Laurel and Calle San Juan. See page 170.

**León**. The open secret here is that the tapas are free. Start in the Barrio Humedo then move on to the Barrio Romántico. See page 245.

**Vigo**. Fish and other seafood are to the fore in this port city and oysters are a speciality. Calle Bouzas is the best place to head for. See page 265.

**Bilbao**. There are *pintxo* bars all over the city. The old quarter, Casco Viejo, is a favourite but also try Calles Ledesma, Diputación and Poza. See page 180.

## BEST CAMINO DE SANTIAGO STOPS

**Roncesvalles**. This town beneath a mountain pass on the border with France is the starting point of the pilgrimage in Spain. See page 164.

**Puente la Reina**. The two main routes of the pilgrimage meet here to cross a photogenic hump-backed bridge. Just outside the town is the enigmatic chapel of Eunate. See page 159.

**Santo Domingo de la Calzada**. The cathedral here permanently houses a cock and a hen in commemoration of a local miracle by St Dominic. See page 173.

**Estella**. Several remarkable churches and a royal palace draw visitors to this historic town on a meander of the Río Ega. See page 160.

**Astorga**. The Catalan architect, Antoni Gaudí, better known for his work in Barcelona, designed the bishop's palace in this town. See page 248.

*The bishop's palace in Astorga.*

*The Camino de Santiago near Castrojeriz, Burgos.*

*Wild horses rounded up during the Rapa das Bestas (Shearing of the Beasts) festival in Sabucedo, Galicia.*

*Sheep grazing in Parque Natural Bardenas Reales.*

The causeway at Cudillero.

# SPAIN'S NORTHERN KINGDOMS

Northern Spain is a wild and rugged landscape, divided by many mountains, cultures and tongues.

The writer H.V. Morton, visiting the Picos de Europa in the early 1950s, wrote: "Nothing I had seen in Spain impressed me more than this glimpse of the Asturias."

The world's stereotypical image of Spain is all to do with flamenco, bulls, guitars and gypsy folklore, but all of these belong to the south. There is an entirely different country to the north of the great central meseta, around Madrid, which is just as Spanish but less well known. The mountainous topography and cooler, wetter climate, which is influenced more by the Atlantic than the Mediterranean (with the Pyrenees linking the two seas), gives rise to lush landscapes: deep green valleys, forests of conifers, meadows and Alpine pastures.

Yet the north could claim to be more than another Spain. The emergence of the modern Spanish state and the fusion of Islamic and Christian cultures owe much to the tenacity of the northern kingdoms of Asturias, Navarra, Aragón, Galicia, Castile and León, whose legacy is some of the most important medieval palaces, churches and cathedrals in Europe.

Cathedrals Beach, Galicia.

This is a diverse region. The fact that, within just a few hundred miles, no fewer than 14 distinct dialects and languages still flourish is a measure of the remoteness, as well as the fierce individuality of the people. The scenery varies from the desert of Navarra's Bardenas Reales to the forests of Asturias, home to the brown bear.

For the visitor, there are plenty of reasons to spend a holiday in the north. There are fantastic festivals – such as Pamplona's celebrated early morning bull running – and fabulous food fresh from the land and the sea. Hay meadows and fertile valleys produce refreshing wcider and intensely aromatic cheese, as well as some of the best wines in Spain. Wildlife abounds in remoter areas. There are even holiday resorts: smaller, more modest and more charming than those in the south.

### A NOTE TO READERS

At Insight Guides, we always strive to bring you the most up-to-date information. This book was produced during a period of continuing uncertainty caused by the Covid-19 pandemic, so please note that content is more subject to change than usual. We recommend checking the latest restrictions and official guidance.

*Zarramaco, La Vijanera carnival.*

# PEOPLE OF NORTHERN SPAIN

The identity of the people of northern Spain is a complex tapestry formed by history, language and territory in interaction with the modern world.

Cross the bridge from Hendaye into Irún in the Basque Country; or traverse the Minho river to reach Tui in Galicia; or take the coast road from Cerbere to Portbou in Catalonia; or step off the ferry from Britain onto the harbourside of Santander in Cantabria and one thing is sure: you will be in another country to the one you left. The language spoken and written up around you will be different; the shops and bars will be different; and so will be the lifestyle of the people you encounter.

So far, so obvious, but that will only give you the most superficial information about the inhabitants of northern Spain. To get a fuller understanding of their thoughts and motivations, its necessary to answer four questions simultaneously: What makes the Spanish, Spanish? How do the people of northern Spain differ from the people of the rest of the country (the centre and the south)? How do the people of northern Spain differ among themselves? How is the society of northern Spain evolving?

*Basque muscians in Irún.*

## BEING SPANISH

To be Spanish means, of course, to live in a particular unit of political geography that corresponds pretty well to an area of physical geography. Spain is neatly defined by seas and oceans on three sides and the Pyrenees across a fourth – forming as clear a demarcation line as you could wish for across its northern border. Only the frontier with Portugal is the result of rivalry and negotiation rather than topography, sometimes following rivers sometimes not.

The modern nation of Spain is the result of waves of historical unification. Sometimes this has been with the consent of the peoples; sometimes without. The shared capital and seat of central government is Madrid although Barcelona fulfils many of the functions of a joint-capital city, such as hosting the headquarters of the mass media.

The people are therefore held together by common geography, history and politics but the greatest tie between them is the lingua franca of Castilian, known in other countries as Spanish, which has formed the country's lowbrow and highbrow culture.

Another common denominator is religion that, with few exceptions, means Roman Catholicism. Not everyone is a believer and attendance at mass everywhere is very sparse, but the Church still has great influence over society. Catholicism permeates much of life, providing the most common Christian names; the names of streets and squares; and innumerable saying and jokes. Religion also dictates the structure of the calendar: almost all public holidays are connected to holy feast days even if they are celebrated in earthly, secular ways.

The people in Spain also have many daily customs in common, notably their attitude to eating. Mealtimes are often described as "late" for people from other countries and, having eaten dinner at 10pm or later, Spaniards think nothing of going out for the night when other Europeans are going to bed.

It is always a mistake, however, to generalise too far about any country and it is essential to remember the differences between people. The two most significant of these in Spain are gender and age. Despite decades of advances in the rights of Spanish women, their experiences of life can still vary greatly from men's. The deepest division, though, is generational: a clear distinction can be drawn between those who remember life under a dictatorship and have a personal connection to the strife of the past, and those who have known nothing but the freedoms granted by democracy.

*A Coruña fish market.*

## OPUS DEI

Opus Dei, the conservative Catholic lay order, has long been a networking path to success in Spain. Encouraging endeavour in business and the professions, it acts as a kind of masonic lodge. It was founded in 1928 by Monsignor José María Escrivá de Balaguer, son of a shopkeeper from Aragón, and flourished under Franco. Opus members consider their works to be religious statements, and the strictest live in celibacy in the order's private dormitories. Its main centre, the Estudio General de Navarra near Pamplona, attracts the high flyers. Escrivá was beatified in 1992, a record 17 years after his death, and canonised in October 2002.

## THE NORTH VERSUS THE REST

You only have to spend a short while in northern Spain to realise that it does not conform to the image of "typical" Spain: bulls, flamenco, guitars, package holidays, windmills, arid plains and all the rest. There is no exact dividing line between "northern Spain" and the rest of the country but there is certainly a zone of transition somewhere north of a line drawn from Barcelona to Valladolid via Zaragoza (roughly following the Ebro river in the east). Northern Spain begins where the meseta, the great plateau that forms of the centre of Spain, gives way to the mountains of the Pyrenees and the Cordillera Cantabrica.

Heading north off the meseta, there is a definite change in the landscape and climate and this has an effect on how people live. Simply put, northern Spain is cooler and wetter than the rest. Much of it is influenced by the Atlantic rather than the Mediterranean: travelling along the Pyrenees you actually notice the shift from one climate zone to the other. The characteristic types of vegetation of the north are evergreen woods and lush prairies filled with wildflowers.

Whereas in southern and central Spain you actively seek shade, in the north you are grateful to see the sun at all. The south expects and gets little rainfall and life is lived outdoors; in the north people live with one wary eye on the clouds and traditionally they made much larger houses in which to endure the long months of winter. The colder climate allows farmers only a shorter growing season and limits the crops they can plant. All this has made the people of the north generally more introverted and prudent: planning and storing are prized as virtues over spontaneity and exuberance.

*Local villagers mark a wild horse, Galicia.*

## DIVISIONS ACROSS THE NORTH

That's where the similarities across the north end. Now things get more complicated. There is one glaring issue that divides up the people of north: whether or not they describe "Spanish" as their primary form of identity.

At either end of the Pyrenees two great nation groups exist uneasily within the Spanish State. In both the Basque Country and Catalonia, the respective regional language, history and culture are extoled and there are even calls for independence. Galicia also has a strong conception of its own regional identity but to a much lesser extent.

Significantly, both the Basque Country and Catalonia are places of industry and enterprise, and hence prosperity and employment, underpinning the self-confidence felt in these two regions. They are also the only two regions of Spain with easy access to the rest of Europe and they pride themselves on being open to influences from the north more than the south.

## BASQUES

The most conspicuously self-identifying group in northern Spain are the Basques. Just how different they are – whether they can claim to be a separate "race" or not – is a controversial topic. They have certainly preserved their culture for centuries and their own language, Euskara. The only non-Indo-European language still spoken in Western Europe, Euskara is thought to be descended from the language spoken by Aboriginal Iberian peoples. In other parts of Spain, the Basques are frequently portrayed as gruff, grave, dour and not very sociable characters, but also businesslike and efficient. In their defence, Basques say they might not be overly friendly at first meeting, but that when they finally offer you friendship, they give it completely and honestly. Culturally, they value plain talking and physical strength – as demonstrated by their muscle-breaking sports: stone-lifting, wood-chopping, weight-carrying, caber-tossing (see page 116).

## CATALANS

The Catalans have a strong sense of their own history and written culture as being connected to that of Spain but also independent from it. The Catalan language has similarities to both French and Castilian but has been a separate language since at least the 12th century.

Stereotypically, Catalans are seen by outsiders as materialistic, humourless and stingy. But to Catalans, this is to misread their virtues as vices. To them, the essence of being Catalan is *seny*, a term as vague as it is useful, which is usually translated as "profound common sense". Instead of being indolent or frivolous, Catalans like to think of themselves as deeply pragmatic types who are able to exercise sound commercial judgement and prudence. To Catalan entrepreneurs, to have *seny* means to be formal when conducting business, to fulfil all contractual obligations strictly and to treat honourably everyone involved in economic production, from worker to businessman.

*Tapas bar on Calle del Laurel in the old town of Logroño.*

## GALICIANS

Gallegos (Galicians) have the reputation among other Spaniards of being thrifty, energetic characters. But since they inhabit a traditionally impoverished corner of the peninsula that is only now gaining economic power, the term Gallego has also come to mean a boor or country bumpkin. Rural Galicians are often seen as superstitious, mainly because many of them so easily blend their popular form of Catholicism with beliefs about the evil eye, the efficacy of magic, and the existence of witches and sorcerers. General Franco, the dictator of Spain for three and a half decades, was Galician.

## PEOPLE IN BETWEEN

With the Basques and Catalans (and Galicians much less so) getting all the headlines, it is easy to overlook the regions in between them, which have a much less defined sense of identity. Aragón, Asturias, Cantabria, La Rioja and Castilla y León are all autonomous regions in their own right and their inhabitants are proud of where they live but for mainly historical reasons none of them have developed a strong, clear regional cultural identity. They do not claim their particular dialects are separate languages and their local politics are not enlivened by nationalist secessionists but by much more middle-of-the-road regionalists.

## DISCRIMINATED MINORITIES

Because the north is mainly mountainous and communications in many places were difficult in the past, some small communities developed their own curious identities and this has sometimes drawn opprobrium from their neighbours. For instance, on the western edge of Asturias live the Vaqueiros de Alzada, herders who, every April, move their cattle up to the crests and slopes of the mountains to take advantage of the summer pastures. Discriminated against in church, they have developed their own eclectic set of beliefs about the supernatural and about the way the process of dying begins long before the moment of death.

On the southern mountain slopes of Cantabria, meanwhile, the descendants of the Pasiegos live on. Until modernity arrived, the Pasiegos were herders who would keep their cattle continually moving from one pasture to another. In the course of a year, they would move more than 20 times, which is a record among traditional herders throughout the whole of Europe. Their way of life has now practically died out but some of their traditions live on.

Both Vaqueros and Pasiegos were long regarded as being among the *pueblos malditos* (despised people) of Spain. Usually, judgements made about them by outsiders were the result of prejudice rather than fact; often they were given a fanciful origin as a back story. The same applies to the Maragatos, the traditional carters who come from Astorga in the Montes de León (see page 248): it is often said, with very little reason, that they are descended from old Jewish or Moorish communities or some sort of "lost tribe".

## THE EVOLVING SOCIETY

In discussing people anywhere it is easy to get swept up in the past and overlook the present and the future. No society is static and northern Spain has seen big changes in recent decades. The old heavy industries have declined radically and the service sector, with less place-related forms of work and more instable contracts, has grown to fill its place, loosening the binding ropes of tradition. Agriculture and fishing have simultaneously declined as Spain has merged into the EU. These changes have affected whole communities: sometimes the dominant local employer has closed its doors and the young have had to find new ways to make a living.

Migration has always been a theme of Spanish society and this has greatly affected the north. Until about the 1980s, Spain sent emigrants to France, Germany, South America and elsewhere in search of any unskilled work they could find and many came back with wealth and new cultural connections. Then, as the Spanish economy boomed, things switched the other way. Spain in its term has become the receiver of mass migration from South America, Eastern Europe and Africa. This has had a visible impact on society. Less obvious is the amount of internal migration that has taken place over the last decades, especially with people from Andalucia, in the south, moving to the Basque Country and Catalonia where employment prospects are better. All these demographic changes make the cultural mosaic of northern Spain ever richer and more complex.

*Las Marzas rural carnival in the Soba Valley.*

*El Pendo cave paintings.*

# DECISIVE DATES

**800,000 BC**
*Homo erectus* living in the Sierra de Atapuerca, near Burgos.

**200,000 BC**
Cave paintings in Altamira and Tito Bustillo.

**1,000 BC**
Celts arrive, bringing pottery skills.

**600 BC**
Greeks set up trading post at Emporion, on the Costa Brava.

**211 BC**
Romans arrive in Spain and begin 200-year subjugation. Asturias and Cantabria are the last places to be conquered, around 19 BC.

**75 BC**
Pompey founds Pamplona.

**476**
Collapse of the Western Roman Empire. Alans, Suevi and Vandals pour into Spain, followed by the Visigoths, who remain and convert to Christianity.

**711**
Moors enter Spain and defeat Visigoths.

## THE RECONQUEST

**718**
Pelayo, a Visigothic chief, leads first victory against Moors and establishes kingdom of Asturias.

**778**
Charlemagne's troops defeated at Roncesvalles.

*Charlemagne in the battle in the valley of Roncesvalles on August 15, 778.*

**792–842**
Alfonso II builds San Julián de los Prados, Oviedo, Spain's largest pre-Romanesque church.

**813**
Tomb of St James (Santiago) is reputedly found in Galicia.

**842–50**
Normans invade the coast.

**844**
St James apparently aids Ramiro I of Asturias in a victory over the Moors at Clavijo, near Logroño.

**866–910**
Alfonso III (El Magno) moves capital of Asturias to León.

**10th Century**
Moors briefly gain Barcelona, León and Santiago de Compostela.

**910–70**
Fernán González gains autonomy from León for the county of Castile.

**988**
Catalonia claims independence from Franks.

**1000–35**
Sancho the Great confirms and extends kingdom of Navarra.

**1037**
Fernando I of Castile seizes León and unites the two kingdoms.

**1094**
Valencia captured from the Moors by El Cid.

**1126–57**
Under Queen Urraca of Castile, Spain's first navy is formed by Archbishop Gelmírez of Santiago.

**1137**
Petronila of Aragón marries Ramón Berenguer IV of Barcelona, uniting the two houses.

**1143**
Alfonso Henriques, grandson of Alfonso VI of Castile-León, crowned first king of Portugal.

**1158**
The first military order of knights, the Order of Calatrava, established by Cistercians. The Order of Santiago is established 22 years later.

**1205**
León cathedral consecrated.

**1208**
Spain's first university founded at Palencia.

**1212**
The combined forces of Aragón, Castile and Navarra defeat the Moors at Las Navas de Tolosa.

**1229**
Jaime I, El Conquistador of Barcelona-Aragón, begins conquest of Balearic Islands.

**1282**
Sicily ceded to the crown of Aragón.

**1386**
Invasion of Galicia by British.

**1406**
Palace built for Carlos III of Navarra in Olite.

*Signing of the Treaty of Tordesillas.*

## UNITED SPAIN

**1469**
Isabel of Castile marries Fernando of Aragón, uniting Catholic Spain.

**1480**
Inquisition established in Castile.

**1491**
Birth of Ignatius Loyola, founder of the Jesuits.

**1492**
Moors finally driven from Spain by Isabel and Fernando. Columbus reaches the New World.

**1494**
Treaty of Tordesillas divides the non-European world between Spain and Portugal.

**1500**
Juan de la Cosa draws first map of New World.

**1512**
Fernando takes Navarra by force, completing Spain's unification.

## THE HOUSE OF HABSBURG

**1516**
Carlos I lands on the Asturian coast to become Carlos V of Spain, declaring "I speak Spanish to God, Italian to my wife and German to my horse." He becomes Holy Roman Emperor in 1520.

**1519–21**
Unsuccessful rising of *comuneros* against appointment of foreigners to court.

**1521**
Juan Sebastián Elkano returns to Spain, completing Magellan's round-the-world voyage.

**1540**
Basque university founded at Oñati.

**1560**
Madrid established as capital of Spain.

**1580**
Portugal comes under Spanish Crown.

**1588**
Defeat of the Armada, followed by raids on La Coruña and Vigo (1599) under Sir Francis Drake.

**1609**
The remaining Moors expelled from Spain.

**1618**
Spain becomes involved in the Thirty Years' War against France.

**1640**
Revolt and lasting independence of Portugal. Catalonia declared a republic, which lasts 12 years.

**1659**
Peace of the Pyrenees ends the Thirty Years' War and draws

*Philip V of Spain.*

the border between France and Spain.

**1700–14**
War of the Spanish Succession between Habsburg and Bourbon claimants to the throne.

## THE HOUSE OF BOURBON

**1714**
Felipe V (Philip of Anjou) exacts retribution on Catalonia for supporting Habsburg claims in the War of Succession.

**1808–13**
The War of Independence, or Peninsular War, follows Napoleon's invasion and Joseph Bonaparte's accession to the Spanish throne. A Spanish uprising is brutally suppressed. The first British forces under Sir John Moore retreat through La Coruña in 1809. The Duke of Wellington leads a second campaign up from Portugal, gaining a decisive victory at Vitoria in 1813.

**1833**
Poem by Bonaventura Carles Aribau starts Catalan Renaixença (Renaissance).

**1833–39**
First Carlist War. Carlists, supporters of Fernando VIII's brother Carlos, attempt to gain the Crown from Fernando's niece, Isabel. Conservatives rally to Carlos and his stronghold in Navarra. Liberals rally to Isabel, who maintains the upper hand.

**1835**
At the instigation of the Republican chief minister Mendizábal, church property is confiscated and religious orders disbanded.

**1847–49**
Second Carlist War.

**1853–4**
Great Famine in Galicia.

**1863**
*Cantares Gallegos* by Rosalía de Castro is pivotal in the Galician *Rexurdimento* (Renaissance).

**1872–76**
Third Carlist War. Vizcaya, Guipúzcoa and álava are punished for supporting Carlists, and lose their autonomous privileges *(fueros)*.

**1894**
Basque Nationalist Party (PNV) formed.

**1898**
Spanish-American War. Spain loses possession of Cuba, Puerto Rico and the Philippines.

**1909**
*Semana Trágica*, a bloody week of revolt and repression in Barcelona.

**1923**
Military coup of General Primo de Rivera.

**1931–36**
Second Republic. Alfonso XIII goes into exile.

**1931**
Catalonia declares itself a Republic.

**1934**
Revolts in Barcelona and Asturias, where a rebellion of

*Uprising in Valladolid during the Second Carlist War.*

*Protest march following the Catalan independence referendum.*

miners in Oviedo is quashed by the military.

**1936–9**
Civil War. General Francisco Franco leads rebellious troops from Morocco, aided by General Mola in the north, establishing his HQ in Burgos. Madrid finally falls in November 1938 and the legitimate government retreats to Barcelona, which falls in January 1939.

**1937**
The town of Guernica, symbolic home of Basque autonomy, is bombed by Franco.

**1939**
General Franco becomes head of state. Catalonia and the Basque Country lose their autonomy.

**1941**
Much of Santander destroyed by fire.

**1953**
US purchases facilities for air bases in Spain.

**1959**
ETA, the Basque separatist group, founded.

**1970**
The Burgos trials: 15 Basque terrorists' death sentences are eventually commuted.

**1973**
Franco's first prime minister, Admiral Luís Carrero Blanco, assassinated by ETA.

**1975**
Death of General Franco. Juan Carlos I assumes the throne, restoring the Bourbon dynasty.

**1977**
Elections bring Socialists to power.

**1979**
Statutes of autonomy introduced for Basque Country and Catalonia.

**1986**
Spain becomes a member of the EEC.

**1992**
Olympic Games held in Barcelona.

**1997**
Bilbao Guggenheim opens.

**1999**
Santiago de Compostela's jubilee.

**2002**
Spain adopts the euro. Barcelona celebrates Gaudí on the 150th anniversary of his birth in 1852.

**2008**
Financial crisis hits Spain and brings an economic boom to a sudden end.

**2011**
ETA declares a permanent ceasefire.

**2013**
King Juan Carlos abdicates and his son takes the throne as Felipe VI.

**2017**
Indecisive referendum on leads to a unilateral declaration of Catalan independence which is rejected as illegal by the Spanish government.

**2019**
Thousands take to the Catalan streets to protest a Supreme Court ruling sentencing nine Catalan leaders to jail for sedition after the 2017 independence bid.

**2020–22**
Covid-19 hits Spain very hard. Very tough restrictions imposed on movement, causing huge negative economic and social impacts.

*Replica of the cave of Altamira with its prehistoric rock art.*

# CAVE PAINTERS TO COLUMBUS

The earliest Europeans walked in this ancient corner of Spain, and its rugged hills hid the nobles who began the Christian Reconquest of the peninsula.

Archaeological excavations in the Sierra de Atapuerca, just east of Burgos, over the last few decades have revealed some of the earliest evidence of *homo erectus* in Europe, with some fossils dating back 800,000 years.

It seems fitting that Europe's most ancient known inhabitants should have been unearthed here. In the rugged landscape of Northern Spain, for so long on the very edge of the known world, prehistory never seems far away. Dinosaur footprints, dolmens and Celtic ruins are as much a part of everyday life as the timeless thatched huts, stone granaries and granite-poled vineyards.

## MASTER CAVE PAINTERS

The apogee of this local prehistoric culture was undoubtedly the extensive cave paintings at Altamira near Santander. Together with those at Lascaux in the Dordogne in France, they are the finest in Europe and show that around 20,000 years ago this was one of the most culturally advanced regions of Europe. Altamira's nine painted caves depict hunting scenes and its 600-metre/yd entrance hall has been described as "The Sistine Chapel of the Quaternary Era". Bison, deer, boar and horses are painted in rich ochres, manganese oxides and iron carbonate, and outlined in charcoal bonded with animal fat. They are the largest group of prehistoric colour paintings in the world. This is by no means an isolated work: there are other fine rock paintings from around the same era in Cantabria, the Basque Country, and notably in the Tito Bustillo caves near Ribadesella, Asturias.

The peoples who later populated this rugged landscape followed the general continental drift, moving in after the last retreating Ice Age (which ended about 8,000 BC) from across the Mediterranean and settling in valleys or mountain areas as independent people. The Cantabrian people arrived in the Iron Age, and in the first millennium BC Celts brought their skills as potters, mingling with the local people of planters and herdsmen to become the Celtiberians, considered to form the ethnic identity of the Iberian Peninsula. There is still substantial evidence of these early communities, principally in *castros*, huddles of circular stone buildings, seen mainly in Galicia. They traded with the Phoenicians, the world's first great explorers, who had a settlement at A Coruña, where they imported tin. Minerals had been mined since early times, and gold items have been found in burial chambers

*Ruins of an ancient Celtic village in Santa Tecla, Galicia.*

in Galicia and the Basque country. Meanwhile, the Greeks had set up a trading post (or emporium) around 600 BC at Emporion (now, in Catalan, Empúries) on the Bay of Roses beneath the eastern end of the Pyrenees.

The rising power of Hannibal's Punic (Phoenician) offspring colony of Carthage at Cartagena in southeast Spain brought the Romans to the peninsula, landing at Emporion in 211 BC. From here they began their subjugation of the country, which took them longest in the mountains of the north. These eventually fell under the administration of Tarraconensis, modern Tarragona. The Romans set up garrisons and towns and enslaved the natives to exploit the gold and silver mines of Asturias and Galicia. The Seventh Legion, Legio Septimus, gave its name to the town of León, where it was quartered to guard the Castilian plain from attacks by the mountain Asturians.

The Romans were naturally attracted to strategic places, such as Lugo and Ourense in Galicia, and Pamplona in Navarra, guardian of the Pyrenean pass (which was named after Pompey, who camped here). Roman walls remain at Astorga in Asturias and at Lugo in Galicia. At 2km (1 mile) long, the Lugo ramparts are some of the best in Spain, making Lugo a good place to contemplate the Romans. Nearby is the 4th-century church of Santa Eulalia de Bóveda, which was discovered and excavated in the early 20th century. It is an exquisite example of early Christian architecture.

*The still intact walls of Lugo, Galicia.*

Christianity, which swept the Roman Empire after the Emperor Constantine's conversion in AD 314, continued, after a shaky start, to hold sway against the tidal invasion which followed the collapse of the Roman Empire. Alans, Goths, Huns, Suebi, Vandals and Visigoths swept into the vacuum. The Suebi were content to settle in Galicia, founding a kingdom centred on Ourense, but the mountainous north did not interest most of the other invaders as much as the fertile, warmer lands, and few stopped on their way south. The Visigoths, former Roman vassals with their capital at Toulouse and of Arian religion, finally gained complete supremacy in the peninsula when it was united under King Leovigild, their greatest king, in 585. He established his new capital in Toledo and his successor, Reccared I, made Catholicism the state religion in 589, two years after his conversion to Christianity.

Just as the mountainous regions of the north of Spain had largely been bypassed by the barbarians, so it was largely bypassed by the Moors. Following the death of the Prophet Mohammed in 632, their *jihad* spread across North Africa from Mecca. They strode over the Straits of Gibraltar in 711 and in three years had conquered the entire peninsula, defeating King Rodrigo, probably killing him in battle, and driving the Visigothic nobles into hiding behind the Cordillera Cantábrica.

## PELAYO BEGINS THE RECONQUEST

From the mountains of Asturias these committed Visigothic noblemen continued to assail the Moors. In 722 under their leader, Pelayo, a guerrilla band trapped the Moors in ravines at Covadonga in the Picos de Europa, hurling rocks down on them and giving them their first taste of defeat on Spanish soil. A cave there was made into a shrine to the Virgin of Covadonga, who helped Pelayo to victory, and pilgrims have ever since scraped their knees approaching it to give thanks. With Pelayo's victory, the kingdom of Asturias was established, Christians rallied, and the Reconquest began.

The Moorish advance was finally checked at Poitiers, halfway to Paris, by Charles Martel, leader of the Franks. As the Moors ebbed back beyond the Pyrenees, they were pursued by Charles Martel's grandson, Charlemagne, who was the first to attempt the unification of Europe since the collapse of the Roman Empire. In 778, rallying to the defence of Pamplona, he routed the Moors. Before leaving, however, he sacked the town and pulled down its defences, either to weaken its strategic position or to extract payment for his troubles. The irate Basques retaliated in their famous ambush in the mountain pass of Roncesvalles (see page 36). During the following 200 years, the nobility of the mountains, the barons and counts of numberless small fiefdoms, consolidated into the kingdoms of Asturias, León, Navarra and Aragón. As they emerged from their mountain lairs, they grew strong enough to defend themselves, developing their own lore and languages, although they were frequently as much at odds with each other as with the Moors.

*Visigothic Mass was held for 400 years before the Abbey of Cluny in Burgundy linked the Spanish Church to Rome.*

*Illustration of Pelayo (685–737) and his grandson Fruela I (722–68) from an 11th-century miniature.*

In the eastern Pyrenees the Franks gave virtual autonomy to a buffer state under a local count, Guifré el Pilós (Wilfred the Hairy), who

# THE SONG OF ROLAND

**One of the great Pyrenean dramas, the story of Roland has been passed down in verse and song across Europe for centuries.**

*Eight stages of The Song of Roland in one picture.*

This Frankish hero, military chief of the border zone of Brittany, was killed along with the entire rear-guard of Charlemagne's army when they were ambushed by Basques in the Pyrenean pass above Roncesvalles north of Pamplona in 778.

The sole historical document referring directly to Roland is a single line written by the medieval Frankish scholar Einhard as part of his 9th-century biography of Charlemagne. It attests to the hero's Frankish name, Hruodlandus, his rank of prefect or warden of Brittany, and his death in battle in the Pyrenees.

*La Chanson de Roland* (The Song of Roland), the first great text in French literature, is a compilation of fragments of written and oral history that appeared between 1098 and 1100, more than three centuries after the battle at Roncesvalles. Composed in assonant rhyme, it is considered the oldest and best of the *chansons de geste* (songs of deeds or epic poems). Whereas, historically, Roland's defeat at Roncesvalles was at the hands of the Basques in revenge for his tearing down the walls of Pamplona during Charlemagne's invasion of Moorish Spain, the *Song of Roland* adds important dramatic elements to the events. In the poem, Roland is one of Charlemagne's 12 peers and a nephew, possibly the son, of Charlemagne's brother Carloman, who died in 771. Roland's stepfather Ganelon treasonously arranges for the Saracens to ambush Charlemagne's rearguard, which is commanded by Roland with his friend Olivier and Bishop Turpin. The Saracens attack; Roland is too proud to blow his ivory battle horn, Oliphant, to call for help, though Olivier begs him to do so. The Franks fight heroically; Roland finally calls for help, but it is too late. Before dying, he tries unsuccessfully to break his supernaturally potent sword Durandal, even as Charlemagne returns to his aid. Charlemagne routs the Moors and defeats the emir Baligant, who has reinforced the Saracens. Ganelon is tried and put to death. Aude, Roland's true love, dies of a broken heart.

## ROLAND'S LAST STAND

Debate continues over the exact location of Roland's last stand. The monument (erected in 1967), which is visible just below the road to Saint-Jean-Pied-de-Port in the Ibañeta pass, is the traditionally accepted site of the battle. A 30-minute walk on the GR 65 trail starting behind the Colegiata church in Roncesvalles village is the ancient pilgrim route to Santiago and certainly the path Charlemagne's troops would have followed. This Roman route turns east at the Ibañeta Pass, however, and follows a track to enter France through the Lepoeder Pass, skirting the ruined Elizacharre chapel and continuing through the Bentarte Pass. It is here, 4km (2.5 miles) from the monument, that modern scholars place the battle.

The Pyrenees are studded with Roland memorabilia. Pas de Roland, near Itxassou, is a perforated stone said to have been formed by Roland's miraculous Durandal to allow Carolingian troops to advance. The "footprint of Roland" (Pas de Roland) is visible in the stone, though experts agree that Charlemagne's forces were never there. Similarly, the Frankish hero may never have seen the Brèche de Roland – a gigantic natural gateway between France and Spain near the Cirque de Gavarnie – but the myth and magic of Roland is omnipresent here.

founded the House of Barcelona, a 500-year dynasty later joined by the house of Aragón. In the west, Galicia was linked with Portugal and León. States and kingdoms waxed and waned with feuds and wars. Marriages linked houses on both sides of the Pyrenees; deaths divided lands among the heirs.

If the common enemy was the Moor, the common bond was Christianity. But the apparent discovery of the tomb of St James (in Spanish, Santiago) in a field in Galicia in AD 813 affected much more than the spiritual health of the region. From the Dark Ages to the Middle Ages, increasing numbers of pilgrims made the journey across the Pyrenees. Christian centres were set up along the route: Oviedo, to which the Asturian court of Alfonso II moved in 810, remained a centre for the faith for 200 years. Sancho III el Mayor (the Great), who came to the throne of the expanding Basque kingdom of Navarra in the millennial year, brought the Benedictine order into Spain and encouraged the Franks to join him in his expeditions against the Moors.

In 844, St James, according to legend, actually turned up on a battlefield, on a white horse and in full armour, to help Ramiro I of Asturias defeat the Moors at Clavijo near Logroño, just as St George, patron saint of Catalonia, would later appear on the battlefield to assist Jaime I of Catalonia-Aragón.

## LAND OF CASTLES

As the Moors were pushed back, the mountain people moved down on to the high plain of Castile, named after the many castles thrown up on this front line. Castile formed its own kingdom in 950, and in 1037 it was united with León and Asturias under Ferdinand I, who based his court at León and Burgos, creating a base for further expansion.

*Statue of El Cid, Burgos.*

Spain's most renowned crusader, Rodrigo Díaz de Vivar, known as El Cid, was born near Burgos in 1043. Mounted on his charger Babieca, wielding his sword Colada, his beard tied up so no knave could tweak it, he struck terror in the hearts of the infidels and inspired all the faithful who heard *El Cantar del Mio Cid*, the minstrel's poem of his exploits. This is the earliest surviving literary work in Castilian written some 40 years after the death of the great hero.

## THE CONNECTION WITH BURGUNDY

The Duchy of Portugal, which included all Galicia and had a similar language, came under Burgundian rule in 1095 after Count Henry of Burgundy received it as a reward for helping his father-in-law, Alfonso VI of Castile, defeat the Moors at Toledo. It was the great Burgundian abbey at Cluny which then became the champion of Santiago. Merchants set up their stalls along the way and a census in Jaca in 1137 revealed 78 percent of the town's population spoke French. The church hierarchy also became dominated by the French, most from Cluny. Church and crusaders were united in the 12th century under Spain's first military religious orders, the Knights of Santiago, Alcántara and Calatrava, and in 1212 the northern kingdoms' penultimate battle against the Moors was fought. By this time, Castile had rolled its borders back across the high central meseta and at Las Navas de Tolosa the combined forces of Alfonso VIII of Castile, Pedro II of Aragón and Sancho VII of Navarra so decisively defeated Mohammed II Nasir that the Moors thereafter went into decline. Behind the triumvirate, the mountains of Cantabria and the Pyrenees echoed to the victory. The event is celebrated in a stained-glass window in Roncesvalles, and the captured Moorish banner still hangs on a monastery wall in Burgos.

*A map from 1576 showing San Sebastián and Mount Igeldo.*

The opening up of the plains of Castile brought new wealth. A system of tributes *(parias)*, brought Castile gold from the south, making Spain, from the mid-11th century, a financial centre on a par with Flanders and Italy. This prosperity was echoed in the architecture. Cathedrals were built at León (1205) and Burgos (1221). Prosperity was increased by the sheep trade of the meseta, which the Castilian royal treasury controlled. Wool was exported via Burgos to northern Europe through Bilbao and San Sebastián. Iron ore, which also contributed large sums to the Spanish coffers, left through Vizcaya. Reflecting the parallel cultural enrichment, Spain's first university was built at Palencia in 1208, moving to Salamanca in 1239.

## ADVENTUROUS FISHERMEN

As the glory and riches of conquest moved south, Basques, Cantabrians and Gallegans consolidated their power and prosperity in Northern Spain's fertile valleys and rugged sea coast. In the Middle Ages, whaling and deep sea fishing were major activities. Whaling was carried on in ports from Bilbao to Bayonne, with a major centre at Lekeitio (Lequeitio) between Bilbao and San Sebastián. It was a perilous occupation and medieval methods of harpooning were used until the 19th century. Basques were familiar with the fishing grounds of the north Atlantic, and may have touched America's eastern seaboard before Columbus.

Northern Spain, however, also needed to protect itself from the seas. Quarrels occurred not just with its French neighbours, with whom it was so closely allied that rulers commonly held lands on both sides of the Pyrenees, but also from sea-borne intrusion. Ninth-century Norse raids on the coast had been seen off by Ramiro I of Asturias, but it was not until the first half of the 12th century that steps were taken to establish a formal navy, under Archbishop Gelmírez of Santiago. Its first success was at the siege of Seville in 1248. By the 14th century, Spanish maritime trade was largely under the control of the Hermandad de las Marismas, an association organised by the Basque ports.

In 1229 Jaime (Jaume) I, El Conquistador of Barcelona-Aragón, began the conquest of the Balearic Islands, heralding the supremacy of Catalonia in the Mediterranean. A hundred years later the Canary Islands were colonised in the reign of Enrique III of Castile and León.

## THE NEW WORLD AND A NEW SPAIN

It is no surprise to learn that a number of Basques, including the pilot, set sail with Christopher Columbus from Seville on his voyage of discovery to the New World in 1492; or that a Basque, Juan Sebastián Elcano, brought the first round-the-world venture back to Spain after its leader, the Portuguese Ferdinand Magellan, died in the Philippines in 1521. The earliest known map of the New World was made by Juan de la Cosa, a Basque, in 1500.

The year 1492 was one of triumph for Spain. The marriage of Isabel of Castilla y León with Fernando (Ferran) of Barcelona-Aragón in 1472 united the two great houses of Spain. This Union of Crowns was completed in 1512, when Fernando's forces marched into Navarra, taking over the "Spanish" southern half of the kingdom, but allowing it to keep its privileges *(fueros)* as a semi-autonomous state, which it retained until 1841.

These "Catholic Monarchs", with God and the Inquisition behind them, drove the last Moors from the peninsula the same year that Columbus discovered a New World of bigger dreams. The mountain fortresses had served their purpose, and they now began to slip back into the mists of history as the royal court stepped out into the sunshine, moving its capital to Valladolid, Toledo and finally Madrid.

*Portrait of Felipe II of Spain (1628), by Peter Paul Rubens.*

# THE GOLDEN AGE

The arts flourished, but so did warfare. Attacks by English Elizabethans, Louis XIV and Napoleon all put the north in the front line of Spain's battles.

Fernando and Isabel's Union of Crowns was enhanced by both the Discoveries and by the marriage of their daughter, Juana the Mad, to Philip the Fair, son of the Habsburg Emperor Maximilian of Austria. Her insanity was induced by her husband's death and when her father died in 1516, succession went directly to her son, Carlos I. Because he had been brought up in the court of Burgundy, he spoke no Spanish and, aged 17, he landed on the Asturian coast with Flemish-speaking advisers.

His inheritance included the Netherlands, the Franche-Comté and Austria, and in 1520 he took on his grandfather's crown as Carlos V, Holy Roman Emperor. Portugal became an ally through his marriage, and his Carolingian ambitions for a united Europe kept his lands constantly at war. Milan and Naples were added to Spain's territories and, before the ageing Carlos retired to a monastery, the Spanish Empire covered a good chunk of South America, the Philippines, and the Caribbean's two largest islands, Cuba and Santo Domingo.

## NO PROFIT FROM THE AMERICAS

The New World's treasures did very little for Northern Spain for, although the crowns were united, natural antipathies remained and the New World was considered to belong not to Spain as a whole but to Castile. Trading rights were given exclusively to Cádiz and Seville, a decision which harmed the northern Atlantic economy and severely curtailed the fortune of Catalonia-Aragón, which had become one of the great Mediterranean sea powers.

Charles V's wars were a drain on the riches arriving from the New World, as were the profligate court and nobility, and titles were distributed with unheeded largesse. In 1521, the country rose against the king and his avaricious court, demanding the restriction of the powers of the local *cortes* (parliaments). Gonzalo el Guzmán, from the leading noble house of León, was among the more radical of these *comuneros*, but they were soon crushed.

Felipe II (1556–98) inherited all but the Germanic territories from his father and reigned over a continuing Golden Age of the arts and literature, which flourished as the economy declined. Madrid, the exact centre of Spain, he decided, should become the capital of his empire. The New World funded the sombre Escorial, built just outside Madrid as a monument and mausoleum for the Spanish royal family.

*Barcelona's commercial activities in the 16th century.*

Strains on the economy were increased by the activities of English pirates, who considered gold shipments from the Americas fair game. Worse, they were Protestants, the religion of the "heretical" Calvinists in the Netherlands and of Felipe's own sister-in-law, Elizabeth I of England. Goaded by the pirates and fired with a crusading zeal, Felipe decided to invade England. Trees were felled across northern Spain to build an armada capable of landing troops there; he personally masterminded preparations down to the last drop of tar.

The Armada's defeat around the coast of Britain was followed up by a visit to Spain from Sir Francis Drake, who laid siege to A Coruña for 14 days, sacking the lower town and burning the fields for miles around. The city was only saved, it is said, by María Pita, a resident who turned the tide of the skirmish when she cut down the English standard-bearer. On 19 June 1589, Drake sailed into Vigo, ravaged the country and burnt the town. Fearing for their safety, the Church removed the relics of St James from Santiago de Compostela and pilgrimages subsequently dwindled to nothing. The relics were not returned until the late 19th century.

*16th-century engraving of Barcelona's port of embarkation.*

The combined Portuguese and Spanish fleet mustered in Lisbon harbour in 1588. Two squadrons of 19 galleons were from Guipúzcoa and all the Armada's admirals were Basque. The fleet, however, was still short of men and equipment, and this led to the first-ever conscription of Spaniards. Among those rounded up were 400 Galicians, who were sent to Lisbon only to be returned as too old, ignorant and decrepit to be of any use. The fleet sailed up to A Coruña (known to English sailors as The Groyne), where it put in for a refit. There, its seasick commander, the Duke of Medina Sidonia (the title of the Guzmán family), wrote to Felipe to complain how ill-equipped and weak the fleet was. It then sallied forth to its sorry fate.

If the English were one of Spain's problems, the other was the French. Continuing religious disputes contributed to the Thirty Years' War with France under Felipe III and Felipe IV, which resulted in the loss of the Netherlands and Portugal. In the concluding Treaty of the Pyrenees of 1659, signed on the Isla de la Conferencia in the River Bidasoa between Hendaye in France and Fuenterrabía (now Hondarribia) in Spain, the boundary was drawn between the two nations once and for all, ceding Roussillon (northern Catalonia) in the eastern Pyrenees to France, just as in the west Navarra had lost its northern portion more than a century earlier.

When Carlos II died childless in 1700, the struggle was resumed as a war of succession between the ruling Habsburgs and the rival French Bourbons. The Bourbons were victorious and their claimant, Philip of Anjou, became Felipe V, who began the dynasty of Spanish monarchs ruling Spain today. His reprisals against Catalonia for supporting the Habsburgs included the removal of the university to Cervera, 100km (60 miles) west of Barcelona, and the banning of its language, as well as stripping Catalonia of its rights, privileges and autonomous government.

## EMIGRATIONS

Like all mountain regions, Northern Spain has never been able to sustain its population, and its sons have had to sally forth to find their fortunes. At Peña Cabarga near Santander, there is a monument to all those who emigrated to Central and South America. Basques were well established on the American continent and had even managed to secure the monopoly on chocolate exports from Caracas. The Venezuelan capital was also birthplace in 1783 of Simón Bolívar, the great South American liberator, who was of Basque descent.

*16th-century map of Santander.*

## THE INQUISITION

The expulsion of the Muslim people and the unification of Spain under Fernando and Isabel led to a witchhunt of *conversos* – Jews who had officially adopted the Christian faith, but were suspected of practising crypto-judaism. The first *auto de fé* (literally "act of faith" but in fact a euphemism for death by fire) was in Seville in 1481, and by the end of the decade 2,000 had died. This persecution lost Spain many of its brightest and most able subjects. The Catholic monarchs did not invent the Inquisition. It had begun north of the Pyrenees in the Languedoc in the early 13th century, when the Church of Rome, fearing the increasing influence of local Albigensian heretics, instigated a crusade against them led by St Dominic, founder of the Dominican Order. At the time, the Inquisition had little influence south of the Pyrenees.

One of the most feared inquisitors was Thomas Torquemada, a *converso* who had become a Dominican. In June 1490 Benito García, a *converso* and a Christian for 35 years, was arrested at Astorga on his way home from a pilgrimage to Santiago. Under torture he confessed to various heinous and imaginary crimes including the murder of a Christian child – a confession Torquemada used in his relentless pursuit of Jews.

Many returned as rich *indianos* and built villas in smart places such as Comillas. Basques sailed against the British in the American War of Independence, which was supported by Spain.

Spain's own War of Independence, known in Britain as the Peninsular War, was started in 1808 when Carlos IV was lured to Bayonne by Napoleon, who used the ruse that he wanted to move troops through Spain to attack Portugal. Carlos, weak and ineffective, abdicated in favour of Napoleon's brother Joseph. The spontaneous uprising in Spain brought the swift reprisals

*The burial of Sir John Moore at A Coruña.*

painted by Goya, but the heroic resistance continued. The English pitched in against France, but were forced to retreat through Northern Spain, fighting a rearguard action all the way to A Coruña, where Sir John Moore, commander of the troops, was killed and so famously buried without ceremony in his boots and greatcoat.

The Duke of Wellington arrived next, disembarking in Lisbon and fighting his way up through Spain, where he had a major showdown with Maréchal Soult at Vitoria on 21 June 1813, ending the war and sending ex-King Joseph and the remaining French army scuttling for the Pyrenees. The British troops failed to pursue them immediately, helping themselves instead to the booty of the town. Wellington described his army

> *"Not a drum was heard, Not a funeral note, As his corse [corpse] to the rampart we hurried ..." from "The Burial of Sir John Moore after Corunna" (1817), by Charles Wolfe.*

as "the scum of the earth", which they proved to be once again in August when they regained San Sebastián and proceeded to plunder, pillage and rape, leaving the town burning through the night.

But within 40 years, San Sebastián had recovered sufficiently to welcome Isabel II and her court for a summer holiday. Isabel had a troubled, interrupted reign (1833–68). At the end of the War of Independence, parliament had drawn up a constitution for the return of Fernando VII, but he had torn it up and returned to absolutist ways. The resulting struggle between the enlightened liberals and the die-hard conservatives was one that was also going on throughout Europe. Spain, unused to evolutionary social reform, swung to extremes.

## THE CARLIST WARS

The conservatives rallied to Fernando's brother Don Carlos, Isabel's uncle and rightful heir to the throne under the Salic law, which excluded female succession to the crown. Three Carlist wars followed: 1833–39, 1847–49 and 1872–76. Don Carlos made his headquarters in Oñati in Guipúzcoa and in Estella in Navarra. He could find friends here, partly because during a republican interlude in 1841, Navarra was provoked by the loss of the privileges *(fueros)* it had so fiercely held for 500 years. Carlists put on their red berets and conducted guerrilla wars from the hills, but with no major success, particularly in the new towns such as Bilbao, which they attacked but failed to take.

Further pressure was applied by the republicans when, in 1835, their chief minister Mendizábal began a campaign of *desamortización*. This disbanded religious orders and confiscated their property, a draconian measure against institutions that had become rich and privileged without check. Monasteries were closed and many monks left for South America. One hundred years later this unresolved conflict between reactionary church and inflammatory republicanism would reach a chilling conclusion.

*Rural Basques, a romantic 19th-century view.*

*Republican Spanish poster depicting the Asturias Revolution of 1934.*

# CIVIL WAR TO AUTONOMY

The northern regions have experienced the greatest changes in Spain's transition from unitary to federal state.

Literary travellers to Spain in the late 19th and early 20th centuries revelled in their descriptions of the quaintness of Spanish rural life, where villagers worked the soil in ways hallowed by time. But what to these educated but ignorant outsiders seemed a pleasingly backward and almost feudal way of life was, to those who lived it, an iniquitous system of inequality which subjected the majority to penury, misery and early death.

Throughout the 19th century, liberal reformers attempted to alleviate the lot of the poor by progressively selling off the large tracts of land entailed by the Church. But, rather than enabling a much broader distribution of land ownership, as they had hoped, these sales led to the rise of a new socially powerful group: the bourgeoisie, who accumulated enough surplus money to buy extra land which could then be worked for them by sharecroppers or day labourers.

On top of that, in the north of the country, peasants living in those areas where the Carlist wars had been most intense (the Basque Country, Navarra, Catalonia) had also to make good their losses caused by the depredations of war. At the same time, their town halls, often bankrupted by the cost of supporting occupying armies, auctioned off part of their commons, so denying locals access to land which had traditionally been for the benefit of all within each municipality.

## THE SWORD AND THE PLOUGH

In many areas, this tightening of the economic screw forced peasants into ploughing up parts of the remaining commons in order to survive. These illegal actions brought them into conflict, sometimes armed, with their respective municipal authorities, who always had recourse to the armed forces of the state.

*The aftermath of the bombing of Guernica in 1937.*

Conventional politics showed little sign of assisting these sections of society, as national debate in Madrid was controlled during this period by a pair of liberal factions which alternated in power (the system of "turns"). At the local level, the vote was controlled by *caciques* (bosses), powerful landlords who wielded their economic might to ensure that those they controlled voted the way they were told to. It was during this time of increasing dissatisfaction with the system of central government that political forms of nationalism began to arise in the Basque Country, Catalonia and Galicia.

In these circumstances, it is understandable that so many peasants chose to migrate to Latin America or to those cities experiencing industrialisation. But conditions there were little better, if at all. It is not surprising, therefore, that Bilbao (which in the last two decades of the 19th century underwent the most rapid rate of industrial growth in the world) became the cradle not only of Basque nationalism but also of Spanish socialism, while Barcelona, with its booming textile factories, proved fertile ground for anarchists and radical workers' movements. This increasing politicisation of certain sectors of the population sometimes had disastrous consequences. In Barcelona, for example, at the turn of the 20th century, extreme left- and right-wing groups formed terrorist gangs, while wealthy industrialists surrounded themselves with *pistoleros* for their own protection. In 1909, these tensions culminated in the *Semana Trágica* (Tragic Week), when a popular revolt and general strike were quashed by the army at a cost of more than 100 lives.

*Communist Party members march through Bilbao in 1932.*

The first three decades of the 20th century may be viewed as a period of cumulative division between the left and the right – powerful conservative interests continued to block the necessary and overdue reforms of the land ownership system, while an irresponsible king, Alfonso XIII, changed governments according to his whim. The progressive extension of the vote during this time to previously unenfranchised sections of the population served only to increase social tensions, as it raised popular expectations but did little to help turn these hopes into reality.

The Church could have been a particularly powerful force for social justice within this political scene, but its leaders repeatedly chose to side with those upholding the status quo and so, gradually but irreversibly, came to lose the respect of and its influence over large sections of the poorer strata of Spanish society. In Barcelona, left-wing activists established the tradition of burning churches and convents in times of civil disorder. In the Basque Country, however, the torching of religious establishments did not become the custom, as the Church there was peculiarly well-rooted in the popular life of the area, many local families having at least one member of their kin serving as a priest, monk or nun. In this region, fears about the increasing degree of social disorder often found religious expression: for instance, in apparitions of the weeping Virgin calling for the faithful to defend her house.

At the end of World War I (in which Spain did not take part) the system of government came under increasing strain as parliamentary political groups (now expanded to include, among others, nationalists of various colours and socialists) repeatedly failed to form strong, long-lasting governments, while workers' associations demonstrated their muscle by staging strikes of greater and greater scope. By 1923, the system had become so enfeebled that the king looked well upon a military coup staged by General Primo de Rivera.

But the General did not have the ability to succeed where other, much more talented politicians had failed and he fled in 1930. Municipal elections were held the following year and the King, taking the results as a referendum on his own monarchy, went into exile when it became clear that republican parties had won the day.

God-fearing but otherwise politically moderate Spaniards. Within two years, they were replaced in office by a rapidly assembled coalition of the Right, which sought to counter its predecessor's legislative reforms. Popular expectations, however, could not be maintained. In October 1934, there were revolts in both Asturias and Barcelona. The Catalan uprising was quickly snuffed out, but the mass rebellion by miners in Oviedo proclaiming their region a socialist republic was only quashed after a bloody military campaign by Francisco Franco.

*A house in ruins following the bombardment of San Sebastián by insurgent warships in 1936.*

*Aged just 34 when he was appointed brigadier general in the Spanish Army, Francisco Franco was the youngest European general since Napoleon.*

## EQUALITY'S FALSE DAWN

The Second Republic (1931–36) was a time of the greatest of hopes and the most acute of tensions. Many in the left-wing coalition which came to power in 1931 saw this as their opportunity to usher in the new dawn of social equality and an end to injustice. But their fatal mistake, in their rush for change, was to brand the Church as the enemy, and so alienate a large number of

In the elections of February 1936, the right was swept from office by the Popular Front, a coalition of left-wing Republicans and Socialists. The Socialists then refused to help form a government, and the unrepresentative government that did take power spent the following months desperately trying, and conspicuously failing, to prevent the country spiralling ever downwards into violent disorder. Factions on both sides prepared for the armed conflict they knew was imminent and had foreseen several years before.

In July 1936 rebel factions of the army launched an armed coup d'etat against the elected government. Franco and his henchmen thought that they would seize power within a matter of weeks, if not days. But the steadfastness to the Republic of the navy and certain sections of the paramilitary police forces, plus the popular support for it in Madrid and Barcelona, where arms were issued to the people, meant that the insurgents' dream of a speedy outcome was not to be realised. Both sides, each with about half of the country, prepared themselves for a civil war.

In Navarra, the pre-trained Carlist militias, the *Requeté*, soon suppressed the regional left wing and then, together with sections of the army, moved on to the Basque Country. The

*Aftermath of the car bomb which killed Prime Minister Luís Carrero Blanco in 1973.*

*It is estimated that 35,000 foreigners fought for the Republican cause in the International Brigades.*

Basque Government wanted to stay out of the war, but the advance of Franco's forces left it no option. The offer by the Republican Government of a Statute of Autonomy swayed it to the Republican side. Bilbao fell to Franco in June 1937, and regions to its west shortly afterwards.

In Catalonia, the forces of the Republic imposed themselves within days and Barcelona became enormously important as the point of entry for material and for members of the International Brigades and, from October 1936, as the seat of the government. With Zaragoza secure from the beginning of the war and with the north and northwest now in their hands, Franco's troops moved eastwards. The battle of the Ebro (July–November 1938) was the bloodiest of the war, and the Republicans' defeat in it led to the collapse of their armies in Catalonia.

The legacy of the war was a totally disrupted, drastically impoverished country barely able to feed itself. The 1940s were *los años de hambre* (the hungry years), when the majority went short. Perhaps the only sector of life where it was almost "business as normal" was the Church, the prospect of a materially good life stirring vocations in some adolescent hearts. As old villagers say today, a child entering the church meant reflected prestige on them and "one less mouth to feed".

Franco's policy of "autarchy", national self-sufficiency as far as economically possible, chimed with the political isolation of Spain throughout the early years of his dictatorship. Then in the 1950s, when Franco's tottering regime was propped up by American assistance because the US saw the dictator as an ally in the fight against Communism, his advisers persuaded him to shift to a policy of liberalisation and openness to foreign investment. The result was a tourist boom along the Mediterranean coast, an industrial revival in Barcelona and Bilbao, which mushroomed with migrants seeking work and the first, faltering signs of a consumer society.

## RISING PROTEST

The achievement of economic well-being did not, however, stifle political protest – rather the opposite. In the 1960s, nationalist activists emerged in the Basque Country, Catalonia and Galicia, spearheaded by the audacious acts of the Basque separatist group, ETA. In 1973, ETA scored a spectacular coup in the blowing up of Admiral Luís Carrero Blanco, Franco's prime minister and political heir apparent. By the early 1970s, it had become difficult for the state to contain the ever-rising level of protest. Franco was by now an infirm old man and the opposition knew it would not have much longer to wait. He died on 20 November 1975.

Within a few years the regime he and his cronies had so carefully maintained was dismantled and replaced with a social democracy, headed by a constitutional monarchy, along standard West

European lines. It has been argued that "the Transition" was as smooth as it was because of a general recognition that the regime was absurdly outdated and that, in order to avoid another civil war, all the parties involved had to negotiate collectively, and peacefully, a common way towards a new, much more representative system of government. The role of the young king, Juan Carlos I, in steering this negotiation was crucial. Despite grumblings from within the ranks of senior officers, nationalist politicians managed to force constitutional reform to their own benefit.

The Spanish economy boomed in the late 1990s and early 2000s, on the back of a prodigious amount of house-building, but crashed spectacularly in the financial crisis of 2008 leading to much unemployment and misery.

Meanwhile, Spanish society changed radically. The old generation remember having to emigrate to richer countries in search of a living; the younger generation have grown used to foreign travel as a pleasure, while a relatively prosperous Spain has become used to receiving migrants from Africa and South America.

*Workers at a tuna-canning factory in Puebla del Carminal, Galicia in 1996.*

Instead of the monolithic state imposed by Franco, in which, according to the official dictat, all separatism was "an unpardonable crime", Spain became a "State of Autonomies", with all its provinces grouped into self-governing units. The regions of Spain have their own governments, but the Basque Country and Catalonia have special arrangements for extensive home rule.

## THE PROBLEMS OF DEMOCRACY

Much has changed since the re-implantation of democracy. Spain joined the EU in 1986. This brought an injection of capital for new transport infrastructure but even more importantly created a sense that Spain was an integrated part of the new western European order.

Politically, much has evolved too. Basque terrorism ended with a ceasefire in 2010, although tensions between the regions and the central government have not entirely gone away. In the autumn of 2017 a pro-separatist government in Catalunya challenged Madrid by organizing a referendum on the region's future and even went as far as unilaterally declaring independence (see page 58), resulting in a political crisis and a general reexamination of what it means to be Spanish. While younger generations want radical solutions to today's problems, older people urge them not overlook the fact that a country which was a dictatorship within living memory has been successfully transformed into a democracy with all the associated benefits and problems that that entails.

*"Basque Celebration (Dance at El Antiguo, San Sebastián)" by Darío de Regoyos, 1888.*

*Catalans celebrating the "Diada Nacional".*

# NATIONS WITHIN A STATE

Two of Spain's autonomous regions have pretensions to independent statehood and this is the cause of much political and cultural tension.

Spain's most successful home-produced film is *Ocho Apellidos Vascos* (literally, "Eight Basque Surnames", but known as *Spanish Affair* in English). It is a romantic comedy about the difficulties of a Basque woman to have a successful love affair with a man from Seville. The joke is that they are of incompatible "nationalities". The film plays mercilessly on stereotypes – the happy-go-lucky Andaluz and the dour, humourless Basque – but everyone in Spain recognises a deeper question: can Spain survive intact in the 21st century when two regions of the north – the Basque Country and Catalonia – won't stop talking about separatism and are in eternal conflict with the central government and the rest of the country?

History, language and culture are the driving force behind the Basque and Catalan independence movements. To a much lesser extent, Galicia also has a sense of national self-identity but few people consider the region could ever be a viable breakaway state.

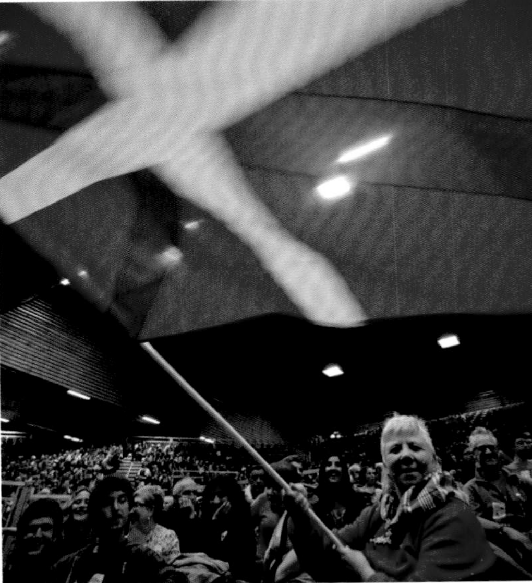

*Waving the Basque flag at a political meeting.*

## THE ROOTS OF BASQUE NATIONALISM

In the late 19th century in the Basque Country, the rise of coal mining, steel making and shipbuilding led to extremely fast industrialisation. Towns were rapidly turning into unplanned cities filled by migrants from other parts of Spain and by rural Basques deserting their villages for the sake of jobs. Members of the local, highly Catholic petite bourgeoisie correctly perceived this upheaval as a real threat both to their own position in Basque society and to the traditional way of life. These pioneer nationalists propounded a purist, backwards-looking political creed to check the destructive effects of laissez-faire capitalism within their own land.

This early nationalism, using the racial terminology of the day, saw the Basques as a separate race, morally united by blood and traditional commitment to the Church. Their ideas soon found an appreciative audience within large Basque towns.

By the 1910s, thanks to determined work in smaller towns and villages, they had extended their support into the countryside. By the 1930s, they were sufficiently strong to be able to demand from Madrid the establishment of a self-governing Basque region. But they were not granted it until late 1936, when the Civil War had already been raging for several months and, even then, it was on condition that the Basques allied with the Republican forces to fight Franco's troops.

Triumphant, Franco suppressed all nationalist activity so successfully that it was not until the late 1950s that Basque youths began to organize themselves politically.

## REIGN OF TERROR

ETA (*Euskadi ta Askatasuna*, The Basque Country and Freedom) started as a broad cultural and humanist movement, but evolved gradually into a terrorist organisation with separatist and revolutionary socialist ends. ETA was so successful at challenging the State-imposed status quo that by the late 1960s it had become hugely popular nationally as one of the leading groups in the militant opposition to the regime. Its most spectacular coup, the blowing up of Admiral Luís Carrero Blanco, Franco's prime minister and political heir apparent, is – with the benefit of hindsight – widely seen as the death-knell for the possible survival of the regime after the dictator's death.

In the long term, Franco's repressive policies boomeranged. By treating not just ETA activists, but almost all Basques as traitors and deserving of the bullying behaviour of his heavy-handed paramilitary police, he ended up politicising a broad swathe of the local population. This, in turn, enabled the fantastically rapid revival of the centre-right BNV (Basque Nationalist Party) during the last years of his rule.

During the transition to democracy, the nationalists successfully forced the central government to establish the three Basque provinces of Vizcaya, Guipúzcoa and Álava as the self-governing region of Euskadi or, in Spanish, El País Vasco (the Basque Country) in 1979. In the ensuing years, the Basque Government won further powers, increasing its autonomy.

*Pro-independence rally in Barcelona.*

Despite these real gains, however, ETA's campaign of "armed struggle" continued well into the new millennium. Although the violence has officially ended, the feelings that inspired it may take a generation or more to be worked through.

## THE CATALAN APPROACH

The Catalan experience has been rather different. In the mid-19th century, the Catalan bourgeoisie, then rapidly enriching itself from the proceeds of the booming local textile industry, fomented and sponsored *La Renaixença*, the renaissance of Catalan culture. The Catalan language, use of which had been confined to the lower classes for several centuries, came into fashion for the well-to-do. Modern versions of medieval contests between troubadours, the *Jocs Florals*, were staged annually. Playwrights and novelists began to produce works in Catalan. Others published literary and satirical magazines in the language. The wealthy also ensured, through their patronage, the rise of a broad artistic but specifically Catalan movement, *Modernisme*, today best remembered for the buildings produced by its architects (most notably Antoni Gaudí).

four provinces accepted the government offer for provincial administrations to pool their resources in conglomerate units called *Mancomunitats*. But this experiment only lasted until 1923, when General Primo de Rivera seized power in Madrid. His repressive policies, however, only served to boost support for Catalanism. So when his departure (in 1930) was followed the next year by that of the king, Catalanists felt sufficiently strong to proclaim a Catalan Republic. Another year later, however, the new central government

*Clashes between police and citizens during the Catalonia independence referendum, 2017.*

## TOWARDS SELF-RULE

In the 1880s, this predominantly cultural form of Catalanism was given a political edge as local businessmen, keen to protect their economic interests, began to call for Catalan self-rule. The next three decades saw the rise (and fall) of a spectrum of Catalanist parties whose main aims were protectionist legislation and regional autonomy. Their efforts achieved little because the fragile coalitions they formed could not contain the differences between left- and right-wing Catalanists and because members of the urban proletariat, well organised in workers' associations, were not attracted to the cause.

Catalonia did finally gain some degree of autonomy in 1914, when the leaders of its forced them to back down and only granted them a Statute of Autonomy, which included the establishment of a Catalan government, the Generalitat.

In 1934, a power struggle between right-wing Catalans and the left-wing Catalanists controlling the Generalitat led to its President proclaiming, once again, a Catalan Republic. This time, the effort was quashed by the Madrid government. The entire Generalitat was imprisoned.

On the election, in 1936, of a left-wing government in Madrid, they were all released and the Statue of Autonomy was restored. But Catalanist aspirations were soon frustrated again, this time by the victorious Franco, whose troops entered Barcelona in late 1938. As in the Basque Country, all forms of regional cultural activity – including the speaking of Catalan – were suppressed, though some of the repressive measures were later eased somewhat.

During the Franco dictatorship there were spasmodic, even mass demonstrations of opposition to the regime, but Catalunya did not produce an armed organisation on a par with ETA.

When Franco died, there was a resurgence of Catalan pride and hope. Key to the successful transition to democracy was the creating of a constitution that granted extensive autonomous powers to Catalunya but kept it within the Spanish state. The constitution was assented to by a majority of Catalans.

*Display Day in Irún.*

Over the next two and half decades, Spain's federal structure seemed to work reasonably well for most people in Catalunya. There were demands for more power to be devolved to the region but aspiration to full independence was reduced to a vigorous but always minority political cause.

## THE CRISIS OF 2017

However, resentment at the centralised Spanish state nominally ruling over Catalan affairs from distant Madrid generated increasing support for separatist parties in the first decade of the new millennium and politicians in Barcelona felt obliged to respond. In 2014 the Catalan government held a controversial consultative referendum on independence. This was won by the separatists but on a very low turnout.

After elections in 2015 a coalition of pro-independence parties took control of the Catalan government and its victorious leaders declared that they now had a duty to hold a binding referendum. The Spanish government expressly prohibited this to go ahead because it was illegal under the constitution. On 1 October 2017 the referendum took place under chaotic circumstances, partly due to the ad hoc organisation and partly due to heavy-handed policing ordered by Madrid.

> *Fewer than 30 percent turned out to vote on home rule in Galicia in the 1980 referendum.*

The confused referendum delivered a confused stalemate. Should the separatist leaders issue a unilateral declaration of independence or not? If they didn't declare independence, they would betray their supporters; if they did the Spanish government would have the legal power to suspend Catalan autonomy.

Outside Spain, the cause of Catalan separatism was attracting international sympathy but the European Union made it clear it could not and would not recognise an independent Catalunya.

Ironically, one of the separatists' principal promises was that an independent state would be more prosperous but the prospect of erecting borders and custom posts caused many of the biggest Catalan businesses to fear that they were about to be cut off from their markets in the rest of Spain. Many subsequently moved their headquarters and their capital out of Catalunya altogether.

On 27 October the Catalan separatists ceased procrastinating and declared the birth of the independent Republic of Catalunya. The Madrid government reacted immediately by dismissing the Catalan government and scheduling fresh elections. In 2019 tens of thousands of Catalans took to the streets to protest the Supreme Court ruling that saw nine Catalan leaders sentenced to long prison terms.

The main effect of these events has been the polarisation of Catalan society into two roughly equal camps, for and against independence. The issue may never be satisfactorily resolved.

## GALICIAN MODERATION

Galicia has only a weak nationalist movement. It has its origins in a late 19th-century literary renaissance, *El Rexurdimento*, of works in the Galician language. Though this movement began to take on political tones in the 1890s, continuing arguments between its members meant that a fully fledged Galician nationalism did not take form until 1916, with the founding of the Irmandades (Brotherhoods). But this region-wide network of nationalist organisations, primarily composed of members of the urban petite bourgeoisie, only lasted until 1923, when Primo de Rivera came to power.

After the declaration of Spain's Second Republic in 1931, nationalists regrouped and formed the Partido Galleguista, the first Galician nationalist body which attempted to be of popular appeal and cross-class in social composition. During the Republic, it negotiated a Statute of Autonomy for the region with the central government but the Civil War ended any chance of its being put into effect. It was not until the 1950s that nationalism began timidly to revive, with the establishment of groups for the promotion of Galician culture.

Today, Galician nationalists maintain a strong showing in regional politics and typically win a handful of seats in parliament but are divided in their exact aims and together are unlikely to gain a majority or push forward a serious project for independence.

## THE ETERNAL TROUBLES OF FEDERALISM

It is easy to assume that all the answers to the question – should the Basque Country and Catalunya be independent states – are in the regions themselves but it is important to remember that neither exists in isolation from the rest of the country. People in historically poor Andalucía and on the vast land-locked central meseta of central Spain – not to mention adjoining regions, notably Asturias, Cantabria and Aragon – sometimes look at these two restless northern regions and see not just self-determination but self-obsession. Federalism inevitably means the co-existence of unequal regions and those that are richer or in some way more fortunate have to pull their weight rather than complain.

For good or ill, both the Basque Country and Catalunya have economic and social histories inextricably entwined with the country of which they form a part. The rest of Spain has long served them as a domestic market for goods produced and sent a steady stream of migrant labour to work in the northern factories and mills. While these regions remain a part of Spain, politicians in Vitoria, Barcelona and Madrid must manage the challenges of a federal country as best they can, forever deciding how far to insist on standardisation against local solutions and how far tax should be redistributed.

*Supporters of the Galician Nationalist Block (BNG) celebrate the "Day of the Galician Country".*

As one Basque puts it, "Why should we pay for the waste and corruption in Madrid with our taxes and why should they tell us what to do when we have proven that we are better at organising our own education, transport and health systems without their interference?"

*Fabada Asturian (bean stew).*

# FOOD

Wherever you go in northern Spain, you will eat well. Galician food has an unmistakable flavour, Asturian dishes are hearty, and Basque food is divine.

When Spaniards say, shaking their heads in admiration, that people in the north live to eat rather than eat to live they are not just talking about the size of their appetites. Spend a hedonistic Sunday lunch in a dining room filled with noisy local families, watch housewives pick over produce in the markets or join in one of the popular competitions for the best cook of the local speciality, and it quickly becomes clear that eating well is not just a priority here. It is a way of life.

For a first-time visitor, though, it is the flavours of the green north that are the biggest surprise. Forget the *gazpacho*, *paella* and *pescadito frito* of the hot south. Here, menus offer deep-sea hake simmered in its own juices, casseroles of beans and smoked ham designed to keep out the winter cold, baby spring vegetables, partridge casseroled in a rich chocolate sauce and more than 30 farmhouse cheeses. Such an abundance of local ingredients makes this the heartland of Spanish regional cooking, with three neighbouring cuisines – Galician, Asturian and Basque-Navarrese – having quite distinct repertoires that run the full range from country cooking to haute cuisine.

*Pintxos from San Sebastián.*

## SEA HARVESTS

What the entire northern coast shares, however, is the salty whiff of its Cantabrian and Atlantic ports. Today, even with falling catches and rising prices, three times as much fresh fish is eaten along this coast as elsewhere in Spain. At early morning auctions in the ports – best visited at about 5am – restaurant owners haggle over the night's catch; later in the day it is laid out in iced, marine still lifes on the fish stalls. Whole hake *(merluza)*, monkfish *(rape*, or *pixín* in Asturian), red bream *(besugo)* and conger eel *(congrío)* fix you in the eye. Slabs of white tuna *(atún)* or albacore *(bonito del norte)* are carved up by fishwives in lacy aprons. On other stalls, you can identify the mass of shellfish which come piled high on platters in the restaurants: mussels, oysters, clams and scallops *(mejillones, ostras, almejas* and *vieiras)*, lobsters, langoustines, prawns and shrimps *(bogavantes* or *langostas, cigalas, gambas* and *camarones)*. Less easily recognised and trickier to eat are the crabs *(buey de mar, cangrejo* and *nécora)* and goose-neck barnacles *(percebes)*, the ugly but most prized of all shellfish here.

Order any of these in a restaurant and they will turn up served in deceptively plain ways designed to hide nothing from discerning local tastebuds. Galician oysters and clams come raw with a squeeze of lemon, elvers are tossed for just seconds in hot oil with spicy dried peppers and Cantabria is famous for its *rabas*, dry-fried squid tentacles. Red bream is at its best done the Basque fishermen's way, simply grilled over a wood fire in ports such as Guetaria and Bermeo. Many of the fish stews now found even on the smartest menus – Galician *caldeirada*, Asturian *caldereta*, Cantabrian *sorropotún* and Basque *marmitako*, for example – started life on the boats and are still at their best eaten in small harbour and port restaurants.

*Pulpo Gallego, Galicia's signature dish.*

## GALICIA'S "ENXEBRE" FLAVOURS

The Colombian novelist Gabriel García Márquez, who won the Nobel Prize for Literature in 1982, once wrote that his "homesickness for Galicia started with food even before I had been there". His longing for the taste of the *enxebre*, as the *gallegos* call native flavours, began with his grandmother's *lacón con grelos* (ham pot-boiled with turnip greens), but could have started with other country dishes such as *caldo* or *pote gallego*, which contain the same winter greens, potatoes to soak up the cooking juices, plus a lick of ham and paprika to provide a spicy-hot fillip. That earthy cooking is alive and well in *casas de comida* (everyday restaurants), as well as in the hands of creative cooks, although one dish, *pulpo a feira* (sliced boiled octopus on potato wafers served on wooden plates) is still best eaten straight from the huge copper cauldrons of the *pulpeiros* (octopus sellers).

Baking, perhaps the best in Spain, also keeps its country roots here. Wheels of dark rye, yellow cornmeal and sourdough bread are sold in heavy slabs and make great eating with rich cow's milk cheeses: squishy *tetilla* – called "breast" after its shape, wood-smoked conical San Simón and mild Cebreiro. The *empanadas* (flat pies) in bakers' windows are also at their best from wood-fired ovens whether made with country yeast doughs sandwiching rabbit, pork or sausage-meat fillings, crunchy cornmeal pastry encasing fresh cockles or sardines, or by city bakers who make elegant flaky-pastry encasing scallops or tuna. Filled with moist almond frangipane, *tarta de Santiago* is also at its best from a good bakery and is typically accompanied by a glass of sweet wine. Another well-known Galician dessert is *filloas*, lacy pancakes served with various fillings, but most traditionally with honey and sugar. The sweet chestnut forests of eastern Galicia produce masses of their delicious fruit for roasting in autumn and Ourense is famous for its *marrón glacé*. Alexandre Dumas, *fils* rated it "the most exquisite confection in the world".

Usually, however, it is the sight and taste of Galicia's seafood which imprints itself on people's memories. Here one finds the essence of *enxebre*: good natural ingredients left to speak for themselves. After finally visiting Galicia late in life, García Márquez wrote of eating "fish which, on the plate, still looked like fish" and "shellfish galore, the only live shellfish left in this devastated world". First time round, be prepared to spend your time learning how to pick the flesh from the shells.

Carnivores wishing to taste some of Europe's best beef should visit Lugo, with its large herd of native beef cattle. It is a mecca for traditional cooking and reputed to have more restaurants per inhabitant than any other town in Spain.

## BEANS, CIDER AND CHEESE

As *paella* is to Valencia, so *fabada* is to Asturias: emblematic, celebrated by poets, eaten in vast quantities and endlessly debated by local cooks. In the end, though, it is the quality of the beans *(fabes)*, made buttery soft here by the soil and water, that really counts. A classic *fabada* – as at Casa Gerardo in Prendes or La Máquina in Lugones – flavoured with *chorizo*, black sausage

*Los Beyos, a typical cheese of Asturias.*

## THE BEST CHEESES

**Afuega'l Pitu** (Asturias) cleanly acidic and flavoured with paprika.

**Los Beyos** (Asturias) a creamy yellow goat's cheese with a soft edible rind.

**Burgos** (Castilla y León) ewe's milk; soft, white.

**Cabrales** (Asturias) ewe's, goat's and cow's milk; pungent, blue-veined.

**Camerano** (Rioja) goat's milk; fresh white.

**Cebreiro** (Galicia), a denominación de origen cheese; cow's milk; mild, hard or medium hard.

**Friol** (Galicia) small-scale artisanal; creamy.

**Gorbea** (Basque Country) ewe's milk; hard.

**Idiazabal** (Basque Country and Navarra) ewe's milk; smoked, hard, creamy, delicate flavour.

**Orduna** (Basque Country) ewe's milk; hard.

**Pasiego** (Cantabria) cow's milk; firm, white, fairly creamy.

**Roncal** (Navarra) ewe's with some cow's milk; smoked, hard, sharp.

**San Simón** (Galicia) a denominación de origen cheese; cow's milk; birch-smoked; orange-coloured and conical.

**Tetilla** (Galicia) cow's milk; soft, white; breast-shaped.

**Tupi** (Pyrenees) fermented with eau-de-vie.

**Ulloa** (Galicia) cow's milk; soft; flat shape.

*Of the nine restaurants awarded the coveted three stars by the Michelin guide, four are in the Basque Country (and three more are in Catalunya).*

and other bits and pieces of pig, can be less appealing than the lighter modern gourmet versions flavoured with clams, crab, hare, boar, partridge, lobster and even spinach. Whichever you decide to try, go easy on quantities.

brick-red fish soups, stuffed hake and potatoes with crab *(patatas con centolla)* along the coast. If you are lucky enough to find it, the most delicious of these is an omelette made with the local sea urchins *(tortilla de erizos)*.

## THE BASQUE COUNTRY

Second to none in Spain, Basque cooking can stand comparison to the best in Europe. Fishermen's kitchens, country farmsteads, male-only gastronomic societies, cider-*bodegas*, gourmet *tapas* bars and star chefs set standards across

*San Sebastián is known for its delicious pintxos.*

Asturias is also a cheese-lovers' paradise. Of some two-dozen sheeps', goats' and cows' milk cheeses, the most famous is the blue Cabrales, said by locals to be the original Roquefort copied by French pilgrims when they got home. Genuine farmhouse Cabrales is wrapped in maple leaves after maturing and racked in caves whose microflora give it the veining. Try eating it the local way, with fruitily tart cider. If you want to buy a whole cheese, search out the farmhouse makers near Arenas de Cabrales. It is at its best in summer.

Unlike the Galicians, the Asturians love to play around with their fish in the kitchen. Modern inventions such as *merluza con sidra* (hake cooked in local dry cider) or salmon in creamy sauces are cooked alongside traditional

the board from market bars to haute cuisine. This is the place to splash out on eating well. As French foodies who nip down over the border know, it is difficult to find yourself being served a dud meal at any price level.

One of the keys to the quality of Basque cooking is what food writer José María Busca Isusi called its radius of reach. Atlantic fish and shellfish, game and shepherds' cheeses from the mountains, and asparagus and artichokes from market gardens on the southern plains are supplemented by French foie gras and the Rioja's best red wines. But the Basques' bold inventiveness goes back to the centuries when there was much less to hand. Hence, for example, their ingenious salt-cod *(bacalao)* dishes, such as *bacalao al pil-pil*, in which the fish gelatine is slowly drawn out to thicken an emulsion of juices and olive oil.

San Sebastián, in particular, is a great city in which to eat, with every kind of choice from *asadores* (grills) selling superb beef *(buey)* chops by the gram to the old town's bars where *tapas* are raised to an art form. In the top restaurants, celebrity chefs mix regional classics such as hake with clams and prawns *(merluza con almejas y gambas)*, squid in its ink *(chipirones en su tinta)* and red *piquillo* peppers stuffed various ways with their own creative modern cooking.

Stretching from the Atlantic to the Mediterranean coast, Pyrenean cooking varies from one valley to the next. Each has its specialities: shepherds' cheeses, wild mushrooms, river fish such as trout *(truchas)*, often cooked in lard or with a sliver of bacon inside and, above all, game. Otherwise the everyday casseroles *(chilindrones)*, bean and lentil stews, and shepherds' *migas*, literally fried breadcrumbs, have an air of old frugality. Every piece of sheep and lamb is used, from the feet to the tail (the latter known as *espárragos montañeses*).

*Red peppers from La Rioja.*

## NAVARRA AND THE PYRENEES

Basque cooking shades almost imperceptibly into Navarrese, although certain specialities allow experts to distinguish between the two. Springtime vegetables include baby artichokes, melting white asparagus and borage *(boraje)*, cardoon *(cardo)* and new-season haricot beans *(pochas)*. Mediterranean *pisto* stew becomes a sauce for salt cod in *bacalao al ajo-arriero*. Likewise, southern Navarrese cooking shades into La Rioja specialities. In autumn, long strings of red peppers hang to dry from balconies. Whether sweet or spicy, fresh or dried, they are the defining ingredient of many dishes, above all *patatas a la Riojana*, a masterfully simple potato dish flavoured with *chorizo* and dried peppers.

## CROSSING TO THE MESETA

Plunging south into the northern meseta, you come abruptly to wide-horizoned wheat fields and sober medieval flavours. Roast baby milk-fed lamb, *cocido* (Don Quixote's stewpot) and garlic soup are designed to keep out the freezing cold in winter; *escabeches* (marinated game and trout), for keeping cool in searing summers. The family pig is king here and the region's cured *chorizo* sausages and loin of pork, rusty red with smoked paprika, are still some of the best in Spain. Frontier pockets have hybwrid cuisines. El Bierzo is known for its cured beef *(cecina)* and preserved fruit, southern Cantabria for its *cocido* (hotpot) made with sumptuous mountain beans and cabbage.

*Freshly harvested grapes at the Bodega Lopez de Heria in Haro, La Rioja,*

# WINE

Rioja is one of the best-known Spanish wines, but Northern Spain produces some other great reds, as well as the best white wines in the country.

Among the foothills, valleys and sunny slopes of Northern Spain are some of the most intriguing wine-growing areas of Europe. Most of the vineyards are sited on the steep, sunny slopes of the region's major rivers, the Ebro, Duero, Miño and Sil, and they produce a remarkable variety of traditional and modern wines.

To many, Northern Spain means Rioja, and it is true that this full-bodied red wine has long been a staple of restaurant menus around the world. But a new wine story of Northern Spain is emerging, based in large part on the rediscovery of old varieties of grape, such as the Albariño and Godello, which are currently making Galician white wines the best in Spain.

Also in the ascendancy are Navarra's wines, traditionally *rosado* (rosé), while the Basque's white *txakoli*, tart as Asturian cider and served from a similar height into squat tumblers, is a taste that many people outside the region are beginning to acquire.

Aragón, too, has a good *denominación de origen* wine from Somontano, in the foothills of the Pyrenees east of Huesca, and the slopes of the Alberes mountains in the eastern Pyrenees produce solid table wines as well as a taste of Catalonia's sparkling wine, Cava, at the castle of Perelada (although most cava is grown in the Penedès region west of Barcelona).

Viniculture was spread around the Mediterranean by the Greeks and Romans, but it was the Cluniac monks of the Middle Ages, weaned on the full reds of their native Burgundy, who brought their heady skills to the monasteries and religious houses that grew up along the pilgrims' road to Santiago.

The wines of Northern Spain have not always been great. Galician wine, most of it white, was once drunk from a white ceramic bowl called a *cunca*, and – traditionally – was thick and cloudy. Pyrenean wine was often likened to tar, and a muleteer's song describes the "stenching wine" of Aragón in the following robust terms: "*As dark as blood, As thick as mud, Strong as the flood of Aragon, the noble River Aragon. It was great nature's second course, It had a body like a horse, You had to drink the stuff by force, At Canfranc, Up in Aragon.*"

*A selection of red wines from La Rioja.*

## BORDEAUX AND RIOJA

Until the late 19th century, Spain's wines were by and large locally produced and did not travel. But in 1860, two marquises, exiled in Bordeaux, returned to their native Rioja heady with the notion that they might emulate the great Bordeaux wines by ageing the Rioja wines in oak barrels. This they did and the houses of the Marqués de Riscal and Marqués de Murrieta, still active today in Elciego and Logroño respectively, gave Spanish wines their first reputation abroad. The use of Bordelais oak barrels was decisive in imbuing the wine with its distinctive oak flavour, while also deepening the colour of the whites and turning the reds tawny.

When the phylloxera louse started to devastate the French vineyards around the turn of the 20th century, some French viniculturalists moved down to La Rioja, notably around Haro, to continue their occupation. They were followed by French *négociants* looking for stock with which to replenish their cellars, and thus the name of Rioja was touted further abroad.

*Treading grapes at the Fiesta de San Mateo, Logroño.*

There are 350 wine makers in the Rioja region, which covers more than 500 sq km (200 sq miles). It stretches alongside the River Ebro and is divided into three areas: La Rioja Baja in the east, where the main town is Calahorra; La Rioja Alta, which includes Haro and Logroño – the main wine towns for the whole region; and, bordering the latter to the north, La Rioja Alavesa in the Basque Country, in the foothills of the Cantabrian Mountains.

The main grape grown is the Tempranillo, with small quantities of Garnacha, Mazuelo and, increasingly, a local variety, Graciano. Many modern methods are now employed and stainless steel fermentation vats are more likely to be seen than wooden vessels, but some *bodegas* (wineries), such as López Heredia Viña Tondonia, founded in Haro in 1887, still use wooden barrels as well as wooden vats to collect the grapes, and they continue to clarify the brew with egg whites, as was traditionally done. The introduction of new methods, however, means that there is no longer a common taste to Rioja wines: although oaky and vanilla tastes dominate, each *bodega* produces wine with an individual flavour.

*Galicians drink more wine than anyone else, consuming an average 137 litres (30 gallons) a year, three times more than they produce.*

A word of warning, though: however traditional that taste might be, not all wines from Rioja are guaranteed to have it. Some are changing their methods to compete with the new wines of Navarra and of Ribera del Duero in Burgos, the most significant wine-producing region in Castilla y León. The wines here come from small, family-run *bodegas* in the scattered villages in the more hostile climate on the edge of the meseta, 500–800 metres (1,600–2,500ft) high. Only reds and rosés are made, mainly from the Tinto Fino, the local name for the Tempranillo grape. Though most of the wines are drunk young *(crianza)*, they are fresh and full-bodied and may be mistaken for older wines. Much sought after, they fetch a high price.

In the Rioja Alavesa, a rugged country of twisting lanes, half of the small *bodegas* are run by their owners and many cover little more than half a hectare (one acre). The method of wine-making here predates the French invasion. Bunches of Tempranillo grapes are tossed, uncrushed, into vats where they ferment in about ten days. The bright red, aromatic wines that result need drinking sooner rather than later.

## NAVARRA

The wines of Navarra are light and refreshing and travel well. The region has long produced Spain's best *rosados* – light, dry and with more body than most rosés. These are made mostly from the Garnacha grape, which is harvested early and macerated for only a short time to keep the colour light.

More recently, Cabernet Sauvignon, Viura Chardonnay and Tempranillo grapes have also been used, as the quest for good reds and whites continues.

The five *Denominación de Origen* regions lie south of Pamplona and cover around 190 sq km (73 sq miles). Among the best wine houses here is Ochoa in Olite, the centre of the Ribera Alta region. The Ochoa family claims descent from a 14th-century winemaker and its label carries an illustration of the 16th-century fortress of the kings of Navarra near which the original winery functioned. Ochoa is now making the best of Navarra's red wines, using Tempranillo with Cabernet Sauvignon and Merlot grapes and long maceration and ageing periods.

*The Tasting Room at Bodegas Portia, a modern Ribera del Duero winery.*

### READING THE LABEL

**D.O.** stands for *Denominación de Origen*, and this authority strictly oversees the production of the wine. Each bottle has a number (BQ No.) and a label which names the region in which the wine is produced.

**D.O.Ca.** is Classified Denomination of Origin, a higher classification which only Rioja enjoys.

**Gran Reserva** red wines have spent at least two years in an oak cask and three in a bottle. White and rosé wines have spent four years in cask and bottle, of which six months must be in oak casks.

**Reserva** red wines have spent at least a year in the cask and are at least three years old. White wines must spend six months in the cask.

**Vino de Crianza** has been at least a year in an oak cask and is in its third year.

**Cosecha** has had little or no ageing. *Vino de cosecha* is made to be drunk young.

**CVC** *(Conjunto de Varias Cosechas)* means there has been a blend of several vintages.

**Blanco** is white and is made from white grapes.

**Tinto** (literally "ink") is red, a colour ranging from cherry to black, made from red and black grapes in their skins.

**Rosado** is pink or rosé, made from red or red and white grapes without their skins. In Castilla y León, this is sometimes called **Clarete**.

## COASTAL SPECIALITIES

Some grapes grow along the northern coastal strip to make small quantities of mostly white wine. Best known is the Basque *txakoli*, which is usually white, light (about 10º) and made from the unripened Hondarribia Zuri grape. The Gipúzkoa coast around Getaria is a main provider of this wine, which is drunk everywhere, especially in *tapas* bars where it accompanies the various morsels that tasca-hoppers nibble as they make their midday and evening rounds from bar to bar. In Getaria, every Sunday in August is celebrated as *txakoli* day.

There is also a red *txakoli*, also made from Hondarribia Gori. Until recently, it was only made for drinking at home, as are many pleasant but unremarkable wines made on farms and smallholdings in Asturias.

## THE WHITE WINES OF GALICIA

The commercial vineyards of Galicia stretch along the valleys of the Miño and Sil, and many houses are decorated with vine-covered porches, their neat gardens trailed with vines strung on wires between granite posts.

*Bringing in the grape harvest in the Sil Valley.*

### GOOD YEARS, BAD YEARS

Every year the wine industry publishes and distributes lists of "good" and "poor" years of the *Denominación de Orígenes*. These are often handed out in restaurants and at first glance seem to provide very useful information, but they can at best only serve as a guide. A "poor" year for a good wine can still be better than a "good" year for a poor wine.

Also, the different character of wines from grapes grown only a few hundred metres apart can be important, so although a vintage may be dismissed as poor, or praised as good, not all wines in the area will follow the trend.

The River Sil comes west through gorges in the Cordillera Cantábrica, benefiting the wine region of Bierzo in Castilla y León, around Ponferrada and the attractive small town Vilafranca del Bierzo, which produces good, solid reds from a local black grape, the Mencía. The two rivers meet just north of the town of Ourense, from where the Miño flows west through the Ribeiro and Rías Baixas D.O.s to Portugal and the sea.

The best-known of the new Galician white wines come from these two regions in the valley of the Miño. The story of the revival of the wines of Galicia belongs, as it often does in wine history, to the enterprise of one man.

White wines have been produced here since the Romans introduced the vine. As so many of the valleys where vines are grown are tucked away, many survived the phylloxera blight. However, in the enthusiasm of subsequent replanting many local grapes were torn out in favour of imported phylloxera-hardy Palomino (white, the sherry grape) and Garnacha Tintorera (red). These produced much more juice, at the cost of flavour.

The astonishing success of Rías Baixas as a *Denominación de Origen* in the 1990s put Galician wines on the world map. This was mainly as a result of the efforts of Santiago Ruiz, a retired vintner from Rosal in Pontevedra. He experimented with a local grape, the Albariño, thought to have been introduced some 300 years previously from the Rhine by German monks on their way to Santiago. His experiments paid off and he tirelessly championed the Albariño cause. It was not long before the wines became so popular that they not only merited a new D.O. region, but they also began to undermine the long-held position of neighbouring Ribeiro as the best white wine in Spain.

*The harvest (vendimia) is celebrated in every wine town at grape picking time, in September, though wine festivals are held throughout the summer.*

Albariño is not cheap, but people are prepared to pay for it: gourmet restaurants in Madrid and Barcelona have been knocking Ribeiros off the wine lists in favour of the new Galician labels. A good stopping-off place for visitors to try them out is Cambados on the C-550 north of Ponferrada, where cafés in the town square sell the wine packaged in boxes of three, and serve it chilled as an admirable accompaniment to the day's fish catch.

## SUPERIOR LOCAL GRAPES

In response to the Rías Baixas' success, winemakers in Ribeiro and the other Galician wine regions began looking not just to Albariño grapes with which to make their wines, but also to other local varieties, such as Lado, Torrontés and Treixedura. Ribeiro remains a major white wine producer (it is twice the size of Rías Baixas), but more and more growers – including the big local co-operative, Vinícola del Ribeiro – are turning to local varieties, naming the result "Ribeiro Superior".

The other Galician D.O. regions are following on fast. In the Valdeorras region on the River Sil around O Barca, the best wines come from the prize-winning Bodegas La Tapada in Rubi, Ourense, founded in 1989 by the Guitian family. Their secret is another local grape variant that faced extinction, the Godella, which benefits from a local climate that allows a natural "noble rot" – a fungus which concentrates the sugar in the grape, as it does with French Sauternes.

*Albariño wine from Rías Baixas, Galicia.*

In the Monterrei D.O., not far from the Portuguese border, the appellation "Monterrei Superior" is a guarantee of 85 percent local grapes.

To complete the picture, Cantabria has 10 wineries of its own which are organised into two wine-producing areas and Asturias has a small wine region of its own, Tierra de Cangas. There are also vineyards at the eastern end of the Pyrenees in the Catalan wine region of Empordà.

# CIDER: THE DRINK FROM PARADISE

Cider is the social drink of northwestern Spain. Asturians drink 35 million litres of it every year and Basque "bertsolari" sing its praises in the bars.

A Basque legend tells that cider was made long before wine. Shortly after Adam and Eve were thrown out of Paradise, Eve reached for an apple from a tree. Adam flew into a rage, shaking the crop into a hole in the ground, and after a day the fruit oozed a sweet, golden liquid. The gist of this tale is true. Native, still cider was the staple drink in Asturias and the Basque Country at least a millennium before imported wine became a commonplace tipple. Wheat here was too valuable for beer-making, but apples grew well in the damp, inland valleys. Indeed, historians suggest that Basque fishermen and sailors took the first cider apples to Normandy around the 6th century.

By medieval times, communal orchards and cider-making were governed by strict laws. Each village had the right to ban imports until its own annual supply had run out and to impose fines on the sale of watered-down cider. It was not until the late 19th century that today's *sidrerías* (cider-tasting cellars) grew out of the custom of friends drinking straight from the makers' barrels.

## HEADY EXCURSIONS

A trip to one of today's *sidrerías* is a fine way of joining in with local life. During the short spring and summer season, Basques flock to the *sidrerías*, locally called *sagardotegias*, which are clustered around San Sebastián. In Asturias, the *sidrerías* or *chigres* are found mainly in central mining valleys close to Gijón, Villaviciosa and Nava, the self-proclaimed cider capital, and stay open all year. Real cider-lovers can get into serious tasting at one of the competitions or fiestas (see page 102).

In the Basque *sagardotegias*, you drink and eat standing at long tables, tapping off as much cider as you want for a flat price. The accompanying food is usually a salt-cod omelette, wood-grilled beef chops, walnuts and local cheese.

*Drawing cider from the barrel is an art: the curving jet fresh but not cold, should froth into a head on the side the tumbler, but no more than an inch at a time.*

*Local sidrerías are making a comeback as orchards ar replanted with native varieties of apple that have been genetically improved to give higher yields.*

*At the Sidreria Barkaiztegi, near San Sebastián, cider is fermented in huge oak barrels. During the cider season, visitors.*

*r tastings are often accompanied by hearty country such as wood-grilled beef chops.*

*apples are crushed and pips removed, then left to d before the juice is pressed out and left to ferment.*

## Ciders to suit all palates

There are all kinds of subtle variations evident in the finished cider depending on the localities and producers. Late-harvested apples give fuller flavours. Slow-pressing and clarification during fermentation give a drier finish. Fermentation in Basque oak, Asturian chestnut or modern stainless steel produce different effects. The maker's hand also counts, since the best cider (clear, fruity and lively in the glass) comes from an expert taster blending acidic, sweet and bitter varieties in the press. It is this which makes the opening of the barrels a big crowd-puller, since not even the maker knows exactly how each barrel will turn out.

Apart from the cider, you may also like to try the local apple-based *eau-de-vie*, called *aguardiente de manzana* (Asturias) or *sagardoz* (Basque Country). Both are very strong and highly recommended as a potent souvenir of your trip.

*Bottled cider is traditionally held above the head and poured in brief spurts to give just an inch or so of cider called culin.*

*The now closed Pozo Calderon mine, León.*

# THE INDUSTRIAL LEGACY

A region once reliant on heavy industry, now reduced to the status of history and heritage, has had to find new ways to make a living.

Approaching the coast of northern Spain on the deck of a ferry from Portsmouth is one way to get a sense of the history of the region but you will need a little imagination.

From 30km (20 miles) outside the mouth of the Bilbao estuary, the view on a clear day at first appears unspoilt and pastoral: it encompasses the French coast and the snow-capped Pyrenees to the far left, the green hills of Biscay immediately ahead and, away in the distance to the right, beyond the relatively low coastline of eastern Cantabria, the tall Asturian mountain range of the Picos de Europa.

What you don't see is industry but it is not that long ago that this same route was traced by a stream of grimy coasters bringing coal to Bilbao and carrying iron ore back to Britain.

The port of Bilbao is still the largest handler of shipping on the north coast and the fourth most important port in Spain but these days it caters for containers and tourists rather than the output of heavy industry as it did in its glory days.

A little way up the estuary, Bilbao itself is a testament to post-industrialisation. Its emblematic building is no longer a blast furnace but an avant garde museum of modern art, the Guggenheim, standing on what was once a coaling wharf. The Nervión river has been cleaned up and gardens planted. Heavy industry is nothing more than a memory but it is a vital part of the history of northern Spain.

*Miners demonstrating against reduced pay in Langreo.*

## THE ART OF METALLURGY

The first known ironworks in the Spanish Basque Country – the provinces of Vizcaya (Bizkaia), Guipúzcoa (Gipuzkoa) and Álava (Araba) – date from Roman times and burned the local brown hematite ore and charcoal fuel in an open hearth to produce simple castings for tools, weapons and adornments. By the late Middle Ages, when the art of metallurgy was revived and refined, higher temperatures were achieved with bellows in what came to be known throughout Europe as Catalan forges, also fuelled by charcoal.

The transition from the smelting of iron to the mass production of steel in Spain did not take place until well into the 19th century, when the defeat of the French invaders and the Carlist rebels created suitable conditions for the required capital investment. The Spanish intelligentsia had seen how British industrial development had contributed to its success in the Napoleonic wars and was eager to rid Spain of its image as a reactionary, anti-rationalist theocracy dating from the Inquisition and the religious wars of the 17th century.

There seemed to be just two basic ingredients for industrial revolution: iron ore and coal. Bilbao had plenty of ore, and the coal could be shipped in from Asturias, just 160km (100 miles) to the west. Thus began an industrialisation programme which, despite some temporary successes, never fulfilled the original intention: to provide the goods and wealth required for Spain to regain its former status as a major European power. Only now, when the European nation-state is questioning its role and future, can the visitor see signs of genuine optimism.

*The Bilbao Maritime Museum is located on the site of the former Astilleros Euskalduna shipbuilders.*

The initial error of Spain's planners was pardonable. The wonders of British industrial might had focused people's minds on the availability of the essential feedstocks and of the know-how; what they tended to forget was the profitable disposal of the end product, in other words, a market. Until the end of the 19th century, Spain could still lay claim to the remains of an American colonial empire, but the destruction of its navy at Trafalgar in 1815 meant that Britain and the United States dominated all trade of industrial goods with that region. Spain's internal market could not provide the demand required for mass production of steel. This fact was made clear when, at the end of an ambitious programme of railway construction – 5,000km (3,100 miles) over difficult terrain between 1848 and 1865 – there were insufficient passengers and freight to defray running costs, let alone to compensate the investors.

The second problem can be attributed to bad luck. At about the time the first major industrial projects were getting under way in Bilbao and Asturias, in England Henry Bessemer was perfecting his converter which, by firing air upwards through the charge, transformed a combination of hot metal and pig-iron directly into steel without reheating, thus reducing coke consumption by about half and boosting the potential output of each burn from a few hundred kilogrammes to several tonnes.

The drawback from the point of view of the English steelmakers was that the process required low-phosphorous iron ore, of which England had only a small supply in Cumbria. There was some in Germany, but it was expensive and costly to move. The nearest economic option was Bilbao and it was not long before the first iron-clad bulkers started to make the journey southwards from Newcastle, effectively turning Bilbao ore into a primary feedstock for British, not Spanish, steelworks.

## CAPITALIST EXCESSES

Unlike Germany, Spain had no cash; most of the investment had to come from abroad. Though Bilbao has made great advances in becoming an attractive city to live in, its environmental problems began when it became the victim of some of the worst excesses of laissez-faire capitalism, exercised by people who never came within 500 miles of it. On the other hand, without investment there could be no industry, meaning that the conditions for repatriation of profits and other side-benefits had to be attractive.

Only a few local families, notably the Ybarras and the Chávarris, managed to make good their land rights and participate in profits. For many years, conventional wisdom held that the sales of Bilbao ore to Britain between the mid-1870s and the turn of the 20th century provided the funds to industrialise both the neighbouring province of Guipúzcoa and the coal-bearing regions of Asturias.

According to this thesis, the profits of the mines were split roughly 50–50 between local and foreign firms. However, research at the University of Bilbao has shown that local interests received an estimated £7.7 million, whereas the foreign companies earned £6.6 million. However, the foreigners, in companies such as Bilbao Iron Ore, Levison, Luchana Mining, Triano Ore and MacLennan, sold their ore at a discount to their steelmaking partners in Britain, which means that their group profits were significantly higher.

What really tilts the balance, however, is the money earned from transport. The records of the port of Bilbao show that 90 percent of the iron ore exported was loaded aboard British merchant vessels, meaning gross earnings, at an average freight rate of six shillings a ton, of nearly £20 million for British shipowners compared with only £2 million for Basque owners. At the height of the ore trade, when the ore was brought down river from the mines in barges towed by women under harness, no fewer than 3,000 ships – nearly ten a day – were loading at the lower wharfs of Bilbao.

## THE DIFFICULT MINES OF ASTURIAS

Asturian coal, the second ingredient in the plan, has always been of bad quality and difficult and dangerous to mine. With hindsight, it should have been left untouched. But the coal deep below the valleys behind Gijón might have justified the effort of mining it if, in the first place, the Bessemer converter had not halved fuel requirements for steelmaking and, secondly, if the ships taking ore out of Bilbao had not loaded their holds first with much better-quality British coal. Henceforward, the Asturian mines had to be protected by duties on imports or laws obliging Spanish industry to burn a certain percentage of their coal.

Not surprisingly, questions were raised about the results of Spain's industrial modernisation programme. As a result, the free-market pendulum swung back. The liberals put up a strong rearguard action, but an import tariff on steel was finally imposed in 1891 and stiffened in 1906. As from 1887, all Spanish-registered ships had to be built in national shipyards. In Bilbao, Astilleros del Nervión and La Sociedad Euskalduna de Construcción de Buques were set up as a consequence.

*Coal mounds in Gijón.*

The promise of a protected market produced the three forebears of the Altos Hornos de Vizcaya (AHV) steelworks: La Vizcaya (1882), Altos Hornos y Fábricas de Hierro y Acero (1882) and Iberia (1888). All three enjoyed a short-lived boom in the years leading up to and during World War I, when Anglo-German rivalry and the depreciation of the peseta placed Spanish steel at a premium.

## INTO MODERN TIMES

After a century of protectionism, initiated under the Restoration, consolidated by the 1920s dictatorship of Primo de Rivera and continued after the Civil War by General Franco, Spain's democratic governments have used the free-market decrees of Brussels to engineer a gradual dismantling of the state-owned primary industrial infrastructure.

They've had good reason to. The technological and commercial failure of steelmaking and shipbuilding had created large pockets of unemployment. Jobs needed to come from elsewhere, principally the service sector.

San Mames stadium, Bilbao.

The rest is easily told. A region once powered by its heavy industry has changed radically over the last decades as competition with other countries has made old industries obsolete. Shipbuilding has disappeared. Coal mining in Asturias, much reduced in scale, clings on but is thought to be doomed: it has all but been reduced to heritage, as seen in the Mining Museum of El Entrego. Steelmaking has similarly shrunk. Spain's steel producing businesses were consolidated and taken over, and taken over again. They are now part of the multinational ArcelorMittal, the world's leading steel and mining company, which maintains plants in Aviles and Gijón (in Asturias); Sestao, Etxebarri and Zumarraga (in the Basque Country); and Lesaka (in Navarra), as well as research and development installations. Just outside Bilbao, one lonely blast furnace – *alto horno* – has been left as a rusting landmark to noisier, dirtier but, for some, more profitable times.

Other industries, however, including chemicals and food-processing – connected to the dairy farming industry of Asturias and fishing fleets of Galicia – are thriving. The same goes for industries that serve a modern prosperous consumer society: there are vehicle factories in Palencia (Renault), Vigo (Citröen), Vitoria (Mercedes) and Pamplona (Volkswagen).

For a while the construction industry looked as if it had a promising future. A great number of buildings went up during the early 2000s, including emblematic projects of urban regeneration in Bilbao and elsewhere, but the sudden world economic crash of 2008 brought this to a halt.

## THE ANSWER CARRIED IN THE WIND

The growth industry of the 21st century is renewable power, particularly hydro-electric power (often seen in the Pyrenees) and the much more recent arrival wind energy. Spain is the fifth biggest producer of wind power in the world. After a sustained programme of investment it has a capacity of over 27,000 MW installed. Lines of white wind turbines along the crests of hills are a common sight in many parts of the north. Navarra has particularly taken advantage of this old technology brought up to date and is now thought to cover around 53 percent of its energy needs from renewable sources. Galicia also has numerous windfarms thanks to its strong Atlantic breezes. Surprisingly, perhaps, despite the cloudier climate, the north also has the country's fourth largest solar photovoltaic plant at Arnedo in La Rioja. The 172,000 panels on the site produced a combined output of 34 MW the equivalent of the energy needs of over 11,000 households.

Like many western European countries, Spain has had to cope with the effects of deindustrialisation, which include not only a change in employment structure but also changes to society. The north has borne the brunt of this as communities built around a mine or a mill struggle to adjust to a world in which short, precarious contracts and retraining, rather than jobs for life, are the norm.

*Las Llanes de Codés wind farm, Navarra.*

A fresh catch in Llanes harbour.

# FISHING

Galicia has the largest fishing fleet in the European Union and its fishermen sail the world in the search for new grounds and new fish to catch.

The town of Laguardia, on the southernmost tip of Galicia, just where Spain and Portugal meet, is typical of hundreds of small fishing ports on the northern Spanish coast and not much different from fishing communities elsewhere on the Atlantic seaboard. It is a picturesque spot. Its tiny, narrow streets wend downwards from the town centre to the small, protected harbour from which a dozen or so vessels set out to sea to earn a living in the time-honoured fashion.

Each morning on the *lonxa* (fish market), local housewives and restaurateurs assemble to inspect the day's catch and the competition and loud bartering begins. You can eat delicious fresh fish and shellfish in any of the restaurants that abound along the harbour quay and this is as delightful a place as any in Spain to spend your summer holidays. Tourism is rapidly becoming one of the main money earners of this remote region which, the locals will tell you, sits on the edge of the backside of the world.

Look at any fish market in Spain and what strikes you is the quantity and variety of fish and seafood available. Spaniards are among the world's largest consumers of fish. They devour almost 2 million tonnes each year, three times more than the average for the rest of the European Union. The average selection of tapas is likely to have several exquisite morsels of fish. However far you go inland you are likely to find at least one fish dish on a restaurant menu – either a fresh seawater variety or a locally caught trout – served without fussy sauces or any pretension.

Supermarkets, meanwhile, invariably have a fresh fish stall with a queue in front of it, and rows of canned fish and seafood. Many species sold go by local names and often a phrasebook is no use. You just have to ask what it is you are looking at and how best to prepare it, or take a chance.

*Ships on a traditional procession near Pontevedra.*

## A DEPENDENCY ON THE SEA

There is a fishing industry on a greater or lesser scale everywhere along the coasts of Spain. Often it is a very low-key affair, with only a few boats operating and few people entirely dependent on the catch. There is also a lot of informal fishing – by rod and line or mask, snorkel and harpoon – and seafood gathering at low tide. Some restaurants rely on such ad hoc supplies to provide their customers with daily variety:

they reduce the supply chain to a walk up the beach and proudly advertise this fact.

In Galicia, however, fishing is serious business. The traditional mainstays of the Galician economy are agriculture and fishing – and the latter makes a healthy contribution to the national economy. In the 1950s, Spain maintained the biggest fishing fleet in the world. It still has the largest fleet in the European Union, catching 285,000 tonnes of live weight fish in a good year. Spain is also the EU's largest per capita consumer of seafood and its biggest producer of frozen seafood.

It has been estimated that 400,000 people in Galicia alone (out of a population of 2.8 million) depend on fishing and its related industries, such as food processing, canning and boat building. Fishing is an important if gradually declining industry in coastal communities all along the north coast and in the Mediterranean.

Spanish fishing vessels ply the seas of the world in search of a living. Galicia's fishing boats also go to the fishing grounds off the Falkland Islands in the South Atlantic, to the waters off the coasts of Chile and Peru in the Pacific, and

*Vendors selling fresh fish on the market in Santiago de Compostela.*

## DREAMS OF SEA BREAM

Dwindling fish stocks may be a global concern, but shortages in the local waters of Northern Spain are nothing short of a tragedy. Sea bream *(besugo)*, for example, has long been a traditional dish for Christmas and other occasions. A generation ago it was regularly on the family plate. Today it is seen less often and, when it is, it fetches very high prices.

Boats that put out overnight (*pescar bajura* or "lower fishing" as opposed to long-distance *pescar altura*) want nothing more than a prize *besugo del Cantábrico* and if one falls into their nets it is likely to go no further. Crews at Ondarroa, the main Basque fishing port, have their names on a rota and take it in turns to keep any specimen they have the good fortune to catch. There are other *besugo*, of course, which are caught in other parts of the world, frozen and imported. But these are not the same at all.

Similarly, salt cod *(bacalao)* has long been a staple. But now that stocks are low, an imposter has been introduced, the *abadejo* (*Epinephelus alexandrinus*, from the grouper family). This does not have the flavour of cod and its skin is slightly speckled.

*Bacalao* is the main ingredient of such favourite dishes as *bacalao al pil-pil*, made of nothing more than garlic and olive oil, and a sauce produced by steadily shaking the simmering pot for 1.5 hours.

eastwards to the Indian Ocean. Their boats now fish off every continent except Australasia and Antarctica. When refrigerated trawlers were introduced in the 1960s, long-distance fishing became the norm and crews now think nothing of spending six months at a time at sea.

Success, however, has brought a new problem, in that fishing vessels are now so efficient that they can fish for only a few days or weeks a year before their quota is exhausted. They are being forced to move increasingly into the high seas and, sometimes illegally, into the territorial waters of developing countries, provoking conflicts there with traditional fishermen.

*Spaniards are among the world's largest consumers of fish, devouring almost three times more fish than the average European.*

Alongside the search for new fishing grounds, goes the search for new species of fish. Scientists at the Oceanography Institute spend their time looking for alternatives to species which are overfished. One line of research led them to considering the commercial prospects of a fish which is so ugly that it is known in Galicia as "the rat", but is in fact the grenadier, a species which is found at depths of more than 1,500 metres (5,000ft).

## EUROPEAN RESTRICTIONS

The largest part of the Spanish fleet, however, fishes much closer to home. Since World War II, fishermen from all along the coast of northern Spain – from Galicia in the West, through Asturias and Cantabria to the Basque Country – have fished in European waters, mainly off the British Isles and France.

Until 1977, boats from the ports of Pasajes, Ondarroa and Bilbao in the Basque Country, from the ports of Santander in Cantabria and Gijón in Asturias, as well as Galician vessels from Vigo and A Coruña, had virtually free access to the fishing grounds of western Europe, catching cod, hake, dory and other species.

That all changed in the late 1970s, with the formulation of a common European fishing policy, following access of the United Kingdom, Ireland and Denmark to the then European Economic Community. European jurisdictional waters were extended to 200 nautical miles (370km) and the consequences for the Spanish fishing fleet have been felt ever since.

The extension of jurisdictional waters was particularly harsh on the Galician fleet, which had traditionally fished profitably in the Irish Conservation Box. The whole of that fishing ground was rendered out of bounds.

By 1986, the year Spain itself joined the Community, the number of Spanish boats that could legally fish in European waters had been reduced to just over 300.

*King crab for sale at a market in A Coruña.*

Spain, like all other EU member states, is party to the Common Fisheries Policy which has noble utilitarian goals but is much criticised in its application by the fishing community. Its aim is to manage fish stocks according to scientific data for the long-term good of the fishing industry and to the benefit of the consumer. Fish, it reasons, do not follow international frontiers. And fishing people, responding to demand and in competition with each other, will not voluntarily reduce their catches of dwindling fish species.

The primary function of the Common Fishing Policy is to prevent overfishing by setting "total catchable allowances" and encouraging captains to be more selective in what they catch. It also seeks to prevent the landing of immature fish and to eradicate the practice of discarding unwanted fish that have been caught inadvertently. Critics say that application of the Common Fisheries Policy is over-centralised in Brussels where bureaucrats don't understand local conditions in northern Spain and place more value on standards and targets than on the needs of ordinary people trying to earn a living. They also argue that protecting fish stocks has come

*Fisherman washes down his catch in Vigo.*

at the expense of fishing communities, that it favours industrial corporations over small and medium-sized fishing firms, and that it does nothing to stop national governments turning a blind eye to abuse.

For years, the story of the Spanish fishing fleet has been one of constant battles with its European partners. Almost every year, Basque fishermen have been at loggerheads with their French counterparts and fishing "wars" have broken out between the Galicians and the British and Irish fleets.

Joint ventures have been set up and quota hopping, whereby Spanish vessels fly the British flag and fish under licences granted originally to the UK fleet, are two of the most

*Uncertainty over the future of Galicia's fishing industry has led some fishermen to emigrate to Argentina.*

recent developments to cause controversy and litigation within the European Union. Quota busting and the use of illegal nets are also common practices. Spaniards have acquired a reputation for being Europe's most avaricious fishermen.

It is an accusation they resent about their fishing practices. They argue that they are no better or no worse than anyone else, because fishermen the world over need to have something of the hunter in them. To a large extent, however, they are the victims of their own success. Their dedication is second to none and they are prepared to go anywhere in the world in search of fish.

A more sustainable solution is fish farming which has taken off in a big way in Galicia. Many of the mussels eaten in Spain are specially cultivated for consumption rather than gathered wild.

## TOUGH DECISIONS

There is a growing awareness that options for the Spanish fleet may now be running out. With 80 percent of the world's fish resources overexploited, the odds against continuing to find new grounds and new stocks are lengthening. It seems, therefore, inevitable that the Spanish fleet will continue to diminish.

Back in Laguardia, some fishermen have already decided they cannot wait for the outcome of their port's uncertain future and have followed in the footsteps of their ancestors, bucking the trend of recent history, and emigrated to Argentina. That traditional escape route from hard times was supposed to have fallen out of use when Spain joined Europe. But ask any fisherman from any port in northern Spain and his answer will be unequivocal. Far from proving a panacea for the ills of the Spanish fishing industry, membership of the European Union has proved to be a disaster for the fishing industry, but better news for fish conservation.

*Fishing boats in the port of Ribadesella.*

*Pilgrim on the Camino de Santiago in Castile-León.*

# THE PILGRIM ROUTE TO SANTIAGO DE COMPOSTELA

In the Middle Ages, Santiago was Christendom's most popular pilgrimage. Interest sagged after the Reformation – but today the pilgrims are back.

Any pilgrim nervous at the start of his or her great trek to Santiago de Compostela in the Middle Ages would have initial fears reinforced by the world's first travel guide, the *Liber Sancti Jacobi* or *Codex Calixtinus*, written around 1130 by Aymeric Picaud, a monk from Poitou. This tract warns of the murderous nature of the Basques and the people of Navarra who may rob the pilgrims and ride them like beasts before killing them.

The Basques, the book points out, are descended from three races sent by Julius Caesar to conquer the region: the Scots, the Nubians, and people with tails who came from Cornwall. Further, the Navarrese, whose lands have no bread or wine, are described as bestial fornicators who affix locks to the behinds of their mules and horses so that no-one else may enjoy them.

Castile, the guide continues, is a land full of food and treasures, but its people are vicious and evil. Galicia, the goal of the journey, comes off best as a land of abundant rivers and orchards and the people, though irascible and contentious, are judged most like the French.

At the time the book was written, the pilgrims' route to the end of the world was becoming established. Christianity had three Holy Cities: Rome, Jerusalem and Santiago de Compostela. To pilgrims making their lifetime's journey for indulgences, Santiago was soon the most popular of the three and thousands visited the shrine of Sant Iago (St James) every year.

Jerusalem was a more perilous journey, one that anyway precluded Spaniards until they had removed the infidel from their own soil, in the same way that Muslim people in Spain were absolved from visiting Mecca, visiting instead Mohammed's bones in Córdoba. Rome was easier to reach but absolution not always as freely given. The journey across the Pyrenees to Santiago, on the other hand, though undoubtedly no piece of cake, was full of exciting things to see and at the end of it pilgrims would receive their Compostelana, a document confirming their visit, and a guarantee that would halve the time they would spend in Purgatory. If they made the journey during a Holy Year when St James's Day, 25 July, fell on a Sunday, they would receive plenary absolution and their due time in Purgatory would be expunged altogether.

*Pilgrim in Santiago de Compostela.*

## ST JAMES'S STORY

The apostle James the Greater, the Galilean fisherman son of Zebedee and older brother of

John the Evangelist, was known as the Thunderer because of his booming voice. According to a story started in the 7th century, after Christ's crucifixion he was allotted Spain as the territory for his mission. He sailed to the peninsula and came ashore on the mouth of the Ulla in Galicia, staying in the country for seven years, with little success, before returning to Judaea where he was put to the sword by Herod Agrippa to become the first of Christ's apostles to be martyred.

His disciples brought his body back to Spain, returning in a stone boat to their first landing place, Iria Flavia, now called Padrón, on the River Ulla. The pillar to which they tied the boat is under the altar in Padrón's church of Santiago. The resting place of his remains then became forgotten through invasions and diversions, and it was not until 814 that their whereabouts was revealed when a shepherd by the name of Pelayo was guided to the tomb by a shower of stars. This gave the place its name: Santiago de Compostela, St James of the Field of Stars *(campus stellae)*. In Spain, the Milky Way is called the Road of St James *(el Camino de Santiago)*. There is, however, another etymology that points to the necropolis on which the cathedral at Santiago is built: *compostela* is the Latin word for cemetery.

*A pilgrim on the Camino de Santiago, in the historic centre of Burgos.*

Thirty years after this discovery, St James reappeared on a white charger at the battle of Clavijo near Logroño, helping Ramiro I of Asturias to a swift victory over the Moors. As a result, he was no longer a thundering missionary, but was Santiago Matamoros, St James the Slayer of Moors, the symbol of the Reconquest and the patron saint of Spain. Alfonso II had already built a chapel on the site of the discovery of the bones, and this was enlarged by Alfonso III between 874 and 899. The tomb was respectfully spared in a subsequent Moorish attack in 997. The saint's bones were incorporated in the foundation of the rebuilt cathedral in the early 12th century, and they now lie in a crypt under the altar.

The 10th and 11th centuries in Europe saw high excitement in the discovery of saints' bones, and the appeal of relics to the people gave the Church great power over the faithful. The leading Christian institution in this part of the world was the Benedictine abbey at Cluny in Burgundy, a dukedom linked to the Spanish kings. It was certainly in the interests of France to see the Moors pushed out of Spain: they had not enjoyed their earlier visit. French traders were encouraged to set up businesses along the route, and the Romanesque style of architecture started at Cluny spread along the way.

## THE ROUTES

Santiago is approached by several pilgrim routes, coming from different points of the compass. The main one, forged by the French and known as the Camino Francés, starts at the pass of Roncesvalles in the Basque Pyrenees, and heads down to Logroño, Burgos and León in Castile before climbing back into Galicia and arriving, 781km (485 miles) later, at Santiago de Compostela. The *Codex Calixtinus* is primarily concerned with this route, which it divides into 13 days' walking from the border, each day covering no less than 21km (13 miles). But pilgrims were frequently diverted and often took longer.

A coastal route, the Camino del Norte or Camino de la Costa, simply followed the north coast, but it was considered dangerous because of brigand attacks. The Camino de la Plata (the silver route) came from Southern Spain, the Camino Portugués arrived from Portugal and the Camino Inglés was the short haul from A Coruña, where English pilgrims landed by boat.

In France, there were four major starting points: Paris, Vézelay, Le Puy and Arles, through which Dutch, German and Italian pilgrims came. The first three routes converged at St Jean-Pied-de-Port, while the one from Arles (which brought Italians and southern Germans) travelled the Camino Aragonés through the Puerto de Somport. The round journey from Paris took about four months.

The pilgrims were protected by the Knights Templar, principally of the Order of Santiago recognised by Pope Alexander III in 1175, and hospitals were set up along the way, often in the towns where churches existed. The Knights' impressive headquarters, the Hospital de San Marcos in León, and the grand Hospital Real built by Fernando and Isabel in Santiago are now both *paradores*. The journey on the open road was perilous and many sections remained remote. Bells would ring from churches and hermitages when the weather was foul and visibility poor. Many pilgrims would not make the whole journey, which could last several months, especially if they were ill and in search of cures for their afflictions. Thousands fell along the way, and there is a large cemetery at Roncesvalles, before the route has barely begun. If a sick pilgrim reached the Puerto del Perdón in León and could genuinely go no further, he or she would receive full redemption. Another "pardon door" exists at Villafranca del Bierzo.

*Pilgrim monument on the Alto del Perdon (Mount of Forgiveness).*

Although there was money to be made by tradespeople along the route, the majority of pilgrims were poor and in need of alms. It was incumbent upon the local populace to ensure the pilgrims were given food and shelter when they asked for it, and the *Codex Calixtinus* gives examples of the divine retribution – sudden poverty, sickness, even death – on those who closed their doors to requests. Residents may, however, have been as wary of the pilgrims as the pilgrims were of them, for among those going of their own volition were also criminals and social offenders who had been sentenced to make the pilgrimage to atone for their sins.

Pilgrims wore distinctive hats and cloaks, carried sticks and gourds for water, and sported

*Camino waymarker.*

the cockle shell of St James. The selling of these *mariscos* was forbidden along the route and pilgrims, on reaching Santiago, would head for the Barrio de los Concheiros (shell-sellers' quarter) where they would buy a Galician cockleshell and fasten it to their hats as a sign that they had reached their journey's end. Here, they would pass through the Pilgrim's door of the cathedral, pray at the saint's shrine or, after it was put up in the 13th century, touch his statue, now above the high altar. To hide the stench of their journey and their sickness, the *botafumeiro* (the largest censer in the world), held by eight men, would be swung across the nave to bathe the assembled with sweeter smelling incense.

Some pilgrims would find the strength to walk the last few miles to stand at Finisterre (literally "Land's End" before 1492) and watch the sun set at the end of the world.

## DECLINE AND RENEWAL

The popularity of the pilgrimage dwindled after the Reformation and particularly after the saint's bones were removed for safety following a Protestant English attack on the coast in the wake of the Armada. They were returned in time for the War of Independence (1808–14), when the French sacked the cathedral, though they spared the relics. The Camino de Santiago never regained its medieval significance and those who did arrive were often not welcome, which led to the saying: *Los Peregrinos, muchas posadas y pocos amigos* (the pilgrims, with many inns and few friends).

Only in the late 20th century did the Santiago route undergo a revival, not just as a kind of religious tourism – although some people make the journey for spiritual reasons – but, with increasing leisure time and early retirement, the long-distance walk became a recreational challenge.

New hostels were built and facilities added, from simple bunks in old churches to dramatic modern buildings such as La Virgen del Camino just outside León, designed in 1961 by brother Coello de Portugal with striking sculptures by Josep Maria Subirachs, who added the angular figures to the Passion facade of the church of La Sagrada Família in Barcelona.

In 1992, John Paul II paid a visit to Santiago de Compostela, the first pope to do so, adding to the pilgrimage's popularity. The following year, the route was declared a World Heritage Site by Unesco.

The popularity of the pilgrimage routes now seems unstoppable. In winter, a week or two may go by without a single pilgrim to be seen. In summer, the numbers soar and coaches have been known to stop when they see a pilgrim, so that the sightseers can clamber out and take photographs.

Nowadays, to qualify as a genuine pilgrim, you must walk the last 100km (62 miles), or cycle or ride on horseback the last 200km (124 miles) of the official route and carry a record book to be stamped at the *refugios* (hostels) on the way, together with a letter of introduction either from your parish or obtained at the beginning of the route.

*Part of the Camino Francés, near Mercadoiro.*

*Santiago de Compostela Cathedral.*

# ARCHITECTURE

Streets of houses with glassed-in balconies and a rich scattering of exquisite pre-Romanesque churches differentiate the north from the rest of Spain.

A particular delight of northern Spain is stumbling across country churches of mellow, earthy hues and of such satisfying proportions and harmony that feelings of peace and solitude are raised to new heights. And within these buildings' elegant space, there seems to be an answer to everything: a key to the past, an escape from the present and a calm contemplation of the future.

Many of these unique monuments belong to the pivotal era of history between the departure of the Roman forces of occupation and the reconquest of the peninsula by the resident Christians, whose faith could live and breathe in the safety of the mountains. In the few hundred years from the 8th to the 13th century, there was a flowering of a sturdy, eloquent architecture which flowed from pre-Romanesque to Romanesque via Mozarabic. Pagan, Moorish and Christian: many gods inspired the architects' art, and nowhere are the hopes and fears of the medieval mind expressed more clearly than in the lively, sculpted figures that people their masonry.

Nothing comes out of nothing, and artistic threads can be traced back through earlier centuries, to the Neolithic caves, for example, whose inhabitants used rope patterns as decorative motifs that were to develop into the *sogueado* relief work of later churches. Celtic motifs also occasionally occur. The Celtiberians lived in communities of *castros* (circular stone dwellings) and erected long barrows, which they filled with treasures for their dead.

## ROMAN FOUNDATIONS

There is not much evidence of the Roman occupation in this part of Spain – some remains at Astorga and walls around Lugo. Their temples and early churches were often plundered for their masonry, though a curiosity is a paleo-Christian monument from around the 3rd or 4th century near Lugo: the subterranean shrine of Santa Eulalia de Bóveda. It has a baptismal pool and remarkable frescoes showing dancing women and the healing of a sick man.

*Santa Eulalia de Bóveda shrine.*

The departure of the Romans left the way clear for their vassals, the Visigoths, to fill the power vacuum. There is not much more evidence of their 400-year rule – a few pieces in crypts, such as the martyrium in Palencia cathedral and a few sculpted friezes. The best preserved Visigothic work is the 7th-century church at Quintanilla de las Viñas, in an isolated spot south of Burgos. Today, it looks like little more than a solid stone barn, but around its exterior walls are the unmistakable friezes of these Aryan Christians – birds, flowers and geometric patterns – while inside sun and moon symbols show that, though the congregation was Christian, all gods were mingled in the arts.

Out of the Visigothic era developed the pre-Romanesque. As at Quintanilla de las Viñas, most churches were situated away from the conflict of towns, in peaceful valleys and under the natural protection of hilltops. The most striking examples of pre-Romanesque architecture are the 30 or so churches scattered through Asturias, from where the Reconquest began. They have been described as Europe's only surviving coherent stylistic group from the High Middle Ages.

The earliest churches, from the early 9th century, were built with dressed stone, without mortar, and continued the Roman basilica, rather than the emerging cruciform (cross) shape, usually with three aisles and without a belfry. Their vaulted naves were an innovation and reached lofty heights. Windows had lovely lattice work, the arches were simply rounded and the interiors were richly furnished. Paintings covered the

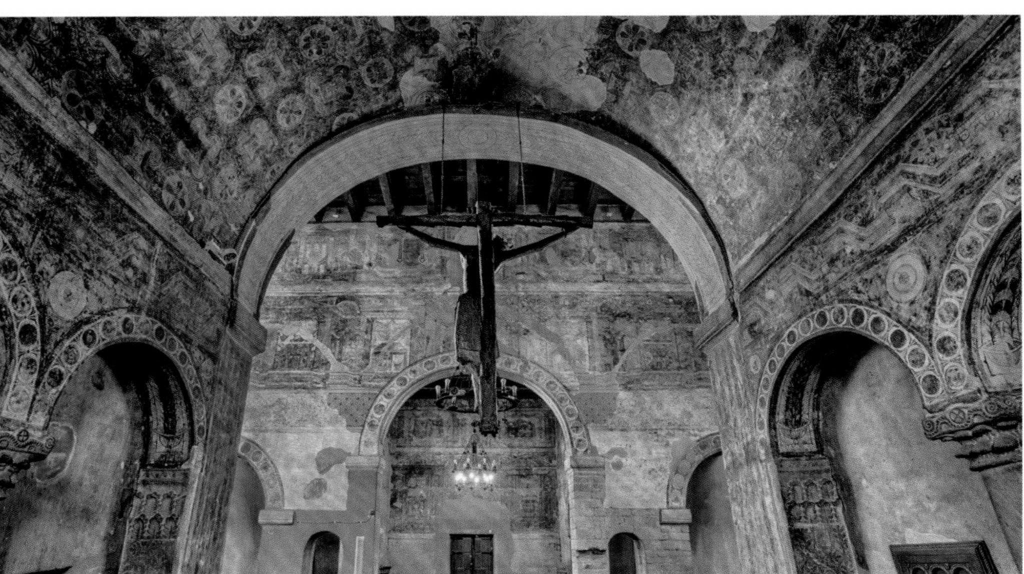

*Pre-Romanesque murals in San Julián de los Prados church, Oviedo.*

## ASTURIAN PRE-ROMANESQUE ART

**San Julián de los Prados**, on the northeast side of Oviedo, dates from the time of Alfonso II (792–842). It is Spain's largest pre-Romanesque church, 30 metres by 25 metres (98ft by 82ft). Roman influence can be detected in its outstanding frescoes.

**Santa María del Naranco**, at the foot of Mount Naranco 4km (2 miles) west of Oviedo. Built for Ramiro I (842–850) as a royal summer palace. The bathroom and living rooms were on the ground floor; above was the large hall with a vaulted ceiling, one of the earliest of its kind. Arcaded galleries at each end of the building give it an opulent air.

**San Miguel de Lillo**, in walking distance of Santa María del Naranco, was also built as a palace. The central nave is exceptionally tall and the aisles are separated by columns. It has fine lace windows, and circus scenes decorate the door jamb.

**Santa Cristina de Lena**, a small hermitage 40km (25 miles) south of Oviedo, is the third of Ramiro's fine buildings and is known as the "church of the corners" because of its many right-angles. Some of its design hints at the incoming Mozarabic style.

**San Salvador de Valdediós**, in a valley near Villaviciosa, was built under Alfonso III (866–910) for his retirement, towards the end of the pre-Romanesque period. It shows clear Moorish influence.

walls (examples can be seen at San Julián de los Prados in Oviedo) and were often first etched in outline on the brickwork so, although the colours have gone, the patterns remain. Ropework motifs were added to the Visigothic relief patterns, human and animal faces were incorporated, and an Eastern style can be detected.

## MOZARABIC

Ramiro I built palaces at Oviedo, following the example of Alfonso II who, in the re-emerging Christian society, wanted to make the Christian capital of Oviedo a match for the former capital of Toledo, which had been lost to the Moors. By the 10th century, when the Christian frontier moved further south and Alfonso III transferred the capital to León, Christians from occupied southern Spain had made their way north to join the young Christian state. They had brought with them Moorish concepts of design, which slipped seemlessly into the architecture, producing a style called Mozarabic.

Moorish influence affected every level of architecture. The monastery of San Miguel de Escalada in León has a most elegant colonnade of Mozarabic horseshoe arches, built by a community of monks who had arrived from the Moorish capital of Córdoba. Other churches, from San Millán de Suso in Navarra to the church in the tiny mountain village of Santiago de Peñalba, near Ponferrada, were clearly built by architects abreast of new trends. Arabic motifs also found their way into church decoration, such as the ceilings of the royal monastery in Burgos, which could have been constructed on the orders of the Caliphate.

## ROMANESQUE

Southern influence was eclipsed with the "discovery" of the bones of St James and the development, by the French monastery of Cluny, of the pilgrimage to Santiago (see page 87). In the scattering of fine churches along the Camino Francés, Romanesque architecture reached its finest expression. San Martín in Frómista is generally held to be the finest example. Though it has a deceptively modest appearance, inside light diffuses across the golden brickwork and the capitals are delightfully animated (visitors are given a leaflet to decipher the tales that unfold in the carvings).

The great era of church building was around the 12th century, and the northern cathedrals all have surviving Romanesque elements which have been built upon by later generations. Many of the region's great churches and monasteries, such as the Monastery of Leyre, were solidly founded on sturdy Romanesque crypts.

Carved capitals and porches are a special feature of Romanesque architecture, and visitors should look out for all manner of beasts and figures – some in the most surprising postures. The most magnificent portals, which often told long and complicated stories, reached dizzying heights of artistry in the Gloria Porch in

*Monastery of San Miguel de Escalada.*

Santiago's cathedral, on the north door of San Miguel in Estella and, most dramatically, in the monastery at Ripoll in Catalonia on the eastern side of the Pyrenees. Catalonia had avoided Mozarabic influence, and had developed its own Romanesque style, highlighted by external bands of blind arches – a concept imported from Lombardy – and featuring vast bell towers, such as those at Taüll and Sant Climent. The interior paintings of these two churches (now in Barcelona's Museu Nacional d'Art de Catalunya) show how shockingly vibrant Romanesque decoration was. The most magnificent in situ work is undoubtedly at the Real Basílica de San Isidoro in León, where the "Sistine Chapel of the Romanesque" was painted around 1160.

## GOTHIC

Maestro Mateo, who designed the Gloria Porch in Santiago, was instrumental in bringing the ogival or "pointed" arch of Europe's Gothic style to northern Spain, and his work was imitated on the Cathedral of Ourense in Galicia, consecrated in 1288. Just as the Benedictines had been influential in spreading Romanesque from Cluny, so the Cistercian monks from Citeaux brought Gothic, notably under an architect called Albert. The pilgrimage of St Francis of Assissi to Santiago in 1214 brought Dominican architecture. The "preaching order" for the first time built churches among the inhabitants: around ports and in "suburban" areas. Gothic really arrived in its full panoply in León and Burgos, where the two cathedrals were constructed in the French style. León, with elegant stained glass windows, has a French atmosphere. Among secular buildings, there is a fine Gothic royal palace in Olite, Navarra, with towers and battlements, built for Carlos III in 1406. Majestic *casonas* (seigneurial manors), such as those at Santillana de Mar, also date from this period.

*"Capilla, hórreo, palomar y ciprés, pazo es" (a manor house is chapel, granary, dovecote and cypress tree).*

*Basilica of St Ignatius de Loyola, Azpeitia.*

## PLATERESQUE AND BAROQUE

Renaissance architecture, with decorated facades, can best be seen at the Basque University at Oñati, built around 1540. Renaissance, however, was soon embellished and decorated to become Plateresque, from *plata* (silver) because the intricate sculpting imitated silversmiths' elaborate work. The Hospital Real in Santiago is a fine example of this style.

Money from the Americas helped to gild the Plateresque lily and turn it into full-blown Baroque, seen in the great *pazos*, country house estates where the nobility retired in summer, such as Pazo de Oca, current home of the Duchess of Alba. Church facades were also treated to Baroque, notably at Logroño cathedral. Its apogee is in the Basilica of St Ignatius de Loyola, the most outstanding Baroque building in Spain.

During the 19th century neoclassical themes were used in civic building, but the most important domestic style was the flourishing of *galerías*, the glass galleries protruding from the first floor of houses. From Hondarribia to A Coruña, arcaded streets with overhanging balconies give the whole of Northern Spain an architectural cohesion.

Interior of Burgos Cathedral.

*Battle of the Flowers parade, Laredo.*

# FIESTAS

A Spanish town or village without its own fiesta is unthinkable. Here we list the calendar's most notable celebrations.

There isn't a town or city in northern Spain that doesn't celebrate at least one fiesta a year. Usually it is held in honour of the local patron saint or of the Virgin Mary; but many fiestas revolve around archaic rites that have clearly survived from pagan times. A few fiestas are secular and modern: they celebrate some sporting event or the culinary delights of the harvest of land or sea.

Whatever the occasion, the festivities will probably include processions or a *romería* – a pilgrimage to a local shrine followed by a picnic. Singing and dancing are vital components of all fiestas and each region has its characteristic instrument and dance. The bagpipes, introduced by the Celts, are heard throughout Galicia and Asturias. In any Basque festival, you will hear the flute-like *txistu*, accompanied by a small drum. In Aragón, Navarra and La Rioja, couples hop to the rhythm of the *jota*, which is danced with hands held above the head. In Catalonia people hold hands, form circles and dance the sedate *sardana* to the piping tunes of a *cobla* band.

There are many more fiestas across Northern Spain than can be mentioned here and even the smallest and least significant of them will give you a rich insight into the local culture. If you are in town during a fiesta, you will inevitably be drawn into the celebrations; you certainly won't be able to sleep or go sightseeing.

## THE NEW YEAR

One of the first feast days of the year is that of St Sebastian. For 24 hours, starting at midnight on the night of 19–20 January, groups of uniformed drummers parade through the streets of San Sebastián in honour of the city's patron.

Two Navarrese hill villages, Ituren and Zubieta (both just west of Doneztebe), hold a joint-carnival early in the last week of January. The central characters of the fiesta are the *zanpantzarres*, who wear large cowbells around their belts and conical hats with ribbons hanging from them. They walk with a peculiar hopping and swinging motion so that their bells ring in unison with a rhythmic beat.

*Ituren locals dress up for a traditional carnival.*

## CARNIVAL

Carnival proper marks the start of Lent, 40 days before Easter, and it always falls in February or March. The Franco regime tried unsuccessfully to suppress it because of its anti-authoritarian nature. In spite of this, some quirky medieval carnival traditions have been preserved (or sometimes revived) in many parts of Northern Spain, especially in Galicia and Navarra.

The best-known Galician carnival takes place in Laza, in the province of Ourense. After midday mass on Carnival Sunday, the *peliqueiros* roam through the town wearing masks painted with fixed grins and Napoleonic mitres adorned with animal motifs. The *peliqueiro* has licence to lash out at bystanders with the riding crop he carries, without fear of retaliation.

Carnival in the town of Lanz in Navarra revolves around a 3-metre (10ft) effigy, the Miel-Otxin, thought to represent a customs guard turned highwayman, who is tried and condemned to death.

In Bielsa, beside Ordesa National Park in the Pyrenees, carnival features the extraordinary *trangas* (characters dressed in ram's fleeces, with huge horns on their heads). Their origin is obscure, but it is thought that they must be part of an ancient fertility rite.

Elsewhere in Northern Spain, especially in the Asturian cities of Oviedo and Gijón, carnival is a more conventional affair of masks, costumes and gaudy street processions. La Junquera, near the French border in Catalonia has a lively carnival when men often dress as women. Carnival in Spain usually ends with the "burial of the sardine" in which a mock fish is ritually burnt or buried, symbolising the end of carnal pleasure and the start of Lenten fasting.

## EASTER

Spring comes later to Northern Spain than to other parts of the country and one of its first celebrations is Easter Week. In the cities of Old Castile – Burgos, Palencia and León – there are solemn processions of hooded penitents carrying highly ornate *pasos*, floats depicting Biblical characters and scenes. In a few places, however, the events of the Passion are remembered in a much more immediate way. In San Vicente de la Sonsierra, in La Rioja, the barefoot, hooded *picaos* whip their own backs until they run with blood as they walk in procession on Easter Thursday and Good Friday.

*Catholic processions held at Easter in Pontevedra.*

Immediately after Easter, the people of San Vicente de la Barquera (Cantabria) set sail on a maritime procession, La Folía. A statue of the Virgin, which is said to have arrived on a boat without oars, sails or even crew, is sailed across the harbour in a fishing boat decked out with flowers and flags.

## MAY

Santo Domingo de la Calzada in La Rioja, on the road to Santiago, commemorates the miracles performed by its patron, St Dominic, with a series of processions ending on 12 May. The most attractive is the Procession of the

Damsels, in which young women dressed in white with long lacy veils carry decorated baskets of bread on their heads.

## CORPUS CHRISTI (MAY OR JUNE)

There are many religious rites around Whitsun and Corpus Christi, both of which fall in either May or June, depending on the date of Easter. On the Sunday between them, Trinity Sunday, the men of Lumbier, southeast of Pamplona in Navarra, next to a spectacular gorge, dress from head to foot in black and go in pilgrimage to a nearby chapel carrying crosses.

In Ponteáreas, near Vigo (Pontevedra), the townspeople create elaborate carpets with flower petals in the path of the Corpus Christi procession.

On the Sunday after Corpus, in Castrillo de Murcia near Burgos, El Colacho, a devil-like figure, jumps over new-born babies laid out on a mattress, which tradition says will save them from hernias and related ailments.

## JUNE

Haro, the wine capital of La Rioja Alta, declares its Wine Battle on the day of St Peter *(San Pedro)*, 29 June. In this messy free-for-all, thousands of people soak each other with red wine. Traditionally, it is squirted from *botas* (leather drinking bottles), but the really serious combatants use crop-spraying equipment. It is traditional to wear white, which means that the clothes will ever after be stained a light purple.

On the same day, an unusual dance, La Kaxarranka, is performed in Lekeitio (on the Basque coast) on a wooden chest held on the shoulders of eight men.

Irún, on the French border, mobilises its men on the last day of June for the mock military parades of the Alarde de Armas de San Marcial, which commemorate the Basques' defeat of an invading French army in 1522.

The eve of St John (San Juan), 24 June, is an important event in the Catalan calendar. Fires are brought down from the top of Mt Canigó, just in France, and spread around the region. General pyrotechnics are accompanied by special *coca* (cake) and *cava* (sparkling wine).

## JULY

One of the most famous Spanish fiestas is Los Sanfermines in Pamplona, which begins on 6 July (see page 105). Huge crowds assemble for the early morning *encierros* (bull runs) – both behind the barricades and in the streets. Although the *encierro* is over in just three to five minutes, it is a thrilling spectacle. The drunken, rowdy celebrations in Pamplona go on almost around the clock until 14 July.

A much more subdued homage to San Fermín takes place in Lesaka, well north of Pamplona, on 7 July, when men dance on the parapets along the banks of the River Onín, which flows through the town.

*Haro's Wine Battle takes place on St Peter's day.*

Throughout the summer, villagers in several parts of Galicia round up herds of small, hardy wild horses that live in the hills so that their manes and tails can be cut, and the year's new foals branded. The biggest and best *rapa das bestas* or *curro* is at San Lourenzo de Sabucedo near A Estrada, in Pontevedra province, at the beginning of July.

All along the Pyrenees there are pilgrimages and other folk events. One of the oldest and quaintest of these takes place at a pass at the head of the Roncal Valley in Navarra on 13 July. The mayors of the towns on the French side of the mountains ceremonially hand over three cows to their Spanish counterparts in accordance with a treaty made between them in 1375.

No one remembers exactly what the tribute is for, but it must be paid in perpetuity.

Throughout the year, but especially in summer, there are fiestas promoting regional dishes and local produce. Depending on where you are, you can feast on eels, oysters, octopus, pig's ear, rice pudding, snails or tripe. Asturian cider is suitably honoured in Nava on the second Saturday in August.

Such recently invented fiestas serve a clear purpose – to eat and drink well in good company – but there are more ancient rituals which have anthropologists baffled. One of the most curious of these takes place on 22 July in Anguiano (La Rioja) when eight young men in yellow skirts descend a steep cobbled street on stilts, spinning dizzily as they do so.

*Pilgrimage of the Coffins in Ribarteme.*

St James's Day (25 July) is, naturally enough, the biggest celebration in Santiago de Compostela and one of the few days a year when you are able to see the giant *botafumeiro* swung in the cathedral (see page 256). There are extra celebrations in a Year of St James, when the 25th falls on a Sunday.

There is no more unusual pilgrimage in Spain than that of the Pilgrimage of the Coffins at Ribarteme (near As Neves in Pontevedra province) on 29 July. By tradition, those who have narrowly escaped death in the course of the previous year thanks to the intervention of St Martha (who asked Christ to raise her brother Lazarus from the dead) are carried in open coffins in procession.

Jaca, in Aragón, stages the Pyrenees Folklore Festival every other year in late July or early August. In the intervening years it takes place on the French side of the mountains.

## AUGUST

The Descent of the River Sella (normally the first Saturday in August) is an international canoe and kayak race from Arriondas to Ribadesella in Asturias. You can follow the multicoloured mass of boats by car or on board a special train along the riverbank. After the race, the fiesta continues in Ribadesella, with singing, dancing and plenty of Asturian cider.

Other canoeing and kayaking competitions take place on a number of rivers in the Pyrenees, such as the Noguera Ribagorzana and the Segre.

The first Sunday in August is Asturias Day, the major festival in Gijón, which is celebrated with a procession of floats and groups in folk costume and folk dances.

All three Basque capitals hold their biggest fiestas in August, beginning with Vitoria. The fiesta of the White Virgin (the city's patron) starts on 4 August with the descent of the *celedón*, a dummy holding an umbrella, which is lowered on a rope from the tower of the church of San Miguel to a house below in the Plaza de la Virgen Blanca. When a man dressed in similar clothes emerges from the house, the crowd applauds and everyone lights a cigar.

Both Bilbao and the popular resort of San Sebastián celebrate their respective "Great Week" (*Semana Grande* or *Aste Nagusia* in Basque) around 15 August (the Feast of the Assumption). That of San Sebastián is much larger and includes an international fireworks competition, which involves a massive display of pyrotechnics on the seafront each night.

Betanzos (in the province of A Coruña in Galicia) celebrates its two main fiestas in quick succession, beginning on 14 August with San Roque (St Roch), when a giant paper balloon is released in the main square. A few days later, there is a pilgrimage on garlanded boats up the River Mandeo for a picnic in the countryside.

The seaside resort of Laredo in Cantabria wages a Battle of the Flowers on the last Friday in August during which floats decorated with flowers are paraded through the town.

*Semana Grande celebrations in San Sebastián.*

## SEPTEMBER

The patroness of Asturias, Nuestra Señora de Covadonga, is fêted at her chapel near Cangas de Onís in the Picos de Europa National Park on 8 September. On the same day, Galicians congregate at their principal shrine, San Andrés de Teixido, in the Rías Altas.

The various wine regions of Northern Spain celebrate the grape harvest in August or September. One of the biggest celebrations is in Logroño, the capital of La Rioja, on 21 September (see page 170).

The Day of the Goose is held in the Basque coastal town of Lekeitio as part of the San Antolin festival (see page 185).

## NOVEMBER

1 November is All Saints' Day, on which people take flowers to cemeteries to remember their dead. On 11 November, several towns in Galicia, including Santiago de Compostela, celebrate Os Magostos, a fiesta in honour of the sweet chestnut, thousands of which are roasted on bonfires.

## CHRISTMAS AND EPIPHANY

Christmas in Spain tends to be more of a family affair rather than a public celebration. The arrival of the Three Kings, however, on the night of 5–6 January (Epiphany) is cause for much celebration because it is then that children receive their presents. Robed kings parade through the streets in processions, throwing sweets into the crowd.

*The Running of the Bulls, San Fermín.*

# RUNNING WITH THE BULLS

Speed, machismo and adrenalin combine in an incredible three-minute drama played out every day during Pamplona's San Fermín fiesta.

Ever since the publication, in 1926, of Ernest Hemingway's novel *The Sun Also Rises* (the British title was *Fiesta*), the early morning events of 7–14 July in Pamplona have formed part of Western mythology. Generations of young – and not so young – Americans, along with French, Germans, Swedes and Britons, have flocked to Pamplona to carouse and watch the running of the bulls. In Spain, *el encierro* is also a major event with live commentaries on radio and television and action replays of the major incidents and casualties on the evening news.

Runners have to keep one eye behind them.

## RITE OF PASSAGE

That this normally quiet Navarran city's purely logistical practice of transferring fighting bulls from the pens at the edge of town to stalls below the bullring has managed to evolve into a world-famous rite of passage for international youths "eager for some desperate glory" is, at the very least, a difficult development to explain. How did this come about?

Bullfights have been held in Pamplona since the 14th century and it is believed that, in one form or another, runners have helped the *entrada* (entry, as it was originally called) of the bulls for more than 600 years. At some point, the runners began to run ahead of the bulls to guide them instead of alongside or behind them. Gradually, it became traditional for San Fermín revellers to run before the bulls for sport, as well as utility, in an outburst of joy, frivolity and daring, and in the general spirit of the fiesta.

It is not surprising to anyone familiar with Basques, who are known as rough and ready types ever willing to demonstrate feats of physical strength and courage, that a potentially brutal event such as the *encierro* should be turned into a popular sport.

Today, the encierro itself is a straightforward enough exercise. Fighting bulls kept in corrals at the edge of town are moved through the streets, accompanied and guided by eight to ten cabestros (steers, also known as mansos, manso meaning "tame") to keep the peace among the bulls. The bulls are herded through the bullring and into the holding pens from which they will emerge to be fought and killed later that same afternoon.

In *The Sun Also Rises*, Hemingway describes the *encierro* (literally, enclosing) in anything but romantic terms. In his first look at the "running of the bulls" as it has (erroneously) come to be known, the character of Jake Barnes hears the rocket go up at eight in the morning, steps out on the balcony of his hotel (Pamplona's La Perla, still available, if somewhat expensively, for a bird's eye view of the *encierro*) and watches the crowd run by: men dressed in the traditional San Fermín uniform of white shirt and trousers with red sashes and neckerchiefs, those out in front running well, those behind running faster and faster, then "some stragglers who were really running", then the bulls "running together". The perfect *encierro*: no bulls separated from the pack, no

*The Chupinazo (opening day) of the San Fermín festival.*

mayhem. The comment, "One man fell, rolled to the gutter, and lay quiet", describes a textbook move, and is a first-rate example of observation and reporting. An American participant was killed because he did not "lay quiet" and let the bulls run by him. Instead, he tried to get up and was, as a result, gored to death. Any native runner would have known to remain motionless, as fighting bulls are attracted to movement.

In the second *encierro* described in Hemingway's novel, a man is gored in the back, the horn penetrating and coming out of his chest. Not very surprisingly, the man dies. Some 20 more are badly injured in the bullring itself, while the steers are worked to lead the bulls through the ring and into the *chiqueros*, the chutes where they stay until the afternoon *corrida* (bullfight or "running", in the correct usage). The waiter at the café, the Iruña, mutters cynically "You hear? *Muerto*. Dead. He's dead. With a horn through him. All for morning fun. *Es muy flamenco*." Hemingway goes on to describe the dead man's widow, his two children and the procession carrying his casket to the train back to Tafalla. This is realism, and anything but a rhapsodic approach to a phenomenon.

Hemingway himself never even considered participating in an *encierro*. And yet men, mostly

> *Statistically, the chances of injury and death are greater on the roads to and from Pamplona than while running the encierro.*

young ones, come from all over the world to run before the bulls, to demonstrate, in the spirit of the fiesta, their temporary liberation from all of the normal preoccupations of real life, and even from life itself, tempting fate by exposing themselves, completely unnecessarily, to danger.

## THE ROCKETS GO UP

Pamplona's morning skies are punctuated by explosions. The first rocket goes up at eight when the corral door opens at the bottom of the Cuesta de Santo Domingo; the second one announces that all six bulls have cleared the corral and are in the streets; rocket number three is fired when all bulls are in the bullring; while the fourth and last rocket confirms that all the bulls have safely passed through the bullring and into the receiving pens.

Though not immediately apparent from the pandemonium of the three-minute run, some 1,000 people, including municipal police, Red Cross workers, ambulance drivers, 16 cattle herders strategically placed in the streets and five *dobladores* (cape handlers) in the bullring, are involved in the effort to get the bulls safely through the mob and into the pens. Estimates on the number of spectators range from 30,000 on weekdays to 60,000 at weekends, including those who have paid to wait in the bullring for the explosion of bulls and runners to come in through the *callejón*, the tunnel through the main entry. Overcrowding has been the most dangerous factor in the *encierros* of the past 20 years. The number of runners varies from day to day, although weekends are the most populous, with French and Spanish workers in full attendance. The total number of runners in the street can range from 500 to 2,000.

The bulls' dash through the streets covers 875 metres/yds in about three minutes over terrain of surprising variety. Each section of the course elicits different behaviour from the bulls and requires a different strategy on the part of the runners. The Cuesta de Santo Domingo, which slopes down to the corrals, is traditionally considered the most dangerous part of the run.

After singing the traditional "*A San Fermín pedimos por ser nuestro patrón, nos guíe en el encierro, dándonos su bendición*" (To San Fermín we pray, for being our patron saint, to guide us in the *encierro*, giving us his blessing), on the eight bells of the hour, rolled-up newspapers on high, the lead runners sprint down the hill toward the advancing bulls until it becomes clear that the chase is on, at which point they turn and run back up the hill. Fighting bulls, their power concentrated in their hind legs, accelerate uphill at great speed, fresh and frightened by the advancing multitude.

The 270-metre/yd Cuesta de Santo Domingo is an all-or-nothing wager high in terror and low in elapsed time. The walls are sheer on both sides, which allows the runners no escape, and the bulls pass at high speed. It's over in seconds, often with an injury or two into the bargain. The great fear on the Cuesta de Santo Domingo is that a bull, as a result of some personal idiosyncrasy, might hook his way along the wall of the Military Hospital on his way up the hill, forcing runners out in front of the speeding pack in a classic hammer and anvil movement.

## MOMENT OF UNBEARABLE INTEREST

The next part of the course, the Mercaderes, cuts sharply left for 105 metres/yds passing in front of the Town Hall before making an even sharper turn right up Calle Estafeta. The difficulty here is to avoid the outside of each turn, where the momentum of bulls and steers, some 10,000kg (22,000lb) of stampeding bovines, can make things – in the words of wordsmith Ethelbert Nevin "unbearably interesting". Being on the inside of the first corner puts you on the outside of the second unless you stay in the middle directly in front of the bulls, which are still moving too quickly to allow anyone to stay ahead of them for long.

Calle Estafeta is the bread and butter of the run, the longest (425 metres/yds), straightest and least complicated part of the course. If the classic run, a perfect blend of form and function, is to remain ahead of the horns for as long as possible, fading to the side when overtaken, this is the best stretch to do it in. The bulls are tiring and the street is nearly flat, equalising speeds of man and beast, and there are no dramatic turns or obstacles for some 350 metres/yds. There are plenty of doorways and shop fronts in which to take refuge (though they are usually well inhabited).

*Encierro Txiki (little bull running).*

A good 400-metre/yd sprinter in top condition should be able to stay ahead of the bulls from the Town Hall into the bullring, though the cobblestones, the other runners, and the need to keep looking back over your shoulder to keep tabs on the bulls following you all combine to make this unlikely.

At the end of Estafeta, the course curves left and descends through the *callejón*, the narrow tunnel, into the bullring. Here, there is often high drama as the course fills with runners trying to time their move with, or ahead of, the bulls through the tunnel and into the ring.

From the end of Estafeta down into the bullring, the bulls move much more slowly, uncertain of their weak forelegs, allowing runners to stay close to them and even to touch their horns as they glide down through the tunnel. The only uncertainty, an important one, is whether there will be a *montón* (pile-up) in the tunnel or not. Some of the most dramatic photographs that have ever been taken of the *encierro* have been taken here, as the galloping pack slams into and through a solid wall of humanity.

Probably the best run, the most complete and fully satisfying, combines Estafeta's smooth going with the drama of the dicey descent into the tunnel and the exhilarating sense of rebirth on emerging from the narrow opening into the bright sunlight and wide open spaces of the bullring. This run starts in front of the bulls for the last 50–100 metres/yds of their advance up Estafeta. The objective is to remain there, just in front of the horns, guiding the pack safely past sprawled and diving runners through the tunnel and into the bullring.

*Runners touch the image of San Fermín before they run.*

Even highly experience runners can get into trouble. Julen Medina, one of the so-called *divinos* (the dozen or so most expert runners) had been perfecting his technique of running for 25 years when, at the age of 41, he was seriously injured for the first time by a bull in the tunnel. "The runners ahead of me were blocked and there was nowhere to go," he explained.

The trickiest part of running with the bulls is splitting your vision so that with one eye you keep track of the bulls behind you and with the other you keep from colliding with or falling over the runners ahead of you. Bulls grouped together and surrounded by steers run through the streets as peacefully as puppies, but if a bull is separated from the pack he quickly turns defensive and lethal.

Joining in the *encierro* for casual, frivolous or spontaneous reasons is frowned upon. The locals know what they are doing and they do not welcome anyone looking for light-hearted experience.

Drunk people and tourists are considered a danger to other runners; the former are removed from the course by police and by other runners, while the latter are instructed, often roughly, in the dos and don'ts of the encierro. The cardinal crime, which is punishable by fines and spontaneous beatings, is to call out in an attempt to attract the attention of the bull, thus removing him from the pack and creating a deadly danger to other runners.

*Encierros* impose a $1,000 fine for distracting a bull during the *encierro*. Inexperienced runners often fail to appreciate how dangerous fighting bulls are, how sharp the horns can be, and what a 40cm (16in) horn wound looks like, especially in the buttocks. There are usually half a dozen *cornadas* (horn wounds), mostly in the buttocks, and a couple of dozen serious injuries requiring hospitalisation.

Since Hemingway first romanticised the fiesta, sixteen people have died by being gored or trampled "all for morning fun".

## MEDITERRANEAN BULL WORSHIP

Bull worship in the Mediterranean dates from before the Greeks as far back as ancient Crete and the Minoan civilisation, worshippers of the Minotaur. Whether imported from Greece when a trading post was established at Empúries on the Catalan coast more than half a millennium before Christ, or (more probably) already in place as an autochthonous Iberian practice, bulls have always played an important role in rituals, ceremonies and festive occasions below the Pyrenees.

The releasing of bulls or wild cows in the streets forms part of fiestas in countless towns

> *Bulls have always played an important role in rituals, ceremonies and festivals in Spain.*

and cities throughout Spain. Navarra, with Pamplona's fiesta as its most famous, dangerous and multitudinous example of the *encierro*, is especially rich in bull-running events, particularly along La Ribera, Navarra's southern Ebro river basin. Tudela, Lodosa, Tafalla, Estella and Sangüesa also have *encierros* or mini-versions of Pamplona's event, though all use wild cows instead of fighting bulls. An hour north of Pamplona, the town of Lesaka also celebrates San Fermín as its patron saint and releases wild cows in its central square during the fiesta, which is known as the San Fermín *txiki* (small) and is held simultaneously with Pamplona's celebrations.

The town of Falces just south of Tafalla has a week of fiestas beginning on the penultimate Sunday of August and runs wild cows down a steep mountain path bordered on one side by the rock wall of the mountain and on the other by a sheer drop into space. With as many as 15,000 spectators, some 200 runners dash the 600 metres/yds down the mountain to the bullring. To date, no serious injuries have been recorded, but the spectacle is hair-raising.

While the bullfight itself has often been vilified, wrongly, as unfair sport rather than the dangerous ritual art that it is, a distinction fundamental to the slightest understanding of tauromachy, the *encierro* has, as well, an ethic and an aesthetic of its own. Spanish philosopher Ortega y Gasset (1883–1955) called it "an artistic model of popular play with bulls".

For *encierro* purists, the supreme achievement is to gain a position in front of the bull's horns from which you can dominate the bull and make him run at your speed, slowing the bull and guiding him forward at an easy pace. During the run, the runner has five key movements or moments, as defined by encierrologist José Murugarren. The runner:

1: sees the bull
2: gets in front of the bull
3: moves at the same speed as the bull
4: imposes his own speed on the bull
5: pulls out to the side to let another runner take over.

In another article entitled "18 Seconds in front of a Bull", Gabriel Asenjo defines the best run as the one that succeeds in spending the longest time, never more than a few seconds, close to the horns – this is not merely a question of speed, but of timing.

*Bulls along Calle Estafeta.*

*Baqueira-Beret ski resort in the Vall d'Aran.*

# OUTDOOR ACTIVITIES

Skiing, hiking and climbing are the principal local pastimes, but there is hunting, shooting and fishing too, and many other outdoor sports.

Northern Spain's mountains, rivers and coasts offer a wide variety of outdoor activities ranging from skiing and climbing at 3,000 metres (9,800ft) above sea level to sailing, surfing or diving in the Atlantic Ocean and the Bay of Biscay. In between are a dozen or more major rivers for angling or kayaking, and some of Iberia's wildest woodlands for hunting and hiking.

## WINTER SPORTS

Skiing, possible from around late November to mid-April, is certainly one of Northern Spain's main sporting attractions. No fewer than 25 of Spain's 30 ski resorts are spread across its northern reaches: one at San Isidro in the Cordillera Cantábrica between Oviedo and León, seven in the Picos de Europa, one in La Rioja's Sierra de la Demanda and the remaining 16 distributed across the Pyrenees. The westernmost of them, Manzaneda, in Puebla de Trives in the province of Ourense, is Galicia's only winter sports station, located 200km (125 miles) east of Pontevedra and the Atlantic Ocean.

The easternmost, Vallter-2000 in Catalonia's Ter Valley at Setcases in Girona province, is just 65km (40 miles) west of the Mediterranean's Bahia de Roses on the Costa Brava, which is visible on the very clearest days. The coldest, highest and most frequently snowy of these ski stations are Cantabria's Picos de Europa, Huesca's Candanchú above Jaca in the central Pyrenees and the Vall d'Aran's Baqueira-Beret, the Pyrenees' only Atlantic-oriented valley as it is drained by the north-flowing Garonne.

The latter is also a favoured haunt of the Spanish royal family. Catalonia's Cerdanya Valley offers skiing in Andorra and France as well as in Spain, multiplying options and opportunities with some 15 ski stations spread over the three nations.

*Sailing near Santander.*

## CROSS-COUNTRY SKI CIRCUITS

Cross country or Nordic skiing is also extremely popular in Spain and, as a result, most of the resorts offer cross country circuits. However, the resorts specialising in Nordic skiing are: Lles in the Cerdanya Valley, Llanas del Hospital at Benasque, Fanlo near Ordesa National Park, and Panticosa.

West of Jaca are the stations of Garbadito near Hecho, Lizara near Aragués del Puerto and Linza near the town of Ansó. In the Picos de Europa, Alto Campóo and Valgrande Pajares are the main Nordic centres. Snow-shoe tours and ski-touring guides are also available for winter travels over the high country.

Although the heart of the ski season extends over the four months from December to the end of March, it is not uncommon for November and April to provide a few weeks of skiing as well. However, in general ski conditions in the Pyrenees are no match for the Alps and the past few years have been especially unpredictable.

## HIKING AND CLIMBING

Hiking and climbing are spectacular and popular activities in the Picos de Europa and the Pyrenees. GR (*Gran Recorrido*, Long Distance) trails are well marked with red-and-white striped marks; maps are available at sports stores specialising in *excursionismo*. Many experienced hikers consider the Pyrenees to have some of the planet's most beautiful hiking trails and even if you're not up for a six week long trans-Pyrenean traverse there are hundreds of spectacular day hikes or shorter, multi-day hikes.

Exploring the highest sections of the *cordilleras* is only possible from June to around mid-October. The lower trails are ideal for spring and autumn walks, through really too hot and dusty in mid-summer.

Equestrian tours of the Picos de Europa and the Pyrenees are another option.

## TROUT AND SALMON FISHING

Cold water fisheries holding trout, sea trout and salmon provide one of the best motives for exploring Spain's northern highlands. The runs of Atlantic salmon into rivers from Galicia's River Miño south of Vigo, all around the peninsula's northwest corner to the River Bidasoa forming the French border at Irún have waxed and waned over the years, but have never been completely wiped out.

*Hiking towards Circo de Soaso in Ordesa National Park.*

> *The largest trout caught in the Pyrenees was from the River Segre – a brown trout weighing 4.8kg (10lb 8oz).*

The best rivers for combining trout, sea trout and Atlantic salmon angling are in Asturias – the Eo, Esva, Narcea, Sella and Deva-Cares foremost amongst them. Although the salmon season begins in early March and the trout season traditionally starts on 19 March, the month of June is prime time on these rivers, some of which (especially the Narcea) offer the triple opportunity of fly fishing for salmon, trout and sea trout on the same day, using the same equipment.

The Asturian Fishing Federation allots the prime reserved beats by lottery; requests are lodged before Christmas. A certain number of spots are, however, reserved for foreigners, and it is often possible to get an excellent stretch of water at short notice. Check with the local fishing federation for details of international angling competitions for Atlantic salmon or sea trout. These tournaments, much less about competition than about camaraderie, provide an excellent vehicle for getting to know fellow anglers from Spain and elsewhere.

The only salmon in the Pyrenees are to be found in the River Bidasoa between Vera de Bidasoa and the estuary at Hondarribia.

*White-water rafting in the Pyrenees.*

Trout fishing in the Pyrenees is excellent. Top rivers include (from west to east), the Baztán, Irati, Ara, Salazar, Esca, Aragón, Gállego, Cinca, Esera, Noguera Ribagorçana, Noguera Pallaresa, Segre, Ter and Ritort. Of these, a shortlist would probably include the Irati, the Gállego, the Noguera Pallaresa and the Segre.

Fishing the tarns and lakes of the upper Pyrenees can be productive as well as stunningly beautiful, though they are not very accessible and can be time-consuming and difficult to fit into a walking tour.

## WATER SPORTS

Sailing, windsurfing, surfing and diving are practised all along the northern coast. While nearly every coastal town has a yacht marina and sailing boats to charter for the day, Cantabria's Santander and Laredo are known as particularly active sailing centres. The beaches of Mundaka (see page 185) and Sopelana, in the province of Vicaya, are the hottest surfing areas on the northern coast, though surfers are active all around Spain's long coast. Surfing breaks out whenever and wherever the Atlantic Ocean provides the weather for it, but autumn and winter consistently provide the best conditions even if high summer offers more warmth! San Sebastián's Playa de la Zurriola, the northernmost of the city's beaches, provides ideal beginner waves. Galicia and Asturias hide many quality spots. Many of these spots are highly fickle and require a great deal of local knowledge.

## WHITE-WATER ACTIVITIES

Other riverine activities are kayaking and rafting. The annual *Descenso del Sella* (Descent of the River Sella) is a multitudinous international kayak race open to anyone wishing to participate in the 25km (15-mile) race from Arriondas to the Sella estuary at Ribadesella. At other times of year you can hire a kayak at Arriondas and paddle down the river at your leisure, to be picked up by a van and trailer further downstream.

A kayak lesson for beginners can be combined with a tour of Vizcaya's Ría de Urdaibai estuary, a natural reserve and one of the most beautiful spots on Spain's northern coast.

In the Pyrenees, there are white-water rafting and kayaking outfitters in Aínsa on the River Ara, in Llavorsí on the Noguera Pallaresa, and at La Seu d'Urgell.

## GOLF

There are plentry of golf courses to be found near to urban areas all over northern Spain.

*Northern Spain's coasts offer a wide variety of outdoor activities from sailing to surfing or diving in the Atlantic Ocean and the Bay of Biscay.*

Some may be closed from December to April, depending on the snowfall. Pontevedra, Oviedo, Santander, Zarauz, Hondarribia, Pamplona, Jaca, Benasque and Puigcerdà all have fine golf courses, two of which (Santander's Pedreña and Zarauz) have produced, respectively, Masters champions Severiano Ballesteros and José María Olazábal.

## HORSE RACING AND RIDING

One of Spain's three main horse racing tracks is located near San Sebastián at Lasarte – not surprisingly, considering the Basque Country's love of competition and betting. Horse racing is also available to watch and bet on in the French Basque Country at Biarritz. There are stables *(hípicas)* throughout Northern Spain where it is possible to hire a horse by the hour or the day.

## WILDLIFE WATCHING

Spain is one of Europe's top wildlife watching destinations. Several rural hotels are ideally placed for excursions on foot into unspoilt countryside in search of curious critters. The Pyrenees are excellent for birdwatching and wildflower hunting at high altitude. Somiedo nature reserve in Asturias is a good place to head for, although you will need patience and luck if you want to see a bear. The Picos de Europa is known for its many varied butterflies as well as for its botanical riches. From April to October it is possible to take a boat trip from Bilbao out into the Bay of Biscay to see whales and dolphins. Keep alert wherever you go – the best sightings are often by chance when you are least expecting them.

## SPORTS FEDERATIONS

The following organisations are a useful source of information on where to practice sports in Spain.

**Royal Spanish Sailing Federation** C/Luís de Salazar 12, 12002 Madrid; www.rfev.es

**Royal Spanish Tennis Federation** Passeig Olimpic 17–19 (Olympic Stadium), Barcelona; www.rfet.es

**Spanish Canoeing Federation** C/Antracita 7 28045 Madrid; www.rfep.es

**Spanish Fishing Federation** C/Navas de Tolosa 3, 28013 Madrid; www.fepyc.es

**Spanish Flying Federation** C/Arlabán 7 28014 Madrid; www.rfae.es

**Spanish Golf Federation** C/Arroyo del Monte 5 28049 Madrid; www.rfegolf.es

**Spanish Horse Riding Federation** C/Monte Esquinza 28, 28010 Madrid; www.rfhe.com

**Spanish Mountaineering Federation** C/Floridablanca 84, 08015 Barcelona; www.fedme.es

**Spanish Underwater Activities Federation** C/Aragó 517, 08013 Barcelona; www.fedas.es

**Spanish Winter Sports Federation** C/Avenida de Cerro de Aguila 15–17, 28709 Madrid; http://rfedi.es

*A young woman riding on a beach in Baiona.*

# GAMES THE COMPETITIVE BASQUES PLAY

There is only one thing Basques like more than a sporting competition – putting money on it. Feats of strength, cooking and poetry are all worth a wager.

Basques are known for near-pathological levels of competitive spirit. Even traditional events, such as Lekeitio's goose festival – in which men hang from the necks of dead geese suspended from a cable over the harbour to see who can hold on the longest – are inspired by this competitiveness and love of betting rather than any pagan or seasonal rite.

*Herrikirolak*, popular sports, include everything from sheep dog trials and weight-hauling oxen to men lifting stones, dragging sleds, scything fields or chopping wood.

*Bertsolaris* (versifiers) compete at impromptu poetry recitals and chefs compete at concocting *marmitako*, the mariners' tuna stew. The competition is spiced by the fact that Basques will bet on just about anything that moves.

## STRENGTH AND SPEED

Raw strength is the prerequisite in most of these events, which are regularly held around the country. Basques are also good at team sports. Their footballers are known for a physical and primarily defensive style of play, supplying famous goalkeepers for the top national teams, while Atlético de Bilbao and Real Sociedad, with homegrown talent, are first-division stalwarts.

Competition starts at home: in the centre of every village is a *frontón* or wall to play *pelota* against. Like *jai-alai* this is a fast game, played not with gloves or rackets but with bare hands. With teams of two players, points are scored by propeling the ball so that it rebounds between the low and high lines marked on the court.

In "Australian style" wood chopping, the *aizkolari* has to keep his balance as he chops his way down to the ground.

*Idi probak (Basque for 'oxen tests') is a rural sport th… involves oxen dragging a stone from one side of a tow… square to the other.*

*Harrijasotzaileak have lifted as much as 325kg (715lb… time. Cubic stones, cylindrical stones, rectangular st… or balls are raised in time and absolute weight trials.*

The Basque game of pelota is played in a two-walled court called a frontón.

## Fast and furious jai-alai

"Happy festival", "lively celebration", "joyous game"... perhaps "fast sport" is the best way to translate *jai-alai*. With balls hurled at speeds of up to 240kph (150mph) from a hook-like wicker basket or glove called *guante laxoa*, the popular Basque game of *cesta punta* is mesmerising to watch. It is played on a three-walled court called a *cancha*, about 53 metres (175ft) long and 17 metres (56ft) wide, with the side walls some 12 metres (40ft) high. The object is to hurl a hard rubber ball against the front wall so it cannot be returned. The ball may hit a side wall before striking the front. *Jai alai* can be played as singles or doubles and the first to reach the required number of points – around seven in singles, as much as 25 in doubles – wins. Betting is very much a part of *jai-alai* and courtside wagers are brokered with speed comparable to the game.

n Sebastián the annual whaler race, called oadak, brings out the entire fleet. Each boat in the etition starts out with 13 oarsmen and a coxswain. urbulent Cantabrian seas make these regattas a and tumble affair.

emale competitors saw through a wood log at the ie Strong Man games in Bilbao.

Aizkolaris, the wood chopping competition, is in classical Basque style. Balance is needed as well as strength, plus, of course, a good eye and aim that will keep the axe clear of the toes.

*Chamois in the Parc Natural del Cadí-Moixeró, Catalonia.*

# WILDLIFE

"Green" Spain has a wild Atlantic coast, rich hay meadows and rugged alpine summits, all of which contribute to a wide diversity of natural habitats.

The north coast of Spain is isolated from the rest of the country by the mountains of the Cordillera Cantábrica, a westerly extension of the Pyrenees that runs parallel with the coast and then curves south to meet the Portuguese border. The Atlantic-influenced climate and vegetation have more in common with northwestern Europe than with the warmer, drier realms which characterise the bulk of the Iberian peninsula. Low population density and traditional farming methods mean that the balance between man and his environment is still relatively harmonious, with the result that the profusion of wildlife found here is without equal in Europe today.

## COASTAL BIRDS

Along the Atlantic coastline windswept headlands jut into the open ocean, sheer cliffs secrete small, pebbly coves and have spawned a rash of offshore islets, sweeping sandy bays are backed by extensive dune systems, and submerged river valleys – known as *rías* – widen into estuaries harbouring intertidal saltmarshes and mudflats.

The wave-lashed coastal cliffs and offshore islets which are scattered along the length of the north coast may seem inhospitable habitats, but they support important seabird colonies, especially in Galicia. On the west coast, an early-summer visit to the offshore Islas Cíes, in the mouth of the Ría de Vigo, the Isla de Ons, in the Pontevedra estuary, or Cabo Vilán, further north, will be rewarded with the sight of huge numbers of yellow-legged gulls, noisily jostling for nest sites among the tussocks of thrift and rock samphire. Unfortunately, the burgeoning gull colonies have all but ousted the rare Iberian race of guillemot from this coast, although the modest shag populations have remained healthy. Kittiwakes and lesser black-backed gulls are recent colonisers, the latter in their most southerly nesting grounds in the world.

*Little owl (Athene noctua) preening feathers, Aragon.*

At the eastern end of the Bay of Biscay, the headlands between Cabo Villano and Cabo Machichaco in the Basque Country support breeding storm petrels, shags, yellow-legged and lesser black-backed gulls, peregrines, rock doves and rock thrushes, while the limestone promontory of Monte Candina in Cantabria is home to the only coastal colony of griffon vultures in Spain.

More varied birdlife can be seen on passage, especially from the headlands of Cabo Fisterra and Punta de la Estaca de Bares in Galicia, Cabo Vidio, Cabo de Peñas and the nearby Punta de la

Vaca in Asturias, and Cabo Mayor in Cantabria. A spectacular fly-by of an estimated 100,000 pelagic birds occurs at the Estaca de Bares observatory in Galicia between September and November: principally gannets, Manx, Cory's, great and sooty shearwaters, Arctic skuas, grey phalaropes, razorbills, guillemots and puffins, as well as large numbers of scoters, gulls and terns.

## ESTUARIES AND MARSHLANDS

Estuarine habitats – particularly Ortigueira in Galicia, Villaviciosa in Asturias, Santoña in Cantabria and Urdaibai in the Basque Country – are best visited between September and March. Although wintering waterfowl are not present in huge numbers, the diversity on offer is high, with the chance of seeing a range of species scarce elsewhere in the Iberian peninsula, such as black-throated, red-throated and great northern divers, red-breasted mergansers, red-necked and grey phalaropes, whooper swans, Brent geese, velvet scoters, scaups and eiders.

Covering some 3,500 hectares (8,600 acres), Santoña, just east of Santander, is the most extensive marshland on the north coast and the most important for wintering wildfowl and waders. The intertidal *marismas* have been colonised by a carpet of salt-tolerant plants such as glasswort, sea purslane and sea milkwort, with colourful sea asters, sea heath and sea lavender in the upper reaches of the estuary. Wintering wildfowl include large numbers of teal and wigeon, as well as pintail, shoveler and pochard, while waders such as oystercatcher, snipe and dunlin also abound. Grey herons and little egrets stalk the shallows, but the most outstanding visitors are the spoonbills – up to 60 at a time – which use the marshes during their autumn migration from the Netherlands to Africa. Other passage migrants include avocets, knots, sanderlings, curlews, sandpipers, black-tailed and bar-tailed godwits and greenshanks.

*Cormorants at sunset on the Ría de Arousa, Galicia.*

Santoña is also one of the few places in Iberia with resident shelducks and curlews, although breeding pairs are rarely seen. However, the freshwater reaches of the marshes do provide nesting sites for little grebes, Baillon's crakes and water rails, with fan-tailed, sedge, reed and great reed warblers rearing their young in the fringing reedbeds and stands of tamarisk. Summer skies see marsh harriers, red and black kites and short-tailed eagles hunting over the estuary, and an occasional osprey dropping in on passage.

Terrestrial mammals which are usually associated with these coastal marshes include stoats, western polecats and otters, with the some of the easternmost systems, such as Urdaibai, just east of Bilbao, harbouring European mink. Although an essentially Eastern European species, this mustelid is also found along the Atlantic seaboard of France and is gradually extending its range westwards. Keep an eye out, too, for harbour porpoises and bottle-nosed dolphins, which commonly frequent estuaries.

## SAND DUNES

Northern Spain's finest sand-dune habitats are found at Liencres in Cantabria and Corrubedo in Galicia. Although the bird interest is minor – only tawny pipits and Kentish plovers regularly breed, with an occasional stone curlew putting in an appearance – the dune flora at Liencres is quite magnificent. Early-flowering species such as brown bee, bee and small-flowered tongue orchids flourish in the dune slacks, with sea bindweed, sea spurge and sea sandwort accompanying the stabilising marram grass on the dunes proper. Later in the summer, sea holly, *Crucianella maritima*, and sea daffodils come into bloom.

The Corrubedo dune slacks are home to such rare plants as adder's tongue spearwort and summer lady's tresses, while the brackish pools nearby provide breeding grounds for large numbers of western spadefoot and natterjack toads, as well as for Bosca's newt, a small, orange-bellied species unique to western Iberia.

*The Parque Natural de las Dunes de Liencres includes a section of Cantabria's breathtaking coastline.*

## MEADOWS AND PASTURELAND

Between the coast and the mountains the land is more heavily domesticated and less interesting from a wildlife point of view, but as you ascend the northern foothills of the Cordillera Cantábrica into the realm of scattered villages, broadleaved forests and traditionally managed meadows and pastures, the diversity of flora and fauna increases dramatically.

These middle-altitude forests, consisting mainly of a mixture of pedunculate oak, ash, wych elm, small-leaved lime, hazel, sweet chestnut and sycamore, represent the surviving fragments of the Neolithic woodland clearance which started around 5,000 BC. The hay meadows which were carved from their midst are still some of the most species-rich grasslands in Europe, particularly those of the Picos de Europa, straddling the borders of León, Cantabria and Asturias.

No two hay meadows are alike. Although sheets of yellow rattle, red kidney vetch and pale flax are among the basic ingredients, other species present vary with altitude, aspect, soil type and climatic factors, as well as with the management regime in place. Atlantic meadows on limestone soils might contain spring squill, Pyrenean lilies and pyramidal and large-tongue orchids, while drier meadows on south-facing slopes and more acidic soils are studded with tassel hyacinths, pink butterfly orchids and white asphodels. Wet flushes teem with colourful globeflowers, marsh marigolds and early marsh orchids, while the highest meadows are the domain of black vanilla orchids, horned pansies, Lent lilies and English irises.

Such botanical diversity is matched by a peerless butterfly fauna: more than 140 species have

*An Adonis blue in the Picos de Europa.*

been recorded in the Picos de Europa alone. Cleopatras, brimstones, swallowtails and scarce swallowtails appear first, to be joined by a huge variety of blues – Adonis, turquoise, long-tailed, mazarine, idas and chalkhill – later in the summer, which are accompanied by sooty, scarce, purple-edged and purple-shot coppers. At the peak of the season, rarities such as black-veined whites and large tortoiseshells join the fray, along with a profusion of marsh, meadow, knapweed, Queen of Spain and Glanville fritillaries.

Wetland habitats within this woodland-meadow mosaic are home to the sylphlike golden-striped salamander, unique to northwest Iberia, and the attractive black-and-green marbled newt, usually more abundant on the southern flanks of the Cordillera Cantábrica, as well as to the more widespread palmate newt, the males of which are distinguished by their "webbed" hind feet. Midwife toads are common throughout these mountains, though rarely seen, but their electronic-sounding "beeps" are often heard at dusk. Painted and parsley frogs, both of which occur only in Iberia and France, are among the rarer amphibians here.

*Every village has its resident white wagtails, black redstarts and serins.*

A wide variety of reptiles inhabits the drier, rockier reaches of Northern Spain, outstanding among which is the stunning ocellated lizard, bright green and up to 80cm (32in) long. Schreiber's green lizard, which is rather similar but smaller, with the males having bright blue heads, is confined to the northwest quarter of Iberia, as is Bocage's wall lizard, a much smaller species with a brownish back and orange-yellow belly. The most widespread and abundant reptiles here are common wall and Iberian wall lizards, as well as grass, viperine, smooth and southern smooth snakes, all of which are harmless. Although Seoane's viper – a species of adder which is endemic to northern Iberia – is venomous, it rarely exceeds 60cm (24in) and is a timid beast which is much more wary of man than vice versa.

## VILLAGE VISITORS

The tiny villages scattered across the Cordillera Cantábrica are as good a place as any for spotting some of the colourful smaller birds of the region. Every village has its resident black redstarts, white wagtails and serins, and many are also home to spotted flycatchers, cirl buntings, redstarts and barn owls. Middle-spotted woodpeckers and wrynecks, which prefer more remote woodlands elsewhere in Europe, often nest in the fruit trees around these villages, particularly in the southern reaches of the Picos de Europa.

Venture out into the patchwork of meadows and forests which surrounds the villages and you are likely to encounter red-backed shrikes, bullfinches, rock buntings, pied flycatchers and tree pipits, with rocky outcrops providing nesting sites for crag martins. The unmistakable calls of cuckoos and quail break the silence, and hunting raptors fill the skies overhead: buzzards and kestrels are ten-a-penny, with booted and short-toed eagles, Egyptian vultures and red and black kites also commonly in evidence.

Although rabbits are rare in the Cordillera, having been severely affected by myxomatosis, brown hares, red squirrels, foxes and weasels frequently venture out during the day, while badgers and wild boars are sometimes encountered on remote roads at night. The smaller mammals tend to be rather secretive, but both common and Iberian blind moles – the latter with flaps of skin growing over their deep-set eyes, hence the name – are occasionally seen in the meadows when their excavations lead them to the surface. Approximately 20 species of bat are to be found in these mountains, but their identification is virtually impossible without the aid of a sophisticated bat detector.

*The brown bear (Ursus arctos) is found in the mountains of Cantabria.*

## FOREST LIFE

Huge tracts of forest still exist in the more remote reaches of the Cordillera Cantábrica, composed mainly of beech, silver birch, sessile oak and holly on the north-facing slopes and Pyrenean oak on the southern flanks. They are home to such shade-tolerant, saprophytic herbs as the bird's-nest orchid and yellow bird's-nest, which overcome the lack of light by obtaining nutrients directly from the decomposing leaf litter. Where more light penetrates, look out for martagon lilies, Welsh poppies, hepatica, Pyrenean squill, herb Paris and whorled Solomon's seal.

Among the best-preserved forest enclaves – most of which are heavily protected today – are the Sierra de Ancares in Galicia, the Bosque de Muniellos (the best-conserved oakwood in Spain), the Parque Natural de las Fuentes de Narcea, Degaña e Ibias, Degaña e Ibias and the Parque Natural Somiedo in Asturias, the Parque Regional de los Picos de Europa in León (including Riaño and Mampodre), and the Parque Natural de Fuentes Carrionas and the Parque Natural de Saja-Besaya in Cantabria.

These forests represent the last refuge for a whole series of vertebrate species which can only thrive beyond the reach of human activity, foremost among which is undoubtedly the brown bear. Here represented by the subspecies *pyrenaicus*, which is unique to the Cordillera Cantábrica and the Pyrenees, the northern Spanish population of brown bears is estimated at around 400 individuals, but the population is growing steadily. Most of these bears live in the area around Somiedo, although a smaller nucleus is centred on the area around Riaño and Fuentes Carrionas.

Apart from the brown bear, the Somiedo beechwoods are also a good place to look for grey wolves (the number and range of which is expanding fast) and smaller carnivores such as wildcats, genets, western polecats, European badgers and pine and beech martens. As most of these creatures are extremely wary of man, as well as being nocturnal, their observation in the wild requires considerable time and dedication. You are much more likely to come across some of the non-carnivorous inhabitants of Somiedo, such as red and roe deer, wild boars, edible and garden dormice and red squirrels, or even Castroviejo's hare, unique to the Cordillera Cantábrica, which usually inhabits broom and greenweed thickets.

*Northern Spain has around 150 species of butterflies, some unique to the area.*

*The Pyrenees are home to an abundance of wild flowers, such as the great yellow gentian (Gentiana lutea).*

The bird interest of these forests is also high, with important breeding populations of capercaillie: one of the highest concentrations of these blackish, almost turkey-sized grouse is found at Riaño, where 180 males preside over the communal display grounds, or leks, every spring. Six species of woodpecker breed in these forests, the most impressive of which is the black woodpecker: a huge, sooty bird, almost half a metre (20in) from beak to tail, with a splendid red crown. Lesser birds such as crested tits, citril finches, goldcrests, treecreepers and woodcocks provide food for sparrowhawks and goshawks, while honey buzzards, with their pigeon-like heads, feed largely on bees and wasps.

Typical butterflies of forest habitats in the Cordillera Cantábrica include such attractive species as the purple emperor, white admiral, Camberwell beauty, cardinal, the misnamed Duke of Burgundy fritillary and a wealth of true fritillaries – silver-washed, pearl-bordered, marbled and dark green – as well as one of Europe's most endangered butterflies: the woodland brown, an exquisite creature identified by the "blind" ocelli on both upper wings.

## ALPINE AREAS

The mountains of northern Spain reach their zenith in the Pyrenees with the 3404m bulk of Aneto. As a result, the truly alpine animals and plants are encountered primarily in Aragon, Navarra and parts of Catalonia, as well as the mountains of Asturias, Cantabria and the northernmost reaches of Castilla y León (with the showpiece of this part of northern Spain undoubtedly being the limestone bulk of the Picos de Europa).

Particularly associated with these high-level pastures and rock gardens are the gentians – spring, trumpet and great yellow, among others – and the dwarf narcissi, such as hoop-petticoat daffodils and Asturian jonquils. Other exquisite mountain plants found here are alpine snowbell, moss campion, Pyrenean fritillary, spring, alpine and red pasque-flowers, snow cinquefoil and dog's-tooth violet, as well as a wealth of saxifrages. Some of the species are unique to the Cordillera Cantábrica, such as the diminutive columbine *Aquilegia discolor*, the attractive white-flowered anemone *Anemone pavoniana*, and the houseleek *Sempervivum cantabricum*.

Rather different assemblages of species are found in the peatbogs which have formed on more acidic uplands with poor drainage. Some of the more notable plants of such conditions are insectivorous species such as round-leaved sundew and large-flowered butterwort, which thrive amid snow marsh and fringed gentians, marsh felwort, grass-of-Parnassus, marsh cinquefoil, starry saxifrage and hairy stonecrop.

Several species of butterfly are unique to the high mountains of Northern Spain, including the diminutive Gavarnie blue, Lefebvre's and Chapman's ringlets, the latter of which is endemic to the central part of the Cordillera Cantábrica. Perhaps the most distinguished high-altitude butterfly, however, is the enormous, satiny-white apollo, whose 8cm (3in) wingspan is sparsely decorated with red and black "eyes". Emerging in July, the apollo vies for airspace with a seemingly infinite number of ringlets, including large, silky, common brassy, mountain, almond-eyed, Piedmont and de Prunner's.

Montane habitats are also home to a number of amphibians and reptiles which are adapted to a life at altitude. Even at heights of more than 2,000 metres (6,600ft), you can expect to find fire salamanders, resplendent in black and gold, and Iberian frogs, which are confined to the northwestern quarter of the peninsula. Alpine newts, with their black skin, whitish eyes and luminous orange bellies, are the most typical denizens of the glacial lakes, but midwife toads are also found around permanent water at altitudes of almost 2,000 metres (6,600ft). Iberian rock lizards are perhaps the most noteworthy of the high-level reptiles, as they occur only in the Cordillera Cantábrica, the Pyrenees and the Sierra de Gredos northwest of Madrid: the males are often bright green above, while the young usually sport vivid blue tails.

*An Iberian frog (Rana iberica) in the Parque Natural de Somiedo, Asturias.*

The Pyrenees and Picos de Europa are home to all the truly montane birds which are found in northern Spain. The most altitude-adapted species are the snowfinch, which rarely nests below 2,000 metres (6,600ft), and the wallcreeper, that most sought-after and elusive of birds, which disappears into the highest crags during the summer months, but can be seen in the limestone gorges in the winter. Alpine accentors, wheatears and water pipits are found throughout the Cordillera Cantábrica all year round, albeit usually at heights of 1,500 metres (5,000ft) or more. Rock thrushes, however, are summer visitors, while ring ouzels and bluethroats pass through on migration, sometimes staying for the winter.

Typical birds of prey of the high mountains include golden eagles, griffon and Egyptian vultures and peregrine falcons all year round, with merlins appearing only in the winter. Both choughs and alpine choughs, the former with red bills and the latter with yellow, are common throughout the mountains of Northern Spain, descending to lower altitudes in huge mixed flocks when bad weather is on the way. The massive lammergeyer (now officially known as the bearded vulture), is confined to the Pyrenees, but again, this population is expanding.

The mammalian king of the Cantabrian peaks is undoubtedly the chamois: an agile, stripe-faced, goat-like creature with hooked horns, which is at its most abundant in the central massif of the Picos de Europa. Their usual haunt is the highest peaks of the lunar landscapes, and they only come down below the tree line in bad weather. Other mammals particularly associated with alpine habitats are the snow vole, which creates extensive networks of barely subterranean tunnels through the high-level pastures, and its main predator the stoat, which swaps its brown coat for a white one in winter, for better camouflage when hunting.

*A griffon vulture (Gyps fulvus) taking flight, Aragon.*

## MOUNTAIN STREAMS AND RIVERS

The Pyrenean desman, a bizarre, mole-like creature with a trumpet-shaped snout, webbed feet, and a flattened, rudder-like tail, has one of its strongholds in the crystal-clear, high mountain streams of the Cordillera Cantábrica. The world distribution of this primitive mammal is restricted to the northern half of the Iberian peninsula, including the Pyrenees, although a related species occurs in Russia. Lower reaches of these rivers teem with trout, such that otters, too, are plentiful, although highly secretive; those watercourses that flow north and discharge into the Atlantic are among the southernmost salmon rivers in the world.

## NORTHERN MESETA

If we follow the south-flowing rivers from the high peaks of the Cordillera Cantábrica, we drop down into a very different world: the northern meseta. Sheltered from the worst effects of the weather systems which sweep in from the Atlantic, the climate here is essentially Mediterranean, even though the average height of the land is more than 800 metres (2,600ft). Evergreen forest predominates in the hills and gorges, with flatter areas supporting sheep pasture and low-intensity cereal cultivation, teeming with rare arable weeds. Wildlife which is more typical of the rest of Spain can be found here.

The limestone gorges of the Sierra del Courel, on the borders of Galicia and León, are inhabited by Bonelli's eagles, alpine swifts, red-rumped swallows, blue rock thrushes and rock sparrows, while the meseta's characteristic patchwork of Mediterranean forests and agricultural land supports subalpine warblers, hobbies and Montagu's harriers.

The southern foothills of the Cordillera Cantábrica host the northernmost breeding populations of the white stork in Spain, particularly around the Riaño reservoir northeast of León.

*Northern Spain's mammals have remained virtually unchanged since the Ice Age.*

To the east, where the land drops towards the River Ebro, colourful Mediterranean birds, such as hoopoes, golden orioles, great grey shrikes and bee-eaters, make an appearance.

On the upper reaches of the Ebro itself, magnificent river gorges – as at Orbaneja del Castillo north of Burgos and Sobrón in the Basque Country – have outstanding raptor populations, particularly of griffon and Egyptian vultures, short-toed and golden eagles and peregrines, as well as eagle owls.

The limestone plateaux, known as *páramos*, which top the gorges, are a botanist's paradise of dense-flowered Provence and lady orchids, which are interspersed with clumps of blue aphyllanthes and shrubby pimpernel.

The southern flanks of the Cordillera Cantábrica are best visited in spring, while early summer sees the glorious hay meadows at their best. The high-level rock gardens peak in July and August, while keen ornithologists who come in autumn and winter will be rewarded by the bird activity on the coast.

*The Pyrenean desman (Galemys pyrenaicus) is found in the high mountain streams of the Cordillera Cantábrica.*

*Grape harvest in the vineyards of Gómez Cruzado in Haro.*

Playa de la Concha beach,
San Sebastián.

*Hikers in the Roncal Valley in the Pyrenees.*

A Coruña's old town.

# INTRODUCTION

A detailed guide to the entire region, with principal sights cross-referenced by number to the maps.

*Bardenas Reales in Navarra.*

In many ways this is not an easy region for the traveller. As the eagle flies, it is a little more than 1,000km (620 miles) from Cap de Creus, Spain's easternmost point just north of Cadaqués, where the Pyrenees fall into the dazzling Mediterranean, to the Atlantic at Finisterre, "land's end", where, according to Galician legend, the souls of the dead must be laid to rest less they be reincarnated as reptiles. This thin strip of land, between 42 and 43.5 north, is not a straight run. The Pyrenees are cut by mountain rivers, and the Cordillera Cantábrica forms a formidable barrier between the Costa Verde and the high central plains.

*Galician coast.*

Often it is easier to go down one valley and up the next, instead of crossing at the shortest point. Roads are always winding and turning. In winter some are closed because of snow, and in summer, mists can make motoring along high ground still slower. Even the coast roads twist and turn, and the fjord-like *rias* of the northwest are particularly dramatic. Only up on the meseta of Castilla y León does the land flatten and become easy – and not quite so exciting.

This guide shows the diversity of the region: what is within your reach, and what you may be missing. It includes the most important sites, but the writers know their ground, and they take you to some unexpected places to share secrets they have discovered and come to enjoy themselves.

The chapters in this guide have mostly been divided into provinces, as this is the easiest way to explain the region. Two exceptions are the Eastern and Central Pyrenees which run from Catalunya into Aragon and the Picos de Europa, shared by Asturias, Cantabria and León: administrative borders often fail to take geography into account.

There are many ways of exploring the region. To reach some places, a car is indispensible, though public transport is geared to take walkers to the main spots. Walking or cycling the pilgrimage route of the Camino de Santiago is perhaps the most rewarding, but also the most arduous, way to get the full flavour of Northern Spain.

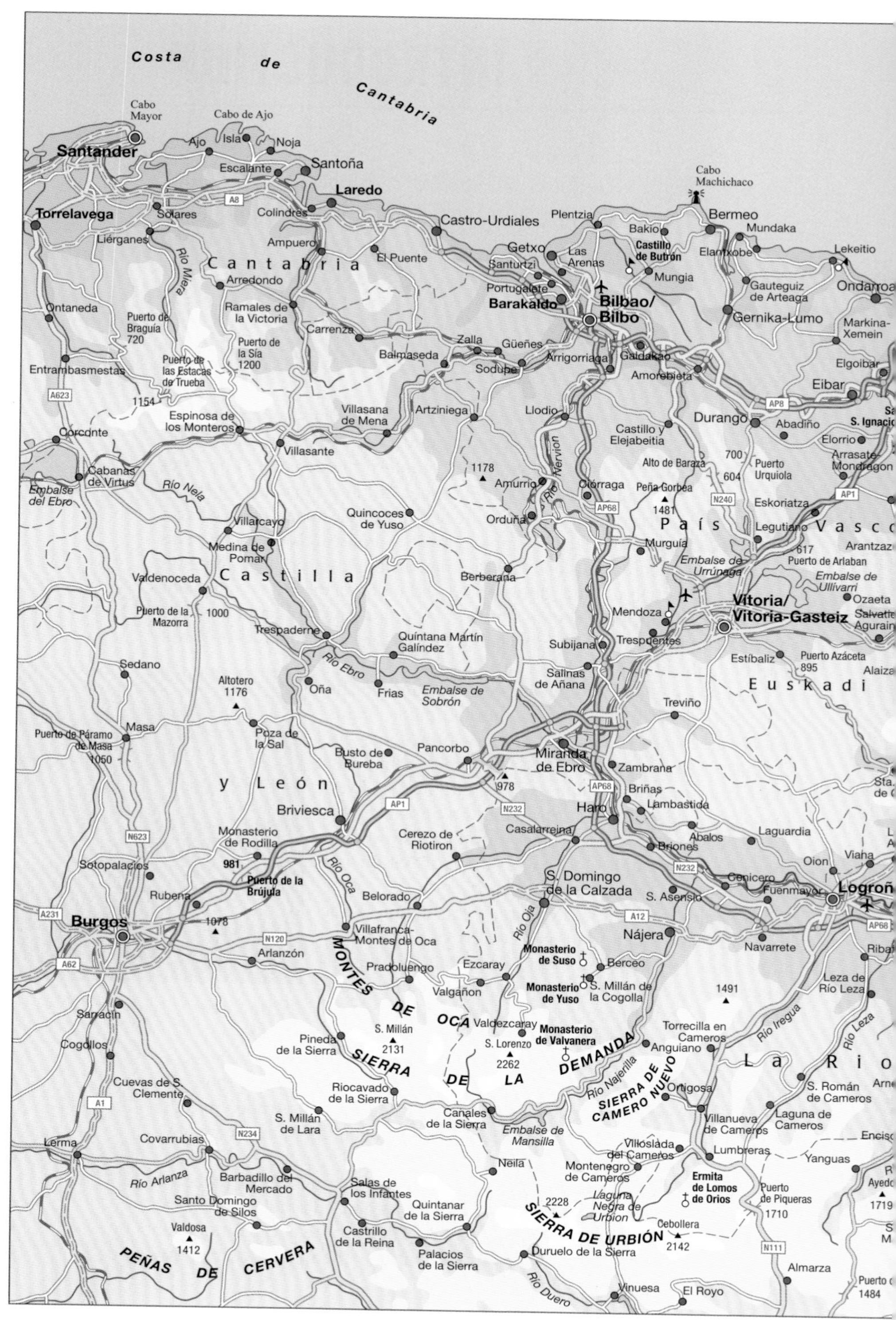
Costa de Cantabria
Cabo Mayor
Cabo de Ajo
Santander
Ajo
Isla
Noja
Santoña
Escalante
Laredo
A8
Torrelavega
Solares
Colindres
Castro-Urdiales
Plentzia
Cabo Machichaco
Bermeo
Mundaka
Bakio
Castillo de Butrón
Elantxobe
Lekeitio
Liérganes
Ampuero
Río Miera
Cantabria
El Puente
Getxo
Las Arenas
Santurtzi
Mungia
Gauteguiz de Arteaga
Ondarroa
Arredondo
Portugalete
Barakaldo
Bilbao/ Bilbo
Gernika-Lumo
Markina-Xemein
Ontaneda
Puerto de Braguía 720
Ramales de la Victoria
Carrenza
Puerto de la Sía 1200
Puerto de las Estacas de Trueba
Zalla
Güeñes
Balmaseda
Sodupe
Arrigorriaga
Galdakao
Amorebieta
Elgoibar
Entrambasmestas
Eibar
A623
1154
Espinosa de los Monteros
Villasana de Mena
Artziniega
Llodio
Castillo y Elejabeitia
Durango
Abadiño
S. Ignacio
AP8
Corconte
Villasante
Río Nervion
Elorrio
Alto de Barazá
700
Puerto Urquiola
Arrasate-Mondragon
Cabanas de Virtus
Río Nela
1178
Amurrio
Orozko
Peña Gorbea 1481
604
Embalse del Ebro
N240
Eskoriatza
AP1
Quincoces de Yuso
Orduña
AP68
País Vasco
Legutiano
Villarcayo
Murguía
617 Puerto de Arlaban
Arantzazu
Medina de Pomar
Embalse de Urrúnaga
Embalse de Ullívarri
Valdenoceda
Castilla
Berberana
Ozaeta
Vitoria/ Vitoria-Gasteiz
Puerto de la Mazorra
1000
Mendoza
Salvatierra Agurain
Trespaderne
Quintana Martín Galíndez
Subijana
Trespuentes
Sedano
Río Ebro
Estíbaliz
Puerto Azáceta 895
Alaiza
Salinas de Añana
Altotero 1176
Oña
Frias
Embalse de Sobrón
Euskadi
Treviño
Puerto de Páramo de Masa 1050
Masa
Poza de la Sal
Busto de Bureba
Pancorbo
Miranda de Ebro
Zambrana
y León
978
Briñas
Labastida
Briviesca
AP1
N232
Haro
N623
Monasterio de Rodilla
Cerezo de Riotiron
Casalarreina
Abalos
Laguardia
981
Puerto de la Brújula
Río Oca
Briones
Oion
Viana
Sotopalacios
Rubena
Belorado
S. Domingo de la Calzada
N232
Cenicero
Fuenmayor
Logroño
S. Asensio
A231
Burgos
1078
Villafranca-Montes de Oca
A12
Río Oja
N120
Nájera
AP68
Navarrete
A62
Arlanzón
Monasterio de Suso
Berceo
Montes de Oca
Pradoluengo
Ezcaray
Monasterio de Yuso
S. Millán de la Cogolla
Leza de Río Leza
Valgañon
1491
Sarracín
Valdezcaray
Monasterio de Valvanera
Torrecilla en Cameros
Río Iregua
Río Leza
S. Millán 2131
S. Lorenzo 2262
Cogollos
Pineda de la Sierra
Anguiano
Sierra de la Demanda
Río Najerilla
La Rio
Sierra de Camero Nuevo
Cuevas de S. Clemente
Riocavado de la Sierra
Ortigosa
S. Román de Cameros
A1
S. Millán de Lara
Canales de la Sierra
Villanueva de Cameros
Laguna de Cameros
Embalse de Mansilla
N234
Lerma
Covarrubias
Villoslada del Cameros
Lumbreras
Yanguas
Neila
Montenegro de Cameros
Río Arlanza
Barbadillo del Mercado
Salas de los Infantes
Ermita de Lomos de Orios
Puerto de Piqueras 1710
Laguna Negra de Urbion
Santo Domingo de Silos
Quintanar de la Sierra
2228
Sierra de Urbión
Cebollera 2142
Valdosa 1412
Castrillo de la Reina
N111
Peñas de Cervera
Palacios de la Sierra
Duruelo de la Sierra
Almarza
Río Duero
Vinuesa
El Royo
1719
1484

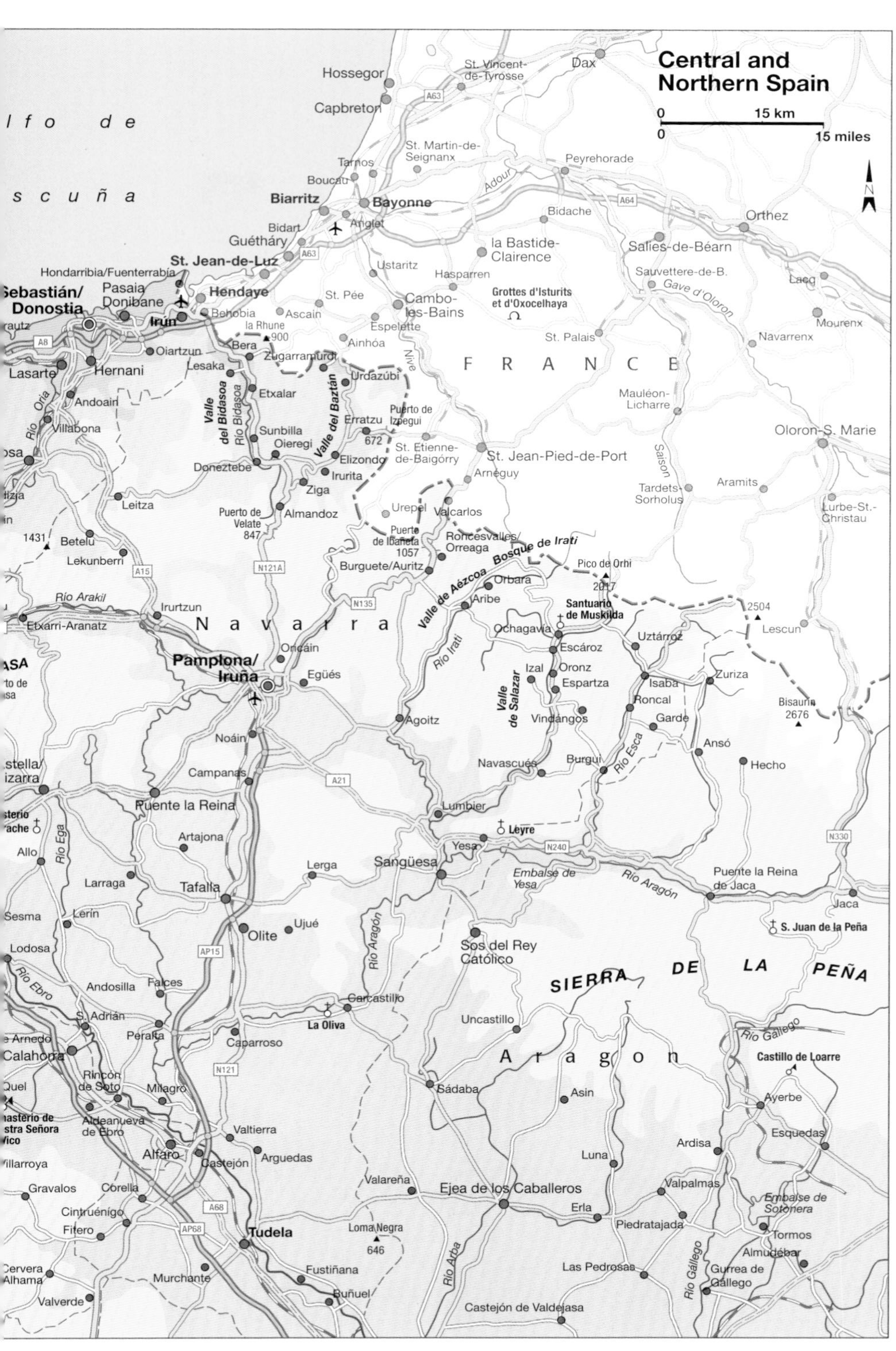
Central and Northern Spain
0 15 km
0 15 miles
Hossegor
Capbreton
St. Vincent-de-Tyrosse
Dax
St. Martin-de-Seignanx
Peyrehorade
Tarnos
Boucau
Biarritz
Bayonne
Anglet
Bidache
Orthez
Bidart
Guéthary
la Bastide-Clairence
Salies-de-Béarn
St. Jean-de-Luz
Ustaritz
Hasparren
Sauvettere-de-B.
Hondarribia/Fuenterrabía
Pasaia Donibane
Hendaye
Grottes d'Isturits et d'Oxocelhaya
Gave d'Oloron
San Sebastián/ Donostia
Irún
Behobia
Ascain
St. Pée
Cambo-les-Bains
Espelette
Mourenx
la Rhune 900
Ainhóa
St. Palais
Navarrenx
Bera
Oiartzun
Zugarramurdi
Lesaka
Lasarte
Hernani
Urdazúbi
Nive
F R A N C E
Etxalar
Andoain
Valle del Bidasoa
Río Bidasoa
Valle del Baztán
Puerto de Izpegui
Mauléon-Licharre
Río Oria
Villabona
Erratzu
Sunbilla
672
Oieregi
St. Etienne-de-Baigórry
Oloron-S. Marie
St. Jean-Pied-de-Port
Elizondo
Doneztebe
Irurita
Arnéguy
Saison
Zig a
Aramits
Leitza
Tardets-Sorholus
Urepel
Lurbe-St.-Christau
Puerto de Velate 847
Almandoz
Valcarlos
Puerto de Ibañeta 1057
Roncesvalles/ Orreaga
Bosque de Irati
Betelu
Lekunberri
Burguete/Auritz
Pico de Orhi 2017
Valle de Aézcoa
Orbara
Río Arakil
Irurtzun
Aribe
Santuario de Muskilda
2504
Etxarri-Aranatz
N a v a r r a
Ochagavía
Uztárroz
Lescun
Oricáin
Escároz
Pamplona/ Iruña
Izal
Oronz
Río Irati
Egüés
Espartza
Isaba
Zuriza
Valle de Salazar
Roncal
Bisaurin 2676
Agoitz
Vidángos
Garde
Noáin
Ansó
Río Esca
Navascués
Burgui
Hecho
Campanas
Puente la Reina
Lumbier
Leyre
Artajona
Yesa
Río Ega
Allo
Lerga
Sangüesa
Embalse de Yesa
Río Aragón
Puente la Reina de Jaca
Larraga
Tafalla
Jaca
Sesma
Lerín
Olite
Ujué
S. Juan de la Peña
Lodosa
Río Aragón
Sos del Rey Católico
SIERRA DE LA PEÑA
Río Ebro
Andosilla
Falces
Carcastillo
S. Adrián
Uncastillo
La Oliva
Peralta
Río Gállego
Caparroso
Calahorra
A r a g o n
Castillo de Loarre
Rincón de Soto
Milagro
Sádaba
Asin
Ayerbe
Aldeanueva de Ebro
Valtierra
Esquedas
Alfaro
Arguedas
Ardisa
Castejón
Luna
Villarroya
Valareña
Valpalmas
Gravalos
Corella
Ejea de los Caballeros
Embalse de Sotonera
Cintruénigo
Erla
Fitero
Tudela
Loma Negra 646
Piedratajada
Tormos
Almudébar
Cervera
Alhama
Murchante
Fustiñana
Las Pedrosas
Río Arba
Gurrea de Gállego
Río Gállego
Valverde
Buñuel
Castejón de Valdejasa
A63
A64
A8
A15
N121A
N135
A21
N240
N330
AP15
N121
A68
AP68

*The jagged, snowy peaks of the Pyrenees.*

# EASTERN AND CENTRAL PYRENEES

Running from the Atlantic to the Mediterranean, the Pyrenees are still spectacularly wild in parts, with fascinating towns and monasteries. The area includes the Principality of Andorra.

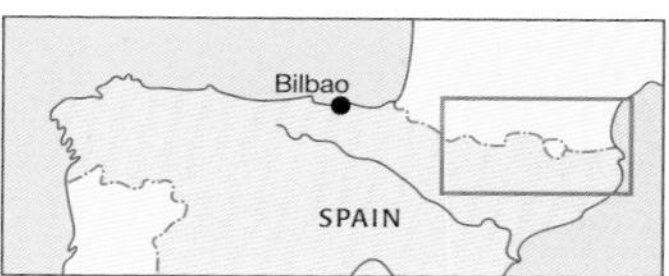


he Pyrenees are one of the world's reat mountain chains, stretching 40km (275 miles) from the Catalan lediterranean to the Basque Atlan- c and defining the border between rance and Spain. In the wildest and ıost spectacular Central or Aragonese yrenees, peaks reach heights of 3,404 ıetres (11,168ft) at Aneto and 3,355 ıetres (11,007ft) at Monte Perdido. The alleys have nurtured unique species of ora and fauna and produced anoma- es such as the Principality of Andorra. he survival of a handful of dialects and ınguages shows just how cut off from ıe world these valleys have been. The ıountains extend in foothills – the pre- yrenees – to the south and these are arved into valleys making east–west rogress slow, even at lower altitudes.

## HE CATALAN PYRENEES

t the Mediterranean end of the chain, ıe Catalan Pyrenees can be said to egin at **Cap de Creus ❶**, the Iberian eninsula's easternmost point and the tarting or finishing point of the GR11 ng distance, trans-Pyrenean footpath ee page 153). This is the book-end to ıatch the Cabo de Higuer lighthouse ıst west of Hondarribia on the Atlantic ɔast. The most appropriate approach the Cap de Creus from France, but ot the fastest, is along the winding ɔast road from Banyuls-sur-Mer.

Near the cape is **Cadaqués**, a white-washed, flower-covered coastal village of great charm that is associated with the Surrealist painter Salvador Dalí (1904–89). His house at neighbouring **Port-Lligat** has become a museum of the artist's life and work (https://www.salvador-dali.org; daily mid-June–mid-Sept 9.30am–9pm, mid-Sept–early Jan and mid-Feb–mid-June 10.30am–6pm; closed some Mon; online booking advised).

Southwest of Cadaqués is the resort of **Roses**, at the top of the sweeping Bay of Roses, which supports the most

**Main attractions**

- Cadaqués
- Sant Pere de Rodes
- Teatre-Museu Dalí, Figueres
- Aigüestortes National Park
- Vall de Boí
- Ordesa National Park
- San Juan de la Peña
- Sos del Rey Católico

Map on page 140

*Cadaques and Cap de Creus.*

> **Tip**
> In winter, check that mountain roads will be open before heading for the hills.

important wetland site on the Costa Brava, the **Parc Natural dels Aiguamolls**. Nearby are the Græco-Roman ruins of **Empúries**, where both the Greeks and Romans first set foot in Spain (daily). A Greek harbour wall is still lapped by the sea and the extensive site is wonderfully set by the sandy shore.

A short way inland from the cape, in the hills above the resort of **Port de la Selva** are the massive ruins of the monastery of **Sant Pere de Rodes** (Tue–Sun June–Sept 10am–8pm, Oct–May 10am–5.30pm). Dating from the 9th century, the monastery used columns from the Roman Temple of Venus Pyrenea, which once stood on this site overlooking the last heights of the Pyrenees as they fall into the sea.

Continuing west but not yet in the Pyrenees proper, you come to **Figueres** ❷, at the centre of the Alt (high) Empordà region. Here is Dalí's most spectacular memorial, the **Teatre-Museu Dalí** (Plaza Gala-Salvador Dalí 5; https://www.salvador-dali.org; Mar–Oct 9.30am–6pm, Nov–Feb 10.30am–6pm; closed some Mon).

One of the finest medieval towns i the region is **Besalú** ❸, 24km (15 miles west of Figueres on the N-260. Its for tified bridge, with crenellated battle ments, is much photographed and i has two fine churches in Sant Vicen and Sant Pere as well as a rare 11th century *mikvah*, Jewish bathhouse discovered in the late 1960s. **Olot** ❹ 20km (12 miles) west of Figueres, is th capital of the volcanic Garrotxa region. I is a tidy town with some lovely corner and the famous **Museu Comarcal de l Garrotxa** (Carrer de l'Hospici 8; Tue–Fr 10am–1pm and 3–6pm; Sat 11am–2pr and 4–7pm; Sun 10am–2pm), whic shows works of the landscape artist of the 19th-century "Olot School". Als displayed in the museum are sculpture by Miquel Blay (1866–1936), whos maidens support the balconies on Olot' main street.

## VALL DE CAMPRODÓN

North of Olot climb the scenic Col lado de Capsacosta or go through th Capsacosta tunnel to **El Vall de Cam prodón**, the easternmost Pyrenea

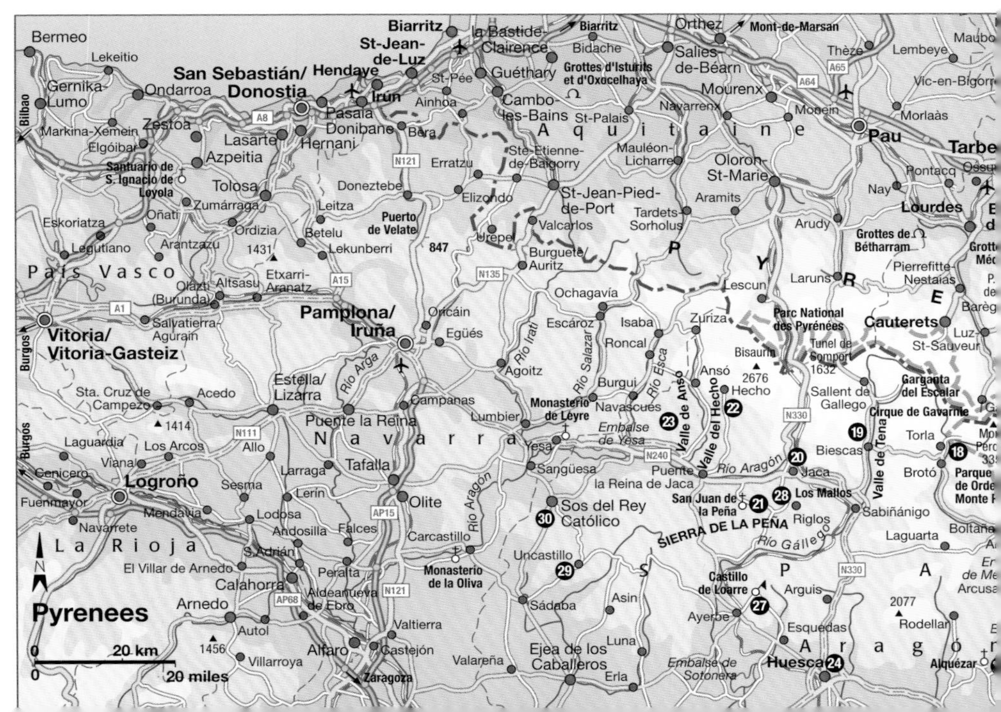

alley. **Camprodón** 5 is at the junc-ion of the Ter and Ritort trout rivers, panned by a graceful 12th-century tone bridge, and the constant flowing vater gives Camprodón a lively, musi-al quality. The composer Isaac Albé-iz, born here in 1860, made his piano lebut at the age of four, perhaps influ-nced by this water music.

It is tempting to make a detour over he **Coll d'Ares**, at the head of the Vall le Camprodón, into France to visit **Prats-de-Molló**, a lively mountain own. From here a small road leads up o the cosy hideaway of **La Preste**.

Another detour, this time in Spain, eads down a winding road to **Beget**, 7km (10 miles) east of Camprodón. This is a hidden jumble of stone houses with massive wooden doors and a distinctive golden-ochre hue. Stone bridges cross the trout-filled stream. The 11th-century Sant Cristó-ol Church has a miniature bell tower and a famous Majestat, a 13th-century polychrome wood carving of Christ. The church's interior is a rare survivor of Catalonia's fiery modern history: ask for the key to the church. **Molló**, on the C-38 on the way to the Coll d'Ares, has a 12th-century church with an elegant bell tower. Continuing along the pre-Pyrenees, **Sant Joan de les Abadesses** 6, 14km (9 miles) southwest of Camprodón, was founded in 885 for Emma, the first abbess and daughter of the first count of Barcelona. The 12th-century church of Sant Joan has a superb polychrome wood sculpture of the Descent from the Cross. The Gothic bridge over the River Ter and the arcaded main square add to the town's distinct medieval flavour.

## CRADLE OF CATALONIA

Emma's father, the first count of Barcelona, was Guifré el Pilós (Wilfred the Hairy), who is revered as the founder of the Catalan nation and a hero of the Christian Reconquest. In 888 he founded the Benedictine monastery at **Ripoll** 7, 10km (6 miles) west of his daughter's abbey and, as a result, the town is considered the *bressol* (cradle) of Catalonia's spiritual birth. It was an early bastion of the Reconquest, a

**Fact**

A figure, one of the two thieves on the 12th-century Descent from the Cross at Sant Joan de les Abadesses, was burnt in the Civil War and has since been replaced. It is difficult to tell which is the new one.

**Quote**

"You have here [the Cerdanya] a small countryside as broad as a small English county might be, full of fields and large enough to take abreast a whole series of market towns."

Hilaire Belloc, The Pyrenees, 1909

centre of medieval religious thought and a cultural hub throughout Roussillon (stretching into France).

Wars and conflict have stripped the interior of the monastery's 12th-century church of **Santa María** (Mon–Sat, Apr–Sept 10am–2pm and 4–7pm, Sun 10–2pm, Oct–Mar 10am–1.30pm and 3.30–6pm, Sun 10am–2pm year round), but the doorway of is one of the greatest Romanesque masterpieces in the Pyrenees. The sculptures decorating this triumphal arch portray the glory of God and all of creation from the beginning. A guide to the portal, the triumphant achievement of the group of sculptors known as the Roussillon school, can be purchased at the church or at the information kiosk nearby. In summer, the attractive cloisters become a music venue. The town also has an excellent folk museum in the former church of Sant Pere opposite Santa María, with artefacts illustrating the shepherd's life in the Pyrenees.

North of Ripoll, the cogwheel train from the mountain town of **Ribes** up to **Núria**, known as the *cremallera* (zip, or zipper), was built in 1917 to connec Ribes with the sanctuary of La Mare d Deu de Núria. It is a spectacular rid with views down the Freser Valley, wit one stop, at **Queralbs**, the end of th road for motorists.

## THE CERDANYA

From Ribes the N-152 twists along th mountain's edge through the Collada d Toses pass to the **Cerdanya**, the wid est and brightest valley in the Pyrenees Said to be shaped like "the handprin of God", the Cerdanya is bordered o both its northern and southern sides b snow-covered peaks. Stretching fron **Martinet** in the Spanish province o Lleida as far as **Mont Louis** in France it was divided between the two coun tries in the 1659 Peace of the Pyrenees *"Meitat de França, meitat d'Espanya, n hi ha altra terra com la Cerdanya"* ("Ha in France, half in Spain, there's no plac like the Cerdanya"). Inhabitants on bot sides of the border speak Catalan. Th Cerdanya's riches are numerous: 15 sk resorts in three countries (includin Andorra), four golf courses, numerou

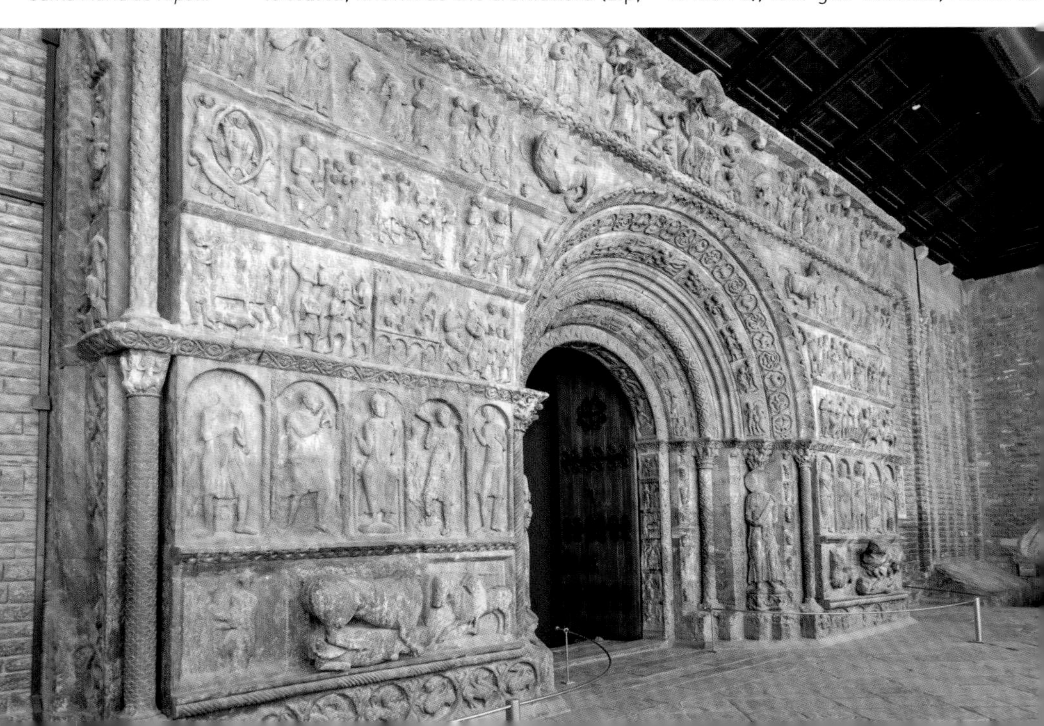

*Santa María de Ripoll.*

rout streams of which the River Segre s the most important, spectacular eaks and hiking routes, thermal baths iscovered by the Romans, unspoiled illages such as Eyne, and fortified owns such as Mont Louis.

**Puigcerdà** ❽, the Cerdanya's biggest own and commercial centre, is built on promontory with views of the valley in ll directions. It marks the international rontier and is paired with the French own of Bourg-Madame. The square round the Romanesque bell tower vith its sunlit and protected pavement afé, the long square (Plaça del Cuarel, site of a very good Sunday market), he arcaded **Plaça Cabrinetty** and the own Hall with a **balcony** looking west cross the valley to the rugged peaks of he Cadí, are the town's best features.

Beyond Puigcerdá, incongruously nside the French border and not vell signposted, is **Llívia**, a Spanish nclave which eluded the 1659 Peace f the Pyrenees that ceded 33 villages o France. Llívia was promoted to the tatus of *vila* (town) by Carlos V after e had spent a happy night there in 1528 and, as no towns were mentioned in the treaty, it remained a Spanish possession. Llívia has a fine fortified church and a pharmacy founded in 1415, the oldest in Europe.

From Puigcerdà, it's an hour's walk (or a 10-minute train ride) to **Latour de Carol** in France where *le petit train jaune* (the little yellow train) leaves daily on its journey to the walled city of **Villefranche de Conflent**. This *carrilet* (narrow-gauge railway) is the last in the Pyrenees and is used for tours as well as for getting around the valley. The tour takes the better part of a day, with stops in Mont Louis or Villefranche, and has an open car in summer. This is the last chance for an easy excursion into France before the increasing height of the peaks makes trans-border crossing difficult.

**Bellver de Cerdanya**, 17km (10 miles) to the southwest of Puigcerdá, is one of the best-conserved stone and slate-roofed Pyrenean towns in the Cerdanya. Suspended over the River Segre, which curves tightly around the base of the town, Bellver is famous for its *coto* (beat) of reserved trout fishing river, one of the

*Puigcerdà's Sunday market.*

**Tip**

The Andorra tourist office supplies a leaflet on what you can take tax-free into Spain: some people stay in hotels just inside the Spanish border and go back and forth to fetch more booty. Petrol is a particular bargain; look out for special offers on all goods.

best in Spain. This is also a starting-off point for exploring the **Parc Natural Cadí-Moixeró**, a protected area of landscape. Bellver's Gothic church and arcaded square in the upper part of town are its best architectural features.

From Bellver, the N-260 continues 32km (20 miles) to **La Seu d'Urgell** ❾, the biggest city in the Catalan Pyrenees. This ancient mountain town has been the seat of the regional archbishopric since the 6th century. The solid mass of the arcaded streets and the gloom under overhanging galleries give La Seu d'Urgell a distinctly medieval feel. The 12th-century cathedral of **Santa María** has a colourful, southeast-facing rose window and a 13th-century cloister with 50 distinctively carved columns. It is widely considered the most beautiful in the Pyrenees. Among the medieval fragments in the **Museu Diocesà** (Diocesan Museum; www.museudiocesaurgell.org; Mon–Sat 10am–1.30pm and 4am–6pm, June–Sept until 7pm) is a beautiful 10th-century copy of an illuminated manuscript from Liébana in the Picos de Europa.

## THE PRINCIPALITY OF ANDORRA

La Seu d'Urgell is the logical point from which to enter **Andorra** 12km (8 miles) north. The Bishop of La Seu has been co-Prince of the Principality of Andorra, along with the Counts of Foix (a title now ceded to the President of the French Republic) since the 13th century. Avoid Andorra at weekends and during holiday periods when its crowded shopping centres generate traffic jams and customs roadblocks.

The upper reaches of the principality, however, with Romanesque chapels and ancient stone houses and bridges, are as lovely as any in the Pyrenees. The main square and the stone bulk of the Casa de la Vall in the capital, **Andorra la Vella** ❿, the 9th-century church at **Santa Coloma**, the Romanesque Pont de Sant Antoni bridge, 3km (2 miles) north of Andorra la Vella on the CG-3, and **La Cortinada**'s Can Pal house and Sant Martí church are some of Andorra's best sights. Spectacular highland touring and hiking routes include the Cercle de Pessons, a basin of Pyrenean tarns under the Pessons peak

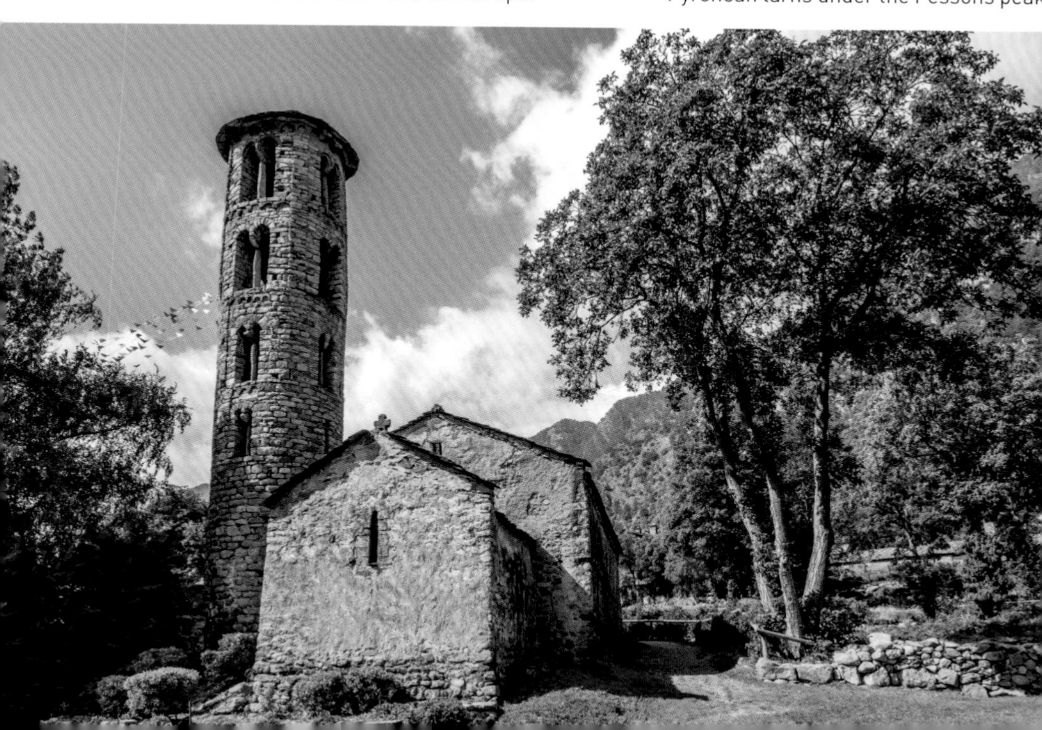

*Church of Santa Coloma near Andorra la Vella.*

n the Principality's southeastern edge nd the route above El Serrat to Port del :at to the northwest.

## IGÜESTORTES ATIONAL PARK

t Andrall, 7km (4 miles) south of La eu d'Urgell, a right turn onto the N-260 eads over the Cantó Pass on the 53km 33-mile) drive to **Sort** ⓫, capital of the 'allars Sobirà (Upper Pallars). This ski- ng, fishing and white-water kayaking entre is the gateway to the Vall de Assua nd Vall de Llesuí to the northwest, a ristine area of untouched mountain illages such as **Sauri**, **Olp**, **Bernui** and **lessuí**, 14km (9 miles) north of Sort on he C-147, at the junction of the Noguera 'allaresa and Cardós rivers. The Vallfer- era valley to the northeast leads up to he villages of Alins and Aneu under Cat- alonia's highest point, the Pica d'Estats 3,115 metres/10,220ft).

The village of **Espot** ⓬, 18km (11 miles) northwest of Llavorsí on the C13, which runs along the Noguera Pallaresa river valley, is at the entrance to the **Parc Nacional d'Aigüestortes**, one of the great treasures of the Catalan Pyrenees. This pristine concentration of woods and meadows tucked under the twin peaks of Els Encantats has more than 150 glacial ponds and lagoons, notably the much-photographed **Estany de Sant Maurici**. The park has rigid rules and regulations prohibiting camping, fires, vehicles in certain areas and loose pets. There are a wide array of way-marked hiking trails with routes lasting anything from a couple of family-friendly hours to a nine day circuit around lake, after beautiful lake.

Continuing north from Espot, the road reaches **Esterri d'Àneu**, a town of stone houses with wooden galleries, and a pivotal point for exploring Pallars Sobirà. There are Romanesque chapels at **Sant Joan d'Isil** and **Alòs d'Isil**, from where a mountain track navigable by a vehicle with reasonable clearance follows the Noguera to the Santuario de Montgarri in the Vall d'Aran.

## THE VALL D'ARAN

Heading west up through the clear mountain air, the C28 crosses the 2,072-metre (6,800ft) Bonaigua Pass into the

*Parc Nacional d'Aïguestorte.*

**Tip**

Several subspecies of butterfly are unique to the Vall d'Aran, which, in late spring and early summer, is a treat for butterfly watchers.

**Vall d'Aran**. Just beyond the pass is the **Baqueira-Beret/Tuca-Betrén** winter sports complex, ranked as the Iberian Peninsula's finest ski resort. Visited annually by Spain's royal family, Baqueira-Beret has more than 40 runs up to an altitude of just under 2,500 metres (8,000ft), thermal baths and a comprehensive tourist infrastructure.

Until the 6km (4-mile) **Vielha (Viella) tunnel** under the Maladeta peak was built in 1948, only one minor road led from Spain into this 600-sq-km (230-sq-mile) northwestern corner of Catalonia, and the valley was cut off in winter. Lying north of the main Pyrenean axis, the Vall d'Aran is the Spanish Pyrenees' only Atlantic valley, drained by the River Garonne flowing northwest across the plains of Aquitaine and into the Atlantic north of Bordeaux. The Atlantic character of the Vall d'Aran is palpable in its wetter and colder weather, and audible in its language – Aranés, a dialect of Gascon French. Originally part of Aquitanian Comminges, the Vall d'Aran had feudal ties to the Pyrenees of Aragón, joining the kingdom of Catalonia-Aragón in th 12th century. In 1389 the Vall d'Ara formally became part of Cataloni Gray slate roofs, conical church tow ers, dormer windows and a certai orderliness all contribute to a sens that, even more than Andorra, the Va d'Aran is a separate country with a cul ture that is more French than Spanish

**Vielha** (Viella) ⓭, capital of the Val d'Aran, is a lively town of 5,400 inhab itants bursting with visitors during th winter ski season and summer hikin season. The Romanesque church o Sant Miquel has an octagonal 14th century bell tower and is the town' chief architectural treasure. The 12th century Cristo de Mig Aran polychrom wood carving displayed under glass a Sant Miquel is one of the Pyrenees' bes medieval sculptures. Vielha's Museu d la Vall d'Aran has historical and ethno logical items, as well as butterflies some of which exist only in this valley.

The **Joeu Valley**, above the town o Es Bòrdes on the N-230 north of Vielha provides a look into the Vall d'Aran' river systems. As one of the two mai

*Vielha in winter.*

sources of the Garonne, the River Joeu flows through Artiga de Lin and crashes down the Barrancs waterfalls to the Garonne. The origin of this hydraulic mystery was finally confirmed using dyes that showed the subterranean stream came from the Aneto glacier miles west in the next valley.

## ROMANESQUE VALLEY

South from the Túnel de Vielha, the N-230 follows the River Noguera Ribagorzana (Ribagorçana in Catalan), which forms the border between Aragón and Catalonia. Running parallel just to the east is the **Vall de Boí**, reached by taking a right turn into the valley of the River Noguera de Tor 2km (1 mile) north of **Pont de Suert**. Here is the best concentration of Romanesque art and architecture in the Pyrenees.

Built in the 11th and 12th centuries, the churches of the Boí valley form a superb matched set. The bell towers are tall and slender, towering over miniature, rounded stone apses and slate roofs. **Sant Climent** in the town of **Taüll** ⓮ is the best known, its six-storey belfry emblematic of the Boí valley and of Catalan Romanesque art. The famous Pantocrator, a brilliant painting of Christ covering the apse wall, is the church's most famous mural, though it is now a copy as the original was removed in 1922 for safety reasons and installed in Barcelona's Museu Nacional d'Art de Catalunya.

Other fine examples of the Boí Romanesque are the church of **Santa María**, also at Taüll, the **Església de Santa Eulàlia** at Erill-la-Vall, and the churches of **Santa María** at Coll, and **Sant Nicolau** in the Sant Nicolau Valley at the entrance to the Parc Nacional d'Aigüestortes. Just 6km (4 miles) north of Taüll is Caldes de Boí, with two hotels open in summer for thermal bathing treatments. The **Boí-Taüll ski resort** is at the head of the Sant Nicolau Valley.

## THE PYRENEES IN ARAGÓN

The Central or Aragonese Pyrenees are the highest, wildest and most spectacular section of the mountain chain. From the Ansó Valley in the west to the valley of Benasque at the border with

**Tip**

Abundant rushing water makes the Pyrenees a source of hydroelectricity. Water power was first harnessed in the 11th-century "farga catalana", an iron forge which can be seen in the museum at Ripoll.

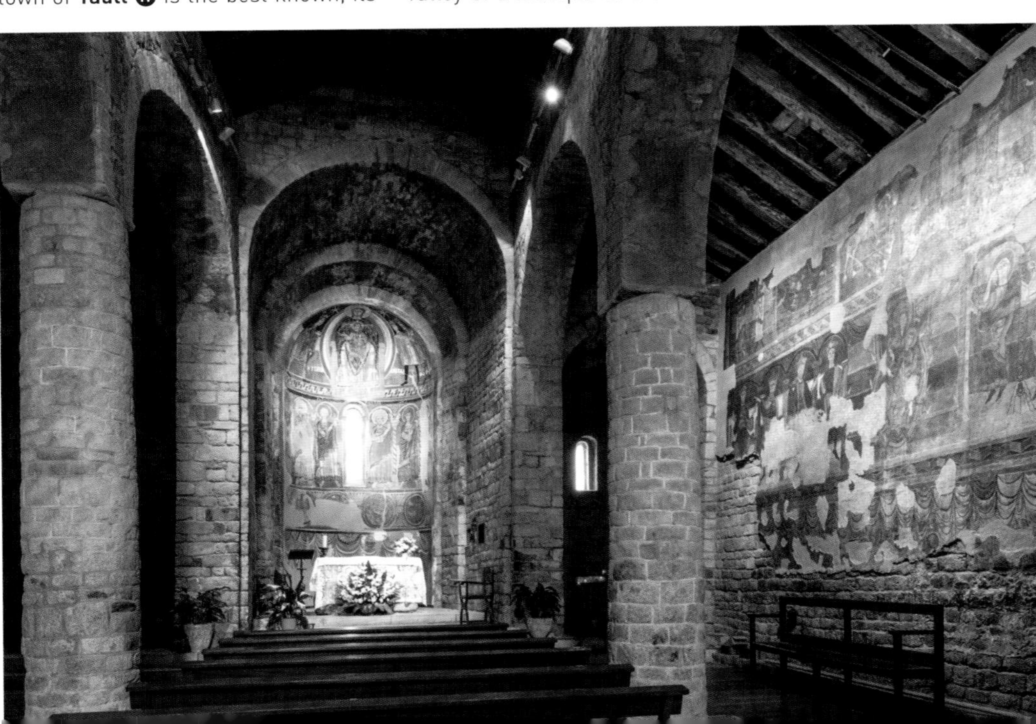

*Romanesque murals decorate the walls of Santa María de Taull.*

> **Tip**
> Maps from the Ordesa National Park visitor's centre, north of Torla, show which trails are easy and which are hard, and indicate the sites of the *refugios*, necessary shelters if the weather suddenly turns bad. Some of these are manned and meals are available but advance reservations are always required.

Catalonia are nine valleys with distinct traditions, dialects and identities. Jaca is the capital of the Central Pyrenees, a busy mountain town pivotal to Alto Aragón (Upper Aragón), the northern part of Aragón's province of Huesca. It has the highest peaks in the Pyrenees: Monte Perdido (3,355 metres/11,007ft), Posets (3,371 metres/11,060ft), Maladeta (3,308 metres/10,853ft) and Aneto (3,404 metres/11,168ft). The valleys, perpendicular to the cordillera's east–west axis, were formed by glaciers at their highest parts, while the deep canyons and gorges below were carved by rivers and snow run-off.

Communications between the valleys were minimal until the second half of the 20th century and much of Alto Aragón had never seen a motor vehicle before that. Until the early 20th century, there was no crossing at all over the 150km (93-mile) French border between Portalet de Aneu and the Vall d'Aran.

At the eastern end of the region is the Aragonese Ribagorza on the A-139 around **Castejón de Sos**, which leads to the Vall de Benasque, Aragón's easternmost valley. **Benasque** ⓯, a town of 2000 inhabitants, has a few stately mansions, notably the Renaissance Palacio de los Condes (Palace of the Counts of Ribagorza) on Calle Mayor and the 13th-century church of Santa María Mayor. Most people come to Benasque either to ski in the nearby Cerler ski resort or to make hiking excursions into the **Maladeta Massif** the **Refugio de la Renclusa** and up to the **Pico de Aneto**, where a once-famous glacier has been reduced to a scrap of grey snow.

Down a little road from Benasque is the exquisitely restored village of **Anciles**, a collection of stone farmhouses of typically solid yet graceful Pyrenean design.

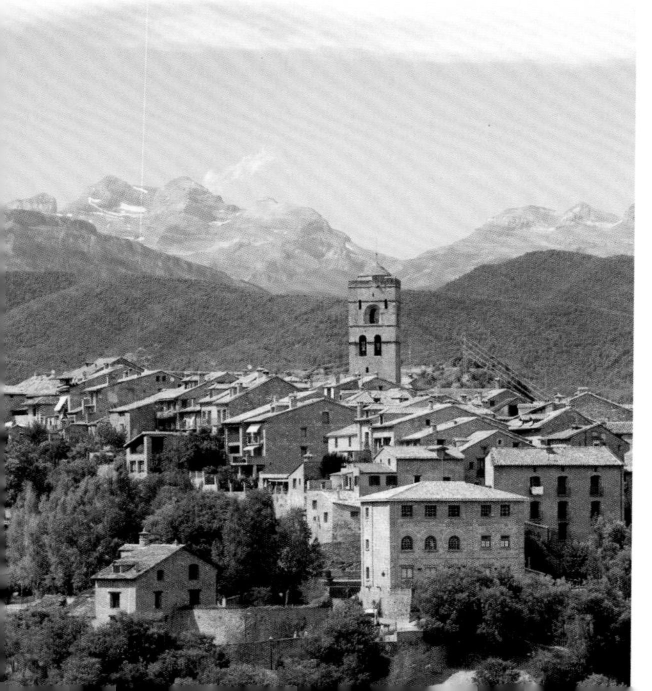

*The view over Ainsa.*

## ORDESA NATIONAL PARK

From Castejón de Sos, the 16km (10-mile) drive south passes through the Congosto de Ventamillo, a spectacular cut through solid rock along the River Esera. Just below the village of Campo, a right turn on to the N-260 leads 32km (20 miles) west to **Aínsa** ⓰. It has a 12th-century church and an arcaded central square with massive arches over lovely, low, heavy porches.

There are two points of access to the Ordesa national park. One is **Bielsa** ⓱, north of Ainsa, which also has arcaded *plazas* and a medieval, mountain feel. Striding the confluence of the Cinca and Barrosa rivers, it is the gateway to the Monte Perdido glacier and the Pineta Valley. The Parador Nacional Monte Perdido is at the head of the Cinca Valley and from here you can take walks up to the Larri valley, which is an easy family-friendly walk. Or the lakes of Munia or Marbore, both of which are far more serious goals involving significant climbs and a lot of effort. Marbore, right at the icy northern foot of Monte Perdido, offers one of the most extraordinary views in the Pyrenees, but the length of the walk (which is really only suitable for very experienced mountain walkers) means it's best to take a tent. North of Bielsa, the road leading to the French border passes **Parzán** in the **Barrosa Valley**, and the villages of **Chisagües** and **Urdiceto.**

Just 8km (5 miles) south of Bielsa is **Salinas de Sin** and the road up the River Cinqueta, which drains the Gistaín Valley, flowing through the attractive mountain villages of **Sin**, **Señes**, **Saravillo** and **Serveta**. The towns of **Plan** and **San Juan de Plan** are at the head of the valley. San Juan de Plan has a Romanesque church and an Ethnographic Museum (July–Aug 10am–1pm and 4.30–8.30pm).

The **Parque Nacional de Ordesa y Monte Perdido**, which occupies the **Valle de Ordesa** between the Valle de Bielsa and the Valle de Tena, was created by royal decree in 1918 to protect the natural patrimony of the Central Pyrenees. Since then it has increased in size tenfold to encompass **Monte Perdido**, the **Pineta Valley** and the canyons of **Ordesa**, **Escuain** and **Añisclo**. The Ordesa Valley forms the southern side of the famous **Cirque de Gavarnie** across the French border. Rich in woodlands of pine, fir, larch, beech and poplar, and endowed with streams, lakes, waterfalls and high mountain tarns, Ordesa has abundant protected wildlife including Capra pirenaica, a mountain goat exclusively found in Ordesa, along with deer, vultures, eagles, otters, mink, snow partridges and capercaillies. Hiking routes cross the park on well marked and well maintained mountain trails to lookout points and sites such as caves or the famous 70-metre (230ft) *cola de caballo* (horse tail) waterfall. The best months to come are mid-May to mid-November.

From Aínsa, the N-260 and then a minor road go up into the park along the River Ara through **Boltaña** up to **Broto** and **Torla** ⓲, which are overshadowed by 2,848-metre (9,344ft) Mondarruego and make a good base for visiting the park. Guidebooks are available at the information centre in the Ordesa Valley 9km (5 miles) north of Torla. All of these villages have interesting mountain architecture of slate roofs and simple stone walls; Broto has the region's

**Fact**

Ramiro II massacred rebellious nobles who had met under the pretext of casting a giant bell. The Spanish expression "como la campana de Huesca" (like the bell of Huesca) has since been used to describe an event of great resonance and some irony or a big surprise.

*Parque Nacional de Ordesa y Monte Perdido.*

**Fact**

News that the Holy Grail could be seen at San Juan de la Peña diverted pilgrims en route to Santiago. The vessel was in fact a gold and agate Roman chalice, which was later moved to Valencia cathedral.

characteristic conical chimneys and fine manor houses.

## THE WESTERN PYRENEAN VALLEYS OF ARAGON

West of Broto, a small winding mountain road reaches **Biescas** 19 in the **Valle de Tena**, a valley formed by the River Gállego and its two tributaries, the Aguaslimpias and the Caldares. A glacial valley surrounded by towering peaks such as the 3,298-metre (10,820ft) Vignemale, the Tena valley is a lively centre for tourists in search of outdoor activities. **Sallent de Gállego** at the head of the valley is a traditional base camp for excursions to **Aguaslimpias**, **Piedrafita** and the Gállego headwaters at **El Formigal**.

The historic town of **Jaca** 20 stands at the head of a parallel valley to the west of Tena. It is the first major town that invaders, pilgrims on the route to Santiago de Compostela and merchants used to reach after crossing the Puerto de Somport traversing the Pyrenees – the pass has since been supplanted by an 8km/5-mile tunnel). Jaca's 11th-century **cathedral** has a **Museo Episcopal** (Mon–Sat 10am–1.30pm and 4.30–7pm, Sun 10am–1.30pm) containing fine Romanesque and Gothic murals. The Ciutadella (Tue–Sun 11am–2pm and 4–7pm; July–mid-Sept until 8.30pm) is an excellent example of 17th-century military architecture, as is the Rapitán garrison, which is located just north of town. Don't miss Jaca's lively music bar scene, or the famous garlic and olive oil potatoes served at La Campanilla. The ski resorts of Candanchú and Astún are 32km (20 miles) north on the road to Somport.

The magnificent **Monasterio de San Juan de la Peña** 21 (daily 10am–2pm and 3–7pm, June–Aug until 8pm), southwest of Jaca, was the spiritual centre of Christian resistance during the Moorish occupation. The monastery's origins can be traced back to a monk who settled on the peña (cliff) of the Pano Mountain during the 9th century. In 920, a monastery was founded in a secluded place in a dramatic place under a great rock overhang. Some buildings are cut out of the rock itself. It was here that the Latin Mass was introduced to Spain. The monastery is

*San Juan de la Peña, last resting place of the first kings of Aragón.*

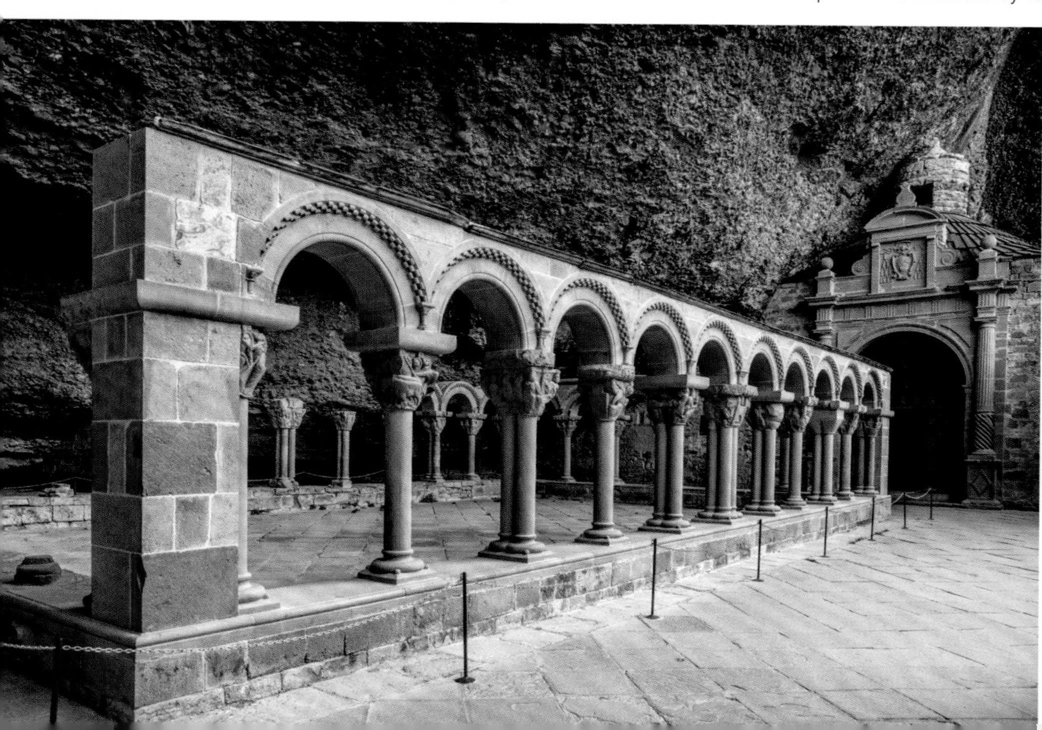

also purported to have been the guardian of the Holy Grail: a replica is on display. The 12th-century cloister built under and into the cliff has intricately carved capitals of biblical scenes. A pantheon of early kings of Aragón adjoins the church.

**Puente la Reina de Jaca** is 10km (6 miles) further west, and is the starting point up the **Valle del Hecho**, one of Aragón's most picturesque valleys and home of the Cheso dialect, still kept alive by ethnographers, linguists, writers and poets. Southeast of the village of **Hecho** ㉒ are mountain roads leading across to the villages of **Aragüés**, **Aisa** and **Borau**. **Aragüés del Puerto** is typical of these compact mountain villages, huddled stone houses ribboned by alleys and unexpected corners.

Aragüés is known for the *palotiau*, a version of the *jota* dance performed exclusively here. Above the village looms the Bisaurin Peak at 2,668 metres (8,753ft). The **Lizara** cross-country ski area is on a plain between the Aragüés and Jasa valleys where you can also see megalithic dolmens.

Just above the town of Hecho is the **Monasterio de Siresa**, a 9th-century retreat with only the 11th-century church still intact. At the head of the valley is the **Selva de Oza** (Oza Forest), reached through the so-called **Boca del Infierno** (Mouth of Hell), a narrow cut where road and river barely squeeze through. Above the forest is a Roman road which was built to connect the region with France across El Palo Pass, one of the first Pyrenean routes on the Santiago pilgrimage.

Just to the west of the Valle del Hecho is the parallel **Valle de Ansó** ㉓, Aragón's northwestern limit. This valley is known for its abundant wildlife, featuring wild boar, chamois and *Capra hispanica*. Halfway up the valley lies the village of Ansó, whose patron saint is honoured in the Santuario de la Virgen de Puyeta in nearby Fago. Close to the head of the valley, above Zuriza, are three cross-country ski areas: the **Pistas de Linza**.

## THE PRE-PYRENEES

**Huesca** ㉔, due south of Biescas and Sabiñánigo, was briefly the capital of Aragón from 1096, when Pedro I of

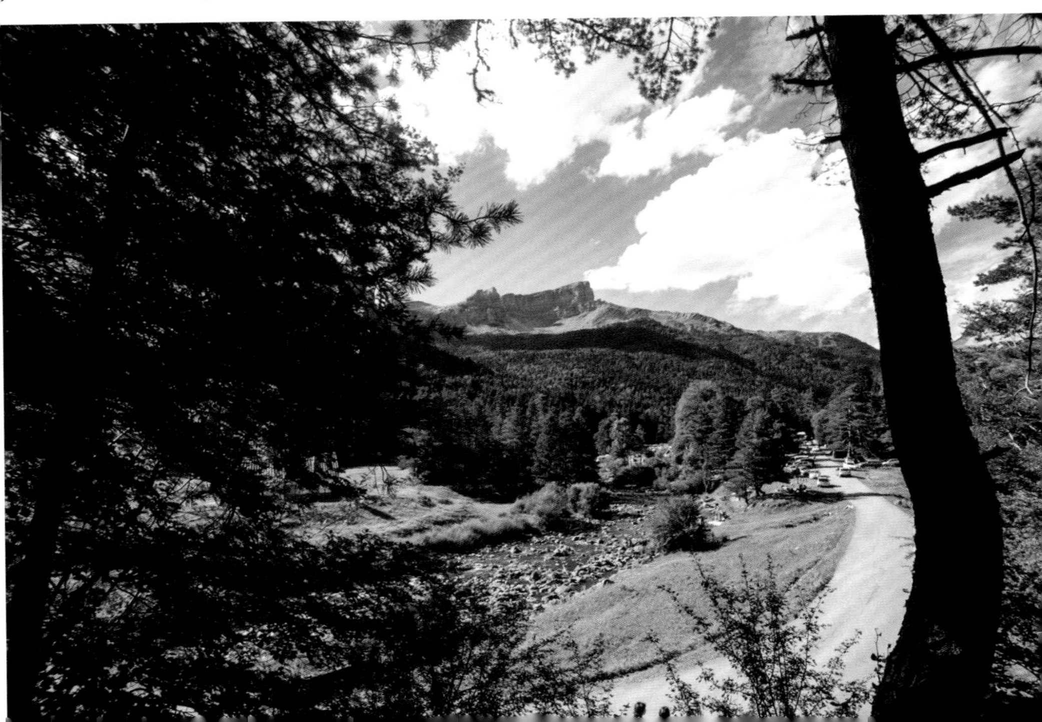

*The Selva de Oza.*

Aragón liberated it from two centuries of Moorish rule, until the royal court moved to Zaragoza in 1118. Huesca today is a bustling farming town of 50,000 inhabitants. The 13th-century Gothic **cathedral** is at the heart of the lovely old quarter, with its weathered floral facade distinguished by an unusual sculpted wooden gallery. The limestone statuary is badly corroded, but the tympanum has scenes recognisable as the three kings and the apparition of Christ to Mary Magdalene. Damián Forment, a disciple of Donatello, created the alabaster altarpiece depicting scenes from the crucifixion. It is the masterpiece of the cathedral. Also worth seeing is the former monastery church and cloister of San Pedro el Viejo, a fine example of Aragonese Romanesque.

The Ayuntamiento (Town Hall) opposite is an elegant Renaissance building. The **Museo de Huesca** (Plaza de la Universidad; Tue–Sat 10am–2pm and 5–8pm, Sun 10am–2pm) occupies the old university buildings and consists of an octagonal patio surrounded by eight halls including the Sala de la Campana (Hall of the Bell), scene of some famous beheadings, shown in a 19th-century painting in the town hall.

The city makes a good base from which to explore the Pre-Pyrenees, a broad swathe of territory running from beneath the major peaks to the north and the basin of the River Ebro to the south.

Immediately to the northeast of Huesca is the Sierra de Guara, which reaches heights over 2,000 metres (6,500ft). It has many rivers flowing north to south through gorges making it a popular destination for canyoning. It's most picturesque town is **Alquézar** ㉕ where hundreds of wild griffon vultures are fed by the local authorities every other Wednesday. Further east is the remote Isabeña valley in which stands **Roda de Isabeña** ㉖, a village of 40 people living around a Romanesque cathedral.

Going east from Huesca brings you the **Castillo de Loarre** ㉗, a well-preserved and stunningly located 11th-century castle with a view over the lowlands beneath it. Just beyond Loarre, the town of **Riglos** ㉘ stands under a curious rock formation, Los Mallos, whose sheer sides attract rock climbers.

From Ayerbe a long, peaceful, beautiful backroad takes you west through Biel which has a disproportionately large castle, to the charming town of **Uncastillo** ㉙. As its name suggests this town gathers around a ruined castle but it also have several Romanesque churches to visit and, more interestingly, a medieval Jewish quarter including a synagogue. Behind the main church is a delightful hotel, the Posada la Pastora.

Nearby Sádaba has a magnificently intact castle. To the north, over a mountain pass, is **Sos del Rey Católico** ㉚, a much visited cluster of medieval streets. The town received its name because it was the birthplace, in 1452 of Fernando II of Aragon, one of the two so-called Catholic Monarchs who unified Spain, effectively expelled all Muslim and Jewish people from their territory and dispatched Columbus to discover the New World.

*Canyoning in the Sierra de Guara.*

# COAST TO COAST WALK

**Many passionate Pyreneists are devotees of the "Transpirenaica", the 40–50-day Pyrenean trek from Mediterranean to Atlantic (or vice versa).**

The thrill of crossing this magical and mysterious cordillera, compendium of so much history, culture, legend and unspoiled natural splendour, is unforgettable.

Basques generally prefer to cross by train to the Mediterranean and, starting from Spain's easternmost point at Cabo de Creus above Cadaqués, work their way back west and homeward to the Bay of Biscay. Catalans do it in reverse, starting at the Cabo de Higuer lighthouse just west of Hondarribia and walking east over "the dragon's back" to the Mediterranean. Pyreneists from neutral points seem to agree, however, that the west-to-east crossing is easier on the mind and body than walking east to west (plus most of the hiking guidebooks covering this route are written for people walking west to east).

There are various theories as to why this might be: leaving the drier and hotter final week's trek to the Mediterranean for last, having reached peak condition during the weeks of walking; avoiding walking into the relentless afternoon sun heading west, instead using this brilliant illumination to make the early evenings stunningly beautiful while heading east. Some even credit the historical pull of the Mediterranean, starting from Atlantic new world and going back to the roots of western civilisation.

## PURGATORY AND ECTASY

"The ones going west," explains an inn-keeper in the Cerdanya, "are just a week or ten days into the trip, having crossed the low country near the Mediterranean. They're weary, not yet in shape, and they have 30 or more days ahead of them over the highest part of the chain. They're still in purgatory. But the ones headed east, having done the hardest part, seem invigorated, empowered by the mountains. They often seem quite beautiful, physically and spiritually, as if under the spell of some kind of Pyrenean ecstasy."

Whichever way it is walked, the GR11 route is a test of stamina and endurance because it descends into and climbs out of numerous deep valleys that run perpendicular to the line of summits.

A parallel, and longer footpath, the GR10, runs the length of the range on the French side from Hendaye to Banyuls-sur-Mer. There are connecting trails between the two. A third trans-Pyrenean route, the HRP (Haute Randonnée Pyrénéenne), keeps high in the mountains as much as possible. It's a wilder and tougher walk than the other two and a good sense of orientation is required. You will also need to be totally self-sufficient for certain sections.

Walking the GR11 takes much physical and logistical preparation. A variety of books and websites – mostly in Spanish – offer advice to anyone undertaking the route for the first time. Excellent English language guidebooks to either the GR11, GR10 or the HRP are published by Cicerone Press (www.cicerone.co.uk).

*The descent from Port de Ratera in the Pyrenees.*

*Running of the Bulls, Festival of San Fermín, Pamplona.*

# NAVARRA

The ancient kingdom of Navarra straddled the western Pyrenees. Today the Spanish region of the same name has a little of every kind of landscape – except a coastline.

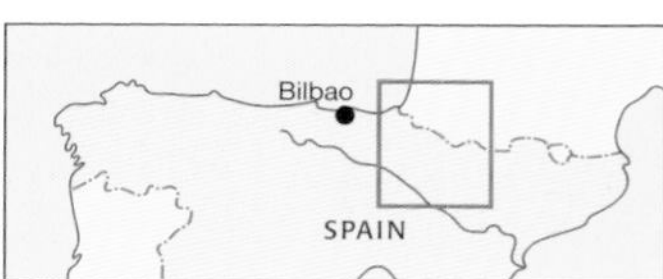


**Main attractions**

Pamplona
Puente de la Reina
Estella
Olite
Bardenas Reales
Roncesvalles
Monasterio de Leyre

ounded by the Pyrenees to the north nd the Ebro river basin to the south, avarra is one of Spain's most hisorically independent regions. Part asque, and for centuries connected ) France, Navarra was a separate ngdom until well into the 19th cenry, enjoying special rights or *fueros* cluding its own parliament, currency, x system and customs laws. Even the ranco regime permitted Navarra, a ronghold of the religious right, some egree of autonomy, while today's emi-borderless European Union has l but restored the age-old Navarrese eam of a trans-Pyrenean state.

With more than half a million asque and Spanish-speaking inhabants spread over 10,500 sq km (4,050 q miles) that range from Pyrenean eaks and forests to river-valley vineards and desert-like meseta, Navarra a microcosm of the Iberian Peninıla. Only a coastline is missing: Navra's closest point to the Atlantic, the idasoa estuary at Irún, is 10km (6 iles) short of the sea.

## ISTORIC RIGHTS

rior to the Roman invasion of the 2nd entury BC, the region was inhabited / Iberian and Celtic peoples. The ırvival of the Basque language in orthern Navarra suggests successl local resistance to the Romans in the Pyrenees. Later on, Basque tribes, the Vascones, fought off Frankish and Visigothic invasions. By the 6th century, Christianity had taken root and by the 8th century, an independent Christian nucleus was consolidated in Pamplona, simultaneously resisting Frankish and Moorish encroachment.

In 778, the Basques defeated the Frankish leader Charlemagne at Roncesvalles in the historic battle chronicled, and somewhat fictionalised, in *La Chanson de Roland* (see page 36). In 906, Sancho Garcés I became King of

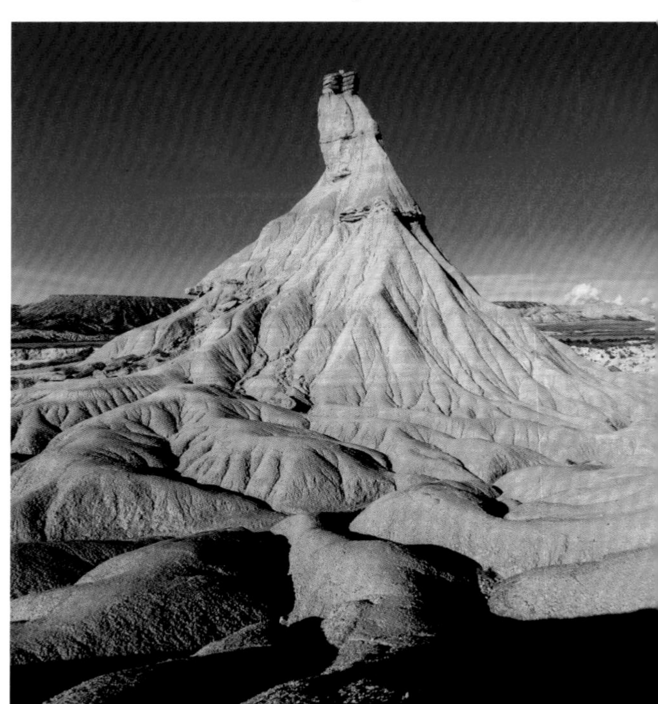

*A cabezo (hillock) in Bardenas Reales.*

**Fact**

Ernest Hemingway (1899–1961), who won the 1954 Nobel Prize for literature, was an ardent bullfight fan. Pamplona was a backdrop to his first major work, *The Sun Also Rises*.

Pamplona, establishing ties with the Frankish Carolingian line as well as to the Spanish Jimena dynasty. Under Sancho III – el Mayor (the Great) – King of Pamplona from 1004 to 1035, Navarra's hegemony extended into Gascony and throughout Christian Spain, but its destiny varied over the following five centuries: Aragón, France, civil war and finally, in 1515, Castile prevailed over it. Within the Habsburg kingdom of Spain, Navarra remained a region apart, maintaining its civil and penal institutions.

After the Bourbons took over the monarchy in 1714, local powers throughout Spain were restricted or suppressed, creating a century and a half of discord until the 1833–39 First Carlist War, when Navarra was declared a *"provincia foral"*, from the word *fueros*, meaning special rights. During the Franco regime, Navarra was the sole autonomous region in Spain. In decentralised, democratic, modern Spain, Navarra's special status as a *comunidad foral* is an uncontested reality.

## THE CAPITAL OF THE KINGDOM

**Pamplona ❶** (Iruña in Euskara) ha always been Navarra's principal cit and the seat of the Navarran kingdon Elevated on a terrace and tucked int a sharp bend in the River Arga, Pam plona was named *Pompaelo* in 74 B by the Roman general Pompey. Afte falling to Franks, Visigoths and Moor (though never under their dominatic for long), the city was taken by Cha lemagne in 778. He immediately raze its walls then retreated, but his rea guard was ambushed and slaughtere on its march back through the Py enean pass at Roncesvalles. Today Pamplona, with 198,000 inhabitan and an important university, is a vit town with a booming student life. Eac year the town hits the world headline during the 7–14 July San Fermín fiest Ernest Hemingway's description of th fiesta's "running of the bulls" in h 1926 novel *The Sun Also Rises* (pub lished in the UK as *Fiesta*) was the fir dispatch to broadcast the town's no famous fiesta.

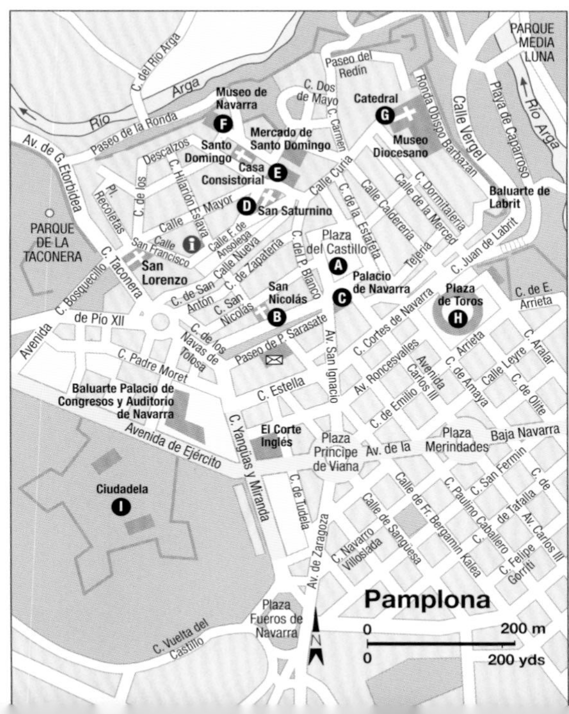

The **Plaza del Castillo** Ⓐ is the ·erve centre of Pamplona, ringed by afés and the Hotel La Perla – the ·ity's oldest and Hemingway's chosen ›dging place. Calle San Nicolás, west f the Plaza del Castillo, is lined with opular taverns and restaurants. The ɔugh-hewn, 13th-century church of **an Nicolás** Ⓑ at the end of the street ; one of Pamplona's finest medieval 'orks.

The baroque **Palacio de Navarra** Ⓒ \vda Carlos III 2; visits by arrange- ıent with tourist office) is also near ıe Plaza del Castillo. It has an impres- ·ive, plush, maroon-and-gilt throne ›om and a portrait of Fernando VII by oya. North of the palace is the 13th- entury **Iglesia de San Saturnino** Ⓓ, ear the spot where the saint allegedly aptised 40,000 pagans. Just to the orth, in the Plaza Consistorial, is the ıost notable civic architecture in Pam- lona, the baroque **Casa Consistorial** ●, used as the Ayuntamiento (Town all). This 18th-century building has ːquired a black patina over the years, ːrikingly emphasised by gilt ironwork and trim. The wood-and-marble interior is also powerfully opulent but simple, the essence of Navarra. Along the Calle Santo Domingo, in a 16th-century hospital used by pilgrims, is the **Museo de Navarra** Ⓕ (Cuesta de Santo Domingo; Tue–Sat 9.30am–2pm and 5–7pm, Sun 11am–2pm), with its collection of local archaeological finds and historical costumes.

Just to the east, near the city walls and the Arga River, is Pamplona's ochre-coloured **Cathedral** Ⓖ (Apr–Oct 10.30am–7pm, Nov–Mar 10.30am–5pm), built between 1387 and 1525, but adorned with a neoclassical facade in the 1780s. It is notable for its superb Gothic cloister and the alabaster tombs of Carlos III, the Noble (1387–1427), and his wife, Leonor de Trastámara. The grille enclosing the Capilla de la Santa Cruz (Chapel of the Holy Cross) in the cloister is made from iron melted down from Moorish tent chains captured at the battle of Las Navas de Tolosa in 1212 (see page 38). The **Museo Diocesano** has a collection of

*Plaza del Castillo.*

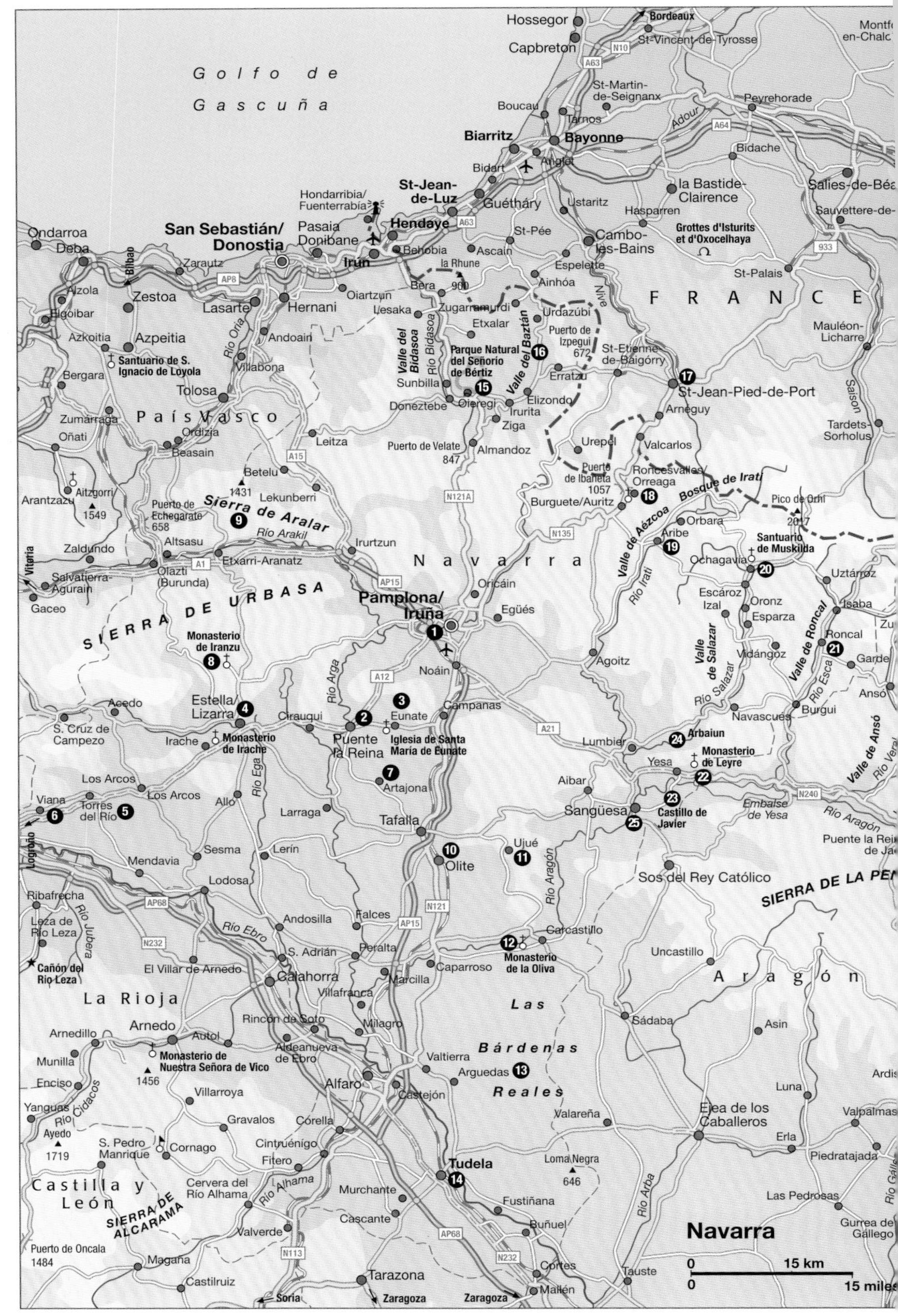
Golfo de Gascuña
Hossegor
Capbreton
Bordeaux
St-Vincent-de-Tyrosse
N10
A63
St-Martin-de-Seignanx
Peyrehorade
Boucau
Tarnos
Adour
A64
Biarritz
Bayonne
Bidache
Bidart
Anglet
St-Jean-de-Luz
Guéthary
la Bastide-Clairence
Salies-de-Béa
Hondarribia/ Fuenterrabía
Ustaritz
Hasparren
Sauvettere-de-
Pasaia Donibane
Hendaye
A63
St-Pée
Cambo-les-Bains
Grottes d'Isturits et d'Oxocelhaya
San Sebastián/ Donostia
Irún
Behobia
Ascain
933
Ondarroa
Deba
Bilbao
Zarautz
AP8
la Rhune
900
Espelette
St-Palais
Bera
Ainhóa
Zestoa
Oiartzun
Zugarramurdi
FRANCE
Alzola
Elgoibar
Lasarte
Hernani
Lesaka
Urdazúbi
Etxalar
Nive
Azkoitia
Azpeitia
Andoain
Puerto de Izpegui 672
Mauléon-Licharre
Santuario de S. Ignacio de Loyola
Río Oria
Valle del Bidasoa
Río Bidasoa
Parque Natural del Señorío de Bértiz
Valle del Baztán
St-Etienne-de-Baïgorry
Bergara
Villabona
Sunbilla
Erratzu
St-Jean-Pied-de-Port
Tolosa
Doneztebe
Oieregi
Elizondo
Saison
Irurita
Arnéguy
Zumárraga
País Vasco
Ziga
Tardets-Sorholus
Oñati
Ordizia
Leitza
Beasain
Puerto de Velate 847
Almandoz
Urepel
Valcarlos
A15
Betelu
Puerto de Ibañeta 1057
Roncesvalles/ Orreaga
Aitzgorri
1431
Lekunberri
Bosque de Irati
Arantzazu
1549
Puerto de Echegarate 658
Sierra de Aralar
N121A
Burguete/Auritz
Pico de Orhi 2017
Altsasu
Río Arakil
N135
Orbara
Zaldundo
Irurtzun
Valle de Aézcoa
Aribe
Santuario de Muskilda
Vitoria
Olazti (Burunda)
A1
Etxarri-Aranatz
Navarra
Ochagavía
Salvatierra-Agurain
AP15
Oricáin
Río Irati
Uztárroz
Gaceo
SIERRA DE URBASA
Pamplona/ Iruña
Escároz
Izal
Oronz
Isaba
Egüés
Esparza
Monasterio de Iranzu
Valle de Roncal
Valle de Salazar
Roncal
Agoitz
Vidángoz
Garde
Noáin
A12
Río Arga
Río Esca
Ansó
Acedo
Estella/ Lizarra
Río Salazar
Eunate
S. Cruz de Campezo
Cirauqui
Campanas
Burgui
Navascués
Valle de Ansó
Irache
Monasterio de Irache
Puente la Reina
Iglesia de Santa María de Eunate
A21
Lumbier
Arbaiun
Monasterio de Leyre
Yesa
Río Veral
Los Arcos
Río Ega
Artajona
Aibar
N240
Viana
Torres del Río
Allo
Larraga
Sangüesa
Castillo de Javier
Embalse de Yesa
Río Aragón
Logroño
Tafalla
Puente la Rei de Ja
Mendavia
Sesma
Lerín
Ujué
Olite
Sos del Rey Católico
Lodosa
Río Aragón
SIERRA DE LA PE
Ribafrecha
AP68
N121
Leza de Río Leza
Río Jubera
Andosilla
Falces
AP15
Río Ebro
N232
Carcastillo
Peralta
S. Adrián
Uncastillo
Cañón del Río Leza
El Villar de Arnedo
Calahorra
Caparroso
Monasterio de la Oliva
Aragón
Marcilla
Villafranca
La Rioja
Las Bárdenas Reales
Rincón de Soto
Sádaba
Arnedo
Milagro
Asín
Arnedillo
Autol
Aldeanueva de Ebro
Monasterio de Nuestra Señora de Vico
Valtierra
Munilla
Arguedas
1456
Ardis
Enciso
Alfaro
Castejón
Luna
Villarroya
Río Cidacos
Yanguas
Ejea de los Caballeros
Valpalmas
Gravalos
Corella
Valareña
Ayedo 1719
S. Pedro Manrique
Cornago
Cintruénigo
Erla
Loma Negra 646
Fitero
Piedratajada
Tudela
Castilla y León
Cervera del Río Alhama
Río Alhama
Murchante
Fustiñana
Las Pedrosas
SIERRA DE ALCARAMA
Río Arba
Cascante
Río Gállego
Buñuel
Navarra
Gurrea de Gállego
Valverde
AP68
Puerto de Oncala 1484
N113
N232
0 15 km
0 15 miles
Magaña
Cortes
Tauste
Castilruiz
Tarazona
Mallén
Soria
Zaragoza
Zaragoza

eligious art from the Middle Ages to he Renaissance.

A few blocks south, at the corner of Carlos III and Roncesvalles, is a bronze sculpture of two men, rolled-up newspapers in hand, running just ahead of a bull. Behind them is the **Plaza de Toros** ⓗ (bullring), presided over by a massive figure of Ernest Hemingway. The **Ciudadela** ❶, the city's fortress built in the reign of Felipe II (1556–98), is a pleasant park: join the *pamplonesas* here on their early evening stroll, or *paseo,* to get the feel of this provincial capital.

## PUENTE LA REINA AND ESTELLA

Pamplona makes a central base for exploring the rest of Navarra. Fast routes radiate from the capital to north, south, southwest and southeast. These can be connected up by scenic backroads if you don't want to return to Pamplona each night.

One main road goes southwest in the direction of the pilgrimage route to **Puente la Reina** ❷ which is named after its majestic bridge over the Arga built in the 11th century for pilgrims on the orders of Sancho the Great. At the edge of town, a bronze pilgrim points to the meeting point of the two routes to Santiago, one through Jaca, the other through Pamplona. The **Iglesia del Crucifijo** (Church of the Crucifix) outside the town walls was built by Knights Templar and has a 12th-century nave and a Y-shaped cross with an excruciatingly expressive 14th-century wooden sculpture of a suspended Christ. The narrow Calle Mayor, lined with elegant houses of golden, weathered brick, crosses the bridge and leads to the **Iglesia de Santiago**, which has a golden sculpture of St James (Santiago). Five kilometres (3 miles) east of Puente la Reina is the **Iglesia de Santa María de Eunate** ❸, an octagonal Romanesque structure apparently used as a funerary chapel for pilgrims. Just west of Puente la Reina is **Cirauqui**, a well-restored village of diminutive houses, elaborately sculpted and emblazoned, connected by tiny streets and stairways. The church of San Román at the top of the village has a lovely fluted 13th-century doorway.

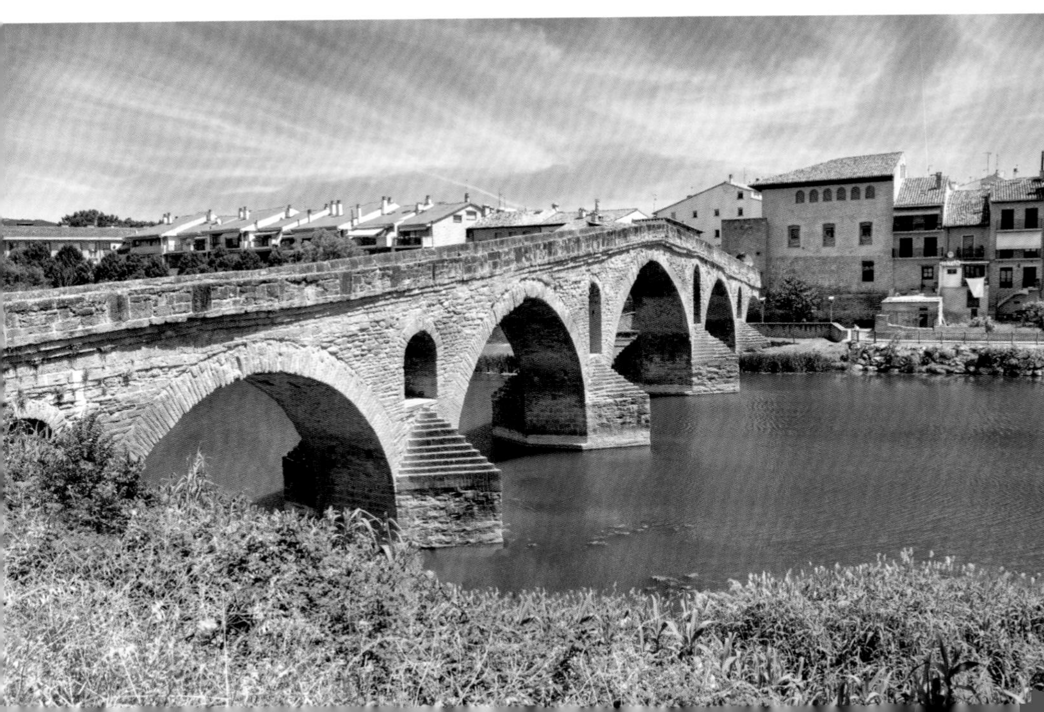

*Puente la Reina.*

**Estella** (Lizarra) ❹, further west, is built in a narrow valley. Sancho the Great boosted the city's fortunes in the 11th century when he routed the Santiago de Compostela pilgrims through Puente la Reina and Estella. Seat of the royal court of Navarra during the Middle Ages, Estella was a *carlista* stronghold during the 19th-century dynastic conflicts following the death of Fernando VII in 1833.

The **Plaza de San Martín**, with arcaded porches, is the centre of Estella's oldest quarter. The 12th-century **Palacio de los Reyes** (Kings' Palace), the 17th-century **Ayuntamiento** (Town Hall) and the church of **San Pedro de la Rúa** with a superb cloister and doorway are the architectural gems. The **Iglesia del Santo Sepulcro** (church of the Holy Sepulchre) has an elaborately fluted doorway, while that of **San Juan Bautista** near the Plaza de los Fueros has an important Romanesque portal. On the other side of the Puente de la Cárcel over the River Ega is the church of **San Miguel**, a jumble of vaults and rooftops with an elegant Romanesque doorway portraying the Archangel S Michael battling a dragon, the symbo of Satan or evil. **Santamaría Jus de Castillo**, now in a dilapidated state, wa converted into a church honouring Al Saints in 1145. It had previously been synagogue and is the sole remnant o the town's ancient Jewish quarter.

Places to visit close to Estell include the **Monasterio de Nuestr Señora de Irache** 3km (2 miles) southwest of town, a Gothic Cistercian monastery which has a tap set into a wal supplying wine to pilgrims.

Continuing southwest of Estella but this time on a minor road, is **Torres del Río** ❺ which has a small bu highly unusual octagonal Romanesque church, **Iglesia del Santo Sepulcr** (you have to telephone the number or the door to get the caretaker to come and open up).

Another 11km (7 miles) southwest is **Viana** ❻ which possesses the stunning **Iglesia de Santa María**, parish church of the Principado (Principality) de Viana, created during the 15th century by Carlos III el Noble as a title to be

Viana city hall.

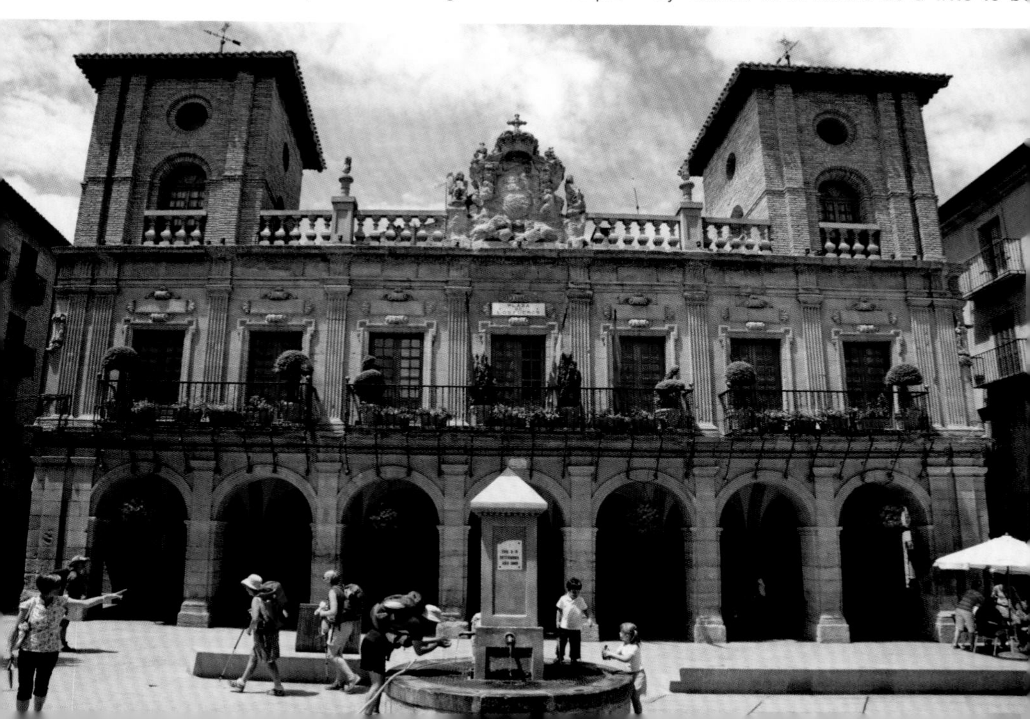

eld by the heir to the throne of Navarra. Cesare Borgia (1476–1507), the scheming son of Pope Alexander IV, is buried in front of the church.

If you want to continue touring and avoid returning to Pamplona, you have two choices. One is to take the cross-country route from Estella to Tafalla and Olite, making a detour to see **Artajona** ❼, protected by walls and towers built in the 12th century.

The other, much longer route is north from Estella on the NA-120, stopping at the 12th-century Cistercian **Monasterio de Iranzu** ❽. The NA-120 continues north over the Sierra de Urbasa via the Puerto de Lizarraga, which is picturesque, especially in autumn. From Uharte-Arakil a very small road winds into the beautiful **Sierra de Aralar** ❾, a vast upland that spreads across the border into the Basque Country. At its heart is a medieval shrine to St Michael. Hidden among the beech and oak woods are numerous caves and dolmens. After the shrine, the road takes you down to Lekunberri. Turn north up the motorway and then east on the NA-170 to get to the Bidasoa valley north of Pamplona.

## SOUTH OF PAMPLONA TO OLITE

Heading south from Pamplona takes you directly to **Olite** ❿, an ancient town founded by Romans. The **Palacio Real de Olite** (daily Jul–Aug 10am–8pm, Apr–June and Sept 10am–7pm, Jan–Mar and Oct–Dec 10am–6pm) with fairytale conical watchtowers and battlements was built over Roman ruins at the beginning of the 15th century by Carlos the Noble. Next door – and half built into - the castle is a parador hotel. On the other side of the castle public, the 13th-century church of Santa María la Real next to the castle has a superbly sculpted portal and facade, while the 14th-century church of San Pedro has elaborately worked Romanesque cloisters and portal.

Close to Olite is the hilltop village of **Ujué** ⓫, one of Spain's best-preserved villages, a maze of cobbled streets and stairways. Every 25 April, pilgrims in black tunics, many of them carrying

**Tip**

In Olite, head for the Bodegas Ochoa (calle Miranda de Arga 35, www.bodegasochoa.com). This family winery dates back to the 14th century, and today it makes some of the best wine in Navarra. It's open for visits with advance bookings.

*Palacio Real de Olite.*

> **Fact**
> San Francisco Javier, founder of the Jesuit order with Ignatius Loyola, spent much of his life teaching in India and Japan. He died in 1552 while waiting to be secretly put ashore in China, then closed to foreigners.

crosses, come in silence to visit the Virgin of Ujué. A minor road leads from Ujué to Sangüesa, one of the gateways to the Pyrenees of Navarra.

The **Monasterio de la Oliva** ⓬, 28km (18 miles) southeast of Olite, is a 12th-century Cistercian monastery near the village of Carcastillo. Today the monks survive by selling honey, wine, cheese and lodging.

South of the monastery the landscape opens out into the desert-like **Bardenas Reales**, an arid area of eroded mudslides and Wild West hills very different to the rest of Navarra. The best approach is from **Arguedas** ⓭. Past the visitor information centre the road turns into a dirt track but it is only a short way to the best scenery, around a rock formation known as Cabezo de Castildetierra. It is, however, possible to drive right through the Bardenas Reales on a passable unsurfaced track, emerging in the north near Carcastillo.

**Tudela** ⓮, 52km (33 miles) south of Olite, is Navarra's second city, with a population of 35,000, and the capital of La Ribera, the Ebro rive basin. Although undistinguished mod ern architecture is what you will firs see, the inner city is a dense networ of ancient alleys with several feature of great charm. The well-preserve Moorish and Jewish quarters serv as a reminder that this provincial cit some 1,200 years old, predates man Spanish cities, including Madrid.

The 12th-century **Cathedral** has a intensely sculpted doorway portrayin the Day of Judgement with more tha 100 groups of figures. The Roman esque cloister was built around a 9th century mosque and a Mudéjar chape the latter probably used as a syna gogue and testimony to the religiou tolerance that reigned here at the en of the first millennium, a lull befor the storm of persecutions, horrors an holocausts that would trouble the nex 1,000 years.

The **Plaza de los Fueros** is Tudela' pivotal square, the balconies deco rated with taurine themes in memor of the bullfights held there until th 18th century. Other sights include th

*Plaza de los Fueros, Tudela.*

2th-century Iglesia de la Magdalena at the Plaza de la Magdalena with another, smaller, but equally powerful, sculpted doorway; the nearby 3th-century bridge spanning the Ebro with 17 eccentric arches; and on Calle Herrerías the 18th-century **Palacio del Marqués de Huarte**, now the municipal archives, with extraordinary frescoes showing caryatids, fauns and rearing horsemen. Cuisine in Tudela makes the most of vegetables, especially asparagus and artichokes. One renowned dish is *menestra de verdura* (steamed assorted vegetables), while asparagus, in season between April and June, is the chief local delicacy, consumed on its own or with oil and vinegar.

## THE PYRENEES OF NAVARRA

The main road north of Pamplona towards Irun (the N-121a) is the best way to start a tour of the valleys of Navarra that form the western Pyrenees. After crossing the low pass of the Puerto de Velate (or Belate) you descend into the **Valle del Bidasoa.** The first point of interest is the **Parque Natural del Señorío de Bértiz** ⓯, a protected area of natural beauty rich in flora and fauna created around a 19th-century country estate. The park's highest point is at the Castillo de Aizkolegi, a 20km (12-mile) round-trip walk from Oieregi.

Etxalar, Arantza, Igantzi, Lesaka and Bera de Bidasoa are collectively known as the **Cinco Villas** (Five Towns). **Bera de Bidasoa** is the northernmost of them. It has some fine *caseríos* including the former home of the Basque novelist Pío Baroja (1872–1956), which later became the residence of his nephew Julio Caro Baroja (1914–95), the foremost Basque ethnologist. **Lesaka** stages a San Fermín Txiki (Little San Fermín) fiesta at the same time as the more famous one in Pamplona. It is also noted for its traditional *caseríos* (country houses) and for its lovely Casherna or fortified medieval manor house in the centre of town. **Etxalar** is known for its popular *palomeras,* a 1,000-year-old autumn pigeon-hunting ritual.

The beautiful upper valley of the river of Bidasoa is known as the **Valle**

**Fact**

The Bidasoa valley is known for its *caseríos*, traditional Basque farmhouses. Animals lived on the ground floor, the family on the first floor, and their combined heat allowed the top floor to be used for drying.

*Valle del Baztán.*

**Fact**

The chains from the Moorish King Miramolin's tent, captured at the Battle of Las Navas de Tolosa in 1212, are kept in Roncesvalles: together with the emerald the king wore in his turban, they form part of Navarra's coat of arms.

**del Baztán** ⓰. A good but curving road, the N-121b, departs from Oieregi on the N-121a. It is signposted all the way to the French border crossing at Dancharinea.

The Baztán Valley is conspicuously well-kept and well off. Baztán families have traditionally been *hidalgos* (noblemen), as evidenced by the many emblasoned manor houses in both the towns and countryside. Land was exploited communally and administrated by a Junta General (General Assembly), a model of Basque social structure optimistically studied by Marxist theorists. The village of **Irurita** has two fine *palacios* (manor houses). **Arraoiz** is the site of one of the loveliest structures in the Baztán – the *casatorre* (fortified farmhouse) of Jaureguizar, built in wood and stone with cupola and porches. **Lekaroz** used to have a renowned boarding school run by Capuchin monks but all that is left of it is the church. **Elizondo**, the valley capital, has a series of elegant town houses as well as the majestic Casa Consistorial, or Town Hall. **Arizkun** is characterised by its lovely wooden eaves and balconies.

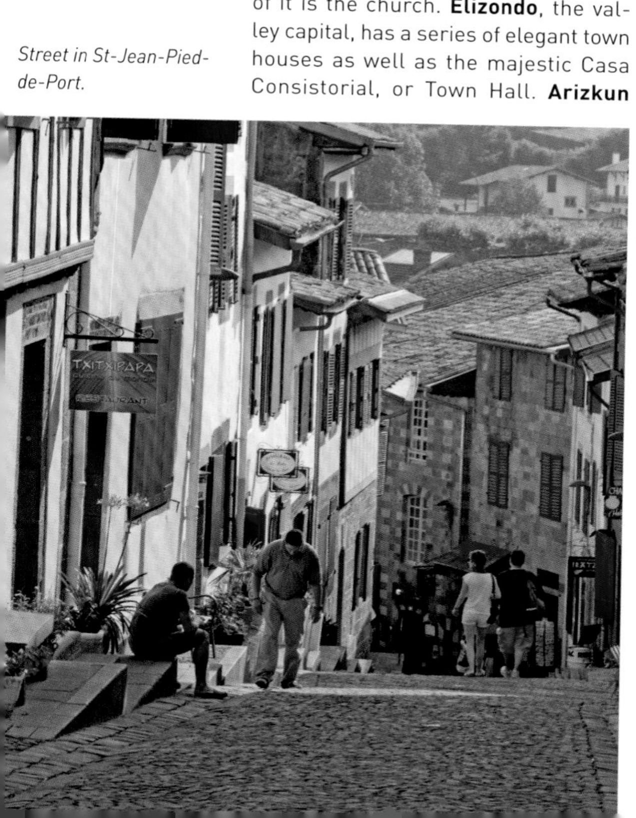


*Street in St-Jean-Pied-de-Port.*

On a back road very close to the French border is **Zugarramurdi** outside of which is the "Cuevas de Brujas" (Witches' Caves), a vast open ended cavern where witchcraft was allegedly practised in the early 17th century. More than 300 people were arrested in 1609 and 1610, and 12 were burned at the stake in an *auto-da-fé* at Logroño. A small museum (10.30am-1pm & 4-5.30pm Wed-Sun) in the village explains more about the areas spooky goings-on.

To carry on touring the Pyrenean valleys of Navarra it is best now to slip across the border into France. The mountains by now have reached low altitudes and many little roads wind gently across the frontier past abandoned customs posts. The main Baztan road leads to the immaculate town of Ainhoa in the French Basque Country. From there it is an easy run via Espelette (renowned for its red peppers), Cambo-les-Bains and the main road up the valley of the River Nive to St-Jean-Pied-de-Port. An alternative way to get to the same destination from Baztan is from Erratzu over the Puerto de Izpegui to **St-Etienne-de-Baïgorry**.

Although the picturesque riverside town of **St-Jean-Pied-de-Port** ⓱ is in France, it is symbolically connected to Spain. This is where most pilgrims walking to Santiago de Compostela choose to start their journey. They follow the footpath back into Navarra but you will need to take the road. Either way, you cross the **Puerto de Ibañeta**, the pass where the events of the 11th-century *Chanson de Roland* (see page 36) were played out, to reach the first town on the other side of the Pyrenees, **Roncesvalles (Orreaga)** ⓲ built around the 13th-century **Colegiata.** The treasures of this collegiate church include the alabaster effigy and tomb of the victor of the decisive battle against the Moors at Las Navas de Tolosa in 1212, the giant Sancho IV el Fuerte (the itrong), measuring 2.1 metres (7ft). 'here is also a fine enamel reliquary, :nown as "Charlemagne's chess set" n the local museum.

The next village south on the N-135, **Burguete** (Auritz), was where, in *The Sun* *lso Rises*, Hemingway's character Jake nd his friend Bill spend a few days trout ishing in the River Irati before returning o Pamplona for the San Fermín fiesta. Hemingway's room at the Hostal de Bur-uete is still the way he knew it.

The **Valle de Aézkoa** is the next val-ey east, on the NA-140. **Aribe** 19 is the rst important town along it, known for :s graceful medieval bridge and dis-inctive Pyrenean *hórreo* (grain store, ee page 252). Further north along the River Irati is the town of **Orbara** with a 3th-century church, two *hórreos* and medieval bridge. **Orbaitzeta** was ne site of a munitions factory, now in uins, established by the Spanish state 1784. The road up to the Irabia res-rvoir passes through the **Bosque de rati**, one of Europe's great stands of eeches and pines covering more than 0 sq km (23 sq miles). It's at its best in early-mid October when the trees turn a flaming orange. Red and roe deer as well as lots of wild boar roam freely in the forest; just before dusk is a good time to see them at close range. The River Irati is an excellent trout stream. A *camino forestal* (forest track) leads from Orbara to the hermitage of La Virgen de las Nieves (the Virgin of the Snows), from where a footpath winds down to Ochagavía.

## MOUNTAIN TOWNS AND VALLEYS

Further east again are two long paral-lel north-south valleys. **Ochagavía** 20 is the most populous and most beautiful town in the **Valle de Salazar**. The River Salazar starts life in the town where the Zatoya and Anduña rivers meet. A jumble of cobbled streets, stone houses and slate roofing, it has six bridges, two over the Zatoya and four over the Anduña. The nearby sanctuary of **Santa María de Muskilda**, with its unusual conical tower, is a celebrated landmark. Ezcároz, Jaurrieta, Esparza, Sarriés and Izal are attactive towns and villages

**Quote**

"The pursuits of the chase, smuggling, with a dash of robbery form their [the highlanders of Navarra] moral education"

Richard Ford, 1855

*Snowfall in Ochagavía.*

south of Ochagavía, but the most spectacular way over to the neighbouring Roncal valley is northeast along the River Anduña on the NA-140 through the **Sierra de Uztárroz** to **Isaba**.

The **Valle de Roncal** is Navarra's easternmost Pyrenean valley, synonymous with a popular sheep's milk cheese and historically associated with the *almadieros*, rafters expers at transporting tree trunks on the fast-flowing rivers to the sawmills. The valley is drained by the River Esca, a trout stream. **Isaba** is the most populous town. It stands at the confluence of the Belagua and Uztárroz rivers, which form the Esca. **Uztárroz** has a 16th-century church, Santa Engracia, which has a notable altarpiece and organ.

Other villages include **Burgui**, the southernmost, which has a Roman bridge. **Vidángoz** and **Garde**, northwest and northeast of Burgui, are interesting side trips. **Roncal** ㉑ is the valley's central town.

An unusual fiesta, the Tribute of the Three Cows, has been held at the head of the Roncal valley every 13 July since 1375. The mayors of the valley's villages, dressed in one of Navarra's most peculiar traditional gowns gather at the pass of San Martín to receive the symbolic payment of three cows from their French counterparts in redress for ancient border disputes over pasturage and water rights.

Rafters on the River Esca, near Burgui.

From the southern end of the Salazar and Roncal valleys there is easy access to the motorway back to Pamplona but there are a few more things to see first.

The **Monasterio de Leyre** ㉒ (www.monasteriodeleyre.com; daily 10am–7pm) overlooks the Yesa reservoir. It was founded in the 11th century by Sancho the Great, who made it the spiritual centre and pantheon of the royal family of Navarra. It now includes a modest hotel. The Gregorian chant of the monks during the church services is hauntingly beautiful in this stark and peaceful setting, and can be heard at Laudes (Mon–Sat 7.30am, Sun 8am), Misa (Mon–Sat 9am, Sun 11.30am), Vísperas (daily 7pm) and Completas (daily 9pm). The nearby **Castillo de Javier** ㉓ (daily 10am–6.30pm) was the birthplace in 1506 of San Francisco Javier, co-founder of the Jesuit order and patron saint of Navarra. The 13th-century castle is now a Jesuit school.

Not far away are two spectacular gorges, those of Lumbier and, a little further away, **Arbaiun** ㉔, carved by the rivers Irati and Salazar respectively. Both gorges are impressive natural spectacles and they are also important for their wildlife, including large colonies of vultures. Arbain has a spectacular viewing platform extending over it.

If you want to join up with the southern route out of Pamplona you can do so via **Sangüesa** ㉕ where the church, the south portal of the 12th-century Iglesia de Santa María la Real is crowded with sculptures showing a variety of different subjects. It is also a short step from here to Sos del Rey Católico (see page 152), just over the regional border in Aragón.

*The Arbaiun Gorge.*

*Vineyards near San Vicente de la Sonsierra, La Rioja.*

# LA RIOJA

Spain's smallest region is synonymous with its best-known product, wine. It is also famous for trout streams and dinosaur footprints.

La Rioja is a small region tucked below the Basque country on the edge of the meseta (tableland) that forms the centre of Spain. It lies along the southern bank of the Ebro basin, separated from the Duero watershed by the Sistema Ibérico (Iberian mountains) to the south and from the Atlantic by the Sierra de Cantabria to the north. Renowned as Spain's most prestigious wine-producing area, this 5,000-sq-km (1,930-sq-mile) region of highlands, plains and vineyards is bordered by the River Ebro to the north and by Burgos, Soria and Zaragoza to the south and east. La Rioja's population of 316,000 is primarily concentrated along the Ebro in the major cities of Logroño, Haro and Calahorra.

## A LAND DIVIDED

Originally part of Old Castile, La Rioja combines in its culture and in the taste of its wines influences from both the Atlantic and the Mediterranean. Added to that is a hint of the neighbouring Basque Country and the sweep and force of Iberia's central meseta. Drained by the rivers Oja (from which the region took its name: *Río Oja*), Najerilla, Iregua, Leza and Cidacos, the region subdivides into the Rioja Alta (Upper Rioja) in the humid and mountainous western part, and the Rioja Baja (Lower Rioja) in the arid and almost flat eastern half beyond the River Leza, which has a semi-Mediterranean climate. Logroño, the capital, stands between the two zones.

La Rioja has been a perennial crossroads with periods of domination and occupation at the hand of Gascons, Romans, Moors, Navarrans and Castilians. From 573 to 711 La Rioja was part of the duchy of Cantabria, which extended down both sides of the Ebro from Las Conchas de Haro to Calahorra. The Asturian kings took La Rioja in 1023 during the Reconquest, but by 1076 Alfonso VI, because of its strategic significance, had incorporated it

### Main attractions

Logroño
Haro wineries
Sajazarra
Santa María la Real, Nájera
Santo Domingo de la Calzada
Monasterio de Suso

Map on page 170

*Grape harvest, near Haro.*

**Drink**

Calle Laurel in Logroño's old town is a great place to bar hop and try the local wines. To buy, try Casa Ortiz, Avda de Madrid 32, which stocks 350 different wines.

into the Crown of Castile. La Rioja was divided into the counties of Nájera, Grañón, Calahorra and Arnedo, a situation that endured through the Middle Ages. From the 15th century to the end of the 18th century, La Rioja was divided between Castile and Navarra and later, as part of a united Spain, between the provinces of Burgos and Soria.

When Spain was reorganised into 52 provinces in 1822, one of them was Logroño, including all of the 8,000 sq km (3,090 sq miles) of La Rioja. Fernando VII retouched the map of Spain the following year, reducing Logroño to 5,030 sq km (1,940 sq miles) and declaring it a part of the historic region of Old Castile. During the remainder of the 19th century, no progress was made in re-establishing La Rioja's medieval integrity, nor did petitions prosper for special rights or *fueros*, such as those enjoyed by neighbouring Álava and Navarra. Only in 1980 was La Rioja once again established as the official name of the region, and in 1982 La Rioja became an Autonomous Community complete with a charter approved by the King of Spain.

## LOGROÑO, THE CAPITAL

Lying on the River Ebro, **Logroño** ❶ the capital city of La Rioja, is a bus industrial city of some 150,000 citizens The streets of the old quarter bordere by the Ebro between two bridges an the curving trace of the medieval tow walls along Bretón de los Herrero and Muro Francisco de la Mata, hav the most archaic charm. Traditionall a stopping-place for pilgrims travellin to and from Santiago de Compostela many of Logroño's best monuments such as the graceful **Puente de Piedr** (stone bridge), have pilgrimage links.

Four of them are among La Rioja' finest religious structures. Prominen among them is the church called **Imperial de Santa María del Palacio** (the original building was once part of the palac of Alfonso VII of Castile and León, 1127-57), which is mainly 16th–18th century but retains a 45-metre (150ft), early 14th century spire known locally as *La Aguj* (The Needle). The single-naved **Santiag el Real** was reconstructed in the 16t century and has a famous equestria statue of Santiago Matamoros (Sain

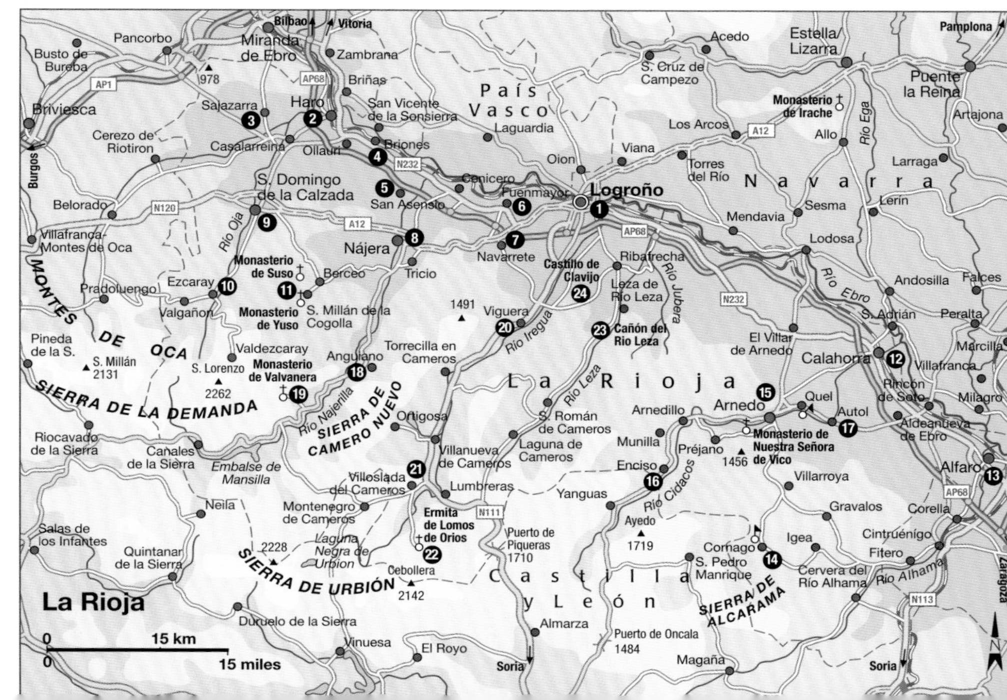

ames the Moor-slayer) over the main oor. **San Bartolomé** is a 13th–14th-cen- ıry French-Gothic church with an 11th- entury Mudéjar or Moorish-influenced ɔwer but is especially distinguished y its intricately sculpted 14th-century othic doorway. **La Catedral de La edonda** has twin baroque towers that, ɔr better or for worse, are the outstand- ng features on the skyline of Logroño's ld quarter. The **medieval walls**, the **uerta del Revellín** and the **Palacio del spartero** complete the list of Logroño's nost important historic sights.

## TOURING WINE COUNTRY

'he renowned vineyards lie along the River Ebro in an area 90km (56 miles) ong and 30km (17 miles) wide, cover- ng 20 percent of La Rioja's cultivated and and supporting more than 2,000 *odegas* (wineries), many of which are ɔpen to visitors who want to taste and ɔuy their wares. Logroño marks the niddle of the wine-growing area and it as many wine shops and warehouses **Haro** ❷, however, is regarded as La Rioja's wine capital. Many of the winemakers offer guided tours and tastings, which are organised through the local tourist office (Plaza de la Paz; www.haroturismo.org). The 29 June *Batalla del Vino* (Wine Battle) on the Bilibio hill on the city's outskirts is a bacchana- lian drenching of epic dimensions, a free-for-all of freely distributed wine. The town's main monuments are the flamboyant Gothic, single-naved Santo Tomás church, built in 1564, and the 18th-century Basílica de la Vega con- taining a figure of the patron saint of the valley, both of which are set among the old quarter's stunning aristocratic man- sions such as the 16th-century Palacio de Paternina and the 17th-century Pala- cio de la Cruz. Beyond Haro, to the west, is **Sajazarra** ❸, a beautiful medieval town built around a restored castle.

On the way back from Haro to Logroño there are a number of interesting places to visit. **Briones** ❹, 7km (4 miles) east of Haro, is a perfectly conserved, walled town with fine mansions dating from the 15th–18th centuries. The 16th-century Gothic parish church of La Asunción has a Plateresque doorway, a stunning

### Eat

The best place to eat in Haro is Terete, Calle Lucrecia Arana 17, which has been in business since 1877. Wood-fired ovens produce succulent lamb served with good local Rioja on long wooden tables.

*Calle del Laurel in the old center of Logroño.*

altarpiece and a slender Baroque church tower. The winemaker Vivanco (10am–6pm Tue–Fri & Sun, 10am–7pm Sat, www.vivancoculturadevino.es) has a superb museum dedicated to the culture of the vine. **San Vicente de la Sonsierra**, north of Briones, has a Roman bridge and hermitage, but it is best known for Los Picaos, a medieval Easter ritual of self-flagellation. **San Asensio** ❺, to the south, is known as *la cuna del clarete* (the cradle of claret) and has a lively harvest festival. As well as sampling its wines, be sure to look at Davalillo castle and the Monasterio de La Estrella. Closer to Logroño, **Fuenmayor** ❻ is an historic wine-making centre with an exceptionally attractive old quarter. To the north of the Ebro valley, the vineyards of La Rioja merge into those of the Basque Country (see page 194).

## LA RIOJA ALTA

La Rioja Alta is, in all ways, the richest part of the region. Extending from the Ebro river to the Sierra de la Demanda highlands, it has the most fertile soil, thus the best grape harvests and wines and has traditionally had, as a result, th strongest economy and the best castle and monasteries, all boosted, through-out much of its history, by the economi boon of the Camino de Santiago, the pil-grim route to Santiago de Compostela.

To see the most interesting sight of La Rioja Alta, drive southwes from Logroño to **Navarrete** ❼, wher there are noble houses and a Churri-gueresque altarpiece in the church o the Asunción. Beside a main road out-side the town is a curiosity that is ofte missed. The cemetery has a magnifice Romanesque portal replete with carv-ings. It was brought here piece by piec in the 19th century from the ruins of th Hospital de San Juan de Acre, a medie-val hospice for pilgrims. The sculpture show a variety of themes connected t the life of the pilgrimage, including a pilgrim struggling against sins.

Another 15km (10 miles) in the same direction is **Nájera** ❽, once the cour of the Kings of Navarra. This was the capital of Navarra and La Rioja unti 1076 when La Rioja was assimilated by Castile, whereupon it became the

*San Vicente de la Sonsierra village and castle in La Rioja.*

ɜsidence for Castilian royalty. The ɪonastery of **Santa María la Real** 'ue–Sun 10am–1.30pm and 4–6pm), ɪe "pantheon of kings" has an 11th-ɜntury Gothic cloister – the Claustro ɜ los Caballeros – with Plateresque indows. The tomb of Doña Blanca of avarra, (wife of Sancho III of Castile), :ulpted in the 12th century, is the fin-ɜt of the many sarcophagi.

Just outside Nájera, at Tricio, is the ɪost unusual Visigothic church, con-dered the oldest religious monument La Rioja. **Santa María de Arcos** (tel: ɜ1-361057 for opening times) was uilt over a Roman mausoleum and corporates many architectural com-ɔnents, such as slices of fat fluted ɔlumns, from that original building.

Further west is **Santo Domingo de Calzada** 9 which stands on the dge of La Rioja's plains. It lies astride e Camino de Santiago and since the me of Santo Domingo (St Dominic) in e 11th century, it has been one of e towns most dedicated to the wel-re of pilgrims. Castilian churchman ɔmingo de Guzmán started these good works in 1044 by having a bridge of 24 arches built over the River Oja and the road *(calzada)* improved. He also built a hospital for sick travellers, which has become a Parador. The cathedral is a Romanesque-Gothic hybrid containing Santo Domingo's tomb, murals in the choir and an intricate walnut altarpiece carved by Damià Forment in 1541. The Plateresque *gallinero* (chicken coop) in a wall in the south transept houses a live hen and rooster commemorating a local miracle when a roasted cock and hen got up and crowed to prove the innocence of a pilgrim who had been hanged for stealing. The town itself has a picturesque medieval and Gothic quarter.

For a probe into La Rioja's **Sierra de la Demanda** take the LR-111 south 14km (9 miles) up the valley of the Oja to the town of **Ezcaray** 10 with its many emblazoned, aristocratic houses. The best is the palace of the Count of Torremúzquiz, built in 1766. From here, the Romanesque church of Tres Fuentes at Valgañón, the source of the River Oja at Llano de la Casa and the ski resort

**Tip**

Look out for the initials "CR", which denote Casas Rurales, ideal country places to stop for the night.

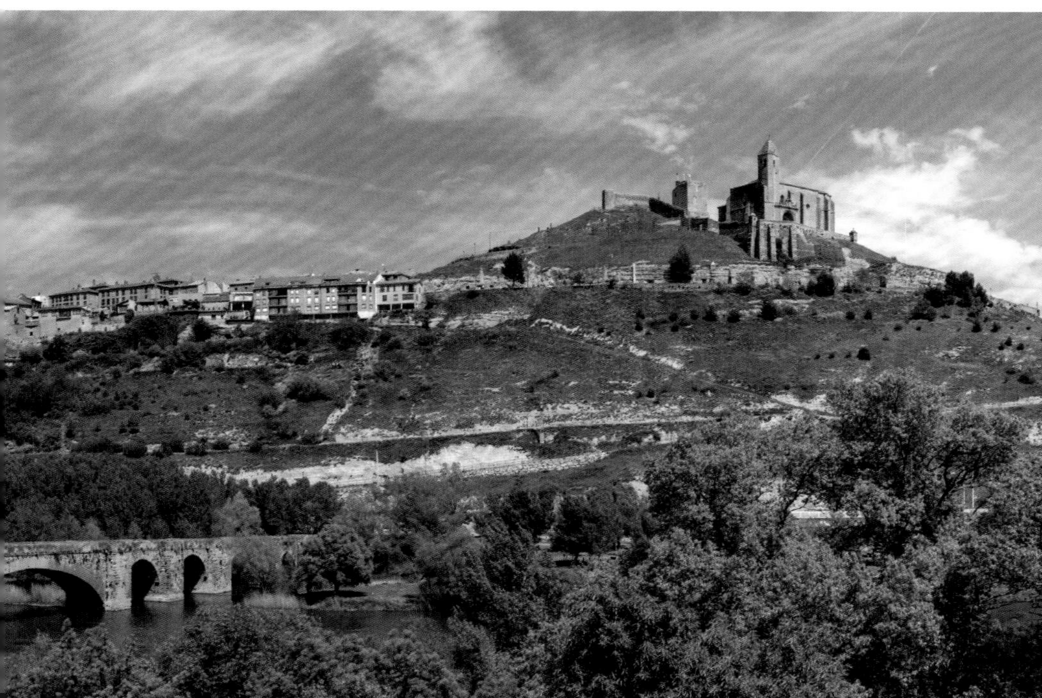

**Fact**

La Rioja Baja has the greatest concentration of dinosaur tracks in Europe. The largest are 30cm (12in) across.

of Valdezcaray are the *de rigueur* side trips. The latter lies just below La Rioja's highest point, the 2,262-metre (7,415ft) Pico de San Lorenzo.

To get to the next place of interest, San Millán de la Cogolla, return to Santo Domingo de la Calzada and take the LR-309 southeast through Berceo. Although unexceptional today, Berceo was the birthplace (in around 1197) of the poet Gonzalo de Berceo whose work is considered the first authenticated use of Spanish (Castilian) as a literary language.

**San Millán de la Cogolla** ⓫ grew up close to two monasteries, known as the Lower (Yuso) and Upper (Suso), both inspired by San Millán (St Emilian, AD 473–574) who spent most of his long life in local caves. The 16th-century Monasterio de Yuso is famous for a 10th-century manuscript on texts by Saint Augustin, the *Glosas Emilianenses*, containing the first words ever written in Castilian Spanish. The nearby Visigothic **Monasterio de Suso** is where, in the 12th century, Gonzalo de Berceo, recognised as the earliest Castilian poet, first recited in *román paladino*, c the clear romance dialect that evolve into the Castilian tongue. Several the monastery's chapels were create from grottos in the hillside into whic the church was built. Visitor number to Suso are strictly limited and it is nec essary to book in advance (www.monas teriodesanmillan.com).

## LA RIOJA BAJA

The lower Rioja, the region's eastern most section, is more Mediterranean i climate and vegetation, a border countr between the flatness of the Ebro Val ley and the tablelands of Navarra, Sori and Aragón. Its main river, the Cidacos joins the Ebro at **Calahorra** ⓬, La Rioja' second city with a population of 24,000 The city was founded by the Romans a Calagurris 2,000 years ago and was th birthplace of the rhetorician and orato Quintilian (teacher of Tacitus) and th Latin poet Prudentius. The rich lode o Roman and medieval remains are bes explored with the help of a leaflet enti tled *Ruta Arqueológica e Histórica* avail able at the Ayuntamiento (Town Hall)

*The main square in Ezcaray.*

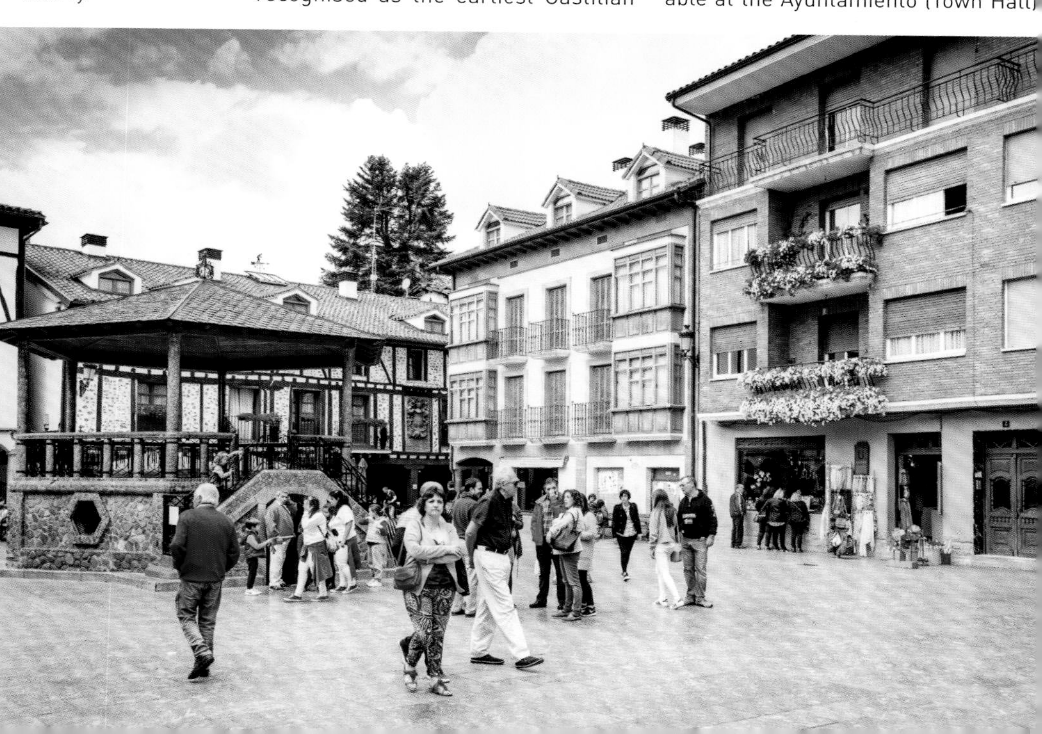

guides you to the Roman walls, the statue of Quintilian, the Jewish quarter and the *casco antiguo* (old town), as well as the later churches of San Andrés, Santiago and San Celedonio.

Calahorra's chief artistic and architectural treasures are concentrated in the 12th-century cathedral of **Santa María**, reconstructed in 1485 and finally completed in the 16th century. It has been an episcopal seat since the 5th century. The choir is surrounded by an elaborately ornate screen; the Gothic side chapels have spectacular altarpieces; a 15th-century, gold-and-silver *custodia* (monstrance), El Ciprés, is the high point of the sacristy; and the chapter room has paintings by Titian and Zurbarán. The Plateresque cloister houses a museum of artistic religious objects.

A tour of the most interesting villages of La Rioja Baja can be made by first following the meandering line of the Ebro river downstream from Calahorra and stopping first to see the medieval houses and church of San Miguel at **Alfaro** ⓭ at the extreme eastern edge of the province.

From here small roads lead southwest through the spa of Fitero to see the Palacio del Marqués de Casa Torre at **Igea**; the four-towered (three conical, one rectangular) castle at **Cornago** ⓮; and the Monasterio de Vico at **Arnedo** ⓯.

**Enciso** ⓰, further into the hills from Arnedo, has some of the best preserved dinosaur footprints embedded in its rocks and also a palaeontological theme park, El Barranco Perdido (www.barrancoperdido.com). You will now need to backtrack through Arnedo to reach the castle ruins at **Quel** and the curious natural limestone towers at **Autol** ⓱ known as El Picuezo y la Picueza after their resemblance to a human couple. Picking up the motorway at Calahorra is the best way to get back to Logroño.

## LA RIOJA'S HIGHLANDS

The rivers forming the seven main valleys south of Logroño, in the half of the Ebro basin occupied by La Rioja Alta, rise in the province's mountains – a region that feels a world apart from its lower-lying winelands. There are three main massifs: the western Sierra de la

**Tip**

Wine festivals are a great time to visit La Rioja. You can catch them on the following dates: **11 June** Logroño; **29 June** Haro; **31 Aug** Calahorra; **5 Sept** Cenicero; **19 Sept** Logroño

*Life-size Brachiosaurus at El Barranco Perdido.*

Demanda drained by the Oja and the Najerilla; the central Sierra de Cameros drained by the Iregua, the Leza and the Jubera; and the eastern Sierra de Alcarama drained by the Cidacos and Alhama. La Rioja's best hunting, fishing, crafts and most timeless villages are tucked away in the highlands.

One approach is to take the road due south from Nájera which later follows the Najerilla river, good for trout fishing. **Anguiano** **18** is the scene of the fiesta of the *Danza de los Zancos* (Stilt Dance) held every 22 July, when dancers on wooden stilts plunge down a steep street to be caught by the crowd in the town square below.

The **Monasterio de Valvanera** **19** stands in the upper Najerilla Valley in the high and dramatic Sierra de la Demanda. It is La Rioja's prime Marian and mountain retreat, the home of the Virgen de la Valvanera, a 12th-century, Romanesque-Byzantine wood carving of the Madonna and Child.

The road up the valley continues over the mountains towards Santo Domingo de Silos in Burgos (see page 242) but if you want to carry on touring in La Rioja you can return down another valley.

Not far from the turn off for Valvanera, a minor road sets off in the other direction over a pass towards Villanuev de Cameros. On the descent you pas through Ortigosa and eventually reac on the N-111, the north-south main roa down the Iregua valley. North takes yo to Logroño through **Viguera** **20** whic has a Roman bridge and a viewpoint.

Heading south instead you can mak a detour through **Villoslada de Cameros** **21** where textile workers mak *almazuelas*, patchwork quilts typical o La Rioja. A lonely road leads from her to the isolated hermitage of the **Ermita de Lomos de Orios** **22**.

The slow way back towards Logroño and the Ebro from the upper part of th Iregua valley is to follow the River Leza In the lower part of the valley the rive flows through the **Cañón del Río Leza** **23**, a dramatic gorge. A detour from th bottom of the valley leads to the **Castillo de Clavijo** **24** where legend places th apparition of Santiago the Apostle wh helped to defeat Moors in 844.

*Monasterio de Valvanera.*

*Danza de los Zancos folk dance, Anguiano.*

*Rugged coastline, near Lekeitio.*

# THE BASQUE COUNTRY

World-class modern art in the Bilbao Guggenheim, excellent surfing, fiercely competitive sports and the best food in Spain are the attractions of this green and rugged land.

ordered by the Ebro River basin to ıe south and the Bay of Biscay to the orth, the Basque Country is a nation vithin the Spanish state, a separate culure with another language: Euskara. El País Vasco" in Castilian Spanish, it ecomes "Euskadi" in the Basque lanuage. The traditional "four plus three quals one" (4 + 3 = 1) graffiti seen in the egion refers to the cultural unity of the ıree Spanish Basque provinces of Vizaya (Biskaia), Guipúzcoa (Gipuzkoa) and lava (Araba), parts of Navarra (the 4th), lus the three French Basque provinces abourd, La Soule and Basse-Navarre.

Basque identity is clearly foreign to astile's arid *piel de toro* (bull-hide) nage or southern Spain's flamenco nd bullfighting stereotype. Basques roudly consider themselves unsuled by Iberia's two most important ultural upheavals (Romanisation in ıe 1st–4th centuries and Arabisaon in the 8th–15th), and this probbly explains the existence of Euskadi. amón Menéndez Pidal (1869–1968), ıe eminent Spanish philologist, in *En orno a la Lengua Vasca (On the Basque anguage)*, cites Basque toponyms ıroughout the Iberian Peninsula as vidence that Euskara, or some form f it, was probably a language used by ıe Iberian people who best defended emselves against Romans and Moors ı this remote corner of the peninsula.

### THREE CAPITALS

San Sebastián (Donostia), Bilbao (Bilbo) and Vitoria (Gasteiz) are the capitals of the three Basque provinces; Vitoria is also the seat of Basque Autonomous Government. Of the three cities, San Sebastián is the most elegant, offering a combination of beaches and gastronomy that has made it a magnet for visitors. Bilbao, traditionally the *barrio industrial* (industrial quarter), once an industrial city with steel mills, and shipyards and a rustic *casco viejo* (old quarter), is fast becoming one of

**Main attractions**

Bilbao and the Guggenheim Museum
The Basque Coast
San Sebastián
Hondarribia
Vitoria
Laguardia

Maps on pages 180, 182, 188, 192

Getaria harbour.

> **Tip**
>
> Tickets to see Atlético de Bilbao can be bought at San Mamés stadium ("La Catedral"), a 10-minute walk from the town centre on Rafael Moreno Pitxiti Kalea. Matches are usually played on Sundays. For more information see www.athletic-club.eus.

Spain's most modern lively cities. The Basque coast between Bilbao and San Sebastián is perhaps the Basque Country's finest treasure, a series of colourful fishing towns and secluded coves beneath rolling green hills. Vitoria is the most underrated of the Basque cities, with a lovely old section.

## BILBAO (BILBO), SPAIN'S FOURTH-LARGEST CITY

Bilbao, which has undergone major urban renewal in the last couple of decades, has been the industrial and financial centre of the Basque Country since the mid-19th century, when iron ore began to emerge from the mines of northern Spain and the city planted itself firmly in the vanguard of the nation's industrialisation. Steel mills, shipyards, chemical factories and other heavy industries soon lined the banks of the Nerbioi (Nervión) estuary. Bilbao had been an important fishing and trading port since late medieval times when it was among those that handled Spain's export of wool from the vast flocks of sheep kept on the Castilian mesetas. The new iron steamships o the Industrial Revolution had too dee a draught to reach the old wharves, s new ones were built at the mouth of th Nervión. Much of the iron used in Grea Britain during the 19th century cam from Vizcaya province. Santurtzi (San turce), the passenger ferry terminal fo the Bilbao–Portsmouth run across th Bay of Biscay, is a continuation of th long-established business connection between Britain and Northern Spain.

**Bilbao** ❶, Spain's fourth-larges city, has a population of 346,000, but million people – nearly one-half of th Basque Country's total of 2,100,00 – make up the greater metropolita area encompassing the dozen town ships on either bank of the *ría* whic have merged to form 30km (20 miles of urban sprawl down to the sea. Now in common with other European citie formerly reliant on heavy industry, Bil bao's wealth is being created by lighte modern manufacturing and a rapidl developing insurance and financia sector, while chimneys, factories an railway sidings from the old days hav

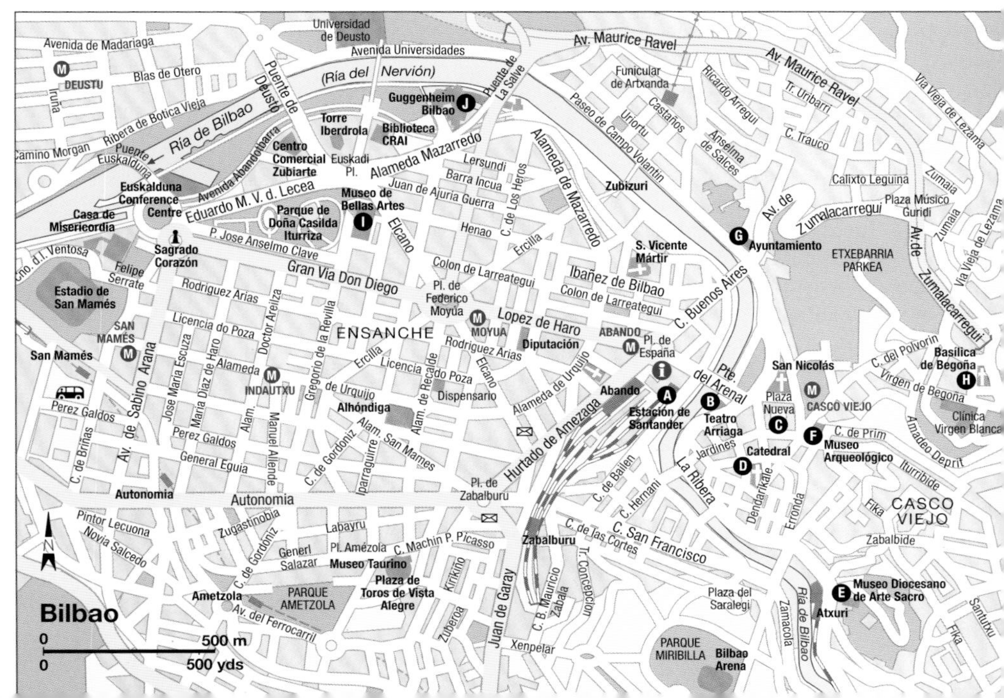

been pulled down. Bilbao has become one of Spain's most forward-charging cities, now well-endowed with cultural resources and state-of-the-art architecture. The Frank Gehry-designed Bilbao Guggenheim Museum has become the symbol of 21st-century Bilbao. Add to this a metro system designed by Norman Foster, a technology park and Santiago Calatrava's airport, plus the dramatic clean up the Nervión estuary (the Ría de Bilbao), and Bilbao shows all the signs of a city on the move.

The wide and elegant avenues of the 19th-century new town are laid out on the left bank of the River Nervión, and one of its planners, Severino de Achúcarro, also designed the cheerful Art Nouveau **Estación de Santander** Ⓐ (now called Bilbao-Concordia) next to the much larger station of Abando, not far from the Arenal Bridge. The bridge leads over to the beautifully refurbished, 1890 Art Nouveau **Teatro Arriaga** Ⓑ, the adjacent Tourist Information Office and the narrow streets of Siete Calles (Seven Streets), or the Casco Viejo, the old town that was fully walled until the 19th century. Leading from the Plaza Arriaga in front of the theatre is the **Plaza Nueva** Ⓒ, with 64 arcades and a Sunday morning open-air market, and the delightful small streets of the old town clustered around the **Catedral de Santiago** Ⓓ. This church, begun in 1379 and rebuilt after a fire 200 years later, was a stop for pilgrims on the way to Santiago de Compostela. The outdoor arcade is its best feature.

The **Museo Diocesano de Arte Sacro** Ⓔ (Diocesan Museum of Sacred Art; Plaza de la Encarnación 9; Tue–Sat 10.30am–1.30pm and 4–7pm, Sun 10.30am–1.30pm) opened in 1996 after restoration work was completed on its 16th-century cloister. The inner patio alone is worth the visit. The displays include religious plates, sculptures and paintings dating from the Romanesque period. Ancient mansions and balconies with fine ironwork are characteristic of the old town, which leads down to the Mercado de la Ribera, the large covered market by the waterfront. Much of the area was rebuilt after floods in 1983 and it is now a chic shopping district

**Tip**

The *Semana Grande* (Great Week, mid–late August) is a good chance to sample the city's best cuisine, concerts and theatre. Bullfights here are renowned for oversized bulls.

*Puente del Arenal, Bilbao.*

**Tip**

Bilbao's metro, designed by Norman Foster, puts the coast within easy reach of the city, with stations at Algorta and Plentzia.

with bars, restaurants and an active nightlife. The **Museo Arqueológico F** (Museum of Basque Archaeology, Ethnology and History; Calzada de Mallona 2; Tue–Sat 10.30am–2pm and 4–7pm, Sun 10.30am–2pm) is housed in a lovely 16th-century convent and has artefacts pertaining to local crafts, fishing and agriculture.

Downriver, close to the bridge known as the Puente del Ayuntamiento (Town Hall Bridge) is the riverside **Ayuntamiento G** built in 1892. Before reaching it, take the elevator (at Calle Esperanza 6) up to the **Basílica de Begoña H**, the massive bulwark overlooking Bilbao and the serpentine Nervión. Its Gothic hulk was begun in 1519 at the spot the Virgin Mary is said to have once appeared and is named after the Virgin of Begoña, patron of the province.

Back over the bridge in the Ensanche, the expanded 19th-century town, is the **Museo de Bellas Artes I** (Fine Arts Museum; www.museobilbao.com; Wed–Mon 10am–8pm) in the Parque de Doña Casilda Iturriza, a 30-minute walk west of the Old Quarter. It has a sizeable collection of works by Flemish, French, Italian and Spanish painters (including El Greco, Goya, Velázquez, Zurbarán and Ribera); 20th-century artists such as Gauguin, Bacon and Tàpies and modern Basque artists including Zuloaga, Regoyos and Echevarría.

Down by the river, five minutes' walk away, is the "titanium whale" of the **Guggenheim Bilbao J** (www.

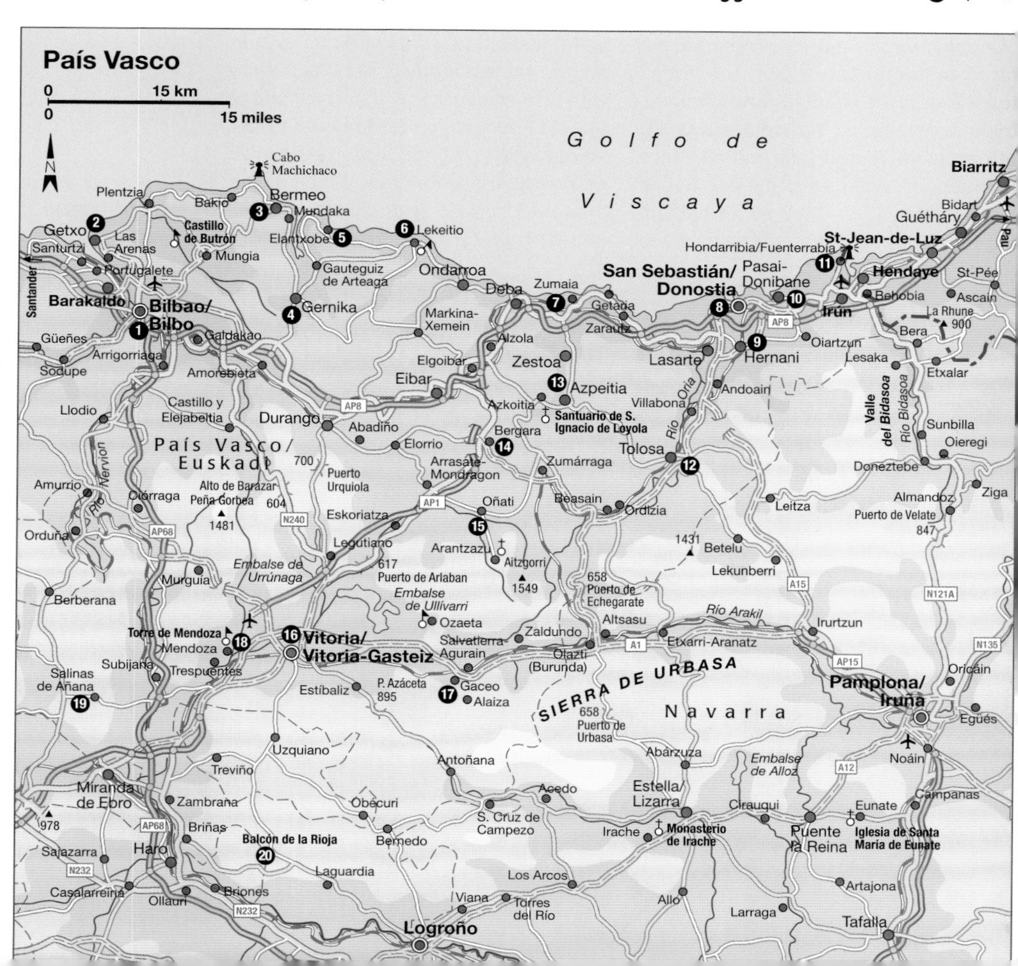

uggenheim-bilbao.eus; Tue–Sun 10am–8pm; see page 196), the high spot of any visit to the city. Built on the site of the defunct Euskalduna Shipyards, its shimmering, flowing lines are an invitation to see modern works of art in a stunning setting. Its collection is shared with its sister galleries in New York and Venice, and is displayed in one of the world's largest exhibition spaces.

Some 8km (5 miles) downriver is one of the city's most curious phenomena, the Puente de Vizcaya or *Puente Colgante* (Hanging Bridge), constructed in 1893. The gondola hanging from cables "ferries" cars and passengers between exclusive Las Arenas on the right bank and, on the left, Portugalete, birthplace of Dolores Ibarruri (1895–1989), the fiery Spanish Civil War orator known as "La Pasionaria". It is possible to take a lift and walk across the upper beam of the bridge, 45m (150ft) above the water (daily 10am–7pm). In the harbour area of Santurtzi, a 20-minute walk from Portugalete, is the quayside restaurant Hogar del Pescador, famous for *besugo* (sea bream) and fresh grilled sardines.

## THE COAST FROM BILBAO TO SAN SEBASTIÁN

The 176km (110-mile) Basque coast offers many picturesque corners. Starting from Algorta, follow the Nervión estuary past the fine beaches north of **Getxo** ❷ towards Plentzia, 13km (8 miles) away, with its bustling port on the estuary of the River Butrón. It is worth a ten-minute detour upriver to take in the Castillo de Butrón, a 600-year-old castle rebuilt in the 19th century.

The corniche road then leads past Armintza beach and steep cliffs to the fishing village of Bakio, also known for its excellent beaches. One of the most picturesque sites on the north coast is San Juan de Gaztelugatxe, an island with a tiny chapel perched on it. The island is reached from the car park by a narrow path and a bridge. The Matxitxako (Machichaco) lighthouse close by also offers panoramic views.

A little further east is **Bermeo** ❸, one of Spain's most important fishing villages, its harbour filled with brightly coloured wooden boats of all sizes

*Ayuntamiento, Bilbao.*

# GUERNICA

**Picasso's moving depiction of the bombing of the town of Guernica during the Spanish Civil War has become a symbol of the fight against facism.**

In 1937, Pablo Picasso, then 56, was commissioned to produce a work supporting Spain's legitimately elected Second Republic against the military rebels who had instigated the 1936–9 Spanish Civil War. The poster-like drawing that he created in protest at the German Condor Legion's "experimental" bombing of a Basque village subsequently became one of the most famous and most fought-over 20th-century works of art.

The town of Guernica (now called Gernika-Lumo), 20km (12 miles) east of Bilbao, has been a symbol of Basque autonomy since the 14th century when the feudal lords of Vizcaya swore on the *Gernikako Arbola* (Tree of Guernica) to respect Basque rights and privileges. When on 26 April 1937 General Franco approved the Condor Legion's saturation bombing of Guernica to take place that same day, he knew the strike would be a blow to Basque national sentiment, a warning to nearby Bilbao and a demonstration of the brutality in store for civilians supporting the Republic. It was Tuesday, market day, and the town was filled with farmers and livestock. There was a high proportion of women, children and the elderly, as most of the young men were at the front. By the time the bombers, unopposed, had dumped their deadly cargo, more than a thousand civilians lay dead or dying in the rubble.

*Detail from the tiled reproduction in Guernica.*

Picasso's painting began its singular odyssey as part of the Spanish Pavillion in the 1937 International Exposition in Paris, where it was only a moderate success. The French architect Le Corbusier recalled: "*Guernica* saw nothing but the backs of the visitors, who were repelled by the painting." The painting returned to Picasso's studio until after the fall of the Republic in 1939 when he turned it over to New York's Museum of Modern Art. He expressed a wish that the painting eventually hang in Madrid's Prado Museum, but only after Spain had returned to democracy.

As Picasso's fame grew, so did *Guernica*'s, both as a work of art and as a symbol of Spain's suffering under a totalitarian regime. Picasso died in 1973, two years before Franco. Negotiations with his heirs for the painting's return were already underway as Spain's transition to democracy developed. Within Spain, civil discord broke out among towns associated with the picture: Málaga, as Picasso's birthplace; Barcelona as his adoptive city and scene of his formative years; Guernica, the work's inspiration; and Madrid, designated in the legacy. Madrid prevailed, and on 10 September 1981, the painting arrived at Barajas airport and was installed in an armoured, bomb-proof building in the annexe next to the Prado.

In 1992, after Barcelona's request to display the *Guernica* canvas as part of the cultural Olympics held parallel to the Olympic Games was refused, the painting was moved to the Museo Reina Sofía in Madrid. It has resided there ever since – a 1997 request to include *Guernica* in the Bilbao Guggenheim's inaugural collection of the world's greatest works of art was also denied.

nd shapes crammed together in neat anks. The Museo del Pescador (Fisherman's Museum) and the fishermen's quarter on Bermeo's Atalaya promontory are two possible visits before a top at nearby Mundaka. At low tide, n big (normally winter-only) swells he barrelling lefthander here is one of he best – but most fickle – surf spots n Europe. This is also the entry point or a visit to the Reserva de la Biosfera de Urdaibai, the most important wetand and bird sanctuary in the Basque Country, extending from Cabo Matxtxako across the Gernika (Guernica) estuary to Cabo Ogoño.

An 11km (6-mile) drive south along the Gernika estuary leads to the town of **Gernika-Lumo** ❹, better known as Guernica, inspiration for one the most famous paintings ever committed to canvas. On Monday 26 April 1937 the Nazi Luftwaffe's Franco-approved experiment with saturation bombing of a civilian target destroyed Gernika, the traditional seat of Basque autonomy, killing more than 1,000 citizens. Since medieval times, Spanish kings had sworn under the famous Gernikako Arbola (Tree of Guernica) to respect the Basque *fueros*, or local rights. When the Republican Government commissioned Pablo Picasso, then living in Paris, to produce a painting supporting the democratically elected government against the military rebellion led by Franco, Picasso chose the bombing of Guernica as his theme. There is not much left of the original Guernica to see, although the Casa de Juntas (Meeting House) and the stump of the sacred oak are places of pilgrimage for Basque patriots.

The **Santamamiñe Cave**, 5km (3 miles) northeast of Guernica at Kortezubi, offers an opportunity to see prehistoric paintings thought to be 13,000 years old, dating from the Cro-Magnon epoch. The cave itself has a spectacular array of stalagmites and stalactites (arranged visits and guided tours only). Modern art is also on hand at the nearby Bosque Pintado de Oma (painted forest of Oma), a stand of pines painted with brightly coloured stripes by the artist Agustín Ibarrola.

## FISHING VILLAGES

**Elantxobe** ❺ (Elanchove), one of the gems of the coast, can be reached by continuing down the eastern side of the Guernica *ría*. It is a diminutive fishing village with houses stacked up a steep cliff, best viewed from the upper village. The nearby Cabo Ogoño is the highest point on the Cantabrian coast. **Lekeitio** ❻ (Leiqueitio) is the next important sight to the east along the coast road after driving through the villages of Ea and Ipáster. Lekeitio is famous for its September *fiesta del ganso* (goose festival), part of the San Antonlin festival, when contestants hang over the estuary from dead geese tied to a cable hoisted in and out of the water by teams of men at either end. Leikeitio's old quarter, with narrow, cobbled streets, is the part of town to find and see. The site of a castle above the town provides excellent views over Bilbao, the Nervión

*Elantxobe.*

**Eat**

In a region full of culinary delights, San Sebastián ranks as a "gourmet world capital".

and much of the surrounding coast. There are also two attractive beaches here separated from one and other by a small island with a sand spit.

**Ondarroa** is 12km (8 miles) east, another picturesque town with a busy fishing fleet brightly painted in the once forbidden colours of the *Ikurriña*, the red, green and white Basque flag. After passing through Mutriku (Motrico) and Deba (Deva), you arrive in the pretty summer resort and fishing town of **Zumaia** ❼ (Zumaya). The Espacio Cultural Ignacio Zuloaga (www.espaciozuloaga.com; Apr–Sept Fri–Sat 4–8pm) just east of town was once the house of the best-known Basque painter of his era (1870–1945). Zuloaga's subjects were society portraits, Spanish peasant genre works and landscapes, all of which are represented in the museum, as well as paintings by Zurbarán, Goya and El Greco. Sculptures by Rodin and by Zuloaga's friend and Zumaia native Julio Beobide (1891–1969) make this an ambitious collection for a little fishing village.

Zumaia offers several options for trips along the Urola river estuary or up the Urola Valley to Zestoa (Cestona – a spa resort in the Belle Epoque) and Azpeitia to see the stunning Baroque Santuario de San Ignacio de Loyola (see page 191).

Zumaia beach.

## THE KITCHEN OF GUIPÚZCOA

**Getaria** (Guetaria) can be reached either on foot over the hills via Azkizu or by car 7km (5 miles) northeast on the coast road. Famous locally as "*la cocina de* Guipúzcoa" (the kitchen of Guipúzcoa province), it has many excellent restaurants and the air is usually thick with the fragrance of *besugo* (sea bream) or *txuleta de buey* (steaks) cooking over coals outside restaurants. Getaria is also the centre for the production of *txakoli*, tart young white wine made from grapes grown on the hillsides over the Atlantic. Juan Sebastián Elcano, Spain's most famous navigator, who completed Magellan's voyage around the world, becoming the first man to circumnavigate the globe, was a native of Getaria. The biannual early August town fiesta celebrates Elcano's return in 1522. Getaria has a fine port and its 15th-century church of San Salvador is reminiscent of a galleon.

**Zarautz** (Zarauz), 4km (2 miles) east of Getaria, is a bright and bustling summer centre with an immense beach (Guipúzcoa's longest) and lively café life in and around its central square; all in all a good place for a run on the sand, a swim in the surf and a beer on an outside terrace. Orio, 5km (3 miles) east along the winding N-634 coast road, is another fishing village well known for excellent dining opportunities. Orio and *besugo* are all but synonyms in this part of the world; a stroll around the harbour or along the estuary of the Oria is the perfect prelude to a *txakoli*-accompanied feast.

Usurbil, the next town to the east, is noteworthy for its excellent cider bar, Sidrería Ugarte. Cider-tasting accompanied by copious portions of beef and cod omelettes is an important winter event.

## SAN SEBASTIÁN (DONOSTIA)

It has long been said that Spain's "Four S" are its most beautiful provincial cities: Sevilla, Salamanca, Santiago de Compostela and **San Sebastián** ❽. Called Donostia in Basque, the town has a resident population of 186,000 and is Spain's quintessential summer resort, built around its famous shell-shaped beach, La Concha. Teased by *bilbaínos* as "La Ciudad Jardín" (Garden City) in contrast to Bilbao's utilitarian "El Barrio Industrial" (Industrial Quarter), San Sebastián is a feast for the eye and the palate. As a gourmet world capital, food shares the limelight with sport. Men-only eating societies compete for culinary excellence, while the *txikiteo* (tippling) and *tapeo* (*tapa* grazing) are daily institutions, only interrupted by football matches, pelota games, whaleboat-rowing regattas, wood-chopping and scything contests or improvised poetry competitions (*bertsolaris*).

Though the origins of San Sebastián date back to the 11th century, it wasn't until the Habsburg Queen, María-Cristina, chose San Sebastián as a summer watering spot to cure her daughter Isabela II's skin ailments in the frigid waters of the Atlantic that the city became fashionable. Isabela was joined, after 1845, by much of the Madrid aristocracy, and the city became popular with the wealthy. San Sebastián is surprisingly modern in design, criss-crossed by wide streets on a grid pattern as a result of the dozen or so times it has been damaged by fire. The most recent torching took place after the French were expelled in 1813. English-Portuguese forces occupied and pillaged the city and proceeded to burn the remaining evidence. Modern San Sebastián is a bustling seaside resort that manages to retain its fresh Basque and rural flavour. The María Cristina remains one of the country's top hotels, and the town's lively festivals include Semana Grande in August when Basque culture is on display.

The **Isla de Santa Clara**, in the centre of the inner bay, is largely responsible for the existence of La Concha and, as a result, for San Sebastián's cachet. The

*View of La Concha beach from Monte Igueldo, San Sebastian.*

**Tip**

Come to San Sebastián in July for the jazz festival, in August in Semana Grande, or in September for the film festival.

strategically placed island breaks up the power of Atlantic storms, allowing La Concha to survive quietly at the edge of city streets. Also decisive are the two promontories on either side of the bay. Monte Igueldo, on the northwest side, which can be reached by funicular from the end of the beach, has a **Parque de Atracciones** Ⓐ (amusement park) and panoramic views over the city's tree-lined boulevards, parks, gardens and Belle Epoque architecture. The **Peine del Viento** Ⓑ (Wind Comb, see page 197) by Eduardo Chillida (1924–2002) is a series of a bronze sculptures built into the rocks under Monte Igueldo. The wind resonates musically through the metal structures, which have become as emblematic as any of San Sebastián's more traditional landmarks.

Monte Urgull, on the northeastern side, with the **Castillo de Santa Cruz de la Mota** Ⓒ and municipal park, offers splendid views of the city. Tucked under Monte Urgull just west of the Parte Vieja (Old Town) is the fishing port, another popular stretch of bars and taverns serving fresh sardines. Ther is a small maritime museum here, th **Museo Naval** Ⓓ (tel: 943-430051; http: untzimuseoa.eus; Tue–Sat 10am–2pr and 4–7pm, Sun 11am–7pm) and, jus beyond, an **Aquarium** (http://aquariums com; Jul–Aug daily 10am–9pm; Apr June and Sept Mon–Fri 10am–8pm Sat–Sun 10am–9pm; Oct–Apr Mon Fri 10am–7pm, Sat–Sun 10am–8pm which together give a glimpse of th town's less glamorous, seafaring pas

## THE OLD TOWN

The Parte Vieja (Old Town) is Sa Sebastián's social and gastronomi nerve centre. Most of the city's tavern and restaurants can be found here clustered in the narrow streets aroun the Plaza de la Constitución. The numbered balconies of the apartment around the square are a relic of th days when it served as a bullring. Als in this part of town is **Santa María de Coro** Ⓔ, the city's main church, featuring the familiar sculpture of Sair Sebastian perforated with arrows o the exuberant baroque facade. At th

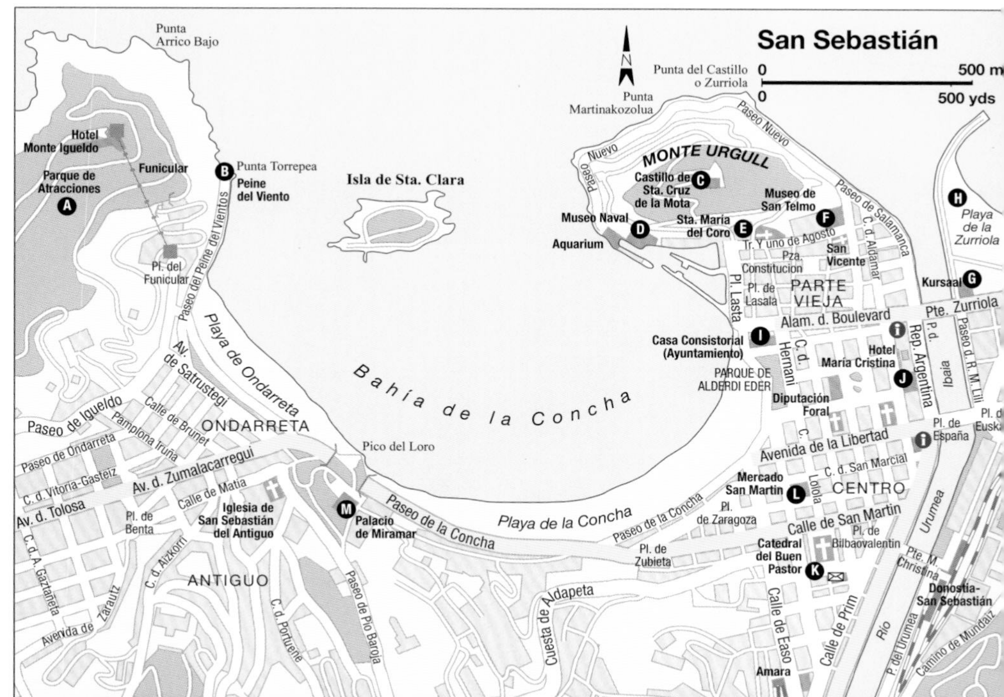

ar end of Calle 31 de Agosto, in Plaza gnacio Zuloaga, is the **Museo de San elmo** F ( www.santelmomuseoa.eus; ue–Sun 10am–8pm). It is installed in lovely 16th-century monastery and xhibits paintings by the pioneers of asque painting, such as Zuloaga see page 186) and Antonio Ortiz de chagüe, works by El Greco, and 16 old- and sepia-coloured murals by atalan Josep Marià Sert (1876–1945), epicting robust scenes from Basque naritime life.

The other side of the Parte Vieja borders the mouth of the Urumea River, ite of some of San Sebastián's finest ourmet restaurants, grouped around he Mercado de la Bretxa. Beyond the Jrumea is **Kursaal** G, Rafael Moneo's tunning translucent cube, now San ebastián's concert hall and convenion venue. Nearby **Zurriola** H, the each on the northeastern side of the River Urumea, is frequented by surfers and is wilder than San Sebastián's other two beaches: Ondarreta, at the western end of town, is low key and, being closer to the university, younger; the sweeping curve of La Concha is quite simply one of the most magnificent urban beaches in Europe.

The elegant **Casa Consistorial** I (Town Hall) is next to the formal Alderdi Eder gardens at the edge of the Concha and the Parte Vieja. Begun in 1887 as a casino, the town council moved there after gambling was outlawed at the beginning of the 20th century. The **Hotel María Cristina** J, one of Spain's grandest, is the venue for the town's international film festival.

The colossal, 19th-century **Catedral del Buen Pastor** (Good Shepherd) K, just behind the **Mercado San Martín** L is the official seat of the Bishopric of San Sebastián. The **Palacio de Miramar** M – built for the royal family in 1889 – overlooks the Concha from the top of the Paseo de Miraconcha.

## AROUND SAN SEBASTIÁN

Just to the south of San Sebastián is **Hernani** 9 where a restored 16th-century Basque *caserío* (farmhouse) is now Chillida Leku, the Eduardo Chillida Sculpture Garden and Museum

**Fact**

Anoeta, east of San Sebastián, caters to the town's love of sport with a modern soccer stadium and Spain's largest indoor sports venue. Horse races are held at Lasarte. The jai-alai centre is on the same route, 3km (2 miles) south of Ondarreta beach.

*Paseo de la Concha, San Sebastián.*

(visited by prior arrangement; www.museochillidaleku.com), a stunning and eclectic collection of the work of Spain's most famous contemporary artist (along with Tàpies).

Back on the coast, **Pasai-Donibane** ⑩ (Pasajes de San Juan), 5km (3 miles) east of San Sebastián, is one of the prettiest fishing villages on the Basque coast. It is known for its excellent seafood restaurants and, in summer, the *txiringuitos* (shacks) where you can sit outside and eat sardines while watching the ships sliding through the *pasajes* (straits) on their way to and from the Atlantic. For the most scenic approach, drive to Pasai San Pedro and take the launch across to Pasai-Donibane or try the well-marked, three-hour walk from Zurriola beach.

**Hondarribia** ⑪ (Fuenterrabía), 12km (8 miles) northeast of Pasai-Donibane on the French border, is another brightly painted village resembling nothing so much as its own fishing fleet. The 10th-century Castillo de Carlos V, now a Parador, is the most important structure, along with the emblazoned 15th-century Puerta d Santa María (St Mary's Gate) leac ing into the old town through ancie walls. The flower-festooned balconie and tiny houses and streets hous many fine taverns and restaurants, th most famous being the Hermandad d Pescadores (Fisherman's Guild).

A *navette* (launch) will take you t Hendaye, in France, for an afternoo on the beach or a three-hour walk u to the picturesque village of Biriato where there are *pelota* games on sum mer evenings. Other nearby attraction include the Cabo de Higuer lighthous at the end of the Bidasoa estuary, an the route over Jaizkibel, the highes point on the Basque coast, a spectacu lar walk or drive between the sanctu ary of Nuestra Señora de Guadalup and Pasai-Donibane.

## THE BASQUE HILLS

It is often said that the highland Basqu is the true Basque, purest and leas adulterated by cosmopolitan coasta influences. The Basque hill countr offers countless *caseríos* (farmhouses)

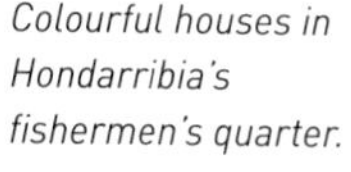

*Colourful houses in Hondarribia's fishermen's quarter.*

ide, solid structures built for livetock as well as their masters. In and round these *caseríos*, rural Basque fe continues, surrounded by traditions nd customs largely unchanged for enturies. Some of the most important pland towns and villages to visit are olosa, Azpeitia, Bergara, Elorrio, Oñati nd Arantzazu, though perhaps the ost authentic slices of rural Basque fe are found by wandering uncharted acks to unnamed *caseríos*.

**Tolosa** ⓬, 26km (16 miles) south of an Sebastián on the N-1, was the capil of Guipúzcoa during the 19th century. his small, industrial, paper-mill town as several interesting buildings, including the 17th-century church of Santa aría, the 16th-century San Francisco onvent, the Town Hall and the Idiáquez nd Atodo palaces. Tolosa is also known r the pure Basque spoken there and for s culinary specialities: *alubias de Tolosa* ed kidney beans) and various sweets cluding *tejas de Tolosa* (almond biscuits), and you can study their history at e Museo de Confitería (Sweet-making useum) in Calle Lechuga.

## IRTHPLACE OF IGNATIUS OYOLA

**zpeitia** ⓭, 28km (17 miles) west of olosa on the GI-2634, is the site of the antuario de San Ignacio de Loyola, rthplace of the founder of the Society Jesus religious order known as the esuits. He was born here in 1490 in a wer house, the remains of which now rm part of the huge sanctuary. The om where he convalesced after being ounded at the siege of Pamplona in 521 and where he began the reading at led to his life's great work is now chapel. The huge Churrigueresque upola and the elaborately sculpted rcular central nave of the basilica, uilt between 1689 and 1738, are the ost striking architectural elements in is impressive structure.

**Bergara** ⓮, 23km (14 miles) southest of Azpeitia on the GI-3750, has one of the best preserved old quarters in the Basque highlands: palaces, townhouses, a Baroque, porticoed Casa Consistorial facing the Real Seminario de Bergara (Royal Seminary), and the churches of San Pedro de Ariznoa (17th-century) and Santa Marina de Oxirondo (Gothic). **Elorrio** is another 15km (10 miles) west on the GI-2632. It, too, has an excellent old quarter with *casas-torres* (fortified townhouses) and the church of Nuestra Señora de la Concepción, a prototypical, solid, Basque structure with heavy columns and a Churrigueresque altarpiece.

**Oñati** ⓯ (Oñate) and Arantzazu form a double destination of great significance to the collective Basque heart and mind. Nestled in the cirque of the Aralar and Arantzazu mountains 74km (46 miles) southwest of San Sebastián, Oñati was for centuries the site of the Basque Country's only university, the Universidad Sancti Spiritus, founded in 1540 and closed at the beginning of the 20th century. Between 1833 and 1839 during the first Carlist War, Oñati was the seat of power for Don Carlos,

*Fishing off the promenade, Hondarribia.*

> **Tip**
>
> The Battle of Vitoria (21 June 1813), one of the decisive battles of the Peninsular Wars, was fought beside the Zadorra river just outside the modern city.

brother of Fernando VII, aspirant to the Spanish throne. The university's Renaissance façade, its chapel altarpiece, the 15th-century Gothic church of San Miguel and the baroque Ayuntamiento (Town Hall) are Oñati's most interesting architectural features.

The drive to the Santuario de Arantzazu 9km (6 miles) south of Oñati runs through the gorges of the Arantzazu river. The Sanctuary is at 800 metres (2,625ft) with the 1,549-metre (5,080ft) Aitzgorri peak behind. The Virgin of Arantzazu, patron saint of Guipúzcoa, was reportedly sighted by a shepherd here in the mid-15th century. The church is a modern structure built during the 1950s; Jorge Oteiza, master and dean of Basque sculpture, created the Apostles on the façade, and Eduardo Chillida sculpted the doors.

## VITORIA-GASTEIZ (VITORIA) AND THE PROVINCE OF ÁLAVA (ARABA)

**Vitoria** ⓰ (Gasteiz in Euskara) is the seat of the autonomous Basque government and, with a population of 244,000, the second Basque city, founded hig on a hill in 1181 by Sancho el Sabio (th Wise) of Navarra. Today Vitoria has surprisingly quiet and elegant *casc antiguo* (old town) tucked inside a mod ern, industrial shell.

The **Plaza de la Virgen Blanca** is the heart of early Vitoria, ringed b ancient houses with galleried porche and balconies. The winged victor monument in the centre of the squar celebrates the 1813 victory of the Duk of Wellington over Napoleonic force (see page 44). The adjoining **Plaza d España** (also known as Plaza Nueva) i an elegant and arcaded neoclassic square redolent of those of Salamanc and Madrid. Medieval Vitoria pen etrates north through the **Plaza d Machete**, named after the weapon o which nobles and officials once swor to uphold the city's laws. The Palaci Villa-Suso stands on the corner of th square on Calle Fray Zacarías Mar tínez, while in the niche outside th main door of the Gothic **Iglesia de Sa Miguel** Ⓑ is an image of the Virge Blanca (White Virgin), patron saint

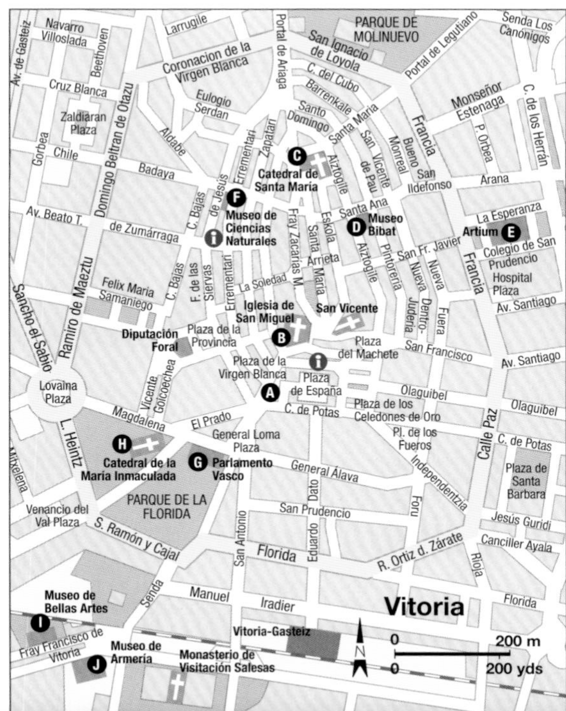

*Catedral de la María Inmaculada.*

toria. Continuing into the egg-shaped ld quarter's narrow streets, the **Pala-io de Escoriaza-Esquibel**, a 16th-entury Renaissance building with a lateresque patio, built for one of Car-os V's physicians, stands at the junc-on of two narrow stairway-streets.

The **Catedral de Santa María** C is ne senior of Vitoria's two cathedrals; specially lovely is the sculpted west-rn portal glowing amber in the after-oon sun.

A short way south is the **Museo Bibat** D (Tue–Fri 10am–2pm and 4–6.30pm; at 10am–2pm; Sun 11am–2pm) vhich combines two previous muse-ms. The Museo de Naipes (Playing Card Museum) occupies the historic 6th-century Palacio de Bendaña. Its ollections derive from Spain's big-est playing-card factory, established n Vitoria in 1868. The exhibits of the Museo de Arqueología – ranging from palaeolithic dolmens to Roman sculp-ures, as well as some intriguing local nedieval finds – are displayed in a nodern extension.

To the east of here is the **Centro Museo Vasco de Arte Contemporáneo - Artium** E (http://artium.org; Tue–Fri 11am–2pm and 4–7.30pm, Sat 10am–2pm), designed by Vitoria architect José Luis Catón as the third leg of the Basque art triangle along with the Bil-bao Guggenheim and San Sebastián's Chillida Leku. Featuring Basque art-ists Jorge Oteiza, Eduardo Chillida, Augustín Ibarrola and Nestor Baster-retxea among others, this is one of the Basque Country's finest collections of contemporary art

Another museum in the city centre is the **Museo de Ciencias Naturales** F (Natural Science Museum; Tue–Fri 10am–2pm and 4–6.30pm, Sat 10am–2pm, Sun 11am–2pm), a collection of local geology, flora and fauna housed in the 16th-century Torre de Doña Otxanta.

Lying on the south side of the old town are the **Parlamento Vasco** G (Basque Parliament) and the new **Catedral de la María Inmaculada** (or Catedral Nueva) H, begun in 1907 but with construction work going on for decades. Two further museums lie just beyond: the **Museo de Bellas Artes** I (Tue–Fri 10am–2am and 4–6.30pm; Sat 10am–2pm and 5–8pm, Sun 11am–2pm; free) has a good collection of Spanish-Dutch paintings, as well as three Riberas and some lightweight works by Picasso and Miró. The nearby **Museo de Armería** J (Arms Museum; Tue–Fri 10am–2pm and 4–6pm; Sat 10am–2pm, Sun 11am–2pm; free) includes mementos of the Napoleonic wars.

## AROUND VITORIA

A good place to start explorations around Vitoria and through the province of Álava is the Romanesque Santuario de Estíbaliz, 10km (6 miles) east of the city just south of the the N-I. **Gaceo** 17, where very fine 14th-century Gothic frescoes decorate the choir in the church of San Martín de Tours, is 25km (15 miles) east on the N-I. Alaiza, 4km (2 miles) south of Gaceo past Langarica on the A-411, also has

*Battle of Vitoria monument, Plaza de la Virgen Blanca.*

a decorated church, the Iglesia de la Asunción, but here the late-14th-century paintings are puzzling, primitive and monochromatic, seeming to represent warriors, castles and churches. The Gothic description beneath them has never been deciphered. For a look through an interesting old quarter, explore Salvatierra-Agurain. The megalithic dolmen of Eguilaz is further east just off the N-I. Known as Aizkomendi, the tomb consists of standing stones with the huge cap stone still in place and is one of the finest in the Basque Country. Now loop north and back towards Vitoria on the A-3012 through Zalduondo (Zaldundo), which contains the Lazarraga Palace and San Julián Hermitage. At Barria there is a Cistercian monastery, and at Ozaeta is the castle of Guevara.

West of Vitoria on the A-3302 is Martioda, which has a fortified medieval mansion, and the **Torre de Mendoza** ⓲, one-time fortress and now home of the Heraldic Museum of Álava. Nearby is the Roman settlement Oppidum de Iruña at Trespuentes. The partial excavations have revealed a stretc of Roman wall, and the remains of tower and some houses. At **Salina de Añana** ⓳, just west of Pobes o the A-2622, ancient salt springs, n longer commercially viable, glisten lik ghostly, scattered diamonds aroun the River Muera.

To the north are the Ullibarri an Urruñaga reservoirs, the largest wet lands in the Basque Country. Town to stop at on the way back to Vitori include Gopegi, (13th-century church Otxandio (the baroque Santa María), an Legutiano (a fortified medieval quarter

*Salinas de Añana.*

## SOUTHERN WINELANDS

South of Vitoria, the Rioja Alavesa, Álava's southernmost area and best win country, lies below the Puerto (Pass de Herrera where the **Balcón de la Rioja** ⓴ on the A-2124 provides a vast panoramic view of the arid Ebro Valley **Laguardia** is the capital of the 15 townships in the Rioja Alavesa, famous fo their *bodegas* (wine cellars), offering tastings as well as meals. Laguardia's oldest building is the 14th-century Casa de la Primicia. There are also sections of the original town walls visible, as wel as numerous 16th–18th-century houses in the old part of the town. The church of Santa María de los Reyes has the only perfectly conserved, polychrome, 14th-century Gothic portal in Spain, protected by a Renaissance facade.

Near Laguardia are two prehistoric sites: La Hoya, a settlement dating back 1,500 years – a museum of finds explains its importance – and the dolmen known as La Chabola de le Hechicera at Elvillar.

That's the remote past. Going towards the future, winemaking firms in the Rioja Alavesa have commissioned some stunning pieces of contemporary architecture. One of the best examples is Bodegas Ysios, just outside Laguardia. Also impressive is the luxury hotel built by Marqués de Riscal at Elciego.

View from the Balcón de la Rioja.

# THE GUGGENHEIM IN BILBAO

The Guggenheim has been an event that has far transcended the art world. This spectacular "titanium whale" has given new life to the city.

The Guggenheim Museum in Bilbao opened in 1997 to a blaze of publicity. The city's US$100-million investment in the spectacular titanium "Metallic Flower" had paid off. Matched by Bilbao's other recent architectural triumphs – including Norman Foster's metro, Santiago Calatrava's airport, the revamped Alhóndiga building (now called Azkuna Zemtroa), the Provincial Library and the Iberdrola Tower – the gallery confirmed the Basques as a people of vision and taste.

Set by the River Nervión and incorporating a busy vehicle bridge, the museum was designed by the Californian architect Frank O. Gehry. It is made up of inter-connected blocks, clad in limestone and topped with a shimmering titanium roof. Light floods through glass walls and a skylight in the 50-metre (165ft) -high central atrium and from here walkways, lifts and stairs lead through the blocks that house the 20 spacious galleries on three floors. Many of the galleries have been designed to take large modern installations, notably the vast boat-shaped gallery built beneath the bridge. For the design of the 24,290-sq-metre (257,000-sq-ft) building, Gehry employed a computer program called Catia, which had been developed by the aerospace industry for mapping curved surfaces.

The Basque administration and the Solomon R. Guggenheim Foundation, based in New York, jointly administer the museum, the Guggenheim providing curatorial and administrative expertise as well as the core art collection and programming.

*Anish Kapoor's "Tall Tree & The Eye" (2009) sculpture outside the Guggenheim.*

*The building occupies a 4.2-hectare (8-acre) site on a bend in the River Nervión, by the busy Puente de la S[illegible] This used to be a run-down dockland and industrial a[illegible] Another renowned architect, César Pelli, designed th[illegible] adjacent waterfront development.*

*"The Matter of Time" (2005) was created by American sculptor Richard Serra. This permanent exhibit weigh[illegible] about 1,200 tons and is over 430ft long.*

'itanium "Metallic Flower" looms up in the heart of
own and is designed to have a 'sculptural presence'
cting the waterfront, downtown buildings and
ounding hills.*

*The museum has a bookshop, café and restaurant, and a 300-seat auditorium with multimedia technology. Note that the Guggenheim closes on Mondays, except during July and August.*

*Peine Del Viento (Winter's Comb) by Spanish Sculptor Eduardo Chillida.*

## 20th-century Basque artists

Eduardo Chillida (1924–2002), sculptor of *Peine del Viento* (see page 188) is the best known of modern Basque artists. He was a member of the Basque School, a movement defined by the 1963 publication of sculptor Jorge Oteiza's *Quousque Tandem*. The title refers to Cicero's first Catiline oration: "*Quousque tandem abutere, Catilina, patientia nostra...?*" (Until when, until when, Catilina, will you abuse our patience?). In a similar tone, Oteiza exhorted Basque artists to define an aesthetic rooted in the Basque character. "Eighty grandmothers connect the Basque Neolithic to Pascuala Iruarrízaga, my wife Itziar's grandmother," he declared.

Chillida's non-intrusive use of space and form illustrates the Basque aesthetic Oteiza identified. "Rejecting the occupation of space, Basque art is natural, irregular," explained Oteiza. "I reject whatever is not essential, whatever fails to respond to constructive truth. This Basque character is already apparent in the *cromlechs*, the rings of sacred stones that lead us into the realm of magic, the basis of our tradition."

Basque art can be seen at the Guggenheim, the Museos de Bellas Artes in Bilbao and Vitoria, and at the San Telmo Museum in San Sebastián. Villa Zuloaga in Zumaia displays paintings by Ignacio Zuloaga and others.

*Jeff Koons's "Puppy" (1992) is a 12-metre (40ft) -high sculpture of a West Highland terrier made out of stainless steel and flowering plants.*

*Medieval buildings and streets, Santillana del Mar.*

# CANTABRIA

Green hills rising up behind long, sandy beaches, colourful fishing ports and remote mountain villages are the backdrop for Romanesque churches and Altamira's incomparable cave paintings.

antabria is a maritime and highland astion historically bound to the kingoms of Castile and León. Wedged etween the Asturians to the west nd the nationalistic Basques to the ast, Cantabrians had to struggle for reir identity as post-Franco Spain has ecome more and more decentralised. antabria was formerly known as Sanınder province and its inhabitants were alled *Montañeses* (mountain people). *ántabros* are descendants of the original inhabitants of the Cantabrian Corillera that runs the length of Spain's oast on the Atlantic Bay of Biscay – *el 1ar Cantábrico* in Spanish. From wild eaches and colourful fishing towns to nspoiled mountain villages, Cantabria as much to explore as well as a rare ense of fresh discovery. The eastern art of the Picos de Europa (see page 11) belongs to Cantabria.

## HE MAIN CITY

**antander** ❶, Cantabria's main city nd passenger port for ferries from ritain, was the Roman *Portus Victoriae*. The early city occupied the igh ground where the cathedral now tands. The abbeys of San Emeterio nd San Celedonio were the earliest enants of this terrain; the name of the ity is, in fact, thought to come from an Emeterio, via Sancti Emetheri and ant Em'ter. By the 11th century, the city's privileged position as a central northern seaport had made it a functioning (though not flourishing) trading centre, and it provided the kingdom of Castile and León with its only seaport. Trade with the New World opened up, a Royal Land and Sea Consulate was established, and wool and grain routes through the mountains connected Santander with Burgos, Valladolid and Madrid. It wasn't until the 18th century that economic prosperity really arrived. In 1754 Pope Benedict XIV made Santander an episcopal seat; the following

**Main attractions**

Santander
Parque de Cabárceno
Santillana del Mar
Altamira
Comillas
Castro Urdiales

Maps on pages 200, 202

*Playa El Camello, Santander.*

> **Fact**
>
> Marcelino Menéndez Pelayo is looked on as the founder of modern Spanish literary history. A traditionalist and committed Catholic, his work included *History of Spanish Heterodoxies* (1881) and *History of Aesthetic Ideas in Spain* (1891).

year King Fernando VI conceded it the title of city. By the end of the 19th century, Santander was booming.

However, two major catastrophes in 48 years slowed the city's momentum. In 1893 the *Machichaco*, a freighter loaded with 45 tons of dynamite, exploded, killing 500 citizens and wounding another 2,000. Forty-eight years later, a fire destroyed most of the city's historic centre, which is why so much seems so new. King Alfonso XIII's early 20th-century visits to Santander "to take the baths" made the city fashionable and gave tourism its start. After the 1936–9 Spanish Civil War, Santander, which had been loyal to the rebel forces led by Franco, remained a much-favoured northern resort of postwar Spain. It is still so today and has a prestigious international summer school (the Universidad Internacional Menéndez y Pelayo), an excellent summer music and dance festival, and no fewer than nine beaches.

The nerve centre of Santander's old town is **Plaza Porticada A**, officially Plaza Velarde and unmistakable for the arcades around its edges. As a venu for the summer music and dance fes tival since the mid-1950s, the squar has become all but synonymous wit Santander in Europe's classical musi circles. Across the lively and com mercial Avenida de Calvo Sotelo is th **Cathedral B**, Santander's oldest build ing, a fortress-like, 14th-century Gothi structure seriously damaged in th 1941 fire and subsequently restored.

In the pretty area a short distanc north of the cathedral are the **Ayun tamiento C** (Town Hall), in front of th daily market; the nearby **Casa Muse de Menéndez Pelayo D**, where th Cantabrian literary critic and great est 19th-century Spanish schola Marcelino Menéndez Pelayo (1856 1912) lived and died (Mon–Fri 10.30am 1pm; and 5.30–8pm, Sat 10.30am–1pm free); and the **MAS Museo de Art Moderno y Contemporáneo E** (Con temporary Art Museum; www.museosar tandermas.es; Tue–Sat 10am–1.30pr and 5.30–9pm, Sun 11am–1.30pm free) a collection of Cantabrian, Span ish and international art.

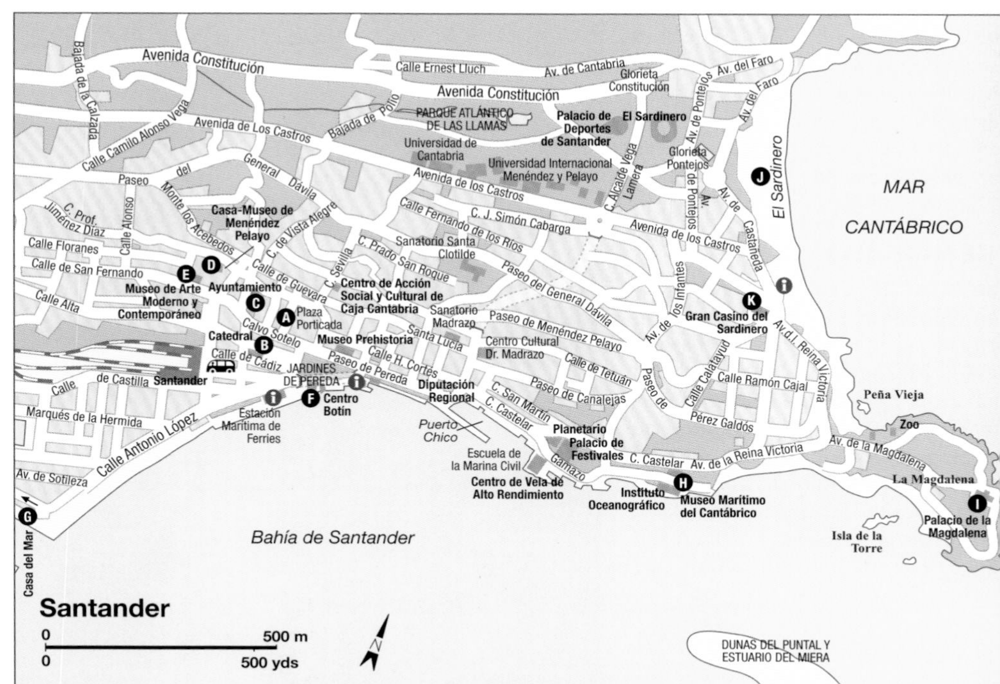

On the waterfront beside the Jardins de Pereda is a striking exhibition centre raised on pillars designed by Renzo Piano, the **Centro Botín** F (www.centrobotin.org; June–Sept 10am–9pm, Oct–May 10am–8pm).

Located east along the waterfront is the Puerto Pesquero (fishing port) and the **Casa del Mar** G, the local branch of the Spanish organisation which looks after the welfare of seamen. The fishing quarter around here is lively with taverns and restaurants specialising in seafood. Past the Puerto Chico yacht harbour is the **Museo Marítimo del Cantábrico** H, displaying model boats and flora and fauna of the deep (Tue–Sun May–Sept 10am–7.30pm, Oct–Apr 10am–6pm).

The seafront road finally reaches the Península de la Magdalena and the **Palacio de la Magdalena** I, or Palacio Real, an elaborate summer residence built for Alfonso XIII and his wife Victoria Eugenia in 1910. **El Sardinero** J, in the bay west of La Magdalena peninsula, is Santander's best beach, anchored by the luxurious **Gran Casino del Sardinero** K seated elegantly at the centre of the city's summer and touristic life; the casino dominates Plaza de Italia.

## AROUND SANTANDER

Just beyond El Sardinero is the **Cabo Mayor** lighthouse and to the west, near the villages of Cueto and Monte, are the wild beaches of **La Maruca** and **La Virgen del Mar**, which has a tiny island chapel. Beyond them is the vast beach at **Liencres**, the second longest in Cantabria, flanked by forest and rippled with dunes. From Liencres, follow the River Pas inland, leaving the wide Mogro estuary to the right, to **Puente Arce** 2, named after its Gothic bridge and known for the best gourmet dining in Cantabria.

From here, continue to **Escobedo**, in the Real Valle de Camargo, which has a hermitage, San Pantaleón, and to the nearby cave at El Pendo, which has prehistoric paintings and engravings. In **Muriedas** the elegant Villapuente Palace serves as the town hall and there is also a folk museum.

*The Gran Casino del Sardinero.*

**Fact**

There are nine sandy beaches in Santander. The largest, Segunda, is where most tourists go. Surfers head for La Primera. To escape the crowds, clamber over the rocks to Mataleñas.

The **Parque de la Naturaleza de Cabárceno** ❸ (http://parquedecabarceno.com; Mar–Oct 9.30am–5pm, Nov–Feb Mon–Fri 10am–5pm, Sat–Sun 10am–6pm), 15km (9 miles) southeast of Muriedas on the N-634, was once a mining area, but now it has been turned into a wildlife park where animals – both European and exotic species – live in relative freedom. There are two points of access to the park, from the north and south. Two cable cars connecting four stations will give you an impressive overview of the landscapes.

## SANTILLANA DEL MAR AND THE WESTERN COSTA DE CANTABRIA

This itinerary is the bread-and-butter of Cantabrian tourism. Its highlights include the lovely architectural treasury of Santillana del Mar, Spain's incomparable prehistoric cave paintings at Altamira, and the towns of Comillas and San Vicente de la Barquera. **Torrelavega** ❹, 21km (13 miles) southwest of Santander, makes a good starting point and has the modest attraction of having a town centre that retain some of its early identity, notably th Town Hall. Good beaches to head fo from here are at the summer resort o **Suances** – one of them, Los Locos, i a favourite for surfers. The fiesta hon ouring the town's patron, Saint Carmen held from 15 to 18 July, is celebrated with an especially colourful processio of decorated boats.

## SANTILLANA DEL MAR AND THE ALTAMIRA CAVES

From Suances, take the road throug the villages of Tagle and Ubiarca t **Santillana del Mar** ❺, which has th most important collection of histori buildings in Cantabria and one of th best in Spain. Two key streets lead ou of Plaza del Mercado (Market Square) one is Calle de Juan Infante; the othe is named consecutively Calle de l Carrera, Calle del Cantón and Call del Río. They are filled with medieval Renaissance and Baroque building and, despite their architectural diver sity, create an overall sense of exqui site harmony. The **Colegiata** churc

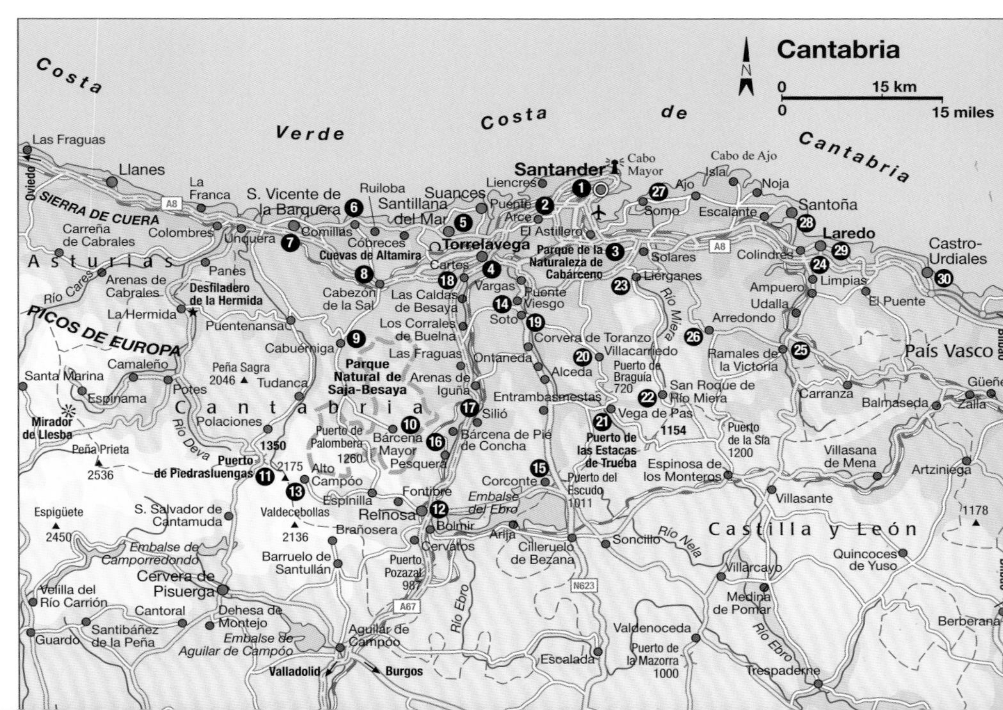

Tue–Sun 10am–1.30pm and 4–7.30pm) ; the best Romanesque structure in :antabria. The earliest capitals of the -iple-galleried cloister are carved with iblical scenes, the Gothic altarpiece as Renaissance paintings embel-ished with Mexican silver, and the outh door has notable sculptures.

Running a close second in merit nd included in the price of the ticket or the Colegiata are the **Museo Diocesano** in the Regina Coeli convent, he **Fundación Santillana** in the Don 3orja house in Plaza del Mercado and he **Museo de las Comarcas** (Counies' Museum) in the Águila and Parra iouses. Potters and other artisans ccupy the ground floors of many of hese buildings. Avoid visiting in high eason, especially Easter and August, vhen Santillana is too small for its own oower of attraction.

About 20 minutes' walk from Sanillana are some of the most famous orehistoric cave paintings in the world. They were discovered at Altamira in 1879, the first to be found in Europe, hough historians refused to recognise that Stone Age people could have painted them until the early 1900s following similar discoveries in France. Altamira has been dubbed the "Sistine Chapel of Stone Age Art". The Museo de Altamira (http://museodealtamira.mcu.es; Tue–Sat 9.30am–8pm, Sun 9.30am–3pm) includes a replica of the original cave, the Neocueva, as well as displays about prehistory and painting techniques. Every Friday morning, a group of 5 adults are chosen by lottery to visit the original cave: to have a chance, you must be there at 9.30am.

On the coast to the west is **Comillas** ❻ which is perhaps the most surprising town in northern Spain, filled as it is with Art Nouveau structures built by Spain's leading architectural exponents of the style, Catalan masters Lluís Domènech i Montaner (1850–1923) and Antoni Gaudí (1852–1926). Catalonia's ornate *Modernista* (Art Nouveau) architecture is unexpected in this part of Spain and this enclave, built by wealthy families as summer homes in the late 19th century, is especially remarkable. Gaudí's

**Fact**

The fabulous paintings at Altamira were first spotted by the nine-year-old daughter of the amateur archaeologist Marcelino de Santuola. He died in 1888, derided by fellow historians.

*Colegiata de Santa Juliana, Santillana del Mar.*

**Eat**

In San Vicente, try a dish of *sorropotún*, a hearty sailor's stew made of tuna, onions, potatoes, tomatoes, peppers, bread and oil.

**El Capricho** (www.elcaprichodegaudi.com; daily Jul–Sept 10.30am–9pm, Mar–June and Oct 10.30am–8pm, Nov–Feb 10.30am–5.30pm), built as a private house and now a museum, is the star attraction. Also worth seeing are Domènech i Montaner's Palacio Sobrellano and, just behind in the Art Nouveau cemetery, the huge figure of an angel by the Catalan sculptor Josep Llimona (1864–1934).

Continue along the coast road across the *ría* (fjord or estuary) of La Rabia, past the Playa de Oyambre area, an important ecological wetlands site for migratory birds, to **San Vicente de la Barquera** ❼, one of the oldest fishing ports on Cantabria's coast. Its importance as a Roman port and, before that, as port for the Orgenomescos, was eclipsed by its years of greater glory during the 13th to 15th centuries. Remains of the medieval walls still stand: the Puerta de Asturias, Puerta de Barreda, and Torre de Preboste. The church of Santa María de los Ángeles, begun in the 13th century, is the town's oldest structure. The Convento de San Francisco and the Ermita de la Virge de la Barquera, on the outskirts, ar other important sights.

The festival of La Folía, held on th first or second Sunday after Easter, i Cantabria's most well-known mari time procession. A colourful fleet c boats delivers a statue of the Virgin c la Barquera, the town's patron sain to the church where dances and song are performed before she is returne to her hermitage.

## THE CANTABRIAN HIGHLANDS

There is a multitude of itinerarie through the uplands of Cantabri within easy striking distance of San tander. The following five suggeste routes cover some of the Iberian Pen insula's most pristine and dramati highlands. It is also possible to add trip through Liébana and the Picos d Europa via Panes to Potes on the east ern side of the Picos (see page 211).

A tour of the **Cabuérniga** and **Nans valleys** can begin either from the bot tom at **Cabezón de la Sal** ❽, halfwa

*Estuary near San Vincente de la Barquera.*

etween Torrelavega and San Vicente e la Barquera, or from the top, coming from Potes at the edge of the Picos e Europa via the Piedrasluengas pass. abezón itself is an important treasury f ancestral heritage well worth sampling. At the Día de la Montaña (Mountain Day) fiesta on 10 August, oxen haul tones and mountain songs are sung. ollow the River Saja, a good trout tream, to **Cabuérniga** ❾ where you can ontinue up the Saja through the forests f the Parque Natural de Saja-Besayu, ome of mountain goat, deer, boar, mink, volf and brown bear (see page 123) to he picturesque mountain village of **Bárena Mayor** ❿, an unforgettable cluster f perfect stone mountain houses.

Alternatively, double back to Cabuéniga and drive up through "La Vueluca" (a sharp bend in the road) to the pectacular **Carmona pass**. The latter oute will give you the oppportunity of exploring the villages of the Nansa basin – **Puentenansa**, **San Sebastián de Garabandal**, **Tudanca** and **Polaciones** – and the **Puerto de Piedrasluengas** ⓫, high and well forested, at the southern edge of the Reserva Nacional del Saja.

## CAMPÓO AND VALDERREDIBLE

This itinerary features some of Cantabria's finest natural and man-made treasures. It centres around **Reinosa** ⓬, which has been important since the 13th century because of its strategic location 50km (30 miles) south of Torrelavega on the Santander–Castile trade route and at the end of the Embalse del Ebro, a reservoir. Its oldest buildings are around the main square. Just south of Reinosa on the Palencia road, a left turn leads to the villages of **Bolmir** and **Retortillo** which have Romanesque churches. Next to Retortillo is the site of the Roman city of **Julióbriga** which flourished from the 1st–3rd centuries and was built over a Cantabrian village. The best of the sparse remains here belong to the Llanuca house with original Roman porch pillars standing in place. Further along this road is a turn for the Monastery and Sanctuary of Montesclaros. Continuing down the River Ebro into the **Valderredible Valley** past Polientes are the pre-Romanesque churches or hermitages at **Arroyuelos** and **Cadarso**, carved into the rock in the 9th and 10th centuries. Near Arroyuelos is **San Martín de Elines**, which has a lovely 12th-century *colegiata*. On the way back through the Valderredible Valley, before joining the Santander-Palencia road, look for **Santa María de Valverde**, the best and largest cave-chapel of all.

West of Reinosa a there-and-back road goes past **Fontibre** and the source of the River Ebro (a brook that becomes Mediterranean Spain's most important river). to **Alto Campóo** ⓭, a ski resort with a complete range of facilities. Rising above it is the **Pico de Tres Mares** (Peak of Three Seas), so-named because the three rivers that begin life on its slopes (Nansa, Pisuerga and Hijas – tributary of the Ebro) flow, respectively, to the Bay of Biscay, the Atlantic and the Mediterranean.

*View from the Carmona Pass.*

**Fact**

Silió has a number of festivals, including las Marzas and the Feast of Maya Arbol. The most colourful is la Vijanera, a pre-Lent carnival, when locals blacken their faces, wear tall pointed hats, sheepskins, and large cow bells, and perform an ancient dance.

## FROM THE RIVER PAS TO THE BESAYA

This loop covers the heart of Cantabria and some of its least-known villages. The best place to start is at **Puente Viesgo** ⓮, 4km (2 miles) south of Torrelavega, famed for its baths, salmon fishing and paleolithic **Cueva del Castillo** cave paintings (June–Sept Tue–Sun 9.30am–3.30pm and 3.30–7.30pm, Oct–May Wed–Sun 9.30am–2.30pm) at Monte Castillo, thought to predate those at Altamira. Continue up the N-623 Burgos road through the Toranzo Valley to **San Vicente de Toranzo** and Agüero, which has a medieval castle-tower. **Alceda** has a set of impressive mansions and palaces. At **Entrambasmestas** you can head east up the River Pas or you can continue over the Puerto del Escudo pass to reach the small spa town of **Corconte** ⓯.

From Corconte, drive west beside the Ebro reservoir to Reinosa before starting down the N-611 (the main road not the motorway-dual-carriageway) through the Besaya Valley, which offers a rich trove of medieval architecture. It was along this route that Romanisatio spread from Julióbriga to the coas with focal points developing at *Portu Blendus* (Suances), *Aracillum* (Aradill and Comillas. Sections of Roman roa are still visible between **Pesquera** ⓰ and **Bárcena de Pie de Concha**. Thi was also the main route from Castil and southern Spain, as the Mozarabi details in the churches at Helguera an Moroso confirm. Romanesque architecture is found all through the valley.

The villages are just off the mai road on either side. **Silió** ⓱ is one o the best, known for its festivals an Romanesque church. **Las Fragua** has an unusual, 19th-century, Roman temple-like chapel, San Jorge. A turn off road to Arenas de Iguña leads t **Bostronizo**, from which a 3km (2-mile walk will take you to the 10th-centur Mozarabic hermitage of San Román.

Continue down the valley toward Torrelavega to find Riocorvo's church of Santa María de Yermo, one of Cantabria's great Romanesque treasures and the town of **Cartes** ⓲ which has a medieval *torreón*, a 15th-century turret-like, fortified townhouse.

*La Vijanera carnival parade.*

## FROM THE RIVER PAS TO THE MIERA

This circular route starts just south o Santander in the lower Pas river valley cuts over to the River Pisueña at Villacarriedo and the upper Pas valley before going over the Estacas de Trueba pass through the neighbouring province of Burgos and descending the valley of the River Miera to Solares.

Your first stop should be the town of **El Soto** ⓳ southeast of Puente Viesgo, notable for its 17th-century Franciscan convent. Then follow signs along the minor road through Villafufre to **Villacarriedo** ⓴ and its 18th-century Palacio de Soñanes, an early Churrigueresque structure considered one of the most important Baroque buildings in northern Spain. The town of **Selaya** just to the south has a number of impressive ouses, especially the austere Dondío palace, which is the most typical f Cantabrian design. After leaving the River Pisueña and crossing over the Puerto de Braguia bridge, you could top in the village of **Vega de Pas** ㉑, which has a perfect Cantabrian central square, to taste the *pasiego* specialities: cheeses and pastries typical of the Pas valley.

Next, cross the pass at **Estaca de Truebas** through the gorge at Las Machorras and turn north through another pass, the Portillo de Lunada, down to **San Roque de Ríomiera** ㉒. Continuing towards Liérganes, the **Salitre caves** have prehistoric cave paintings. The small hot-water spa of **Liérganes** ㉓ has a 17th-century artillery factory and is also notable for its Baroque civil structures, for its Gothic, Renaissance and Baroque religious architecture, and for its Renaissance bridge next to an abandoned mill. **La Cavada** is 4km (2 miles) east, and there is an unusual octagonal church at **Rucandio** nearby. **Solares** has medicinal baths fed by mineral waters.

## THE RIVER ASÓN AND THE SOBA VALLEY

The fifth and last suggested tour of the Cantabrian highlands is a short itinerary that follows the River Asón up from the port of **Colindres** 55km (34 miles) east of Santander through the important town of **Limpias** ㉔, which has impressive palaces, townhouses and hermitages and a sanctuary, Cristo de la Agonía.

**Ampuero**, 2km (1 mile) south, is a small town of traditional glass-balconied houses. It has a distinguished cuisine, with salmon and elvers a speciality, and on 8 and 9 September bulls run through the streets Pamplona-style. **Udalla** and the Baroque sanctuary of **La Aparecida** (Apparition of the Virgin), Cantabria's patron saint, is 6km (4 miles) west. **Ramales de la Victoria** ㉕, named after General Esperato's victory over the Carlists here in 1839, is also known for its paleolithic cave paintings at Haza, Cullalvera and Covalanas: ask at the tourist office for visiting details. The **Soba Valley** west of Ramales is dotted with 26 tiny villages which have lively *fiestas* and

*San Roque de Ríomiera.*

**Tip**

Most roads follow the river valleys. The best view of the coast is from onboard the luxurious Transcantábrico train, which runs from Bilbao to Ferrol in Galicia (see page 273).

*romerías*. Circle around the Sierra de Hornijo to **Arredondo** 26, known for its many *indianos* – emigrants to America who returned rich. Don't miss nearby **Socueva** where the 9th-century Mozarabic cave-hermitage of San Juan has a lovely horseshoe arch. From Arredondo, follow the trout-rich Asón back to Ramales and return to the coast.

## TRASMIERA AND THE EASTERN COAST

Cantabria's eastern coast, between Santander and Bilbao, is centred around the Santoña estuary and the small ports of Santoña, Laredo and Castro Urdiales.

Circle the Bahía (Bay) de Santander through Solares and Villaverde de Pontones to reach **Somo** 27, opposite Santander, where there is an immense beach and the adjacent Ría de Cubas. The beach at **Langre**, protected by the sheer cliff walls behind is just to the east. Further east, the **Alto de Ajo** is a high point, with good views between **Galizano** and **Ajo**, a tourist centre with beaches, hotels and architectural gems both in and around the town. Just 3km (2 miles) north is **Cabo de Ajo** (Cape Garlic), the Iberian Peninsula's northernmost point. Inland at **Bareyo** is the harmonious 12th-century Santa María de Bareyo church. **Noja** has two excellent beaches: Playa de Nueva Berria and Playa de Ris.

**Santoña** 28, at the mouth of the next bay, is on the edge of an important wildlife area (see page 120). This fishing and commercial port is also of historic importance, and is supposed by some historians to be the Roman *Portus Victoriae* cited in Pliny. Santoña has been the base for a significant whaling fleet and for expeditions to the New World and Europe, as well as a shipyard. Juan de la Cosa was born here in 1460: he accompanied Columbus on his second voyage and drew the earliest surviving map of the New World. Today Santoña is also a year-round tourist destination. The church of Nuestra Señora del Puerto is its most important architectural sight, along with the fortresses of San Carlos, La Terrecilla, San Martín and the Fort of Napoleon.

*Laredo.*

**Colindres** is the next large port, its ld section, *"él de arriba"* ("the one up op"), perched over the estuary of the són. The 16th-century church and the emains of the Torre del Condestable re its best buildings.

## APITAL OF THE COSTA VERDE

**aredo** 29, capital of Cantabria's Costa erde (Emerald Coast), has a long and lustrious history, a magnificent beach the 5km (3-mile) La Salvé – and a tiny ight-block network of symmetrical treets in its walled *Puebla Vieja*, or ld town. The section of town known s *Arrabal*, dating back to the 13th nd 14th centuries, has the Convent f San Francisco, the Espíritu Santo ermitage and houses emblazoned ith coats of arms. In the mid-15th entury, Laredo was one of Northern pain's most important seats of power nd was later one of the bases of the *a Invencible*", the doomed Armada. aredo today has much to offer: a uisine featuring a delicious *marmita* tew), spectacular whaleboat rowing egattas, University of Oviedo summer courses, and popular fiestas such as the Flower Battle on the last Friday in August or the San Antonio maritime *romería* (fair) on 13 June.

**Castro Urdiales** 30 is the last large port of Cantabria's eastern coast. It is not unlike Laredo; an ancient and distinguished port; well-preserved medieval quarter) and is the site of Cantabria's finest Gothic church, Santa María de la Asunción, an immense rose-coloured structure looming massively over the port and containing the Christian standard flown at the decisive battle of Las Navas de Tolosa against the Moors in 1212. The semi-ruin next door is a Templar castle converted to a lighthouse. The *Puebla Vieja*, also called the *Barrio de Arriba* (Upper Quarter), retains a dense network of narrow, medieval, cobbled streets. The newer Paseo Marítimo and the Paseo Menéndez Pelayo are lined with a variety of interesting buildings, from typical houses with glassed-in balconies to neo-Gothic and *Modernista* palaces. *Besugo* (sea bream) is the culinary speciality here, along with *caracoles* (snails).

**Fact**

Juan de la Cosa's map of the New World, drawn in 1500, measures 1 by 2 metres (3ft by 6ft) and was discovered in a shop in Paris in 1832. It is now in the Naval Museum, Madrid.

*The Canal de Trea, Picos de Europa National Park.*

# PICOS DE EUROPA

This compact and rugged mountain range is one of the peninsula's most popular hiking areas. It also shelters, at Covadonga, the birthplace of Christian Spain.

ituated at the heart of the Cordil-
ɜra Cantábrica, the limestone turrets
f the Picos de Europa rise head and
houlders above the rest of the range.
hree massifs, divided by precipitous
iver gorges, cover fewer than 500 sq
m (200 sq miles), and yet the terrain
; so rugged that some areas remained
ntrodden by man until the 1960s. The
ighest peaks adorn the central massif,
ulminating in the 2,648-metre (8,688ft)
ulk of Torre Cerredo, which vanquishes
earby Llambrión by a mere 6 metres
20ft). The best-known summit, how-
ver, is the Naranjo de Bulnes (2,519
ıetres/8,264ft), a thickset, sheer-sided
lock of limestone which resisted all
fforts at human subjugation until 1904.

Just inland from the Costa Verde, the
icos de Europa are shared between
sturias, Cantabria and Castilla y León.
he classic route around them passes
ırough the main towns of Cangas de
nís, Arenas de Cabrales and Potes,
om which the best sorties can be
ıade into the mountains. The heart of
ıe Picos de Europa is virtually a lunar
ndscape, strewn with frost-shattered
mestone rubble, studded with pot-
oles and pinnacles, the haunt of cham-
s, wallcreeper and snowfinch. Despite
eing snow-covered in winter and
rought-stricken in summer, crevices
the rocks provide a foothold for all
ıanner of alpine plants, many of which have disproportionately large flowers: Cantabrian bellflower, Asturian jonquil, purple saxifrage and alpine aster are among a number of them that flourish above 2,000 metres (6,600ft).

To the north of these high peaks lie the Asturian valleys of **Cangas de Onís**, **Cabrales** and **Peñamellera**. Poor weather originating in the Atlantic hits them head-on, so rainfall is high, and the vegetation green and luxuriant all year round. By contrast, the southernmost valleys of **Valdeón**, **Sajambre** (León) and **Liébana** (Cantabria) lie in

**Main attractions**

- Cangas de Onís
- Covadonga
- Garganta Divina
- Santa María de Lebeña
- Fuente De cable car

Map on page 212

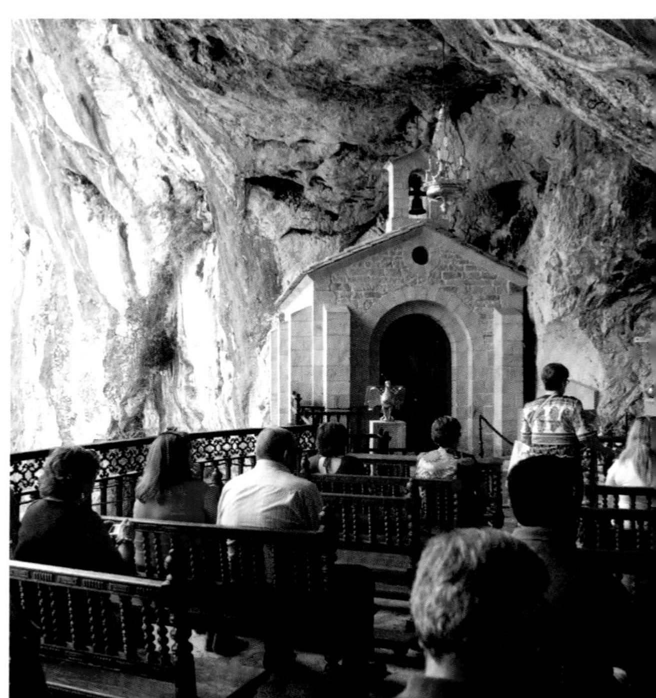

*The Holy Cave of Covadonga.*

the rainshadow, creating a habitat in which animals and plants more typical of Mediterranean Spain thrive.

## TRADITIONAL FARMING

These peripheral valleys still depend primarily on a centuries-old beef-rearing regime. Local breeds of cows – small, red *casinas* with pitchfork-like horns in Asturias, and wide-horned, grey-roan *tudancas* in Cantabria – spend the summer months grazing the high-level pastures known as *vegas* or *puertos*, thus freeing the valley meadows for the production of hay, later used to feed the livestock during the winter. The cattle descend to the valleys with the first snows, spending the winter ensconced in thick-walled barns in the villages. The accumulated manure is spread on the meadows early in the spring, maintaining grassland fertility. The only inputs to the system are energy from the sun and back-breaking human labour, and the "harvest" is a crop of young animals, sold for beef at the autumn *ferias* which take place all around the Picos. This is traditional, low-intensity farming, in which artificia fertilisers and pesticides are almos unknown, and mechanisation is rare.

## WHAT TO SEE AND WHEN TO VISIT

Almost 1,500 species of vascular plar have been recorded from the Picos d Europa, more than a third of whic are found in the superb hay meadow: Orchids, often considered to reflect th health of a natural ecosystem, occu here in abundance, with more than 4 species recorded, including such Euro pean rarities as red helleborine, ear spider and lizard orchids and summe lady's-tresses. Associated with thi botanical diversity are around 140 spe cies of butterfly, several of which ar found nowhere else in the world. Th hay meadows are at their best in ear summer when their sheer colour an diversity is beyond belief. The high level rock garden flora peaks durin July and August, but at this time c year most of the meadows have bee cut and you will also have to conten with large numbers of holidaymakers

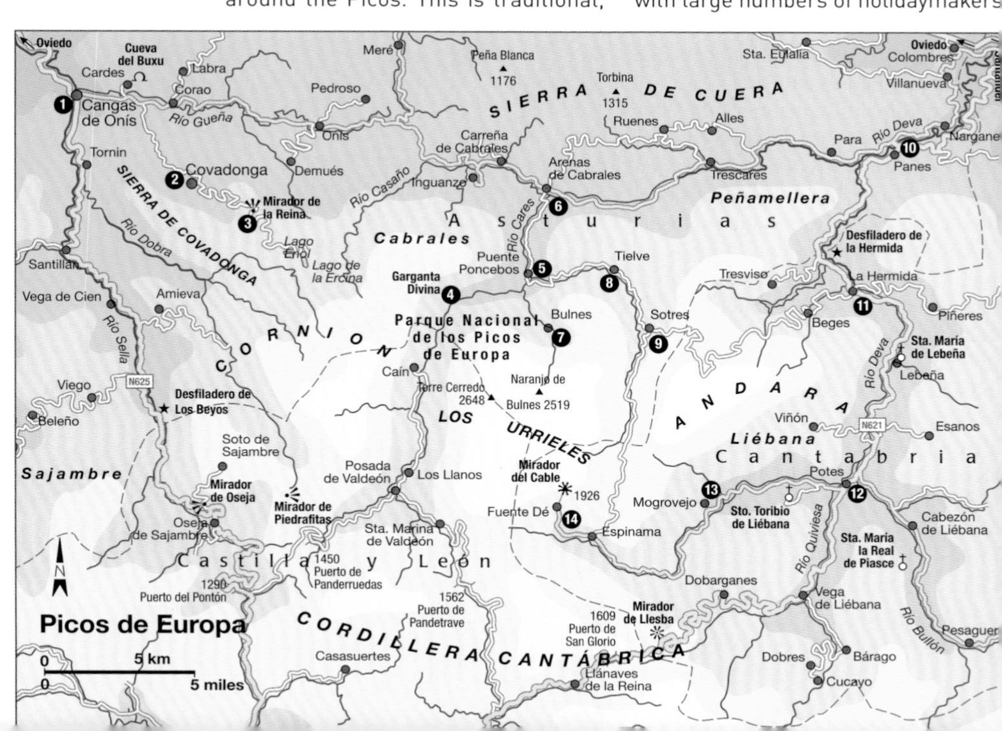

Although the total number of bird spe-ies found in the Picos is not high, the aptor populations are quite exceptional · around 500 griffon vultures inhabit nese mountains, including 170 breeding airs. Birds of prey are particularly com-non in the Liébana valley around Potes: ook out for short-toed eagles, hover-ng like giant kestrels; black-and-white gyptian vultures; light-phase booted agles; and griffon vultures like "flying arn doors". The remote montane beech nd oak forests are a national stronghold or capercaillie and black woodpecker.

The mammalian fauna is also remark-ble in that only two species have been ost from these mountains since the last ce Age: lynx and ibex became extinct t the end of the 19th century. Most nammals inhabit the forest areas, par-cularly such wary creatures as brown ears, grey wolves, pine and beech mar-ens and wildcats, but others, such as yrenean desmans (web-footed, shrew-ke creatures) and otters, thrive in the lear mountain streams and rivers.

However, most of the mammalian nhabitants of the Picos – more than 60 species – are notoriously difficult to find: you'll probably see little more than red squirrels, hares, foxes, roe deer, and some unidentifiable bats around a lamp-post at night. No fewer than 16 species of amphibian and 17 of reptile have also been recorded in the Picos, bringing the total number of vertebrates to more than 250.

## THE NATIONAL PARKS

In the light of this superlative species diversity, it is perhaps not surprising that the mountains of the Picos de Europa are protected by national park status. What is remarkable, however, is that this designation dates only from 1995. Prior to this, only the western massif was protected – as the Parque Nacional de la Montaña de Covadonga – more for historical and religious reasons than ecological ones. The full significance of the immense scenic and ecological value of the Covadonga National Park was not realised until the 1960s, and it is only since then that any real effort has been made to protect its wildlife.

**Fact**

The secret of Cabrales cheese's strong taste, called "picón", is the slow fermentation in local caves.

*Restaurant in Bulnes.*

In 1995, after many years of political shenanigans, the park was finally expanded to cover all three massifs and it is now known as the **Parque Nacional de los Picos de Europa**. Even so, this is a less than ideal situation, as the land within its borders lies mostly above 1,000 metres (3,300ft), thus abandoning much of the mosaic of mixed broadleaved woodlands and species-rich hay meadows to the vagaries of the "buffer-zone" protection measures.

The way into the park from the northwest arrives at **Cangas de Onís** ❶, which is the best place to start if searching for architectural merit. Here you will find the 15th-century Ermita de la Santa Cruz (Holy Cross Chapel), built over a dolmen which remains in the crypt, as well as the probably misnamed Puente Romano (Roman Bridge) that spans the River Sella at the western edge of town; this bridge almost certainly dates from medieval times, although this makes it no less aesthetically pleasing. The powerful Cabrales cheese is a star of the Sunday market here. In the area to the south of Cangas de Onís, *hórreos* – wooden granaries built on rat-proo "mushrooms" – are a common sight Used to store maize, potatoes and othe foodstuffs, it is common to see beans an peppers hanging under the eaves to dr in autumn. Vernacular architecture centres on the intrinsic beauty of the pantiled roofs and the use of local stone, wit many of the larger houses in the regio displaying hand-carved coats of arms.

At **El Buxu**, east of Cangas, a cave containing a small number of Palaeolithic cave paintings can be visite (closed Mon).

From Cangas proceed east 4km (2 miles) on the AS-114 then turn south onto the AS-262 for **Covadonga** ❷, the centre of the former national park and considered the birthplace of moder Spain. This is the site of the battle in AD 718 (some say AD 722), when the Visigothic prince, Pelayo, and his small army faced up to the Moors who had already conquered all the lands to the south, virtually unhampered by Christian forces (see page 35). Although Pelayo was vastly outnumbered and backed into a corner, the Virgin Mary

*Basilica de Covadonga.*

nterceded, causing an avalanche that rushed invaders who were Muslim. The cave where Pelayo fought (now a shrine containing his tomb) and the huge 19th-century basilica next to it have jointly taken on the status of a mini Lourdes, complete with souvenir stands selling religious paraphernalia. Beyond Covadonga, the road runs past the **Mirador de la Reina** ❸, with views out over the Atlantic, before reaching the glacial lakes of **Enol** and **Ercina**. A two-hour circuit of these lakes is one of the classic walks of the Picos de Europa. A bus runs up from Cangas in summer.

## CLASSIC VALLEY WALKS

Walking in the valleys is a delightful experience. You are at liberty to use the extensive network of tracks that give farmers access to the woodlands and hay meadows, so long as you don't jump fences or trample the grasslands themselves, which here have the status of croplands.

Another classic walk is through the depths of the 12km (8-mile) -long Cares Gorge, known as the **Garganta Divina** ❹ (the Divine Gorge), starting from **Puente Poncebos** ❺ south of **Arenas de Cabrales** ❻ (a bus runs between the two in summer) and taking five or six hours there and back.

Another good option is to follow the vertiginous trail from Puente Poncebos up the Arroyo del Tejo valley to the village of **Bulnes** ❼, the most remote village in the Picos. There is no road access to Bulnes but there is a funicular railway (every 30 minutes, 10am–8pm) from Puente Poncebos which is expensive but takes you effortlessly up 400 metres (1,300ft) of height in seven minutes. There are bars here, however, for those who make the two-hour hike, and a hostal for those who want to stay over. The traditional mountain villages of **Tielve** ❽ and **Sotres** ❾ will leave indelible memories before you descend to **Arenas de Cabrales**, where there is an important 12th-century church (Santa María de Llas) and where Spain's most pungent and potent blue cheese is concocted.

## THE LIÉBANA VALLEY

Continuing along the northern perimeter of the Picos will bring you to **Panes** ❿. Turn south here and take the N-621 through the impressive, snaking gorge of **La Hermida** ⓫. It was gouged out by the River Deva, an excellent trout and salmon stream, and is so narrow and steep that its sides are largely devoid of vegetation, while the hamlet of La Hermida within it is sunless in winter.

Most of the village churches in the Picos are Romanesque or a little later, but one of the most outstanding is the Pre-Romanesque church of **Santa María de Lebeña**, a few kilometres south of La Hermida. Built in the 10th century, its main attraction is the 2,000-year-old Celtic altar-stone, only discovered in 1973, although the Mozarabic horseshoe arches and campanile also have much to recommend them. Beyond, lies the valley of **Liébana** – a world of its own with its particular customs, cuisine, crafts and architecture.

*Bridge spanning the Cares Gorge.*

**Tip**

In the high mountains, trails are few and the terrain is inhospitable, so you must invest in a large-scale map. The Miguel Andrados series of 1:25,000 is the most accurate.

**Potes** ⓬ is the capital and pivotal point for the four valleys of this mountain domain. Its *casco viejo* (old town) has traditional *casas señoriales* (stately homes), five ancient bridges, a 14th-century church (San Vicente) and the 15th-century Torre del Infantado, now the Town Hall.

There is an interesting excursion 8km (5 miles) east on the C-627 from Potes to Santa María la Real de Piasca, the hauntingly lovely church of a former monastery described as a "*comunidad dúplice*", meaning that both monks and nuns lived there. The main door of the church is of particular interest. Look for the capital known as "*el beso de piedra*" (the stone kiss), portraying, in clear reference to Piasca's dual nature, a man and a woman kissing.

Just west of Potes is the monastery of **Santo Toribio**, which was founded by the Cluniac order in the 8th century. Its church harbours an ornate crucifix, ostensibly fabricated from the whole left arm of Christ's cross. At the end of the road is the Romanesque chapel of San Miguel, from which there is a fine view of the eastern massif of the Picos.

## THE CABLE-CAR ROUTE TO THE TOP

West of Potes the 23km (15-mile) route continues climbing along the Deva river valley, passing a number of ancient rustic villages where cheeses are made and life continues at a slow pace: any one of them is worth a visit. There is a fine medieval tower at **Mogrovejo** ⓭. The road eventually opens out into a spectacular limestone amphitheatre at **Fuente Dé** ⓮, which marks the source of the Deva. Here is a modern parador and the base station for a cable car to place you atop the central massif of the Picos de Europa.

This is undoubtedly the best way of reaching these dizzy heights, saving you 800 metres (2,625ft) of ascent in about three minutes. Once up here you can plan hikes using the facilities of the mountain *refugios*, ranging from the four-man Cabaña Verónica to the 46-bed, luxury Refugio de Aliva, with bar and restaurant attached. In the high mountains, however, trails are fewer and the intervening terrain is rough and inhospitable, making it advisable to invest in a large-scale map of the area.

*Exploring the old town of Potes.*

*Fuente Dé cable car.*

Decanting cider at Llanes.

# ASTURIAS

Around the Asturian capital of Oviedo are fine pre-Romanesque churches. Inland are miners' valleys and remote villages. The east is known for its cider and its caves.

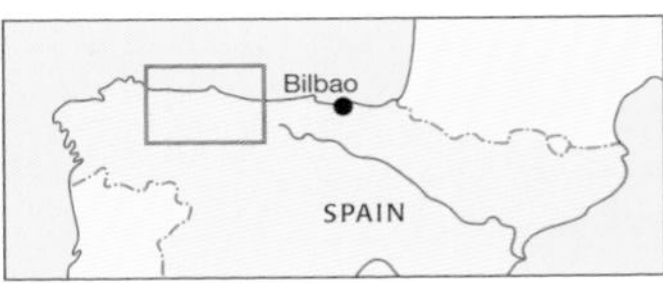


.ush and green, Asturias is an Atlantic asis, a 10,000-sq-km (3,900-sq-mile) tate of mind as well as a principality. 'he Spanish expression *estar en Babia*, to be in Babia", means daydreaming, nd it refers to a mountainous region alled Babia in León in particular nd, by extension, to the mountainous regions of Asturias and León. It vas used to describe the tendency for he monarchs of Spain's Golden Age o become lost in pastoral and sylvan reams while attempting to perform official duties in Madrid. Even today, for nany of the inhabitants of arid Iberia, Asturias remains a verdant northern everie of wilderness and flowing water.

## WHERE THE RECONQUEST BEGAN

Asturias is an Autonomous Community officially known as the Principado de Asturias, and has been a principality since 1388 when Juan I gave his first-born son, Enrique, the title Príncipe de Asturias, which has been the traditional title for the Crown Prince of Spain ever since. It owes its name to the Astures, Iberian people that fought fiercely against invaders. Conquered by the Romans, however, in the 2nd century BC and the Visigoths in the 5th century AD, Asturias became a sanctuary for Christian nobles fleeing the Moorish invasion of AD 711.

Eleven years later the Christian reconquest of the Iberian Peninsula began in Asturias at Covadonga, where King Pelayo organised the first successful resistance to the Moorish advance. It is in fact widely suspected that it may have been Pelayo's stubborn devotion to his favourite hunting grounds, rather than any burning religious fervour, that provided the spark that started the 670-year struggle of *Reconquista*.

Towering heights in the Picos de Europa, rushing rivers, pine and beech forests, apple orchards and apple cider,

**Main attractions**

Oviedo
San Julián de los Prados
Santa Maria del Naranco and San Miguel de Lillo
Santa Cristina de Lena
Parque Natural de Somiedo
Costa Verde
Museo de la Minería
Tito Bustillo Cave

Map on page 220

The fishing port of Luarca.

**Fact**

The cathedral treasures from Toledo include fragments of the True Cross, drops of the Redeemer's blood, scraps of His clothes and crumbs from the Last Supper.

elevated granaries called *hórreos*, haunting pre-Romanesque churches, wild salmon, wild wolves and bears and colourful fishing ports are the characteristic elements of this northern kingdom.

Mining has been the main industrial activity of Asturias, though dairy farming, shipping and fishing are also significant. The Romans were the first to discover rich deposits of coal in the region and exploited them vigorously.

Iron, zinc, lead and manganese have also been found in these green hills, and steel mills and metallurgical industries have been important since the late 19th century. Though many of the mines have closed down, a number of rivers, notably the once salmon-rich Nalón, are still recovering from the environmental effects of industrial exploitation.

## THE CAPITAL OF ASTURIAS

Nearly equidistant from the borders of the neighbouring communities of Cantabria to the east and Galicia to the west, **Oviedo 1** today is a busy industrial and university town of some 220,000 inhabitants, and is known for the manufacture of firearms, gunpow der, textiles and for its service indus tries. In recent history, it bore the brur of the repression of the Asturian mir ers' strike in 1934, and it suffered bad during the subsequent Civil War.

Oviedo's beginnings can be trace back with precision to a monaste founded by a Benedictine monk in c about the year 761 on a hill known a *Ovetum* (from the Latin word for eg *ovum*). The fourth Asturian king, Fruel I, built a palace and a church nearb to form the nucleus of the future cit Oviedo flourished in the 8th and 9t centuries after Alfonso II (792–842 called "The Chaste" for his celibac moved the capital of the Asturia kingdom there in 792, but the city importance faded when the capital wa moved to León in the 10th century. Th University of Oviedo was founded 1604; a lively student life still remair an important part of Oviedo's make-u

To explore Oviedo, it is best to sta at the **Catedral de San Salvador**, ar then walk through the old parts of tow around the Plaza Alfonso II and Pla

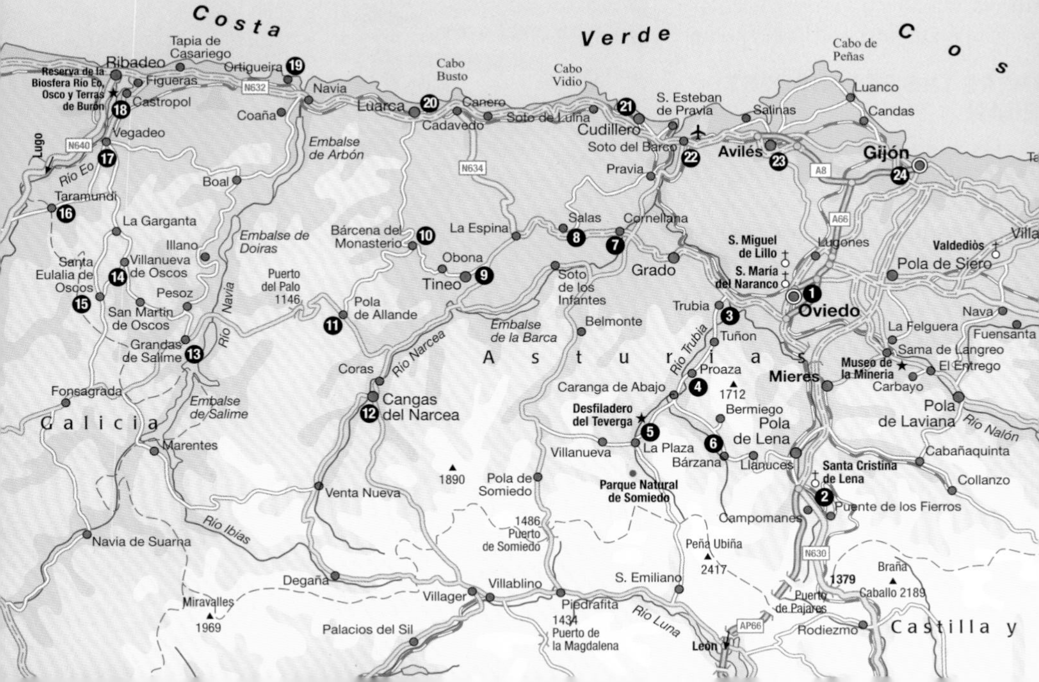

ayor before moving out to the Asturian re-Romanesque churches near the ity's periphery. Built around Oviedo's nost prized treasure, the Cámara Santa Holy Chamber), the flamboyant Gothic athedral started with a 14th-century loister and finished in the 16th cen-ury with the completion of the south-rn tower and arcaded porches. The ntensely decorated, 17th-century side hapel dedicated to Saint Eulalia, with shrine containing the saint's relics, is ne of the cathedral's main sights. The ther is the lateral Chapel of Alfonso , the Chaste, placed on the site of the riginal church. Alfonso constructed he **Cámara Santa** for the safekeeping f the gems and icons rescued from the Christian capital of Toledo after it fell o the Moors. It contains some of the nost remarkable treasures in Spain, rincipally the **Cross of the Angels** and he **Victory Cross**. The former, made of edar covered with gold-leaf and stud-ded with pearls and gemstones, was esigned by order of Alfonso the Chaste n 808. It warns "May anyone who dares emove me from the spot where I have been willingly given be struck down by a divine lightning bolt". The Victory Cross, dating from 908, was carried by King Pelayo at his victory at Covadonga in 722.

Other points of interest in the cathedral are the sculpted capitals in the cloister and the lacy detail of the cloister windows. As you leave the cathedral's main entrance, turn to the right and look for the chancel window of the 9th-century San Tirso church, on the corner of Calle Santa Ana, which is all that remains of the original structure built by Alfonso II. Take a walk along the side of the cathedral into the **Corrada del Obispo**, one of Oviedo's most atmospheric spots.

Around the Plaza de la Catedral, also known as Plaza Alfonso II, are historic buildings and palaces. Directly across the square is the **Casa de la Rúa** (Rua Palace), an austere, 15th-century structure. On the corner opposite is the 18th-century **Palacio Camposagrado**, while across from the **Plaza del Porlier** is the 16th-century **Palacio Toreno**, now a library. On the corner of Calle Ramón y Cajal is the ancient

**Fact**

The miner's strike in October 1934 resulted in a great deal of damage and loss of life. Oviedo university was destroyed and the strikers brutally put down by General López Ochoa.

Church of San Isidoro, Oviedo.

**Fact**

Mines in Asturias are named after saints. The mine at El Entrego, site of the Museo de la Minería, is named after San Vicente.

17th-century **university** building with a plain façade and symmetrical courtyard. The **Plaza Mayor**, with the Town Hall and church of San Isidro, is just a few steps up Calle del Peso. Nearby is the **Plaza del Fontán** where there is a produce market, always a good opportunity to take the true pulse of the city, and, just beyond, the Palace of the Marquis of San Feliz. Working your way back towards the cathedral, with the Plaza Mayor on your left, you will come to the elegant **Museo de Bellas Artes** (Fine Arts Museum; www.museobbaa.com; Tue–Sat 10.30am–2pm and 4–8pm, Sun 10.30–2.30pm) in the 18th-century **Palacio Velarde** at Calle Santa Ana 1. The wooden-balustraded interior rooms and the collection of Asturian and Spanish paintings spanning the 16th to 20th centuries make a worthwhile visit. Finally, behind the cathedral are the **Museo Arqueológico de Asturias** (Tue–Fri 9.30am–8pm, Sat 9.30am–2pm, Sun 9.30am–3pm) in the 15th-century San Vicente monastery and the nearby **Monasterio de San Pelayo** (17th–18th century).

*Restaurant on Plaza del Fontán, Oviedo.*

## AROUND OVIEDO: EARLY CHURCHES AND MINING MEMENTOS

The most important sights of all in Oviedo are its three millenary pre-Romanesque churches, constructed in the 9th century, some 200 years before Romanesque architecture appeared, which have a rustic elegance and simplicity, and a sturdy power bordering on the primitive. Developed in areas unconquered by the Moors and uninfluenced by Charlemagne's Frankish empire to the north, "Asturian art" is mysterious, original, surprising and curiously moving. **San Julián de los Prados** (Mon–Sat May–Sept 10am–12.30pm and 4–6pm, Oct–Apr 10am–noon), also known as Santullano, in the Plaza Santullano northeast of the cathedral is the most spacious of these churches, being 30 metres (98ft) long by 25 metres (82ft) wide. Typical elements include the porch, the three naves, the immense transept, and the three vaulted brick chapels in the apse. The San Julián frescoes are considered the best in Asturian art, remarkably lifelike and only discovered a few decades ago.

**Santa María del Naranco** and **San Miguel de Lillo** (both churches Apr–Sept Tue–Sat 9.30am–1pm and 3.30–7pm, Sun 9.30am–1pm, Oct–Mar Tue–Sat 10am–2.30pm, Sun 10am–12.30pm) stand 4km (2 miles) northwest of the city on Monte Naranco. Santa María del Naranco is the most emblematic example of Asturian architecture. Originally designed by the architect of King Ramiro I as a royal residence with living quarters on the ground floor and a banqueting hall on the upper floor, it is both light and elegant. From the loggias of the upper floor there are views over Oviedo and of the distant Picos de Europa. San Miguel de Lillo, 300 metres/yds uphill and also built by Ramiro I, partly collapsed in an earthquake in the 13th century. The height of the walls is accentuated by the narrow naves separated by pillars. The culptural decoration has circus scenes ith acrobats and animal tamers.

There is another pre-Romanesque hurch worth seeking out on a hilltop Pola de Lena, 40km (25 miles) south f Oviedo on the A-66 motorway. **Santa ristina de Lena** ❷ (Tue–Sun 11am–pm and 4.30–6.30pm) is the third 9th-entury church built by the architect of amiro I. Known as "the church of the orners" because of its numerous right ngles, it has a rectangular nave with our facades, one for each protuberant section. For a sense of the magic nd mystery of Asturian art, try to be here in the late afternoon when the un slants into the intricately arched nd vaulted apse and *iconostasio* (icon oom) through the tiny latticed windows of the west facade.

## ARQUE NATURAL DE SOMIEDO AND SURROUNDING VILLAGES

ying southwest of Oviedo, Somiedo is ne of the Principality's great natural ssets – a remote region of sharply olded mountains with fertile intervenng valleys that were well inhabited in antiquity. The most picturesque approach is to take the main road west from Oviedo and turn left onto the AS-228 towards **Trubia** ❸. Before turning, however, you may want to stop off at the church of San Juan, constructed during the 11th–13th centuries, and the pre-Romanesque San Pedro de Nora, which dates from the first half of the 9th century.

From Trubia continue along the AS-228 through Tuñón, which has a pre-Romanesque church, **San Adriano**, towards **Teverga**. This village is part of a *consejo*, a community which consists of a series of villages in the remote upland valley drained by the River Teverga. **Proaza** ❹, in a neighbouring *consejo*, has a unique circular tower built between the 13th and 14th centuries.

The **"Peñas Xuntas"**, grey limestone cliffs carved out by the River Trubia, mark out the next village, Caranga. **La Plaza** ❺, 10km (6 miles) south, has a 12th-century church, San Pedro, while to the west is the village of **Villanueva** with another Romanesque church, Santa María, notable for its Baroque

**Quote**

"Pelayo's commanders, who hurled rocks down upon Moorish heads and trapped armies in ravines, were the ancestors of those Asturian miners who achieved sinister glamour in the Civil War by their fearlessness and their casual familiarity with explosives."

H.V Morton

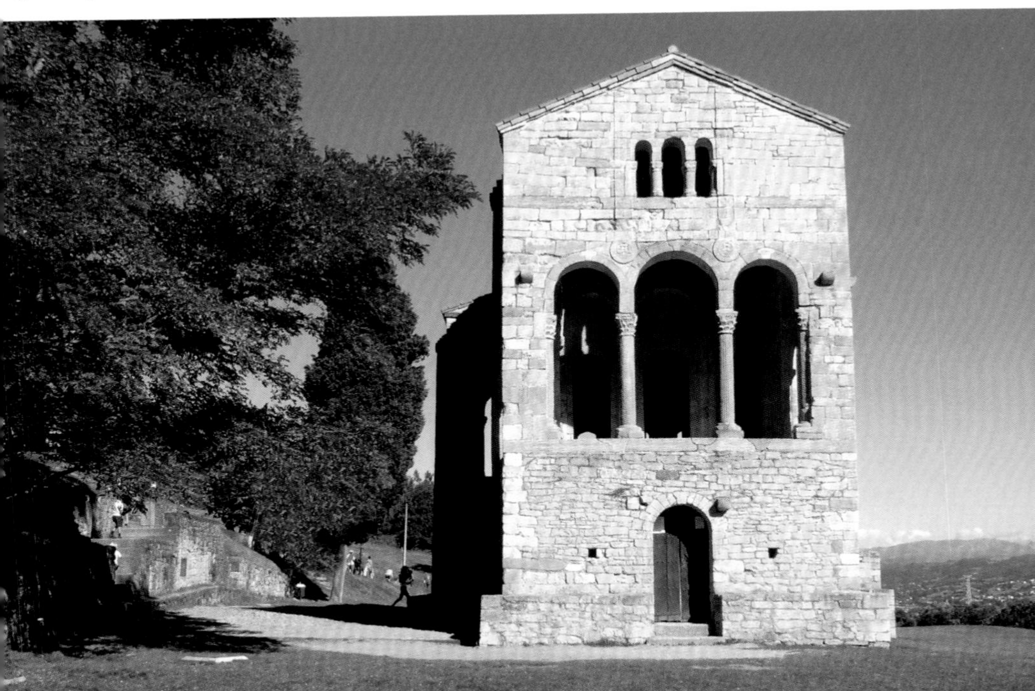

*Santa María del Naranco.*

ornamentation and exceptional capitals and pillar bases.

If you prefer to move about here under your own steam, the route of the old coal-mining railway between Tuñón and Ricabo has been adapted for walkers and cyclists at **La Senda del Oso** (the Path of the Bear). The route is 30km (18 miles) long.

Beyond Villanueva, the road continues into the **Parque Natural de Somiedo** (http://parquenaturalsomiedo.com) covering five valleys which are home to furtive wolves and an estimated population of around 200 European brown bears (see page 123). More than a dozen glacial tarns, ponds and lakes and innumerable *teitos* – thatched huts that provide shepherds with shelter – dot the landscape. There is a park information office at Polares de Somiedo. Twelve marked routes taking from 2 to 8 hours allow you to explore the reserve. You're very unlikely to spot a bear on your own (and its illegal – and dangerous – to disturb them anyway), but by joining an organised wildlife hike with a qualified guide you stand a better than averag chance of seeing a bear.

Return to Caranga and turn righ onto the AS-229 up the **Quirós** valle for **Bárzana** ❻, capital town of the *con sejo*. On the way to Bárzana the roa passes Las Agüeras reservoir and th **San Pedro de Arrojo** church, wher serpent decorations recur in its capi tals and corbels. The Sierra del Aram looms to the north.

Between the two, a side road twist up to **Bermiego**, a real gem of a village A kilometre (half a mile) beyond the vil lage cemetery is a famous yew tree, 6. metres (21ft 8in) round with a 15-metr (49ft) canopy, called "Tenxu l'Iglesia (church yew). Yews were sacred to th early Astures who used them as meet ing places, a function taken up by th church. As a result, as in this case remarkable yews usually stand next t country churches. The road to this yew i rough, so it is best reached on foot – it i easy to walk and the views are stunning

Back on the AS-229, the next tow beyond Bárzana is **Llanuces**. Not far fron it, in a mountain meadow called *pra*

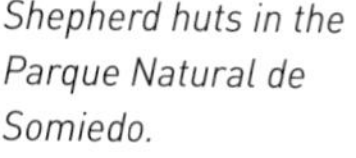

*Shepherd huts in the Parque Natural de Somiedo.*

*agüezos* on the border between the *con-*
*·jos* of Quirós and Lena, there is, near the
ıd of June, a Lamb Festival where spit-
·asted lamb is enjoyed by all-comers.

You can return to Oviedo either by ·ossing the mountain pass between ·anuces and Pola de Lena for a quick )-minute drive back on the A-66 ıotorway, or by retracing your route ack through Caranga and Trubia.

## VESTERN ASTURIAS

**ornellana** ❼, a salmon angler's aven on the River Narcea, 37km (23 ıiles) west of Oviedo on the N-634, is lso home of the 17th-century Monas-erio de San Salvador, which has a two-ered cloister from the 18th century.

**Salas** ❽, 10km (6 miles) further vest, has a memorable old quarter vith a 14th-century tower and a 16th-entury church, Santa María. The Val-és Salas castle, former residence of he Marquis of Valdés Salas, a leader f the Inquisition, is now a hotel and estaurant. From the **Espinas** Pass, vhich has a superlative 360-degree ·iew, descend south to **Tineo** ❾ on the AS-216. Tineo is known for its ham industry and for the 14th-century García-Tineo and 16th-century Meras palaces. The church of San Pedro, once part of a Franciscan Monastery, has a Romanesque porch and doors.

From Tineo, take the minor road to the 12th-century monastery of **Obona** and continue on to **Bárcena** ❿ where there is a 10th-century monastery, San Miguel, and the church of San Pedro. Cross the Alto de Lavadoira Pass to **Pola de Allande** ⓫ to see the Cienfuegos Peñalba family palace and the parish church.

You can make a detour here to **Cangas de Narcea** ⓬ a town which has produced both coal and wine in its time, to see the Monasterio San Juan Bautista de Corias which has been described as "the Escorial of Asturias". It is now a parador hotel but it can be visited on a guided tour (Tue–Fri and Sun 11am, Sat 11am and 6pm).

Continue 45km (28 miles) over the spectacular Puerto de Pola Pass to **Grandas de Salime** ⓭ where there is an excellent ethnographical museum

*Bermiego's famous "Teixu l'Ilesia" (church yew).*

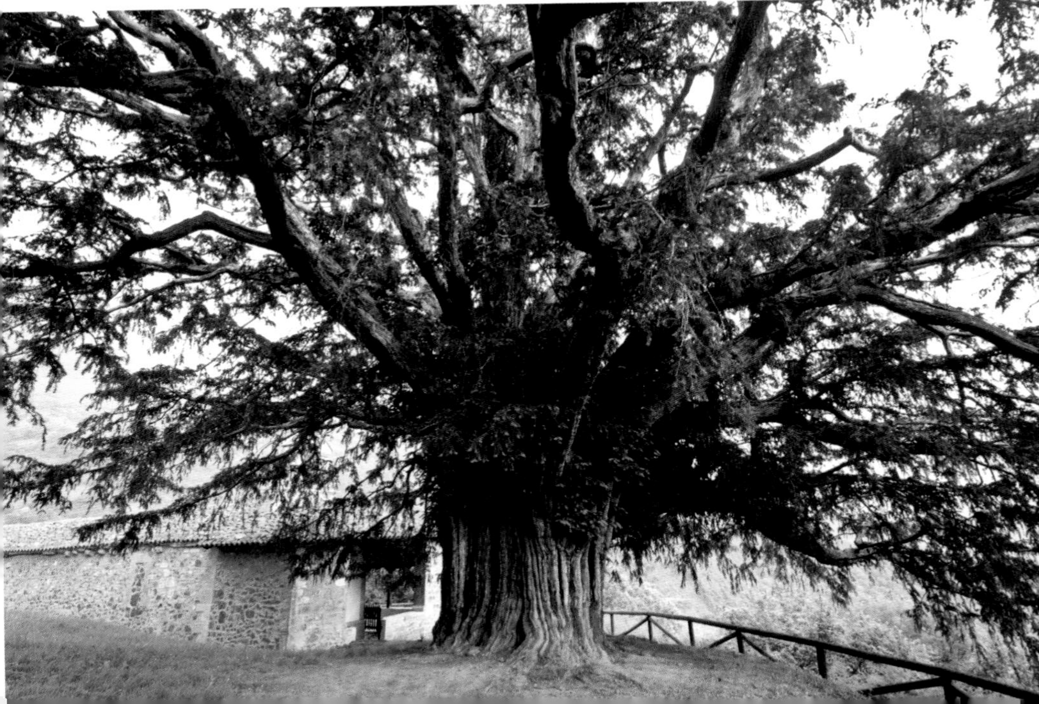

**Fact**

Asturian trees are part of the region's mythology, and some are designated national monuments. The Carbayu (Oak Tree) at Valentín, 15km (9 miles) from Tineo, has a girth of 9.5 metres (31ft) and dates from before the European discovery of America.

(Tue–Sat 11am–2pm and 4–6.30pm, Sun 11am–3pm). Next, on the AS-13, drive into the Los Oscos region to **San Martín de Oscos** to find the 18th-century Palacio de Mon and the Palacio de Guzmán de Vegadeo.

From San Martín, drive west to **Villanueva de Oscos** ⓮ where there is a lovely and rare (for Asturias) Cistercian monastery with a Romanesque church. South of it in **Santa Eulalia de Oscos** ⓯ (Santalla in Asturian) it is worth taking a look at the 18th-century Aquel Cabo house.

**Taramundi** ⓰, 11km (7 miles) west of the junction of the AS-11 and the AS-26, is an important nucleus for tourism because of its long tradition in iron forging. The Romans first mined iron ore here in the 3rd and 4th centuries. The town has a dozen forges and is famous for pocket-knives with elaborately carved boxwood handles. The "mazo de Aguillón" (Aguillón ironworks) is located in a *castro*, the remains of a prehistoric Celtic village.

**Teixois**, 5km (3 miles) south of Taramundi, is another village with a similar *castro* and ironworks, as well as a mi a tool grinder and a display of hydraul devices. "La Rectoral" (The Vicarag in Taramundi was the first rural tou ism centre in Asturias. This hotel an "Action Tourism" centre organises fo est excursions, hiking routes, eques trian outings and other activities, a well as helping to find places to stay.

**Vegadeo** ⓱ is 20km (12 miles) nort of Taramundi through La Garganta Pas on the AS-21. Another approach t Vegadeo (the *vega* is the valley or wate meadow of the Eo) is to head north west through back roads to San Tirs de Abres and El Llano to the N-640 tha descends along the Eo River.

## THE WESTERN COSTA VERDE

The Costa Verde (Green Coast) has n problem living up to its name: verdan meadows grow lushly down to the edge of the Atlantic. From the west the N-634 (now mostly replaced by the A dual carriageway) runs right along i towards the main towns of Avilés and Gijón, a scenic route between sand beaches, rocky cliffs and colourfu

*View of Cudillero's main square and harbour.*

fishing villages, and steep hills, pine forests and grassy farmland.

The *Ría* (estuary) of the Eo, the river forming Asturias's western boundary, is the main marshland ecosystem in Asturias for migrating European waterfowl and forms a central part of the **Reserva de la Biosfera Río Eo, Oscos y Tierras de Burón**, shared between Asturias and Galicia.

The town of **Castropol** ⑱, with narrow and colourful streets overlooking the estuary, has views of Ribadeo in neighbouring Galicia. Castropol is on a promontory in the estuary, highlighted by its 15th-century Nuestra Señora del Campo church and the Montenegro, Valledor and El Pardo palaces. **Figueras**, the next town seawards on the estuary, is a port and boat-building centre. **Tapia de Casariego** on the coast proper is known for its beach and its lively restaurants.

Continuing east towards Navia, a right turn up the AS-12 leads to the Celtic **Castro de Coaña** (Apr–Sept Wed–Sun 10.30am–5.30pm, Oct–Mar 10.30am–3.30pm), an excavated Iron Age settlement dating from the 4th century BC. The site is organised into zones and many of the house were circular.

A left turn at the same intersection leads to the picturesque fishing village of **Ortigueira** ⑲ tucked into a rocky inlet. **Navia** itself, on the eastern bank of the Navia river estuary, is a busy fishing port. The nearby Playa de Frexulfe is a well-known, 700-metre/yd strand of dunes. **Puerto de Vega**, another irresistible port, can be reached by back roads from Navia.

## FISHING FESTIVALS

At the mouth of the River Negro lies the fishing port of **Luarca** ⑳, a slate-roofed cluster of houses dubbed the *Villa Blanca* (white town) because of its white facades. Luarca is a lively, festive village and a good stop-over point. The Marqués de Ferrera palace, with elements dating from the 14th century, is Luarca's most significant building. The Easter Week celebrations and the boat processions on Assumption Day (15 August) are two key events. **Cabo Busto** and **Canero** are the next destinations before passing through **Cadavedo**. At the annual *romería* (open-air fiesta) of La Regalina on the last Sunday in August, dancers in elaborate local costumes perform to bagpipe music. Cabo Vidio is a promontory with panoramic views west to Cabo Busto and east to Cabo Peñas. **Cudillero** ㉑ is the next attraction, an extraordinary Asturian fishing village, with houses hanging from steep rock walls over the ramp leading down to the harbour. Restaurants line either side of this dramatic cut and call for a round of fresh sardines and cider.

From Cudillero, a detour inland provides a brief parenthesis in this coastal tour to see the oldest Asturian Pre-Romanesque church, located 3km (2 miles) from Pravia. **San Juan de Santianes de Pravia**, also known as San Juan Evangelista, was built by order of Silo, sixth king of the Asturian monarchy (774–83), after the court moved from Cangas de Onis to Pravia, and a fragment of stone with the inscription *Silo*

*Locals' daily camino, Cudillero.*

**Drink**

Check out the *sidrerías* (cider bars) in Asturias, and watch the way the drink is poured to make it fizzy. If it's flat, Asturians won't drink it (see page 72).

*Princeps Fecit* (Silo constructed it) was recovered during 20th-century excavations. A copy of it is in the church.

In Pravia itself, significant buildings include the collegiate church, the Moutas palace and the Town Hall, all elegant and aristocratic 18th-century structures around a single square next to the 16th-century Casa del Busto, one of the excellent series of *Casonas Asturianas*, or Asturian Palaces offering dining and lodging. The Plaza de la Victoria (with glassed-in porches over the square), Calle Nueva, Calle de la Victoria, Calle de las Huertas and Plaza de las Madreñas all have 17th and 18th-century houses.

On the way back to the coast, take the *Ruta de los Indianos* to Muros de Nalón through Escoredo and Villafría to see the mansions built by rich *Indianos,* Asturians who emigrated to America, made their fortunes, and returned triumphantly.

Heading back to the coast, **Soto del Barco** 22 has a 19th-century castle and **Salinas**, good beaches. This brings you to **Avilés** 23, the second major Asturian port town after Gijón. Avilés was the principal Asturian steel centre in the early 20th century, but it has a charming *casco viejo* (old town) concealed within its industrial outer shell. The church of San Nicolás de Bari's weathered facade and 14th-century chapel, the San Francisco church and convent, and the area around the Plaza de España are all ancient and intimate and filled with bustling bars and restaurants.

Lastres.

## INDUSTRIAL PORT

**Gijón** 24 (Xixón in Asturian) is the biggest Asturian city, with a population of 273,000 and an industrial port much reconstructed since the Spanish Civil War. The old part of town is located on a narrow isthmus that connects the city with the peninsular Cimadevilla ("top of the town") district. The main sites include the arcaded Plaza Mayor, the 18th-century Palacio de Revillagigedo and the Muro de San Lorenzo promenade. The Museo del Pueblo de Asturias has a bagpipe collection and the Museo Etnográfico next door has artefacts on cider making.

A tour of the coastal towns between Avilés and Gijón is an option to consider: **Verdicio** has an excellent beach; **Cabo de Peñas** is a wind-whipped observation point with panoramic views down the Asturian coast; **Luanco** is a fashionable summer resort; and **Candás** is a quaint fishing village.

## EASTERN ASTURIAS, FOR CIDER AND CAVES

East of Gijón, the coast is less developed. **Tazones** 25 is one of the prettiest fishing villages to visit. **Villaviciosa** 26 has an old town centre that includes the pre-Gothic Santa María de la Oliva church, some Renaissance buildings and the baroque quarter of El Ancho.

Heading inland From Villaviciosa takes you up the Boides Valley to the Pre-Romanesque San Salvador church at **Valdediós** (Apr–Sept Tue–Sun 11am–1.30pm and 4.30–7pm, Oct–Mar Tue–Sun 11am–1.30pm), consecrated in 893 by Alfonso III.

A little further inland is **Nava**, which as Asturias' **Cider Museum** (www.museodelasidra.com; Tue–Sat 11am–2pm and 4–7pm, Sun 11am–2pm; see page 231). Exhibits explain the process of making the local drink.

Further still from the coast, south-west of Nava, is MUMI, the **Museo de la Minería** (Mining Museum; www.mumi.es; Tue–Sun July–Aug 10am–8pm, Sept–May 10am–2pm and 4–7pm; see page 231).

Back on the coast, **Lastres** ㉗ is a fishing village of exceptional charm, notable for the juxtaposition of elegant mansions and fishermen's houses in the colourful streets. The hilltop **Mirador del Fito**, provides views over the coast, the Sella Valley and the Picos de Europa which are accessed via Cangas de Onis.

The next stop along the coast is **Ribadesella** ㉘. A fishing port and tourist resort at the mouth of the River Sella, Ribadesella has a lovely old quarter and important 20,000-year-old cave paintings, discovered in 1968, at the **Tito Bustillo Cave** (www.centrotitobustillo.com; Cave Art Centre Jul–Aug Wed–Sun 10am–7pm; Feb–June and Sept–Dec Wed–Fri 10.30am–2.30pm and 3.30–6pm, Sat–Sun 10am–2.30pm and 4–7pm. Advanced booking is required to visit the cave in groups of 15). These are on an archaeological par with those in Lascaux in France or at Altamira in neighbouring Cantabria (see page 203). Only 150 visitors are permitted per day, so arrive early in high holiday season. There are multitudes of stalactites to see as well as rock paintings.

The Picos de Europe (see page 211) are easily accessed from here. It is an easy trip to Cangas de Onis and Covadonga.

Back on the coast, **Llanes** ㉙, 40km (25 miles) east of Ribadesella, has a medieval quarter rich in buildings of the 13th–15th centuries. Don't miss a walk along the cliffhanging Paseo de San Pedro above the Sablón beach.

Between Llanes and the Cantabrian border, stop in **Vidiago**, famous for its cheese, **Pimiango** where there are more rock paintings at the Pindal cave (but in poor condition, unlit and without guides) and **Colombres** to visit the Archivo de Indianos, a museum which records the lives of Asturian emigrants to America.

**Eat**

Tazones is the place to go to eat lobster. Take your pick from the tank and watch it being cooked in front of you.

*Llanes harbour.*

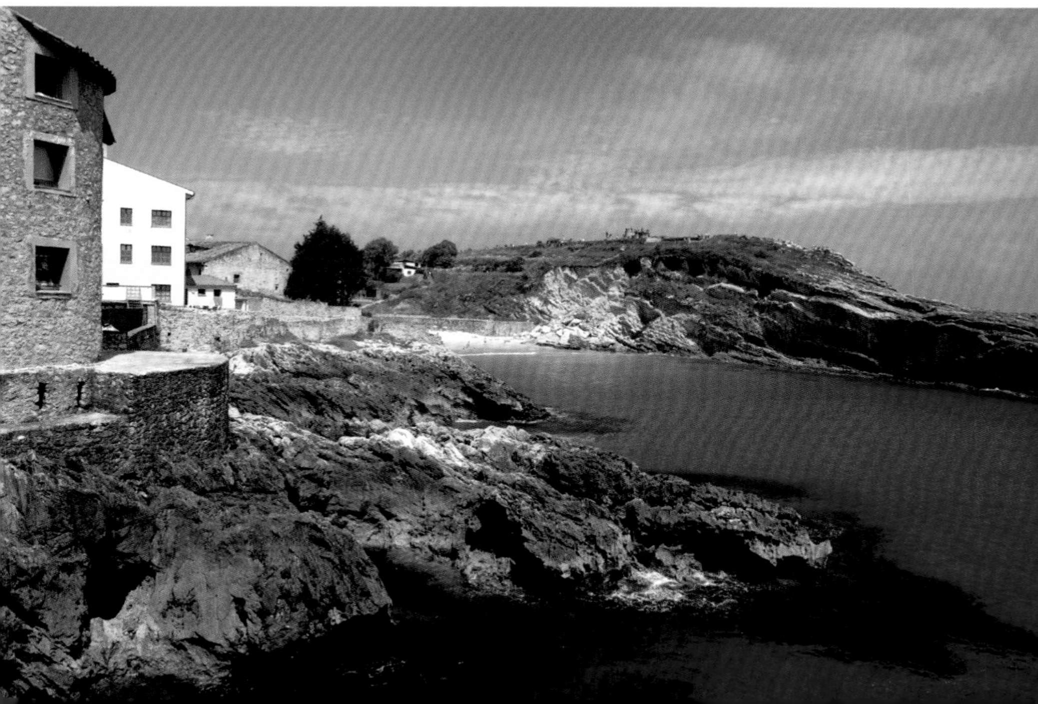

# COUNTRY CRAFTS AND MUSEUMS

Ethnographic museums are a cultural mainstay of Northern Spain. Local artisans are often in residence, keeping local crafts and skills alive.

As ever-shrinking rural communities across the north of Spain struggle to keep their customs and traditions alive, more and better local exhibitions and museums are appearing. Artisans and farmers from highlands and valleys are thriving – just – from a multitude of valleys and villages, each of which has a unique story to tell. These displays and collections offer revealing glimpses into the lives and times of the people who shaped the landscape and knew how to live by its rugged demands.

## TINKER, TAILOR...

Galician fishermen, Asturian knife-makers and cider brewers, Cantabrian sabot cobblers, Basque *txakoli* growers, Navarran shepherds, Aragonese weavers, Aranese cheesemakers, Andorran contraband merchants or Catalan wild mushroom stalkers...there is much to learn from these local crafts and customs stored away in remote treasuries of regional life and lore. Through their lively displays, many rural museums offer a chance to feel, just for an instant, the experiences of tough working lives, from a whaler's terror while approaching his quarry, to a miner's claustrophobia as he descends into the underworld. They capture stories, history and human dramas in an immediate and atmospheric way. Taramundi's Asturian iron craftsmen continue producing knife blades using methods handed down over centuries, while weavers in San Juan de Plan, Upper Aragón, have restored techniques lost for years.

From displays of La Rioja's medieval wine presses to Basque sportsmen and the river log drivers of the Pyrenees, these small-town museums are nearly always worth making time to see. They also offer a chance to purchase hand-made crafts which make excellent souvenirs of Northern Spain.

*The art of ship-building is kept alive at the The Sea Factory of the Basques in Albaola, which is located in renovated shipyard.*

*Knife blades have been a local speciality since the 18 century in and around Taramundi in Asturias. Water h always been a good natural energy source and the ar former mills were powered by water. Today hydraulic power drives the turbine that produces the electricity heat the steel blade this artisan is shaping.*

*The Mining Museum of Asturias, whose complex includes the information on mining activity that developed in the coalfields of the area.*

## The Asturian mining experience

Mining has been a way of life and a part of the local identity in Asturias for nearly 2,000 years. The Museo de la Minería (Mining Museum) at what was once the San Vicente mine in the town of El Entrego occupies a special space in the history of Asturian mining. It was here, in 1934, that the Sindicato de Obreros Mineros de Asturias (Mine Workers Syndicate of Asturias) first wrested control of a coal mine, protesting against the inhuman conditions and poor management. The Asturian coal miners' revolt was a foretaste of the polarisation between workers and government that led to the 1936–39 Spanish Civil War.

Visitors can experience being in an Asturian coal mine for a short while – long enough to see why these workers occupied the vanguard of the labour movement. The primitive mine shafts, the miner's lantern and its evolution, the infirmary, the rudimentary safety precautions and the all-important forum provided by the bath house, all paint a dramatic portrait of this sombre Asturian underworld.

*Sea Factory of The Basques charts the history of que whale-hunting in the Atlantic.*

*se wooden madreñas or galochas were (and still are) n with socks and slippers and provide insulation from w, mud and water.*

*An old mining cart inside the museum of the local mines that is now part of the Picos de Europa National Park.*

*The San Pantaleón de Losa hermitage in the Valle de Losa.*

# CASTILLA Y LEÓN

On the upland plains of the northern meseta, green Spain turns to brown. Here the Reconquest took root, castles and cathedrals were built and the history of Castilian Spain began.

ny consideration of Northern Spain nust involve not only the Green Spain f the coast, but also the northern wathe of Old Castile. This was where he Christian frontiersmen of the Can-abrian mountains established the first ettlements of the 9th-century Recon-uest. The Moors were uninterested 1 much of the region and, as they fell ack, frontier castles were built, giving astile its name. The region possesses ne Visigothic and Mozarabic churches, nd it was here that Gothic architec-ure first appeared on the peninsula, otably in the cathedrals of Burgos nd León. The cities lie on the haunt-ng, unforgiving meseta, Spain's 1,000-netre (3,000ft) central plateau where he extremes of climate can make the ilgrim route a baptism of ice and fire.

In the east, the meseta begins round Vitoria in the Basque country, djoining Burgos province, which is enerally rather flat. More varied are he provinces of Palencia and León, which climb into the Cordillera Cantá-rica to share the Picos de Europa with sturias and Cantabria. In the west, he Montes de León are a foretaste of he mountains of Galicia.

## URGOS: THE BURGHERS' OWN

**urgos ❶** is the solid city implied by s name, which was taken from the burghers who brought trade to the town. They grew rich on the wool trade which flourished until the early 17th century, transporting their commodity from the meseta through Bilbao to Spanish Flanders. Surrounded by the undulating, brown sea of Castile, Burgos has found a niche in the valley of the burbling Arlanzón, overlooked by a castle which the Napoleonic French demolished, blowing a good deal of the town away in the process, and reducing many of the cathedral's stained-glass windows to shards.

**Main attractions**

Burgos
Covarrubias
Santo Domingo de Silos
Fromista
León
Astorga

Maps on pages 234, 238, 244

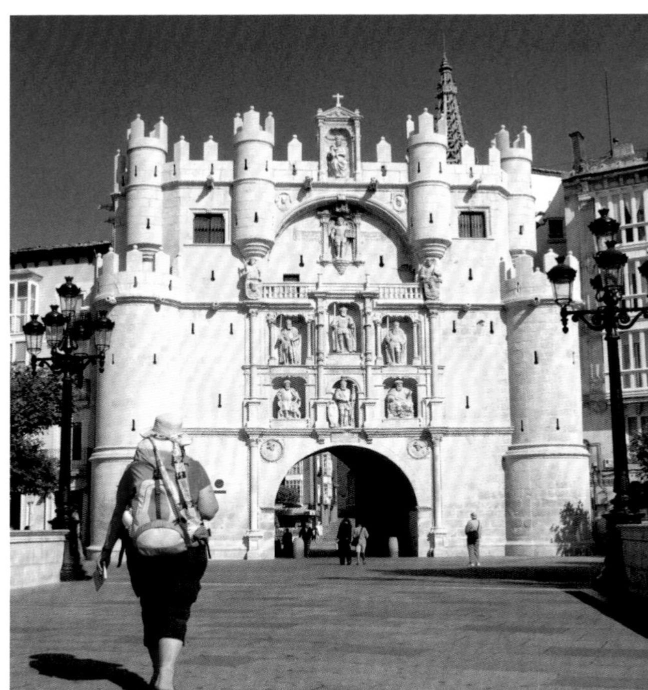

*Pilgrim at the Arco de Santa Maria, Burgos.*

> **Fact**
>
> According to legend, when El Cid was banished from Castile by Alfonso VI, he left Burgos cathedral promising to pay for 1,000 Masses if the Virgin Mary would help him in exile. He did win glory and presented the cathedral with a bootful of gold on his return.

At first, this was a frontier post against the Moors, founded in 884 by Count Diego Porcelos. It grew to become the capital of the kingdom of Castile and León in 1073, which it remained until the Moors were driven from Spain in 1492. All that is missing from towns further north can be found here: the pomp of the Middle Ages, the grandeur of kings, funded by merchants' coffers and embellished by the court painters' brushes. It is a treasure house of the early history of Spain.

There is no overt sign that this is a military town, but the spirit of the conqueror, epitomised in the town's favourite son, El Cid, was grasped in the 20th century by General Franco, who made the Nationalist capital here in 1936. Franco set up his rebel government in the white building called the Capitanía General in the Plaza Alonso Martínez. The city's name was again associated with Franco during the infamous Burgos trials of 1970 in which six Basque separatists were sentenced to death, a sentence later commuted after pressure from world opinion.

All this is not to say that moder Burgos (pop. 170,000) is a gloom place. On a Saturday night, young peo ple out-chatter starlings in the Huert del Rey behind the cathedral and i the Calle Jerónimo and other street in the old town beneath the cathedra where they drift from bar to bar, nib bling tapas and tasting small glasse of wine. The paseo, the stroll besid the river beneath the plane trees in th Paseo del Espolón, is a lively event, toc

## GETTING AROUND BURGOS

The centre of town is signposted an easily found down dead-straight boule vards. Parking during the week may b a problem, but there are several ca parks, the most central beneath th Plaza Mayor. All the places worth see ing are within walking distance wit the exception of the Cartuja de Mira flores monastery, which is nearly 4kn (2 miles) east of the town, though it i a pleasant wooded stroll for those wit time (see page 238).

A good place to begin exploring th city is the **Arco de Santo María** Ⓐ,

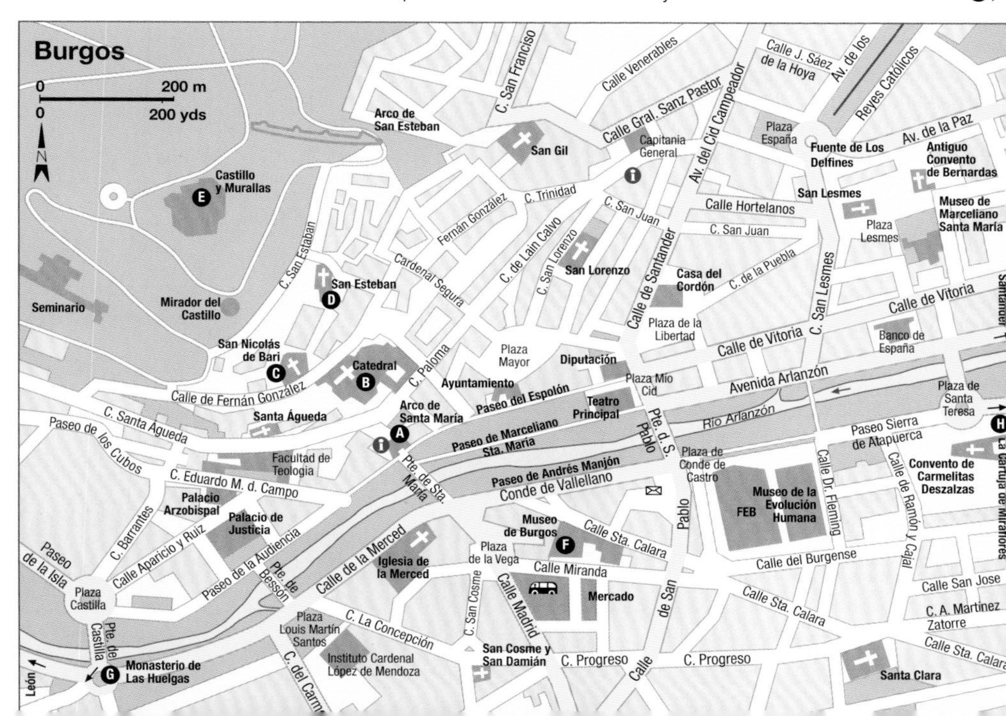

ateway which once pierced the old city walls and remains a plump and satisfied portal which leads from the river to the old town. The sculptures on the front represent the figures of Carlos V, El Cid and Fernán González who, breaking from León, was declared first king of Castile in AD 950. Its interior is now an exhibition space (Tue–Sat 11am–1.50pm and 5–9pm, Sun 11am–1.50pm; free), with a brutish fresco of Fernán González. The Sala de Poridad contains El Cid memorabilia, including a copy of the manuscript of the epic poem, Cantar de Mío Cid; a replica of his sword, Tizona; and an authenticated bone from his left arm. By the next bridge downstream there is a powerful statue of this hirsute warrior, born Rodrigo Díaz de Vivar in 1043 at Vivar del Cid on the north side of the city.

## SPAIN'S FIRST GOTHIC CATHEDRAL

The arch leads through to the Plaza de San Fernando and the **cathedral** Ⓑ http://catedraldeburgos.es; daily 9.30am–5pm; free Tue pm) the first of Spain's great Gothic buildings (it was begun in 1221) and, some might say, a shrine to El Cid. It is worth circumnavigating the whole building first to take in its rather ungainly shape and the whirls and spires of Gothic embellishment – novelties in Spain inspired by contemporary architectural trends in northern Europe. It is a magnificent synthesis of the talents of three generations of a family of builders, originally from Cologne, and of the local Gothic master artisans, the sculptor Gil de Siloé (last quarter of the 15th century), and his son Diego (1495–1563) who was both architect and sculptor. John of Cologne (1410–51), the head of his family's enterprise, was responsible for the west front, where statues of Castilian kings decorate the gallery between the heavily ornamented twin towers. These were built between 1442 and 1558, but the pinnacles were added only in the 19th century, to John of Cologne's original design. The plain lower part of the west front was an 18th-century reconstruction.

Inside, the sense that this cathedral measuring 84 by 59 metres (275ft by 194ft) is the third largest in Spain is not immediately apparent. A **central choir**, with finely carved stalls by the Burgundian Felipe de Vigarni (1498–1543), is boxed off on three sides by a neoclassical wall of panelled doors and Corinthian pillars. The fourth side, like each side chapel and the whole nave, is incarcerated by sky-high iron railings. Many of the side chapels are as big as churches, with vaulted ceilings and intricate decoration. Among the finest is the **Capilla del Condestable** at the back of the ambulatory. It was built by Simón de Colonia (Simon of Cologne) for the commander of the Castilian army, Pedro Hernández de Velasco, and it has an altar by Diego de Siloé.

Light filtering through the star-shaped vaulting of the stunningly intricate lantern, built by Juan de Vallejo to an original idea by Simon of Cologne

**Eat**

A staple in Burgos is *la olla podrida* – the rotten pot – made with pig's ears, ribs, trotters, *morcilla* (black pudding) and red beans from Ibeas. Be sure not to miss it.

*The finely carved stalls of Burgos Cathedral.*

and completed in 1568, illuminates the slab marking the tombs of El Cid and his wife, Ximena. (Their remains were brought here in 1921 from Sigmaringen in Germany, where they ended up after the Peninsular War when they were stolen from the Monasterio de San Pedro de Cardeña 10km/6 miles north of Burgos. Babieca, his horse, remains buried outside the monastery's gates.)

High on the north wall by the west entrance is a curious 15th-century clock. An impish figure called Papamoscas (fly-catcher) pops out to strike each hour. Opposite, in the south aisle, is the Capilla del Santo Cristo, which contains the 13th-century **Cristo de Burgos** dressed in various coloured petticoats depending on the liturgical season. Made of buffalo skin, human hair and fingernails, it must have convinced many pilgrims it was alive, and though it is still said to be warm to the touch, a notice on the chapel door discourages visitors from entering.

The cathedral museum holds some some real treasures including a Bible in the language of the Visigoths (a kin of Latin) and, high on the wall outsid the chapterhouse, the coffer full c sand that El Cid gave to moneylender pretending it was full of gold, to fun his exploits against the Moors.

Behind the cathedral in the Call Fernán González is the church of **Sa Nicolás de Bari** C (Mon–Tue and Thu Sat 11.30am–1.30pm and 5–7pm; fre Mon). It contains a stunning floor-t ceiling alabaster altarpiece by Francisco de Colonia (John of Cologne' grandson). The most impressive o its 36 scenes is the figure of the Virgin surrounded by a fan of nearly 20 angels. Further up the street on th right is **San Esteban** D, which has a collection of altarpieces, mostly with painted panels of suffering saints and a fine cloister. Just beyond, a path goes up to the **castle** E (Sat-Sun 11am–6.30pm), from where there are good views across the town to the surrounding treeless countryside, bu little else. The French made a thorough job of destroying the defences in 1813.

*View over Burgos.*

## CROSS THE RIVER

here are two important museums on ie opposite bank of the river from the ty centre. One of these is the **Museo e Burgos** **F** (www.museodeburgos.com; ue–Sat 10am–2pm and 4–7pm, Sun 0am–2pm; free Sat–Sun). The **Pre-istoria y Arqueológia** section is in the asa de Miranda, an imitation Roman lla built in 1545 on three floors with central colonnaded courtyard. It has good collection from the province, inging from Stone-Age scythes to eautiful Celtiberian necklaces, Ibe-an money and finds from the Roman lla at Clunia. The adjoining **Bellas rtes** section is on three floors and as an exquisite enamel altarpiece om the monastery of Santo Domingo e Silos (see page 242), rare wooden mb effigies, and religious and secu-r paintings.

The other museum is the **Museo de volucion Humana** (MEH; Paseo de erra de Atapuerca; www.museoevolu-onhumana.com; Tue–Fri 10am–2.30pm nd 4.30–8pm, Sat–Sun 10am–8pm), contemporary building explaining the story of human evolution based on the finds in the Sierra de Atapuerca (see page 33). The finds include a sharpened tool of red quartzite that has been nicknamed "Excalibur". You can find out more about the Atapuerca operation at CAYAC, outside Ibeas de Juarros on the N120 towards Logroño, from which there are guided tours to visit the excavations.

On the same side of the river, some 10 minutes' walk through a modern residential area, is the **Monasterio de Las Huelgas** **G** (Tue–Sat 10am–1pm and 4–5.30pm, Sun 10.30am–2pm) a truly intriguing building that makes five centuries slip away. It was founded in 1187 by Alfonso VIII and his wife Eleanor, daughter of Henry II of England and Eleanor of Aquitaine, as a convent for the most aristocratic ladies, but it also became a pantheon for Castilian kings. The building itself is wonderful, with great shining floor planks, while the decoration on the wood panels and the intricate filigree of the Mudéjar door leading into the cloister salutes the art of the Caliphate of Granada.

The power of the monastery can be measured by an unusual statue of St James: the arm which bears a sword can be moved up and down, so that he could dub ruling monarchs, and others, into the Order of the Knights of Santiago. Much of the collection in the monastery is unusual, but the most extraordinary must be actual clothes worn in the 13th and 14th centuries by the monarchs and their children. These are in the form of *pellotes*, thick, woven shifts, which incorporate an Arabic script pattern in the stripes of their simple design.

Beside a pine wood about 4km (2 miles) upstream, and a good walk if it's not too hot, is the city's other great monastery, **La Cartuja de Miraflores** **H** (Mon–Sat 10.15am–3pm and 4–6pm, Sun 11am–1pm and 4–6pm; voluntary donation). It is still in use, and only the church, built by the Colonia family, can be visited. Its great treasure is Gil de Siloé's highly intricate tomb of Juan II, for whom the church was built in 1441, and his wife Isabel of Portugal. Siloé also produced the altarpiece, decorated with gold brought back b Columbus.

## NORTH OF BURGOS

Most of the countryside north of Bu gos is the same as south of it, flat ar treeless, but every now and then the are surprises, such as the Ebro Car yon. Green Spain only gets going in th far north, in the high Cordillera Cant brica, which can be reached in abo an hour by car.

One way into these upper regior is via **Briviesca** **2**, 40km (25 mile northeast of Burgos. This small cou try town has a busy Saturday mark and more history than it looks cap ble of bearing. It was on the Camir Francés until the 11th century whe Sancho the Great re-routed pilgrin through Nájera. Remaining from i pilgrim days are the large convent Santa Clara and adjoining hospital Nuestra Señora del Rosario. Both t town's churches have 16th-centu altarpieces. It was here that the tit of Prince of Asturias was bestowed an heir to the throne for the first tim

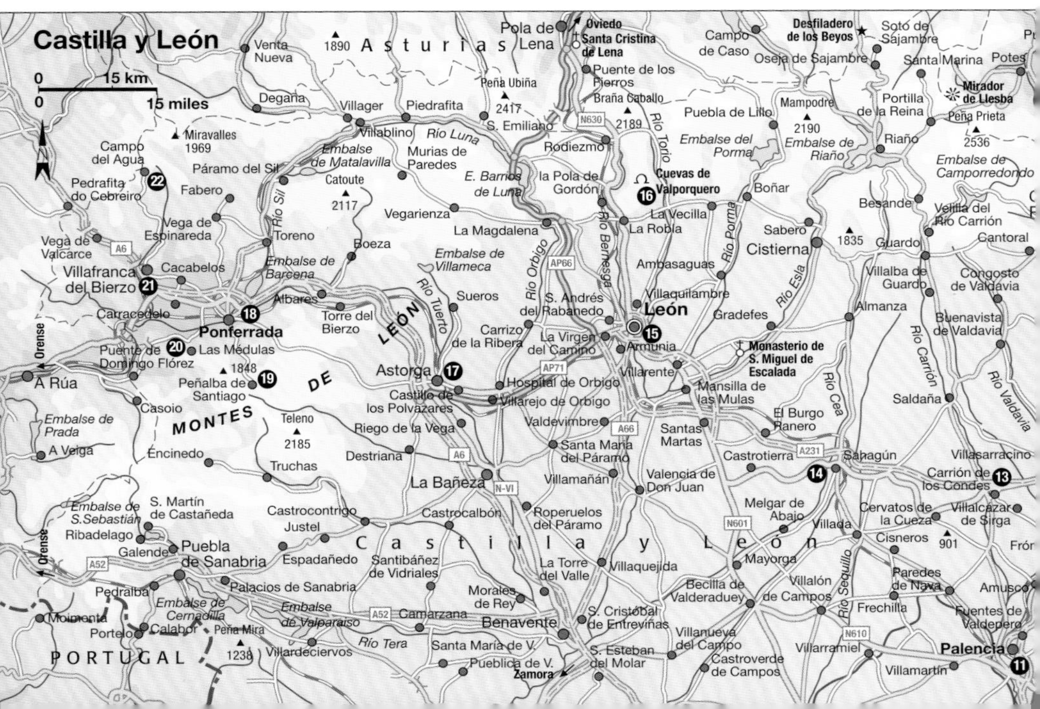

vhen Enrique, son of Juan I, married Catherine of Lancaster in 1381. Spanish heirs have born the title ever since.

From Briviesca, a good road heads traight up to **Oña** ❸, which has a couple of cheap *hostales*. History here is ar more evident than at Briviesca. It vas a Roman settlement, and had one f the first castles of Castile. The monastery church of San Salvador dates rom 1072 and two Romanesque windows on the facade remain. The monastery building is now a hospital, but here are tours of the church (Tue–Sun 0.30am–1.30pm and 4–7pm). This has he Pantéon Real (Royal Pantheon), vith the decorated tomb of Sancho he Great of Navarra, founder of the nonastery, who died in 1035. Some of his belongings are in the museum in he sacristy. The Gothic cloister is by Simón de Colonia.

Above Oña, the N-629 leads along an attractive ravine of the River Ebro for a ew miles before leaving it and heading straight across the pancake-flat sierra to **Medina de Pomar** ❹, whose big box of a castle looms a long way off. It was built in 1390 for Fernando de Velasco, Constable of Castile, and for some time in later centuries its 2.5-metre (8ft) thick walls contained a prison. The town itself is spacious and quiet, its several bars and discos notwithstanding. The central Plaza de Juan Francisco Bustamente looks out over *huertas*, the allotments of a large vegetable-growing area. There is a healthy farmyard smell along the 10-minute walk south to the **Monastery of Santa Clara**. The church is open to visitors, and there is a small museum (daily 10am–8pm) containing an Adoration of the Virgin attributed to Van der Weyden.

## INTO THE EBRO CANYON

To the west lies **Villarcayo,** which, judging by the occasional old facade, might be more attractive had it not been virtually flattened in the 19th-century Carlist Wars. From here the road towards the corner of the province and the Embalse del Ebro (Ebro Reservoir) becomes much more dramatic before connecting with the N-623 from

*Medina de Pomar.*

### Shop

Aguilar de Campóo has one of Castilla y León's sweet-making convents which sell home-made cakes and biscuits. Buying these from an invisible nun through a turnstile window provides a great taste of old Spain.

Santander to Burgos. Travelling south down this road, over the Puerto de Carrales (Carrales Pass), the canyon of the Ebro becomes evident, and a right turn into **Orbaneja del Castillo** ❺ brings you to the heart of this dramatic gorge. Above this hamlet are the battered limestone teeth of the canyon, and walks by the river lead off in all directions. A spring at the back of the village produces a stream that courses through a mill and cascades over mossy stones. The central, low-beamed café, hung with clogs and frequented by monosyllabic locals, has a mountain air.

Further west, **Aguilar de Campóo** ❻, 50km (30 miles) from Burgos, is 2km (1 mile) from another reservoir and a popular centre for exploring the countryside. This is an attractive town spread beneath a ruined castle, with an elongated main square, the Plaza de España, leading to the church. A rich variety of glass-fronted buildings stands on wood, stone and iron colonnades, among them the Siglo XX, a good local café, restaurant and hotel. An inscription in Hebrew over one c the remaining town gates on the sout side bears testimony to the forme Jewish population of Aguilar, whic was built during the resettlement following the Reconquest. A river promenade leads north towards another c the town gates, which frames a fine tree-lined lane to the **Monasterio d Santa María La Real**. This is a centr for studies of Romanesque art, and th church contains several dozen excellent models of examples to be foun in the region. A number of routes ar suggested for you to seek out the mar Romanesque churches scattered abou the region. Beyond the monastery i the **Embalse de Aguilar de Campó** with beaches and watersports for cooling off.

## SANTO DOMINGO DE SILOS AND FERNÁN GONZÁLEZ COUNTRY

To the south of Burgos lies the Benedictine Monasterio de Santo Doming de Silos whose singing monks unexpectedly hit the classical charts wit

*Orbaneja del Castillo.*

ecordings of Gregorian chant in the 990s. The monastery is an hour's irect journey from Burgos, but it is good idea to make a round trip of it, lanning to be there for vespers and aking in three other sights in the day: erma, the would-be capital of Spain the early 17th century; Covarrubias, pretty village that became the last esting place of Fernán González as he olled Castile's frontier southwards; nd a fine Visigothic church at Quinta-illa de las Viñas.

For the round trip, start out on the ast, 35km (22-mile) stretch of the N-1 owards Madrid to reach **Lerma ❼**, tanding in neoclassical pomp just off he main road. It was founded in 978 by son of Fernán González and became he domain of the Lerma family. In 598, the then Count, who was elevated o become the first Duke of Lerma in he following year, thought it was time he capital (always a moveable feast n Castile) settled here. His grandiose lans took root in his mind because he ad just become regent on the death f Philip II and had almost immediately consolidated his position by becoming the young Philip III's favourite and chief minister. Bolstered by extraordinary powers to relieve Moors of their wealth, he planned his city around a vast plaza, with a fitting palace, a cluster of churches and two religious houses. Today, the winds of Castilla blow unkindly on it and the palace is a vast pigeon coop.

Just north of Lerma there is turn off signposted for Covarrubias, an attractive road following the poplar-lined River Arlanza and passing the remains of the monastery of Quintanilla del Agua. **Covarrubias ❽** is on the river, a touristy town that looks quite different from those further north. The vernacular architecture here has shed its stony image for half-timbered buildings propped up by Roman columns. Fernán González's former residence was on the site of the town hall, and the fortification for the town was provided by a 10th-century Mozarabic tower. The church, the **Ex Colegiata de San Cosme y San Damián** is Fernán González's last resting place; his tomb is a simple box

*Covarrubias.*

**Where**

Covarrubias is a good stop-over. There is a pretty hotel in the village square, the three-star Arlanza, and next door the Tiky, an inexpensive bar and restaurant.

compared with the 4th-century Roman sarcophagus picked out for his wife. It is a fine Gothic church with a well-decorated 17th-century organ. The cloisters, verging on the Plateresque, lead to a museum of four rooms containing a mix of treasures, including a 16th-century Flemish triptych which opens from a closed cupboard.

From Covarubbias the road twists through chunky rocks to the village that surrounds the monastery of **Santo Domingo de Silos** ❾ (http://abadiadesilos.es; Tue–Sat 10am–1pm and 4.30–6pm; Mass sung daily at 9am, on festivals at noon; vespers sung daily at 7pm). Saint Dominic of Silos arrived in the 11th century to rescue what was by then a neglected monastery. The most exquisite creation is the cloister, a heady mix of bold Romanesque with a filigree touch to the menagerie which inhabits the capitals, and a suggestion that their creator may have been a Moor. The monastery is a centre for Mozarabic studies and there is a collection of Mozarabic illuminated manuscripts in the museum, where there is also an 18th-century pharmacy. Th 18th-century church where the mon chant is a disappointment, but at lea it does not detract from their conten plative plainsong.

Tres Coronas, a three-star hot across the road, is an excellent place stay, and there are several other hote and hostels in the village. At **Yecla**, mile to the south, is a gorge with wal ways, and Celtic remains.

From Santo Domingo de Silos car on to the N-234 back towards Burgo On the right is a 7th-century Visigoth church just outside the village of **Qui tanilla de las Viñas** ❿ sitting benea the craggy outcrop of the Torre La (Wed–Sun May–Sept 11am–2pm a 4–8pm, Oct–Apr 9.50am–5.10pm). Th is the eastern arm of a larger church, can be seen from the foundations. T rare, tell-tale external friezes are still a good state, and those on the inside a especially rich (see page 93).

## PALENCIA

The province of Palencia is sandwich between León and Burgos and, judg

*Cloisters of the monastery Santo Domingo de Silos.*

jainst its richer neighbours, in most ings it comes in third place. Much of e province is taken up with the vast, at, burnished meseta, but in the north pushes up into the Cordillera Cantá-ica and has many hidden treasures. ne city of **Palencia** ⓫ (population ),000) lies by the River Carrión and centred on a fine main street, Calle ajor, where there is an eclectic mix colonnaded buildings with glass bal-onies. It is not hard to find your way to and out of town, which makes it a ood stop-over, and there are several expensive hotels.

The town started growing rapidly the wake of the Reconquest and pain's first university was sited here 1185, moving to Salamanca 44 years ter. In the 16th century the town ll from grace after the *comunero* volt (see page 41). A subsequent ck of riches may have benefited its thedral, considered the "unknown auty". The simple, white facade des a graceful interior which lacks sitors and postcard stalls. Mainly othic, from the14th century, it has some fine carving around the choir by Gil de Siloé and Simón de Colonia. The side aisles are empty, echoing and lofty, and there is an interesting stucco chapel of the Magi in the ambulatory. Like Burgos, it has a humorous striking clock, this one high on the south tran-sept. Each hour a figure strikes his top hat against the bell.

The church is built over a Visigothic tomb to St Antolín, the church's patron, and is the only known Visigothic mar-tyrium. The cloisters are enclosed and not interesting. Among a few treasures in the Sala Capitular museum is an early El Greco, of St Sebastian, and a strange splash of colour in a glass case which, when viewed through a hole at one end, turns out to be a portrait of Carlos I.

## THE PILGRIMS' ROUTE

The Pilgrims' Route has three impor-tant stops in Palencia province. From Estépar 15km (10 miles) southwest of Burgos, it leads from the A-62 through attractive, bleached, mud-walled vil-lages to **Frómista** ⓬, where you will

**Fact**

Mozarabic liturgical chants can be heard at Venta de Baños, Palencia, on the Sunday following the feast of St. John (24 June), when the Mass has Visigothic and Mozarabic elements.

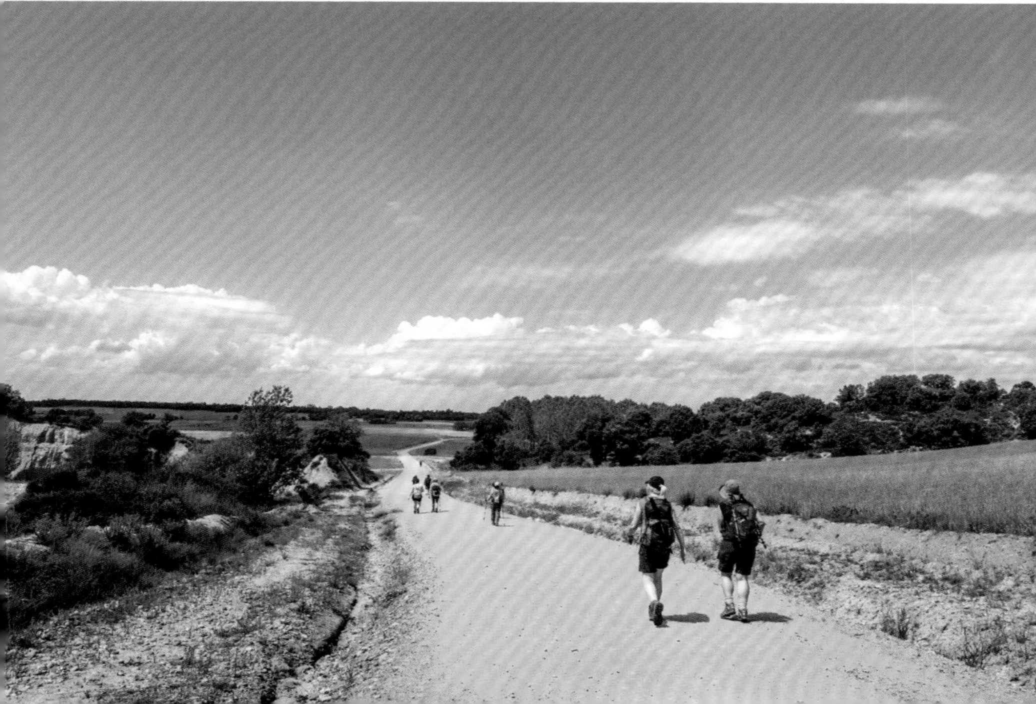

*Pilgrims on the meseta, between Burgos and Astorga.*

find San Martín, thought to be the finest Romanesque church in the world. Built in the 11th century, it was completely renovated at the beginning of the 20th century. In a classic shape of three apses and three barrel-vaulted naves, cupola and lantern, its gold stones and simple space are exhilarating. A leaflet explains the menagerie of figures carved high on the pillars. Also in Frómista is the unusual church of San Pedro, with a colonnaded portico.

The next major stop on the Camino Francés is the busy small town of **Carrión de los Condes** ⓭, with parks graced by willows and poplars beside the River Carrión. Two of the counts of Carrión infamously married daughters of El Cid to get their hands on sizeable dowries. But they treated their brides so badly El Cid made them fight his greatest warriors in single combat. The counts were roundly defeated and the women found more respectful husbands.

On the west side of town and south of the bridge is the Benedictine monastery of San Zoilo, which has Renaissance cloisters by Juan d Badajoz, and a two-star hostel. O the east side is the convent of Sant Clara, which is a pilgrim's rest an has a small museum of religious ar Near Santa Clara is a tourist booth an the church of Santa María del Camin with interesting portals: two horse men on the one on the south side hav lost their heads to buttresses on th narthex. There is also a frieze of th legendary annual gift of a hundred vir gins to the Moors as a tribute. In th centre of town, off the Plaza Mayor, th church of Santiago has a wide frieze c figures and an arch of guild craftsmer

There is a magnificent portal on th church in the former Templar tow of **Villalcázar de Sirga**, 7km (5 mile southeast of Carrión de los Conde Here the mighty church of Santa Marí la Blanca has a miraculous Virgin, an there are fine tombs including thos of the infante Don Felipe (d. 1271) an his wife, Leonora, and that of a knigh templar with his goshawk. The 1st 4th century Roman Villa at **Quintanill de la Cueza**, where there are mosai

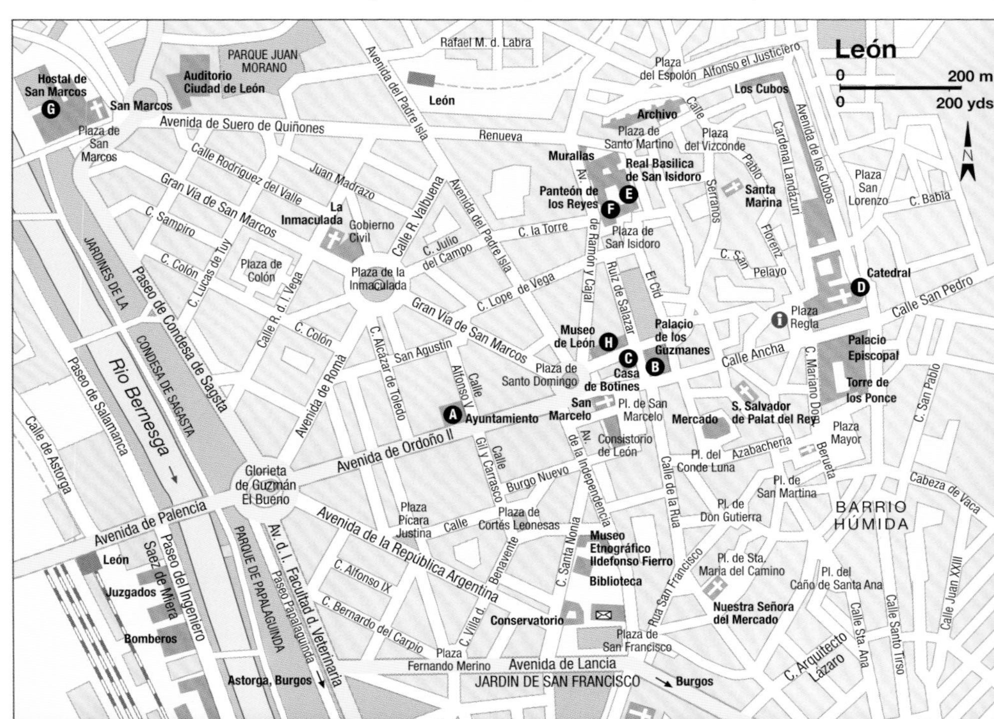

oors, is to be seen 22km (15 miles) orth of Carrión de los Condes.

The churches of **Sahagún** ⓮ (a town n the A-231 between Palancia and eón) are among the most unusual n the pilgrim route. They are all built f red brick, and their interiors were nly recently peeled away to reveal ıe detailed brickwork of their pillars nd arches. San Tirso, with Mozarabic orseshoe arches, dates from before 123 and is generally regarded as he earliest Mudéjar brick building in :hristian Spain. Above it is the Fran-iscan monastery of La Peregrina, ounded in 1217 and abandoned by the nonks in the 19th century. Colourful riezes of Arabic motifs are an aston-shing site in a presbytery. Two other hurches in this sleepy town, which lfonso VI (1163–96) made into a Span-sh Cluny, are also brick built: San Lor-nzo, from the 13th century and, above pleasant central square, the Trinidad, vhich has been converted for pilgrims' ıse and has 40 bunks. Alfonso is bur-ed in the convent of Santa Cruz.

The surprise of the Arabic influence on Sahagún is doubled at the **Monaste-rio de San Miguel de Escalada**, south-east of León. Founded at the end of the 9th century and rebuilt in the 11th by monks expelled from Córdoba, it has an mmaculate row of Mozarabic arches on the porch. Inside it has both Visigothic and Moorish decoration and it is the fin-est Mozarabic building in Spain.

## LEÓN

The two principal reasons for visiting the city of **León** ⓯ (population 139,000) are the cathedral windows and the frescoes in the basilica of San Isidoro, the sight of either of which may cause a momentary intake of breath. There are other reasons to go – the bars in the Barrio Húmedo (Damp Quarter), watering hole of the old town centred on the Plaza de San Martín beside the cathedral, is not a bad one. This is an agreeably active city, with a university, but the wide boulevards and well-spaced squares ensure it is not oppressively crowded.

León was the base of the Roman VII legion and the capital of Asturias from the 10th century until 1282, after which it was left behind as Castilian Spain moved first to Burgos then further south. The legion gave its name to the town which inherited a tradition of straight roads, making it easy to navigate. Street parking is usually available and there is a central car park beneath the Plaza de San Marcelo. Immediately in sight of this central square are the 16th-century **Ayuntamiento** Ⓐ (Town Hall), the complementary **Palacio de los Guzmanes** Ⓑ and the **Casa de Botines** Ⓒ, a neo-Gothic building with turrets topped by witches' hats, created in 1889 by Antoni Gaudí when he wasn't really trying. The Guzmanes Palace houses the government offices and was begun by León's most illustrious family in 1560. They can trace their ancestry back to Guzmán El Bueno (his statue stands on a roundabout near the river) who sacrificed his son to the Moors at

**Quote**

"You then come to prosperous Sahagún (Sanctus Facundus), the site of the field where, it is said, in olden times, the splendid lances which the victorious warriors thrust into the ground in the Glory of God's holy name, sprouted leaves again".

Aymeric Picaud

*The church of San Lorenzo de Sahagún.*

**Fact**

The right-hand entrance to the basilica of San Isidoro is a "Puerta de Perdón", the first "door of pardon" on the Camino Francés. If pilgrims were too weak to travel any further, they would be given the same dispensations as if they had reached Santiago itself.

Tarifa in southern Spain in 1292, but their downfall came when they supported the revolt of the Castilian communes against the crown in 1520–22.

Visible just up the road from this trio of buildings is the **cathedral** **D** (Mon–Sat 9.30am–1.30pm and 4–7pm, Sun 9.30am–1.30pm), dating from 1253, a fine Gothic building outside and in, based on French designs. However, the most remarkable feature of its construction – the way the windows are given preference over walls – combined with the poor quality of the stone used, make it a much less sturdy edifice than it looks, causing worry on the part of the restorers. The triple portal on the west front is contemporary with the first work on the building.

Inside, the colours of the windows dominate everything. Deep blues, ruby reds, vibrant greens, luscious purples and yellows, all give the space immense richness and light. In the 19th century it was cleared of a lot of clutter and the result is that, standing inside the west door beneath the rose window, you can look clear through the choir to the main altar withou interruption, and the light from th windows gives a rich tonal quality tha changes as the sun moves through th day. There are some 1,700 sq metre (18,300 sq ft) of glass, much of it from the 13th century. The lower window depict plants, the sciences, arts, virtues and vices, the triforium has heraldic devices, the upper windows saints prophets and biblical tales.

In the cloisters and museum where there is an eclectic collection of Gothic and Romanesque work, as well as some small gems, in particular a Mozarabic antiphone in which the music is notated in proper notes rather than traditional medieval square blocks, and a Bible from AD 920 in which modern-looking illustrations predate Picasso by a millennium.

From the cathedral, the old Roman wall, fortified by Alfonso V when he made León his capital in 1002, and much rebuilt by Alfonso XI in 1324 heads north via a handful of bastions then turns west and heads south again to encompass the **Real Basílica de**

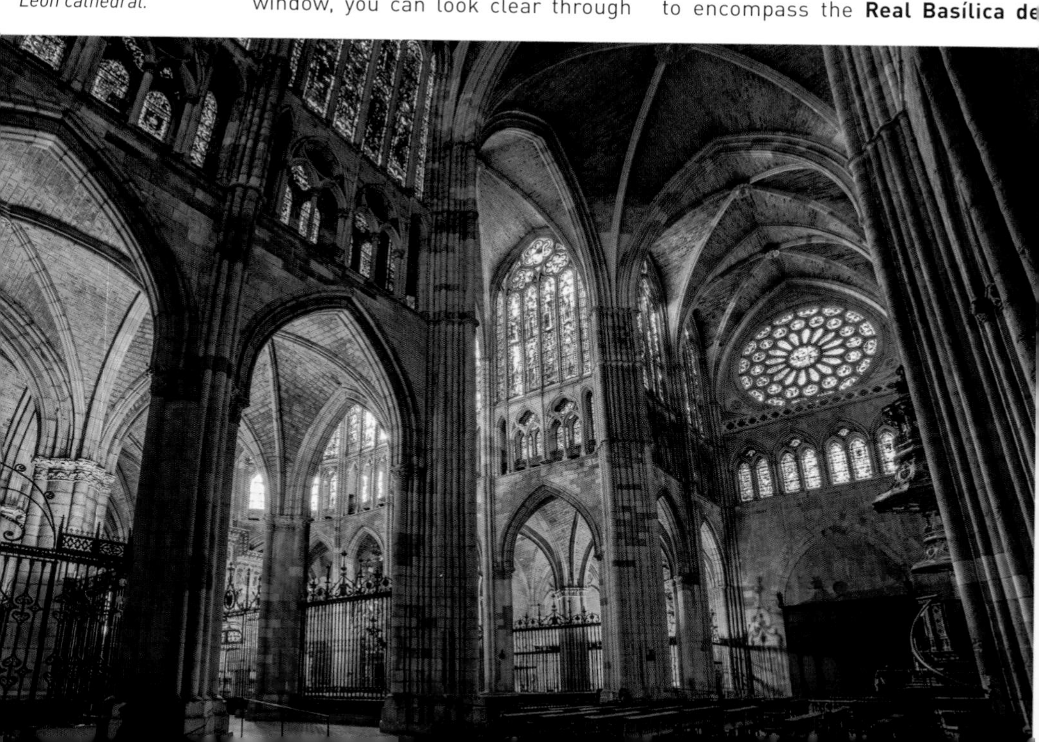

*León cathedral.*

an Isidoro **E**, a few minutes' walk orthwest of the cathedral. The church self is not the reason to come here. he door to the left under a Baroque culpture of Santiago Matamoros leads the museum and the **Panteón de los eyes** **F** (www.museosanisidorodeleon. om; Mon–Sat 10am–2pm and 4–7pm, un 10am–2pm). A guided tour through he rooms of what was Ferdinand I's alace begins with the museum collection that includes the casket which ore the remains of Saint Isidoro from eville in 1063. In the 16th-century brary is a fine collection of Bibles nd choir books, dating from the 10th entury, many of calfskin. Finally and ost importantly are the exceptional nd delightful 12th-century frescoes overing the ceilings and arches of the oyal pantheon, which was once a long ortico of the church. The paintings epict the seasons' tasks, the killing f the first born, and a brilliant Christ antocrator. Around a dozen kings and s many queens once lay at rest in the antheon, but their tombs, too, were espoiled by the French.

It is about ten minutes' walk from San Isidoro to the unmistakeable **Hostal de San Marcos** **G**, a giant of Plateresque vanity beside the River Bernesga and at the far end of the chestnut-lined parade which leads to Guzmán roundabout. Built in 1173 for the Knights of Santiago as a monastery and hospital to shelter pilgrims, it was raised to its present monumental status in 1514, when the Order sold some of its privileges to the crown and made the Hostal its headquarters. Its 300-metre (330ft) facade was continually added to, but in the 19th century it fell into disuse. It is now a handsome, privatised Parador, and anyone can drop in for a coffee to check out its interior, which looks on to the cloisters. These are otherwise reached through the church, which has scallop shells covering the altar wall.

The **Museo de León** **H** is housed in the sacristy and chapterhouse until a new one, designed by Alejandro de la Sota is completed (www.museodeleon.com; Tue–Sat 10am–2pm and 4–7pm, Sun 10am–2pm). High spots of the

*Plaza Mayor, Leon.*

**Fact**

Astorga lies on the Ruta de la Plata, the Silver Route, though its name may derive from the Latin platea, meaning public highway. The route was used to transport minerals to Rome.

collection are a 10th-century jewel-encrusted pendant cross from San Miguel de Escalada (see page 245), and an 11th-century ivory crucifix. There are a few remnants from the Romans.

## AROUND LEÓN

Of all the nine provinces that make up the whole of the *comunidad* of Castilla y León, the greenest is León in the northwest, adjoining Asturias and Galicia. The Cordillera Cantábrica sweeps over its borders and has a second tier in the Montes de León. These mountains produced gold for the Romans and produce coal today. They also harbour remote villages which have sustained highly individual cultures. There are several caves 45km (30 miles) north of León, including the largest in Spain, at **Valporquero** ⓰. Its wonderfully oxide-stained stalactites and other natural formations can be visited in summer.

**Astorga** ⓱, a small town 40km (25 miles) west of León framed by the Montes de León, is a good stopover spot, with more than enough to kee a visitor occupied. It is elevated with a Roman wall and this seems to b where the Romans kept enslaved pe ple imprisoned to work their mines Bierza. Among them were Phoenician and Iberians from whom the Marag tos may have descended. Astorga is th main town of this "lost tribe", whos honesty made them their reputatio as reliable muleteers. Shops sell dol in their traditional dress, and the cloc on the 18th-century Town Hall is struc alternately by a Maragato coupl called Colasa and Zancudo. Maragato are not immediately recognisable, bu they put on their finery to dance at Co pus Christi and Ascension.

The main attraction otherwise i Astorga is the **Palacio Episcopal** (Tue Sat 10am–2pm and 4–8pm, Sun 10am 2pm). This is a work by Antoni Gaud the innovator of the Sagrada Famíli in Barcelona. In his inimitable neo Gothic style, the palace was begun i 1889 when the former one burnt dow His patron, the Barcelona industriali Eusebi Güell, secured him the work

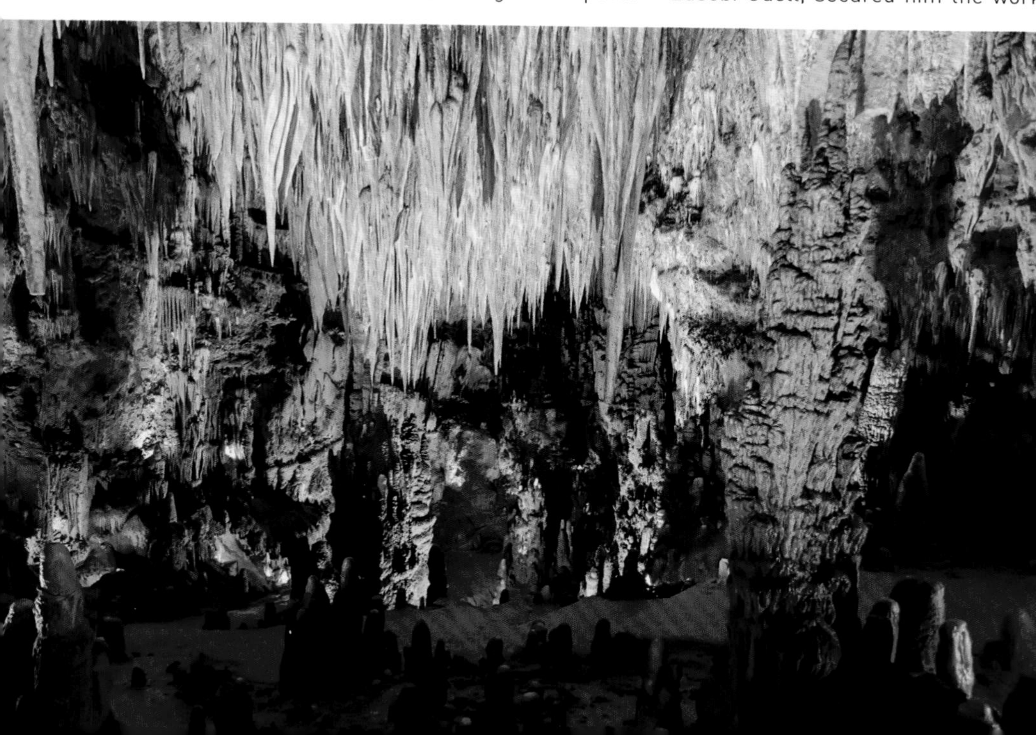

Valporquero cave.

ut Gaudí overspent and apparently o shocked the Astorgans with his uilding that the bishop refused to live nere; this was his loss. The interior eems to owe as much to the Arts and Crafts movement of William Morris as o the *modernista* style of Catalonia to vhich Gaudí belonged. Though he did ot stay long enough to embellish the etails, he left a beautiful building of legant tile-ribbed, vaulted ceilings nd limpid stained glass. It is hard to magine anyone who would not want to it in such a spacious dining room or be levated by such a throne room, both n the first floor. The top floor is a gallery of irredeemable contemporary art nd the ground floor contains an interesting museum of the pilgrims' route. The basement has Roman remains.

The bishop's taste may be explained by he rather brutish **cathedral**, which has a museum beyond it. The tourist office s located in the small church next door, and will provide a plan of a tour of the own's Roman sites, including the slaves' ail. On a sweeter note is the Museo del Chocolate, a private enterprise which traces the history of chocolate-making, for which Astorga was one of the primary centres after Hernán Cortés took his first bite of the cocoa product.

West of Astorga, the pilgrims' route continues towards Pontferrada on the LE-142 up into the uninhabited heights of the Montes de León, where pilgrims add their stones to the mounting pile beneath the **Cruz de Ferro** iron cross. It is worth travelling just a couple of miles down this road to see **Murias** and particularly **Castrillo de los Polvazares**, two typical Maragato villages, the latter much done up, with all its woodwork in matching green. Glowing in the deep orange of its stones and mortar, the buildings that line the main cobbled streets each have large doorways to allow passage to their trusted beasts of burden.

The alternative route west to **Ponferrada** 18 is the A-6 motorway, which climbs higher into the ever greener Montes de León, a few slag heaps notwithstanding. Ponferrada is no bad small town, for all its coal mining. The old and new parts lie on opposite sides

**Tip**

Chocolate from Astorga, home of the Maragatos. A local museum of chocolate shows this was one of the first places to capitalise on the new South American import.

*Castillo de los Templarios.*

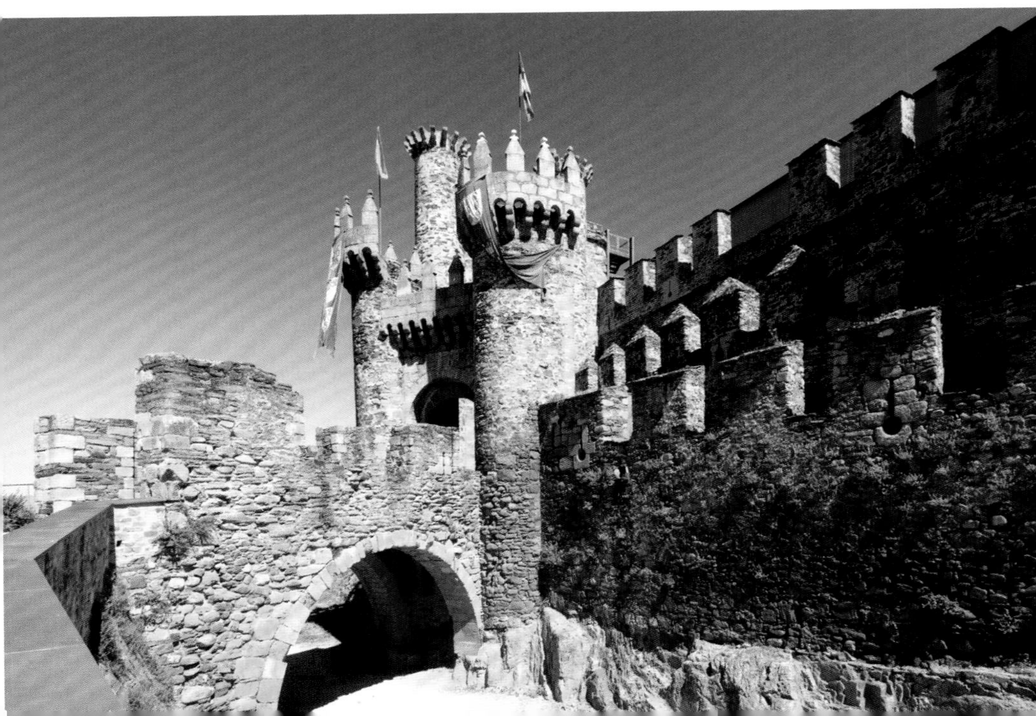

**Fact**

The writer Graham Greene was a frequent visitor to this region. His good friend and biographer, Father Leopoldo Duran, a priest in Astorga, inspired Greene's book *Monsieur Quixote*.

of the River Sil, and access to the old town, centred on a 17th-century Ayuntamiento (Town Hall), is relatively simple. The main interest is in clambering over what remains of the **Castillo de los Templarios** (Tue–Sun 10am–2pm and 4.30–8.30pm). This Templar stronghold, on Roman foundations, dates from the 12th century, and was razed by the French in 1811.

## INTO THE HILLS AND ON TO THE WINE

Just south of Ponferrada is a fine Mozarabic church, **Santo Tomás de las Ollas** (St Thomas of the Pots, after a nearby pottery). Another Mozarabic gem is at **Peñalba de Santiago** 19, in the Valle del Silencio. Although only about 20km (12 miles) south of Ponferrada, at least 40 minutes should be allowed for the journey, as the latter part is a convoluted track. The first few miles roll through the vineyards of the Bierzo region towards **San Esteban de Valdueza**, where the road skirts left through a beautiful valley of sweet chestnuts which have sustained the people of the enchanting mountain hamlets of **Valdefrancos** and **San Clemente de Valdueza**. The road then climbs seemingly to nowhere, past the turn-off to the ruined monastery of the **Montes de Valdueza**. The road ends at the hamlet of Peñalba de Santiago. Dark-slated, balconied and almost deserted, it is a wonder people have ever lived here at all. Their church was built between AD 909 and 916 and has a double horseshoe-arch entrance. Its ground plan is a simple cross and the Mozarabic curves continue everywhere inside. Isolation has kept it wonderfully preserved, though its frescoes have been whitewashed over.

Southwest of Ponferrada, some 20km (12 miles) away off the C-536, are the **Roman gold mines** at **Las Médulas** 20. From the village of Médulas a 2km (1-mile) track goes through an industrial landscape of tunnels, collapsed galleries and caves which claimed the lives of thousands of slaves.

**Villafranca del Bierzo** 21, 28km (18 miles) west of Ponferrada, is a good base for exploring the Ancares Leoneses, a region of mountain hamlets of wood and thatch that are lost in time. The best place to see these Celtic *pallozas* is **Campo del Agua** 22, a good 40-minute, hill-hugging drive up behind Villafranca del Bierzo. Bierzo is an official doc wine region, and several *bodegas* (wineries) are sited a short distance east of Villafranca del Bierzo, at **Cacabelos**. But the wine can also be found in Villafranca del Bierzo, as can other artisanal comestibles, such as wood-fire dried peppers, and cherries and chestnuts soaked in liqueurs. The town is on the pilgrim route, and the church of Santiago beside which the pilgrims' hospital is being resurrected has a Puerta de Perdón, the second after León. The other church above the town is San Francisco, supposed to have been founded by the saint from Assisi on his pilgrimage to Santiago. The town's bulky 16th-century castle is privately owned.

*Old mine at Las Médulas.*

*The rooftops of Peñalba de Santiago.*

# DISTINCTIVE STYLES OF GRANARY STORES

The landscape of Northern Spain is distinguished by oblong "hórreos", granaries built of wood or stone and raised on stilts, with flourishes and decorations.

Whole volumes have been dedicated to studies of the *hórreo*, the *panera*, the *cabazo* and the *granero*, all variations of the granaries of Northern Spain. The aesthetics, materials, forms and functions of these rural outbuildings, which some ethnographers have dubbed "adjectival structures", vary widely from one valley or village to another, depending on terrain, weather and the kind of goods to be stored, as well as on local materials. They need to be tall enough for good ventilation, but not so high that the wind blows them apart. Any *hórreo* still standing was built after the 15th century, though documentary evidence two centuries earlier talks of roofs made of straw or slate and wood or stone floors. The size, shape and material used for the *pegollos* (stilts or legs) or the *muelas* (guards against rodents from climbing the *pegollos*) contributed to the distinctive styles.

The various parts of the *hórreo* are as linguistically colourful as the quirky shapes of the elements they describe. The *colondra* (colander) is the basic container; the *moño o obispo* (bishop's hair-bun) is the top knot, the *subidoría* is the stone stairway placed just far enough from the *hórreo* to discourage unwanted guests. Inevitably, the eye and taste of the builders came into play. The *lauburu*, or Basque cross, is a typical decoration in the Basque Country. *Hórreos* were often more ornate than the farmhouses they served, as they represented the productivity or fertility of farming.

*The distinctive legs of the hórreo are known as pegollas.*

*A traditional stone hórreo in Leis de Nemancos, Galic*

*This hórreo in Carnota, said to be the largest in Galic probably belonged to the local rectory. Rectorial hórr were where the parish priest hoarded his tithe (tenth the farmers' produce, and they often held vast stores*

ͻn hórreo with a curtain of drying garlic. An hórreo hold, as well, dairy products, meat, corn and other · of different types.

ᵗravellers often mistook hórreos for tiny chapels.

*Palloza and horreo in Los Ancares, Piornedo de Ancares, Galicia.*

## Traditional country living

From the circular Galician and Asturian *palloza* or thatch-roofed *teitos* to the Basque *caserío* or the Catalan *masia*, different models of northern Spanish country architecture share many characteristics and at the same time differ widely.

Galician and Asturian farmhouses tend to be smaller than Basque *caseríos* or Catalan *masias*. Catalan and Basque families generally owned their lands, whereas the peasants of the northwest were tenant farmers. In addition, the *minifundio* system of inheritance divided ever-shrinking properties. Catalonia´s *hereu* (heir) and the *latifundio* system left properties intact, all inherited by the first-born.

Popular architecture varies widely within regions. High mountain architecture along the Pyrenees and in the Picos de Europa favours steeper, snow-shedding rooflines, while coastal structures such as the Asturian *casa mariñana* used lower, wider lines. Galician and Asturian houses have little space for livestock and equipment, so more outbuildings and *hórreos*, were built, whereas the Basque *caserío* and the Catalan *masia* lodge animals on the ground floor and the family on the second.

*Crosses and religious ornamentation give the impression of chapels or tombs.*

La Lanzada's long, sandy beach.

# GALICIA

Dubbed the "Ireland of Spain" for its climate, patchwork of green fields and vegetable gardens, alicia is best known for its fjord-like *rías*, its seafood and Santiago's superlative pilgrims' cathedral.

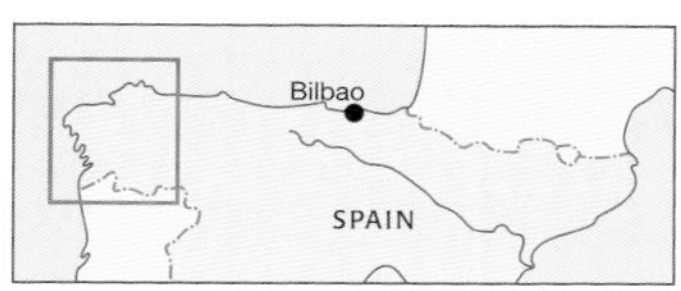


pain's rainy northwestern corner ccupied by Galicia has kept a distinct haracter shaped as much by its mounin and coastal landscapes as its long story of chronic poverty and emigraon. The Romans believed its western oint, Cape Finisterre, to be the end of e world and even today, when motorays slice between the main cities and own the Atlantic coast, it retains tracts spectacularly wild landscape which aze with purple heather and yellow orse in early summer.

Galicians feel a deep attachment to e land, which is farmed in characristic smallholdings averaging just 50 sq metres (2,700 sq ft). These, in rn, are grouped in nearly 4,000 scatred and often isolated parishes. Such agmentation has held back economic evelopment inland, but helped to prerve native traditions such as the alician language *(gallego)*, deeply held eliefs in the spirit world, a lively Celtic usical tradition with bagpipes, and a ewildering range of fiestas. Along e jagged seaboard a denser populaon lives off the highly developed sea conomy, with fishing fleets backed up tourism.

The provincial capitals – Lugo, Ponvedra, Ourense and A Coruña (Orense nd La Coruña in Castilian) – have any marked contrasts but they share eather-beaten stone architecture. Today, the region's largest city is the sprawling industrial port of Vigo (population 290,000), while its administrative capital is its spiritual heart: Santiago de Compostela (population 100,000), Europe's greatest pilgrimage city.

**Main attractions**

Santiago de Compostela
River Sil Valley
Baiona
Pontevedra
A Coruña
Rias Baixas

## SANTIAGO DE COMPOSTELA

Known by locals as the city where rain is art, **Santiago de Compostela ❶** has granite-paved streets that gleam softly under frequent, fine drizzle. The first medieval town grew around the supposed discovery in 813 of St James's

Maps on pages 256, 258, 268

*Cathedral, Santiago de Compostela.*

tomb – an event now firmly debunked by historians as a political manoeuvre by the church. Santiago became a Renaissance university city in 1501 and Galicia's administrative capital in 1981. Today, its character is chameleon-like, sometimes determinedly cosmopolitan and at others marked by its traditional native and spiritual heartbeat.

The **cathedral** Ⓐ has been rebuilt four times. Its golden Baroque shell (1738–50) encloses a shadowy medieval interior (1075–1211) designed to meet pilgrims' needs by travelling French Benedictine architects. Wide unbroken aisles – an innovation at the time – were designed to ease the flow of visitors, sleeping space was provided in the upper galleries and perfume from the famous 70kg (154lb) incense burner smothered the whiff of unwashed bodies; the original was stolen by Napoleon's troops, but a replica still swings dramatically at daily Mass in Holy Years, reaching speeds of up to 70kph (44mph). Today, an estimated 3 million people pour through here every Holy Year. The *botafumeiro* (incense burner) is kept in the **Museo de l Catedral de Santiago** (www.catedralde santiago.es; daily 7am–8.30pm), whic also has a tapestry and archaeologica collection and wonderful 13th-centur stone choir stalls.

Among the cathedral's treasures, it original Romanesque doorway calle the **Pórtico de la Gloria** (1168–88) "Gateway to Heaven" – is an unpar alleled masterpiece. The sculpture friezes carved by Maestro Mateo ar so alive with human detail that each the 200 figures seems to leap out of th stone. A glutton in hell snacks on a pi (right arch); musicians in the heaven choir doze on medieval instrument (central arch). Inside, pilgrims knoc their heads against a statue of Maestr Mateo in the hope of acquiring a sma tering of his genius.

Although the cathedral is Spain single most valuable church propert it buzzes with humanity. Locals pra in the 9th-century Capilla de la Co tizuela, where students leave prayer written on scraps of paper to a Romar esque Christ.

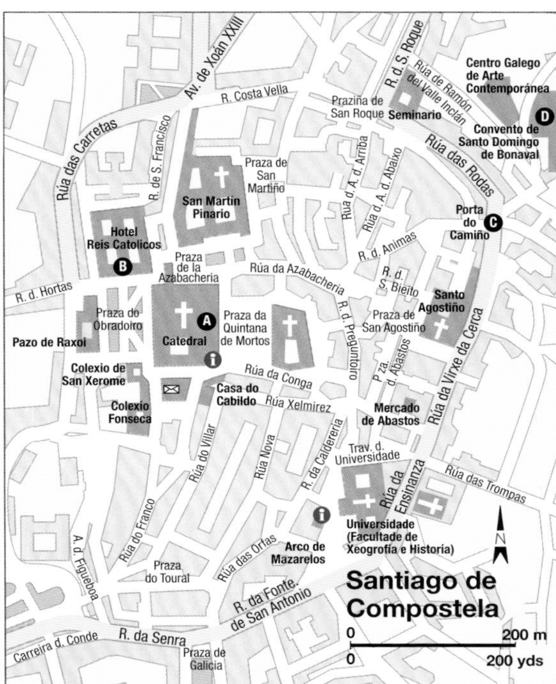

*Statue of St James, inside Santiago de Compostela's Cathedral.*

## ROUND THE OLD TOWN

mong the city's many sights are 73 onasteries, convents and churches, us fountains, workshops and taverns. ne splendid **Praza do Obradoiro**, for enturies the cathedral's building te, is framed on its west side by the enaissance **Hotel Reis Catolicos** **B** Hostal de los Reyes Católicos) pil-rims' hostel built between 1500 and 511, now a sumptuously furnished arador hotel. Two smaller squares *praza* in Galician), Azabachería and raterías, are named after the jet and lver talisman-makers who still sell neir souvenirs to pilgrims there. In the arrow streets you will find all kinds f traditional shopping ranging from logs and candles to umbrellas and, n the market, breast-shaped cheeses *etilla gallega)*, while a mass of taverns nd bars serves good local food.

Just outside the main pilgrims' gate nto the city, the **Porta do Camiño** **C**, tand the adjacent **Convento de Santo Domingo de Bonaval** **D** (14th–18th entury) where there is the lively eth-nographical **Museo do Pobo Gallego** (Tue–Sat 10.30am–2pm and 4–7.30pm, Sun 11am–2pm) and the sleek 1993 **Centro Gallego de Arte Contemporáneo**, which holds regular exhibitions making an interesting contrast. The monastery is backed by a sweep of modern gardens, or you can watch the world stroll by – often clutching umbrellas – in the gardens of La Herradura park.

## PILGRIMS' APPROACHES

As the pilgrims' approach routes to Santiago converge like a star, they trace an architectural pattern. Churches, shrines, hospitals, calvaries, milestones, bridges and monasteries – whether dating from the early Romanesque or later Baroque spurts of building – share a regional style with natural details and an earthy sense of humour. St James pops up everywhere, as pilgrim, warrior and evangelist.

Today most pilgrims arrive along the **Camino Francés** (French Way), which runs in directly from the east through Lugo and La Coruña provinces. There are sections of lovely woodland paths,

**Fact**

The Año Jacobeo (Xacobeo in Gallego) occurs when St. James's day (25 July) falls on a Sunday. Pilgrims visiting Santiago in that year have all their sins forgiven.

*Pilgrims gather outside the Town Hall in Santiago de Compostela.*

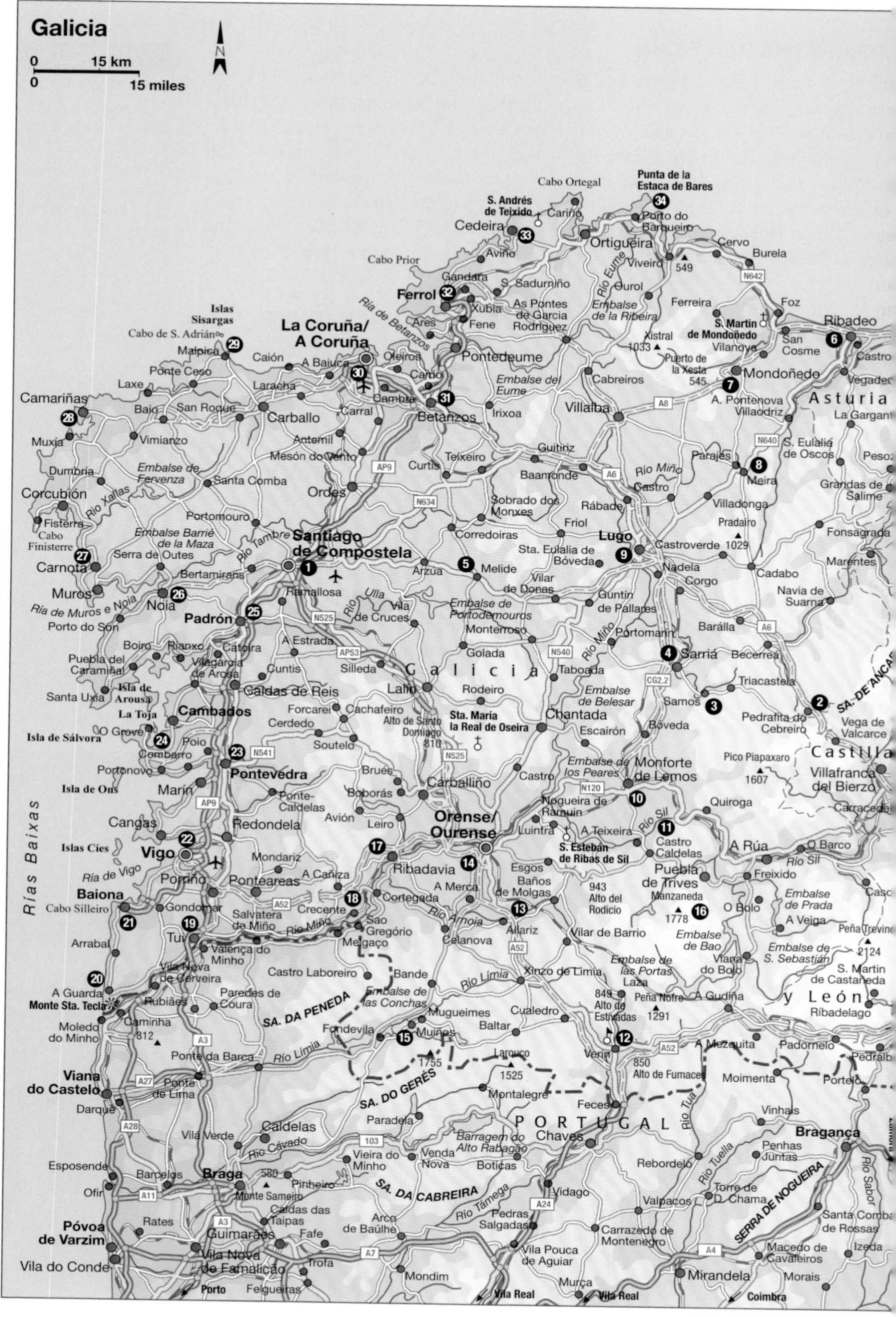
Galicia
0 15 km
0 15 miles
N
Cabo Ortegal
Punta de la Estaca de Bares
S. Andrés de Teixido
Cariño
Porto do Barqueiro
Cedeira
Ortigueira
Cervo
Burela
Aviño
Cabo Prior
Viveiro
549
N642
Gándara
S. Sadurniño
Ourol
Ferrol
Xubia
As Pontes de García Rodríguez
Río Eume
Embalse de la Ribeira
Ferreira
Foz
Islas Sisargas
Ría de Betanzos
Ares
Fene
S. Martin de Mondoñedo
Ribadeo
Cabo de S. Adrián
La Coruña/ A Coruña
Xistral 1033
Puerto de la Xesta 545
Vilanova
San Cosme
Castro
Malpica
Caión
A Baiuca
Oleiros
Pontedeume
Mondoñedo
Vegadeo
Ponte Ceso
Laxe
Laracha
Camio
Cabreiros
Embalse del Eume
A. Pontenova
Villaodriz
Asturias
Camariñas
Bajo
San Roque
Carballo
Cambre
Carral
Betanzos
Irixoa
Villalba
A8
La Garganta
Muxía
Vimianzo
Antemil
Mesón do Vento
N640
S. Eulalia de Oscos
Pesoz
Dumbría
Embalse de Fervenza
AP9
Curtis
Teixeiro
Guitiriz
Parajes
Meira
Corcubión
Río Xallas
Santa Comba
Ordes
N634
Baamonde
A6
Río Miño
Castro
Grandas de Salime
Fisterra
Cabo Finisterre
Portomouro
Sobrado dos Monxes
Rábade
Villadonga
Pradairo 1029
Embalse Barrié de la Maza
Río Tambre
Santiago de Compostela
Corredoiras
Friol
Lugo
Fonsagrada
Carnota
Serra de Outes
Sta. Eulalia de Bóveda
Castroverde
Marentes
Muros
Bertamirans
Arzúa
Melide
Nadela
Cadabo
Ría de Muros e Noia
Noia
Ramallosa
Río Ulla
Vila de Cruces
Vilar de Donas
Corgo
Navia de Suarna
Porto do Son
Padrón
Embalse de Portodemouros
Guntín de Pallares
N525
Monterroso
Portomarín
Barálla
Boiro
Rianxo
Catoira
A Estrada
Golada
N540
Sarriá
Becerreá
Puebla del Caramiñal
Vilagarcía de Arosa
Cuntis
AP53
Silleda
Galicia
Taboada
CG2.2
Triacastela
Isla de Arousa
Santa Uxía
Caldas de Reis
Lalín
Rodeiro
Embalse de Belesar
Samos
La Toja
Cambados
Forcarei
Cachafeiro
Alto de Santo Domingo 810
Sta. María la Real de Oseira
Chantada
Pedrafita do Cebreiro
SA. DE ANCARES
Vega de Valcarce
Isla de Sálvora
O Grove
Cerdedo
Escairón
Bóveda
Poio
Souteló
Monforte de Lemos
Pico Piapaxaro 1607
Castilla
Combarro
N541
Pontevedra
Embalse de los Peares
Portonovo
Brués
Castro
Carballiño
Villafranca del Bierzo
Isla de Ons
Marín
Boborás
Ponte-Caldelas
N120
Nogueira de Ramuín
Quiroga
Carracedelo
AP9
Avión
Cangas
Redondela
Leiro
Orense/ Ourense
Luintra
A Teixeira
Río Sil
Islas Cíes
Vigo
Mondariz
S. Estebán de Ribas de Sil
Castro Caldelas
A Rúa
O Barco
Ría de Vigo
Ribadavia
Esgos
Freixido
Porriño
Ponteareas
A Cañiza
Baños de Molgas
Puebla de Trives
Baiona
Cabo Silleiro
Gondomar
Cortegada
A Merca
943 Alto del Rodicio
Manzaneda 1778
Embalse de Prada
Casoyo
A52
Salvatera de Miño
Crecente
Sao Gregório
Río Arnoia
O Bolo
Río Miño
Allariz
Vilar de Barrio
A Veiga
Peña Trevinca 2124
Rías Baixas
Arrabal
Tui
Valença do Minho
Melgaço
Celanova
Embalse de Bao
Embalse de S. Sebastián
Vila Nova de Cerveira
A52
Viana do Bolo
S. Martín de Castañeda
Castro Laboreiro
Bande
Río Limia
Xinzo de Limia
Embalse de las Portas
Laza
A Guarda
Monte Sta. Tecla
Paredes de Coura
Embalse de las Conchas
849 Alto de Estivadas
Peña Nofre 1291
A Gudiña
y León
Rubiães
SA. DA PENEDA
Mugueimes
Cualedro
Ribadelago
Moledo do Minho
Caminha
812
Fondevila
Muiños
Baltar
A3
Larouco 1525
Verín
A52
A Mezquita
Padornelo
Ponte da Barca
Río Limia
1755
850 Alto de Fumaces
Pedralba
Viana do Castelo
A27
Ponte de Lima
SA. DO GERÊS
Montalegre
Río Tua
Moimenta
Portelo
Darque
Feces
Vinhais
A28
Paradela
PORTUGAL
Bragança
Vilá Verde
Caldelas
Barragem do Alto Rabagão
Chaves
Rio Cávado
103
Esposende
Vieira do Minho
Venda Nova
Boticas
Rebordelo
Penhas Juntas
Barcelos
Braga
580
Monte Sameiro
Pinheiro
SA. DA CABREIRA
Río Tuella
Río Sabor
Ofir
A11
Vidago
Torre de D. Chama
SERRA DE NOGUEIRA
Rio Tâmega
A24
Rates
A3
Caldas das Taipas
Arco de Baúlhe
Pedras Salgadas
Valpaços
Santa Comba de Rossas
Póvoa de Varzim
Guimarães
Fafe
Carrazedo de Montenegro
Vila Nova de Famalicão
Vila Pouca de Aguiar
Macedo de Cavaleiros
Izeda
Vila do Conde
A7
Trofa
A4
Mondim
Murça
Mirandela
Morais
Porto
Felgueiras
Vila Real
Vila Real
Coimbra

ıt the main landmarks are still on the ad from Ponferrada in León province. ·ossing into Galicia the 9th-century ınctuary of **O Cebreiro** ❷ keeps a ıalice said to be the Holy Grail; **Samos** is a riverside town whose lovely enedictine monastery was heavily built after a fire in 1951; **Sarria** ❹ ıs a hilltop fortified watchtower and enaissance monastic hospital; the gion's oldest stone calvary stands at **elide** ❺; and, finally, **Monte Gozo** – ount Pleasure – gives weary pilgrims e first view of Santiago's spires. But early every village and town – **Tri-astela**, **Portomarín** and **Vilar de nas**, for example – has its own small urch or chapel (ask for the key).

Following the other eastern pilgrims' utes is an excellent way of exploring ıgo and Orense, Galicia's least-vis-ed provinces. The original Cantabrian ute was opened by the Asturian yal pilgrims of the Middle Ages. It ns from **Ribadeo** ❻, a tuna-fishing rt on Lugo's northern coast, via **ondoñedo** ❼, a small farming town mous for its deep-dish almond pies, to the capital city of Lugo. Mondoñedo was an episcopal seat until 1834 and its former cathedral, San Martiño, is a gem with an eccentric museum under the rafters packed with naïve rural religious art. From here a detour through the sierra takes you to **Meira's** ❽ fine 12th-century Cistercian church and then to **Castro de Viladonga**, a Celtic settlement dating from the 3rd–4th centuries with an excellent museum, the **Monográfico Do Castro de Viladonga** (daily 10am–7pm), explaining the way of life of the Celtic people who were spread right through Galicia for a thousand years. Above Meira, at **El Pedrigal**, there are fine views at the source of the Miño where its nascent waters rush over boulders.

By the time the Miño reaches the city of **Lugo** ❾ it shows its quiet power, throwing off mists that shroud the entire town in winter. Much of Lugo's charm is in its easy-going country ways, but it is famed for two things: its intact Roman wall encircling the inner town and its superb local beef. Walking around the top of the wall you spy

**Eat**

At O Cebreiro, stop to taste the local cheese, *Queso de Cebreiro*, which, like a good wine, has been given the appellation *denominación de origen* for its excellence. It is traditionally eaten with honey.

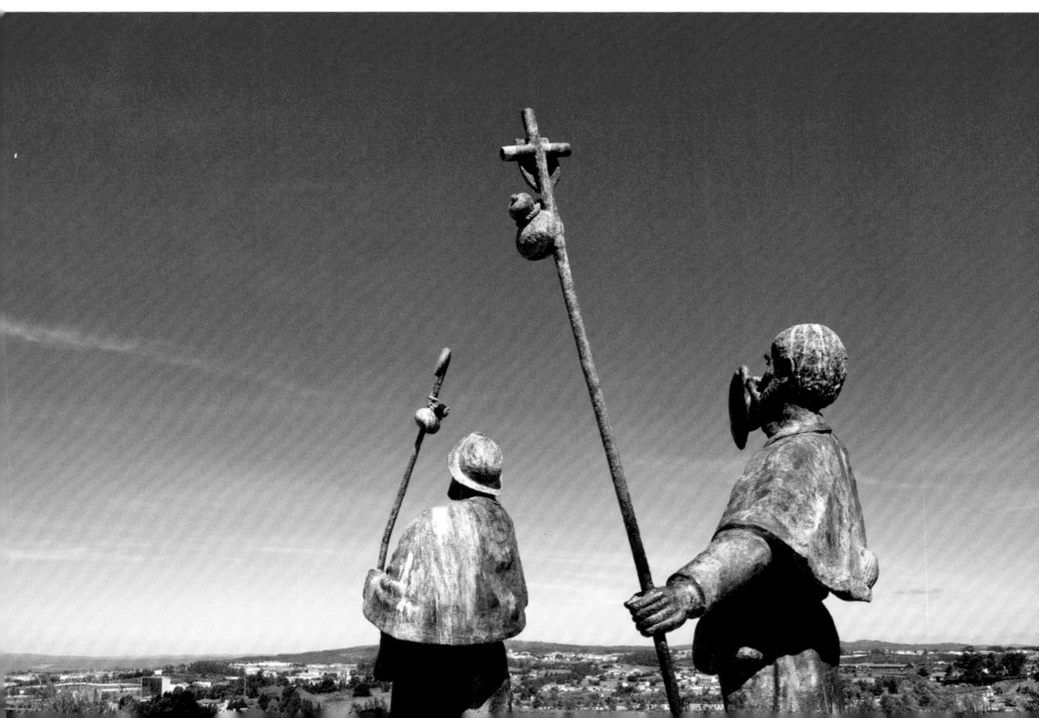

*Bronze statues of pilgrims on Monte Gozo.*

**Quote**

"Any people who have been as badly treated as the Galicians are entitled to be mistrustful, and among other Spaniards they have a reputation for caution and guile. In Castilian, an ambiguous statement is a *galleguismo* (Galicianism)."

John Hooper, "The New Spaniards"

down on the cathedral (12th–18th century), and the **Museo Provincial** (Mon–Fri 9am–9pm, Sat 10.30am–2pm and 4.30–8pm, Sun 11am–2pm).

A focal point in one of the cathedral's chapels is Nossa Señora dos Ollos Grandes (Our Lady of the Big Eyes), a serene Gothic statue surrounded by an extraordinary Baroque frieze of sculptured cherubs. In the narrow network of old streets (Rúa Nova, Praza do Campo and Santa Cruz) locals quaff wine day and night from china cups. Curiously little else remains of the Roman town, built at a road junction on the route from Braga to Astorga, except **Santa Eulalia de Bóveda**, 15km (10 miles) southwest on the Ourense road, a unique 4th-century Roman temple later Christianised with vivid wall mosaics.

## SIERRAS, VINEYARDS, MONASTERIES

Lugo's countryside gives wonderful glimpses of old Galicia. Widows walk solitary cows along the road, chestnut woods drip in the mists and octopus is cooked in copper cauldrons at count markets. At O Piornedo in the **Parqu Natural de Os Ancares**, a spectac larly beautiful mountain region ea of Lugo often cut off by winter snow you can visit the best examples of th pre-Roman thatched stone house *pallozas*, in which mountain familie lived until recently. Os Ancares's wa of life is fast disappearing, eroded a elsewhere by emigration and moder agriculture, but wildlife, including ro deer, boar and capercaillie, remain among its peaks and remote valley Intriguingly, historians suggest th *Don Quixote*'s author, Miguel de Ce vantes, was born in a village here 1547 – his name means "land of th red deer".

The hilltop town of **Monforte d Lemos** ⑩ at a railway junction 66k (41 miles) south of Lugo makes a goo base for exploring the sierras, vine yards and river valleys of souther Lugo province. Above the town stan the crumbling medieval palace an watchtower from which the powerf Counts of Lemos ruled their feud

*Stone bridge at Monforte de Lemos.*

erritory. They also built the fortress t Castro Caldelas on the other side of he River Sil to the south.

In Monforte, Lemos family members ndowed the overpoweringly grandiose 6th-century Jesuit Colegio del Cardeal, nicknamed "the Galician Escorial", nd the apparently modest **Convento e las Clarisas**, or Poor Clares' conent, which accumulated a stunning ollection of 17th-century religious art ncluding a number of gory saints' relcs that can be inspected in the Museo e Arte Sacro (daily 11am–1pm and –6pm). The hilltop Monasterio de San 'icente del Pino is now being converted nto a stately Parador hotel.

## WINELANDS OF THE RIVER SIL

From Monforte there is easy access ither to the walking country of the Sierra de Ocourel, or to the vineyards, gorges and monasteries of the **River Sil Valley** ⓫, which runs westwards nto Galicia from León. The Romans struck gold here, built roads and bridges – at Petín and El Barco – and erraced the vineyards of Valdeorras and Ribeira Sacra, two growing areas which still produce fine wines that are fast becoming collectors' items.

The **Ribeira Sacra** vineyards, which run dizzyingly down a spectacular 50km (36-mile) gorge, may be seen from a river catamaran or the country road between **Luintra** and **A Teixera**. At **Gundivós** craft potters make earthenware jugs and urns for the wines. The area takes its medieval name, the Sacred Riverbank, from a cluster of early monasteries and hermitages on the south bank. **San Estevo (Estebán) de Ribas de Sil** near Luintra is splendidly sited if dubiously restored; here you can rent simple rooms and eat with a panoramic river view. Among the half dozen smaller ruins, **Santa Cristina** (near Parada de Sil) or **San Pedro de Rocas** (reached from Esgos) are outstanding, preserving their primitive beauty and buried in woodland.

## OURENSE AND ITS PROVINCE

Medieval pilgrims heading up to Santiago through landlocked south-eastern Ourense province travelled roads dating back to Roman times. Today, the main route is a lorry-laden highway (the A-52) on which travellers rarely stop, although there are worthwhile things to see. Six kilometres (4 miles) above **Verín** ⓬, near the Portuguese border, stands the splendid triple-walled castle complex of **Monterrei** (13th–18th century), which watched over safe passage of pilgrims through the frontier territory. The country town of **Allariz** ⓭ has six churches and further north a short detour leads to **Santa María la Real de Oseira** (1140), Galicia's first Cistercian monastery, where Benedictine monks will show you round the cloisters, church and superbly carved sacristy.

The city of **Ourense** ⓮ (Orense) is often bypassed, too, but within its modern suburbs is a compact old town with three main sights – the Roman bridge (largely rebuilt), hot sulphurous springs and the **cathedral** (12th–13th

**Quote**

"As I travelled to the west on my way to Coruña I was reminded continually of Galway, and it was not only something in the greenness of the land, in the stone walls, in the wind-swept estuaries, but something also in the bearing and glances of the people.

H.V. Morton "A Stranger in Spain"

*Grape harvest, River Sil Valley.*

century) – all lying within a stone's throw of one another. The largely 12th-century cathedral echoes that of Santiago although it is less heavily rebuilt; gilded decoration runs riot in the **Capilla del Santo Cristo** where a painfully emaciated and revered Gothic Christ hangs. Off the Plaza Mayor, where the bishop's palace houses the Museo Arqueológico (www.musarqourense.xunta.es; 9am–9pm Tue–Sat, 9am–3pm Sun), the pedestrianised streets are packed with elegant shops, such as those of native fashion designers Adolfo Domínguez and Roberto Verino, and a mass of bars serving excellent *tapas*.

Southern Ourense can be explored more fully from **Allariz**, which has excellent family holiday facilities ranging from country sports to workshop-museums, riverside restaurants and bars. From here you can loop west on country roads to **Celanova**, where it is worth visiting the **Monasterio de San Salvador**. This Benedictine edifice grew to house a thousand monks, but its huge cloister is now echoingly empty. In fact the original, tiny, 10th-century Mozarabic chapel of Sa Miguel is as impressive as the grand ose Baroque church. Continuing sout after passing through the village Bande, you come to **Santa Comba**, 7th-century church (rebuilt in the 9t century), which ranks high on the li of Spain's Visigothic buildings. On th opposite side of the reservoir nea which it stands is **Muiños** 15, whic has a beach.

To the east of Allariz stretch wil sierras with the region's only ski station at **Manzaneda** 16. Villages her celebrate Carnival with costume antics, banned under Franco but kep alive in the inaccessible countryside These days, Galicia's fiestas rang from superstitious religious rituals horse round-ups and flower days t festivals of local culture and win binges. Local tourist offices can giv you details of how to join in.

## DOWN THE MIÑO VALLEY

Southwest of Ourense, **Ribadavia** 17 is a picturesque wine town sitting in a bowl of terraced hillsides at the mouth

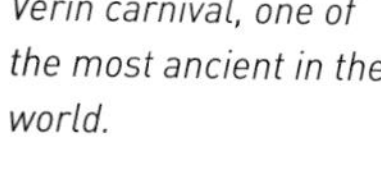

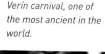

*Verín carnival, one of the most ancient in the world.*

f the River Avia. The town's closely acked medieval quarter, protected y a sturdy castle, was built with profs from the export of the local sweet vine which is said to have left both ohn of Gaunt's and Napoleon's invadng troops legless. Today's maze of lleyways preserves a sizeable Jewish uarter, nine medieval churches and ld town gates. For wine-lovers, a visit o the *bodega* (winery) at the **Museo Etnológico** (Tue–Fri 10am–8pm, Sat–Sun 11am–2.30pm; free), where new vines are experimented with, can be ollowed up by a thorough tasting of the Ribeiro wine tapped from the barrel at O Papuxa, a cellar *bodega*.

There is much else to enjoy here both on land and the river. Winding anes lead to the Cistercian **Monasterio de San Clodio** in **Leiro**, 8km (5 miles) north, the 9th-century Mozarabic church of **San Xéns (Ginés) de Francelos** just downriver and lovely wine villages such as **Pazos de Arenteiro**. The tourist office in Ribadavia can also steer you towards both quality and farmhouse wine-makers, called *colleteiros*, where you can buy the fruity red wines. The river waters can be explored by catamaran, rowing-boat or canoe; or there are serious watersports at **Castrelo do Miño** on the reservoir east of the town. Thermal waters abound and there is a spa for every taste within a few kilometres, from the brand new hotel at **Arnoia** to **Prexigueiro**'s sulphurous river pools, or traditional smaller spas at **Cortegada** and **Berán**.

The journey on down the north bank of the **River Miño** is a beautiful drive at any time of year. In winter mists trail up over the high valley sides; in summer you can cool down with a dip in the river. Shortly before **Crecente** ⓲, small watchtowers and fortresses begin to mark the border with Portugal. The largest is at **Salvaterra do Miño**, where a detour northwards takes you up to 19th-century **Mondaríz-Balneario**, perhaps the most beautiful of all the Galician spa-hotels. **Arbo**, a river-fishing village, holds a lamprey festival in April – although these days the fish are in short supply.

*Ribadavia's medieval quarter.*

**Fact**

An estimated 85 percent of all Europe's cocaine arrives via Galicia's western Atlantic coastline.

## HILLTOP TOWNS

Shortly after Salvaterra the road runs into **Tui** ⓳, which looks over to the geometric, 18th-century fortress walls of **Valença do Minho** on the Portuguese south bank. Linked since 1884 by an iron box-bridge designed by Gustave Eiffel, the towns live as friendly neighbours with crowds flocking over the border to Valença's huge Wednesday street market. Tui's strategic position has made it an important crossroads since Roman times. No surprise, then, that the small hilltop Cathedral, a quirky architectural gem, has such a defensive fortress exterior. Its rich stone carving, paintings, chapels and facades condense every Spanish style from the 12th to the 18th century, when vast stone beams were built across the nave to prevent it collapsing after earthquake damage. The Museo de la Catedral (Tue–Sun 10am–1.30pm and 4–8pm) contains local treasures.

A short walk through hilly streets leads to unexpected quiet corners such as the Convento de Santa Catalina, where you can buy the nuns' biscuits. In spring you can also try tiny transparent elvers, regarded as a great delicacy and priced accordingly. The best vistas back over the town and river valley are just 7km (5 miles) north of Tui, where wild horses run free in the Parque Natural de Monte Aloia.

## THE ATLANTIC PROVINCES

Although the western Atlantic coastline falls into contrasting geographic segments, all are marked by a shared history of centuries living looking out to sea to ward off invaders and earn a livelihood. While its ports grew wealthy on trade, shipbuilding and industry, life in the fishing villages remains hard. So many boats have been lost in the swell or smashed against the raggedy rocks here that every wave is said to carry the soul of a dead sailor. Women run families and work the land while their husbands are at sea for months at a time.

New sources of income – ranging from intensive fish-farming and canning to tourism, wine-making and drug-smuggling – have swept away the old poverty. Many families remain dependent on the sea, but the number of operating fishing boats has fallen dramatically and ports have had to specialise in certain fish catches. Modern times have improved safety at sea but brought new hazards, such as pollution and depleted fish stocks. As a result, even a short visit here will bring you up against sharply felt ancestral memories. Churches up and down the coast remain full of lighted candles and offerings for the sailors' and fishermen's safety.

## A GUARDA TO BAIONA

The southernmost stretch of the coast is pleasantly empty. **A Guarda** ⓴, sitting at the mouth of the Miño estuary, is a characterful fishing port with brightly painted houses round the harbour, restaurants serving spanking fresh lobster and a car ferry service to

## GARDENS AND PARKS

Just inland from the coast the mild but damp Atlantic climate has produced some really wonderful parks and gardens that are particularly verdant and luscious. The **Jardín Botánico** in Padrón has rare subtropical species brought back by emigrants from Latin America. A distinctive style of lush, watery, romantic gardens developed in the *pazos*, manor-houses with farm-estates where the Galician nobility retreated in the summer. They had their own chapels, dovecotes and granaries.

Three of the gardens are now open to visitation by the public. One is Vigo's **Pazo de Quiñones**, where a 500-year-old camellia continues to blossom in the gardens (closed Mon and Sun pm). The **Pazo de Santa Cruz** in Ribadulla, 18km (11 miles) southeast of Santiago on the N-525 (also with railway station) has lovely wooded walks and water gardens (by arrangement, through Santiago de Compostela tourist office). The most beautiful of them all is the **Pazo de Oca**, 8km (5 miles) further on (9am–dusk). Dubbed "the Versailles of Galicia", it was laid out in the 18th century with lakes, a splendid bridge, ornaments, vine arbours and even a church. It is now owned by the Duchess of Alba, whose ancestor was famously painted by Goya.

ortugal. Kiwi fruit and vines flourish
 the subtropical climate, which draws
 mass of migratory birds to the estu-
ry. **Monte de Santa Tegra**, the wooded
nountain behind the town, offers pan-
ramic views and has a large Celtic
xcavation and associated museum
Tue–Sun Mar–June and Sept–Oct
0am–7pm, Jul–Aug 9am–9pm, Nov
1am–5pm). To see these, take the
km (2-mile) walk to the summit along
 path that starts in the centre of A
uarda.

The 40-minute drive north to **Baiona** passes the graceful Cistercian nonastery of **Santa María de Oya**, uilt in 1168. In early summer, wild orses in the sierra behind the coast re rounded up in famous *curros* fes-ivals. Heavy development begins shortly before Baiona, a ritzy resort with a prestigious yacht club, where Europe's first news of Columbus's discovery of the New World was received after the flagship *La Pinta* made landfall here in 1493, disembarking the first Native American. A wooden replica of the boat, looking remarkably small, bobs in the harbour. Above is the jutting headland where the original city fort (now a Parador) was built to repel Berber and English attacks. Behind it lies the old town. In summer boat trips can be made to the nearby Islas Cíes.

## VIGO AND THE RÍAS BAIXAS

A Galician creation myth runs that when God rested on the seventh day he leaned on Galicia and his fingers pressed in to make the *rías baixas*, four fjord-like estuaries slashing the coast between Baiona and Noia. (*Baixa* means lower, *alta* is higher.) Formed by the same geological upheaval which lifted the inland mountains, their fresh and salt waters support rich ecosystems. The rich harvest from mussel and oyster farming platforms, clumped together like houseboats, and from hundreds of shellfish-gatherers on foot makes for some of the world's best seafood restaurants.

**Vigo** ㉒ is Galicia's most dynamic and largest city. As the exit point for nearly all the region's emigrants to Latin America – more than a million

**Fact**

The first recorded sea-bathing in Europe was in Vigo. It is mentioned in the verses of an early 13th-century Galician *joglar*, Martin Codax.

*Celtic village on Monte Santa Tefra.*

made the journey in the 20th century alone – and home to Spain's largest fishing fleet, it has a strong liberal political tradition and the vitality of all great sea-cities. After downing fresh, raw oysters outside the **Mercado de Piedra** market, you can explore the old town and the city's museum inside the **Pazo de Quiñones**, a palatial 17th-century manor-house, where you can see the region's best collection of historical and modern Galician art and then relax in its surrounding parkland (the Parque de Castrelos).

For seaside sightseeing, head towards the Berbes fishing quarter before picking up a boat ride across the *ría* for 14.5km (9 miles) out to the **Islas Cíes**, three islets with sparkling sands. Inhabited since Palaeolithic times, they are now a bird reserve with limited summer access (and a campsite), though they can become crowded at weekends and on public holidays. The Cies, along with three other archipelagos, now form the Parque Nacional Maritímo-Terrestre de las Islas Atlanticas de Galicia.

Galicia's main estuary towns hav all enjoyed heydays as busy ports **Pontevedra** ㉓ bears the title of cit but after being landlocked by estuary mud 300 years ago, lives with relaxed, countrified air. Paved street lead between manor houses, medieva squares with calvaries, six churche and an excellent **Museo de Pontevedr** (Tue–Sat 10am–9pm, Sun 11am–2pm with the contents of a ship's hold Columbus's flagship was built in the dockyards here before being fitted ou at nearby Marín. Just upstream, a contemporary sculpture park with work b a dozen international artists has bee created on the river islet of Xunquiera The lovely 16th-century Colegiata de Santa María church, rich with Plateresque stonework, was built with seafaring wealth. In the old streets belo it there is some good old-fashione food to be had in the bars and taverns.

The patchwork of smallholdings an vineyards running down to the wester shoreline is broken by small ports an seaside resorts. The first of these wa the smart 19th-century spa-hotel or

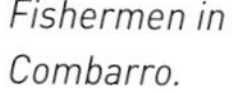

*Fishermen in Combarro.*

he tiny island of **A Toxa** 24 (La Toja), vhere Julio Iglesias' annual visits set he tone, but now the entire headland orth of Pontevedra is clogged with ourists in summer. Opposite A Toxa nd as its less exclusive counterpart, ) **Grove** has established itself as a eafood-lovers' paradise. To the south, round the headland, the open, sandy each at **La Lanzada** ends in a nature eserve of marshland and sand dunes. **:ombarro**, a quaint fishing port, and **:ambados**, an old smuggling town on he opposite side of the peninsula, have istoric centres; the latter is a good pot to stop and try the delicious local Albariño wines. In the hills between the wo is the 12th-century Monasterio de Armenteira – a quieter spot.

**Padrón** 25 and **Noia** 26, the smaller owns of the two northern estuaries, vere the oldest ports till silting up closed them off from the sea. Noia has an interesting guild cemetery, a busy nightlife and delicious cornmeal and clam pies, and also makes a good base for exploration. **Boroña** to the south is the most atmospheric of all the Celtic *castros* (settlements). Padrón, where St James's body landed (see page 87), grows spicy green peppers and has a rich literary inheritance. Rosalía de Castro (1837–85), one of Spain's greatest poets, lived and died here and her home is now the Casa-Museo de Rosalía de Castro (Tue–Sun July–Sept 10am–2pm and 4–8pm, Oct–June 10am–1.30pm and 4–7pm).

Her verse, written in Galician during its literary renaissance, expressed her pain through a melancholy lyricism innate in the Galician spirit. Today she is one of the region's most revered figures. Camilo José Cela, the Nobel prize-winning novelist (1916–2002) has also turned his birthplace into a literary foundation (Tue–Sat 10am–2pm and 4–7pm).

## COSTA DA MORTE

The cooler climate of the coastline bulging into the ocean north of Noia has so far saved it from tourist development. In the south, farmland, forest and moors run down to windswept beaches and fishing villages. **Carnota**

**Eat**

One of the most delicious Galician dishes, as a *tapa* or as an accompaniment to a meal, are the *pimientos de Padrón*. These small green peppers, some of which can be red-hot, are simply grilled and sprinkled with salt.

*Pontevedra's Praza Ferreira.*

㉗ has a magnificent 8km (5-mile) sweep of sand and is a good place for windsurfing. Immediately to the north of that are lethal rock formations which gave this coastline its name: the Coast of Death. **Muros**, **Muxía** and **Camariñas** ㉘ are fishing villages with old mariners' churches and few tourist trappings. Camariñas is also famous for its lace-making – the hand-made bobbin lace is sold by the women from home. The **Islas Sisargas**, lying just off **Malpica** ㉙, are now an ornithological reserve, counting cormorants among its inhabitants.

## LA CORUÑA, A PLACE TO ENJOY LIFE

The solid, 19th-century, bourgeois wealth of **A Coruña** ㉚ has imbued it with an air of the good life. Or, as one proverb puts it: Vigo works, Pontevedra sleeps, Santiago prays – and La Coruña enjoys itself. Summer sunbathers pack beaches lined by glazed facades which bounce back the ocean light, but the port works day and night (you can visit the **fish auctions** Ⓐ from 5am onwards). The city's sights also reveal its past. From here Philip II's ill-fated Armada set sail in 1588. In an ironic juxtaposition of ancient and modern, the remains of the *Mar Egeo*, wrecked here in 1992, sits on the rocks below the 2nd-century **Torre de Hércules** Ⓑ, the world's only working Roman lighthouse. A tram loops round to it along the headland's Paseo Marítimo, where the **Aquarium Finisterrae** (Mon–Fri 10am–7pm; Sat–Sun 11am–8pm) stands, with its vast "submarine" tank full of big sea fish. In the old town, the **Jardín de San Carlos** Ⓒ is built around the tomb of Sir John Moore, who died here in retreat from the French in 1809. Three museums reflect the city's ancient and modern spirit – the 16th-century **Castillo de San Antón** fortress Ⓓ, which incorporates an archaeological museum (July–Aug Tue–Sat 10am–9pm, Sun 10am–3pm; Sept–June Tue–Sat 10am–7.30pm, Sun 10am–2.30pm); the **Museo de Arte Sacro** Ⓔ (Tue–Fri 9am–2pm, Sat 10am–1pm; free) displaying church silver; and **Domus E** (Mon–Fri 10am–7pm

The Torre de Hércules.

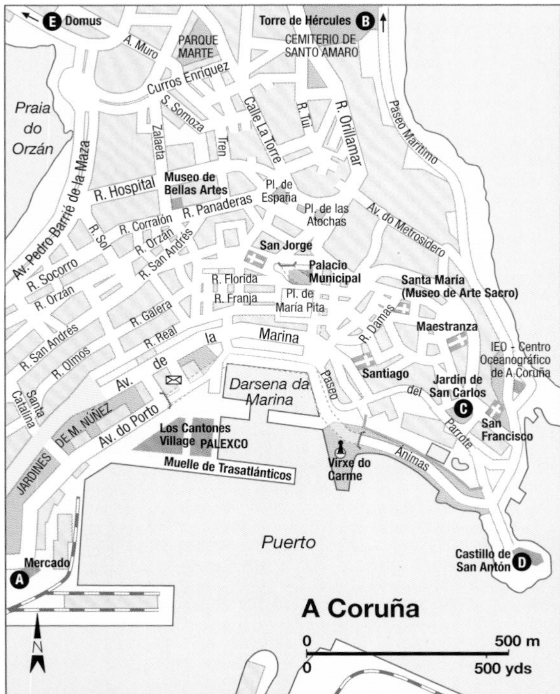

at–Sun 11am–7pm), a striking interctive museum of mankind.

## ŔÍAS BAIXAS: WILD CLIFFS, ;HELTERED PORTS

;edate summer villas and mansions et the tone on the road running round the triple-fingered Golfo de ̀rtabro north of A Coruña. It is worth ausing at the river-town of **Betanzos** **D**, a major port where many northern ilgrims arrived until estuary mud relgated it to a small river town. It has ept a gracious historic centre and hree lovely medieval churches. In )ctober, family *bodegas* start selling he new vintage of the town's rough but ure red wines.

**Ferrol 32** is a drab dockyard town nd naval base, but Spaniards come ıere to visit Franco's birthplace – narked by a plaque at Calle María 136. His father worked here as a naval :lerk. The **Pazo de Meiras**, built by 19th-century feminist novelist Emilia Pardo Bazán, was given to the Spansh dictator by locals as a summer palace and is still owned by his family. The town gives access to Pantín beach, where the national surfing championships are held and where you can pick up the picturesque **railway route** round the coast to **Ribadeo**.

Galicia's northeasterly corner remains spectacularly wild with steep cliffs between the estuaries and their small fishing ports where it is said the region's very best shellfish are collected. Each of the Atlantic ports here – Cedeira, Cariño, Ortigueira and O **Vicedo** – has a different character. **Cedeira 33**, once a whaling port, is especially beautiful. From there a country road gives access to awe-inspiring landscape around **San Andrés de Teixido**, a spectacularly set cliff-top chapel. Legend has it that if Galicians do not make the journey here alive, their spirit must be escorted here from their burial place by a relation or they will be reincarnated as a reptile. Hence the apparently empty but reserved places on the busy pilgrims' buses. Historians suggest this may have been the original pilgrimage, possibly with pagan origins, which was later moved to Santiago.

The road winds on past the **Sierra de la Capaleda**'s highest cliffs (640 metres/2,100ft), wild horses and windmills. The port on the next headland, **Estaca de Bares 34**, is the most northerly of the coast and is thought to have been of Phoenician origin, its vast sea wall now eroded to a mass of huge round boulders. With only a small huddle of houses, it is a magical spot.

Once the quieter Cantabrian sea takes over on Lugo province's coastline, the road runs down gently past busier ports and tamer, low-lying landscapes towards **Viveiro**, a busy family resort. The traffic-free old town throbs with nightlife during the summer and has preserved the widest variety of the northern fishing villages' *galerías* – balconies which are decoratively glazed to keep the wind out.

*Rugged coastline near Cedeira.*

*The stone cross marking the westernmost point of Spain on Cape Finisterre, Galicia.*

# NORTHERN SPAIN

## TRAVEL TIPS

### TRANSPORT



### A – Z



### LANGUAGE



### FURTHER READING

# TRANSPORT

## GETTING THERE

Northern Spain is easily accessible by car from France, by sea from the UK and by air from the UK, the USA and many other countries. The best option to explore the north is often to book a fly-drive deal together.

### By air

The main international airports of northern Spain are Santiago de Compostela, Asturias, Bilbao and Girona-Costa Brava. Barcelona is also a useful point of access, as is Zaragoza, and there are three handy airports just over the border in France: Biarritz, Lourdes-Tarbes and Perpignan. Smaller airports include Burgos, A Coruña, León, Logroño, Pamplona, San Sebastián, Santander and Vigo.

Spain's national airline, **Iberia** (www.iberia.com), serves all these airports and has international routes into Spain from London and many other European departure points. **British Airways** (www.britishairways.com) also serves several Spanish airports. Passengers from North America will probably need to fly into either Madrid or Barcelona for onward connections. **Delta** (www.delta.com) and **United** (www.united.com) serve these two cities.

**Aerlingus** (http://aerlingus.com) connects Ireland with northern Spain.

Many visitors to northern Spain, however, prefer to travel by low-cost airlines such as **EasyJet** (www.easyjet.com), which flies to Barcelona, Asturias, Bilbao and Santiago de Compostela; **Ryanair** (www.ryanair.com), which flies to Asturias, Girona-Costa Brava, Santander, Vitoria and Zaragoza; or **Vueling** (www.vueling.com), and **Volotea** (www.volotea.com), both of which use several northern airports.

### By rail

France's high-speed **inOui** rail network (previously known as SNCF) now extends into Spain, from Perpignan to Figueres, dramatically cutting journey times from Paris and London.

There are two other ways to cross the frontier by train. From the western end of the Pyrenees you can catch Eusko Tren's **"Topo"** service from Hendaye to San Sebastián (www.euskotren.eus). The journey is only 19km (12 miles) and takes a little over 35 minutes. There are departures every half hour depending on the time of day. In the middle of the mountains there is a lesser known rail crossing point at Latour de Carol. For rail routes from France into Spain, see www.voyages-sncf.com.

### By sea

**Brittany Ferries** (www.brittany-ferries.co.uk) operates two routes for cars and foot passengers from Britain to northern Spain across the Bay of Biscay.

Plymouth is linked with Santander in Cantabria (20 hours' sailing time) and Portsmouth with Bilbao (24 hours). The company also offers holidays (with or without a car), including hotel accommodation at various seaside or inland locations.

A much more low-key route into Spain is to take the ferry (*navette maritime*) across the estuary from Hendaye marina to the Basque town of Hondarribia.

*Brittany Ferries ship in Santander.*

Bilbao-Concordia train station.

## ⊙ Transcantábrico train

The most stylish, romantic and leisurely – if pricey – way to see Spain's northern coast is on ***El Transcantábrico***, an upmarket tourist train that runs on a 1,000km (620-mile) route from Bilbao to Ferrol on a narrow-gauge track. The service was initiated in 1983, when some Pullman carriages, most of which were imported from Britain, were refurbished to echo the luxurious atmosphere of the 1920s (when they were first built) and to provide all mod cons.

As speeds rarely exceed 50kph (30mph) and the train stops at attractive towns and for the night, there's time to enjoy the scenery, some off-train sightseeing and local cuisine. The route loops inland to Covadonga in the Picos de Europa. There are coach excursions at either end – to San Sebastián and Santiago de Compostela.

There are now two versions of the train that use the same route. The Transcantábrico Clásico has smaller cabins and offers shorter journeys. The Transcantábrico Gran Lujo – "a five-star hotel on rails", with suites as well as cabins – pulls out all the stops on a journey of eight days and seven nights.

For information and bookings, see www.renfe.com/trenesturisticos (tel: 902-555902).

### By coach/bus

**Eurolines** (http://eurolines.com) has services to northern Spain from many European countries, including the UK. Its destinations include Figueres, Logroño, San Sebastián, Bilbao, Vitoria, Santander, León, Oviedo, Burgos, Ponferrada, Vigo, Ourense, A Coruña and Santiago de Compostela.

### By road

From Calais to the eastern Spanish border, La Junquera, takes around 11–13 hours by motorway, depending on stops. Calais to Hendaye in the west is a slightly shorter journey and typically takes around 11 hours. Be warned that French motorway tolls can considerably add to the cost of a journey.

If you are bringing your own car, check that your motor insurance is valid for travel in France and Spain. An international licence is not necessary. You will need to carry a set of spare bulbs, a warning triangle and a first aid kit, and you must have a yellow reflective jacket in the passenger compartment in case of roadside emergency. Ensure that your headlamps are adjusted for right-hand driving.

## GETTING AROUND

### By rail

Spain's railway network is not dense and is most useful for intercity services or for journeys into urban centres from the outskirts. Most of the country's 12,000km (7,500 miles) of track are of a broader gauge than the rest of Europe but in parts of the north (Galicia, Asturias, Cantabria, the Basque Country and Castilla y León) there is also a sub-network of narrow gauge lines. The best known of these is one that runs along the north coast from Bilbao to Ferrol. When it is not being used by the Transcantábrico tourist train (see box) there are normal passenger services along it, but most cover only short distances and are very slow. Most trains in Spain are operated by **Renfe** (www.renfe.com) but in the Basque Country there is a local operator, **Eusko Tren** (www.euskotren.eus).

In a few places there are novelty and heritage lines such as **La Cremallera** rack railway at Ribes de Freser (www.valldenuria.cat). There are funicular railways at Bilbao, San Sebastián and Bulnes in the Picos de Europa.

### By coach/bus

All smaller towns are connected to the provincial capital cities by regular bus routes. These are operated by private companies and the best way to find out about them is to ask at the local tourist information office or in the local coach station (*estación de autobuses*). Fares are generally competitive with trains.

### By road

Spain has an extraordinarily good road network in general. A few remote back roads may be in bad repair but main roads are well-maintained and reliable. N (*carretera nacional*) roads, marked in red on the map, are preferable for fast travel. "Yellow" roads are generally slower and more scenic. Don't be too ambitious about how many miles you cover on a touring holiday, as the Pyrenees and the Cordillera Cantábrica make for a slow journey: many roads have endless sharp bends and they frequently cross mountain passes.

There are two kinds of motorway: the toll-charging *autopistas* and the free dual-carriageways denominated *autovías*. Signs on all roads conform to European standards.

To hire a car you need to have a valid licence and be over 21.

### Car pooling

Car sharing is an increasingly popular and economical way of getting around Spain, provided you take sensible precautions in choosing your ride (or your passenger). One of the leading providers is **Bla Bla Car** (www.blablacar.es).

### Distances and driving times

**Bilbao–Barcelona** 607km/377 miles (6 hrs).
**Bilbao–Madrid** 397km/247 miles (4 hrs).

*The zero kilometre marker at Cape Finisterre.*

**San Sebastián–Madrid** 488km/303 miles (5 hrs).
**Santander–Madrid** 393km/245 miles (4 hrs).
**Oviedo–Madrid** 445km/276 miles (5 hrs).
**Gijón–Madrid** 474km/295 miles (5 hrs 30 mins).
**Santiago de Compostela–Madrid** 613km/380 miles (7 hrs).

## Taxis

Every large town has at least one taxi company and cities more than one. Taxis can be found in ranks at airports and other key locations, or ordered in advance. Ask the tourist information office or your hotel for the relevant telephone number. They may even call a cab for you.

## Cycling

Spain is more used to cycle road racing than cycle touring and it generally has a poor network of quiet backroads. As northern Spain is so mountainous, you should be prepared for a succession of long climbs and fast descents. Always carry water with you. Increasingly, hotels welcome cyclists. All large towns have at least one cycle repair shop.

## On foot

There are many marked footpaths in northern Spain in addition to the Camino de Santiago (see box). When walking anywhere, you need to have a hat for protection from the sun and to have raingear in your backpack.

### Tips for pilgrims

If you decide to make the pilgrimage from Roncesvalles to Santiago de Compostela, here are a few pointers.

You should be fit before you go. The 800km (500-mile) journey will probably take you five weeks to walk and two weeks to cycle, so put in a bit of advance practice. Hike up a few mountains or go on some long bike rides.

On the first few days of your travels, particularly if you are walking, you are likely to suffer from minor ailments such as blisters and aching limbs. It is essential, therefore, to pack a simple **first aid kit** of a needle, antiseptic cream, plasters and anti-inflammatories.

Of course, the right footwear and clothing will help to limit any physical discomfort. Walkers should wear a pair of **sturdy hiking boots** that are both durable and light; cyclists should wear dedicated cycling shoes. All pilgrims will need a good mix of clothes, due to the various altitudes and terrains through which the route passes. Take light, comfortable cotton clothes so that your skin can breathe, but also carry a warm sweater or fleece, waterproof gear and a hat. You'll also need a sleeping bag, a water bottle, a detailed guide book which is light in weight and, of course, some money. For comfort, independence and privacy you may also want to consider carrying a walking stick (or a long umbrella that can double as a walking stick), a lightweight tent, some cooking gear and a head lamp.

Walkers should not forget that they will have to carry their possessions, so any superfluous items should be rejected. Essential items, such as food, can be bought locally.

**Cyclists** can carry slightly more because they can put their possessions in panniers, but they should still limit themselves to the items detailed above, plus a pump, spare tyres and inner tubes, patches and spanners.

In order to validate your pilgrimage, you will need to obtain a **Pilgrim's Record** (*credencial*) before you set off which you get stamped at the start of your journey, for example at the monastery in Roncesvalles, and at churches, bars and *refugios* (pilgrims' hostels) en route.

Alternatively, you can follow the road to Santiago by **car**, but you will not then be considered a *bona fide* pilgrim and will not be awarded the Pilgrim's Record, which means that you cannot use the network of *refugios*.

These hostels offer basic **accommodation**, hence the need for a sleeping bag, but they are either inexpensive or free (any donations will of course be gratefully received). Some do not even serve food, so basic cooking equipment may also come in useful.

Some of the hostels close in winter, so it is better to make the journey during the "**pilgrimage season**" (between Easter and October). The best months, because the weather is milder, are May, June and September. The main route (*Camino Francés*) becomes very crowded during these months; the Confraternity of Saint James (CSJ) can offer information on alternative routes.

Those who can produce a completed Pilgrim's Record can enjoy a free meal at the luxurious Hostal de los Reyes Católicos in Santiago's cathedral square.

For comprehensive information on all aspects of the pilgrimage, both spiritual and practical, contact the **Confraternity of Saint James** (CSJ; 27 Blackfriars Road, London SE1 8NY; www.csj.org.uk).

The best series of books on the route – by ratio of weight to the amount of information – are the Camino Guides by John Brierley (www.caminoguides.com).

## A

### Accessible travel

Spain is making rapid strides in its services for people with disabilities in line with EU standards, but you may still find things not as you would like them to be. Few restaurants specifically cater for wheelchair-users. The staff may have a ramp to cope with entrance steps but it is rare to find an accessible toilet. However, the Spanish are generally accommodating and it is more likely than not that the staff of a restaurant will help lift a wheelchair in and shuffle tables round to make the user comfortable.

Tourist offices will provide details of wheelchair-accessible hotels, beaches, monuments and restaurants, but it is wise to call in advance if you have additional requirements. Most city buses are adapted for wheelchairs, and you can request a taxi specifically intended for wheelchair-users.

The Spanish tourism website, www.spain.info, has useful pdf guides to download, covering accessible restaurants, accommodation, and sights and activities. There are two useful organisations for travellers with disabilities. In the UK contact **Tourism For All** (www.tourismforall.org.uk) and in the US **SATH** (www.sath.org).

### Accommodation

Places to stay come in great variety and it all depends on your requirements and your budget. Every tourist office can provide a comprehensive list of local places to stay.

Hotels are classed between one and five stars depending on the level of facilities. Note that this system doesn't say anything about charm or quality or personal service.

Some smaller hotels are known as *hostales*, which is not the same as hostel in English. It denotes a cheaper, less fancy place to stay with fewer facilities and comforts than the average hotel. Other names for small rural hotels are also still used, notably *posada* and *fonda*.

Paradors (www.parador.es) are a class apart. They are part of a state-run chain of prestigious hotels that either occupy historical monuments (monasteries, castles and the like) or are purpose-built in exceptional settings – occasionally rather spoiling the look of the exceptional setting. Paradors offer a reliable standard of service but most don't have much personality. Each parador has a restaurant specialising in regional cuisine.

"Green tourism" has been booming in Spain in recent years and there are now a great many charming small rural hotels all across the north. One good place to find them is at www.rusticae.es. There are also a great many self-catering village houses for rent – search for "*casa rural*" or visit www.toprural.com. Backpackers can find cheap places to bunk at sites such as www.hostelworld.com.

Camping and caravan sites are graded from one to three stars according to the facilities they provide. www.eurocampings.eu is a good place to start.

There are refuges for hikers and climbers in the main mountain ranges described in this book, especially in the national parks. Most are only open from spring to autumn. Each has a guardian on hand who will probably prepare an evening meal. Accommodation is in dormitories. Reserve your place in the refuge in advance if you can.

Tourist information offices have lists of all types of accommodation available in their areas on their websites.

### Admission charges

Most of the sights in this book – with the exception of most but not all churches – charge an entrance fee, which is generally not very high. A student card or proof that you are over retirement age may get you a reduction. Some museums are free on a particular day of the month.

## B

### Budgeting for your trip

Once in Spain, your largest expenses are going to be transport and accommodation. You can keep the cost down by concentrating on a small area only, finding a modest hotel to use as a base and making picnic lunches. If you are going to do long-distance drives, remember that you have to factor in motorway and tunnel tolls, and these can quickly add up.

Allow €70 upwards per day for two persons for the least expensive accommodation, which will generally be in a basic *hostal*; €35 per person per day upwards for basic meals or tapas. Wine or spirits will obviously push this up. Public transport is generally inexpensive in cities: allow around €10 for local bus and train and (where applicable) Metro travel.

## C

### Children

The Spanish, in general, adore children and Spain is a very child-friendly place. Children go out with their parents even late at night: babysitters are practically unheard of (although available for tourists at larger hotels). Although you won't find facilities for

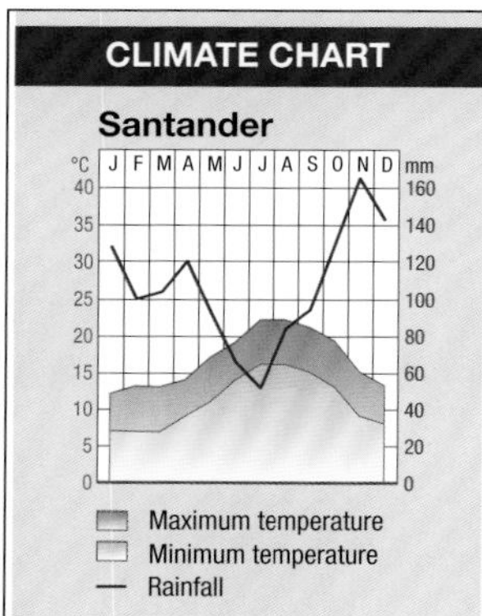


children everywhere, you will almost always find obliging people to provide you with what you want, such as a waiter and chef who will cater for particular culinary requirements. Modern tourist-orientated restaurants have play areas and high chairs, but elsewhere you will need to provide your own folding seat. Baby changing areas are fairly infrequent except in motorway service areas. Very few hotels are adults only. Family rooms are commonly available, and some hotels will allow children to stay in their parents' room at no extra charge.

## Climate

The climate varies a great deal across northern Spain, (both regionally and seasonally), so it is important to pack a suitcase with clothes that will cover all eventualities.

**"Green Spain"**, which stretches from the Basque Country along the Atlantic seaboard through Cantabria and Asturias to Galicia, is obviously so named because it rains a lot, so take waterproofs, umbrellas and suitable footwear – even in summer. Bilbao and Santiago are renowned for being very rainy and the pasture-clad hills are often swathed in mist.

**Winters** in the north and northwest can be *very* wet, and it may snow.

**Summers**, on the contrary, have lavish measures of sunshine and warmth everywhere, increasing in intensity as you travel inland and cross the mountains of the Cordillera Cantábrica. Even in summer, however, it is worth bringing a few sweaters for cool evenings, windy ferry trips or cloudy days – especially if you're intending to go on any excursions into the higher mountains.

The north coast is, therefore, a good destination for a summer beach holiday. There are hundreds of beautiful coves and beaches (many sheltered and backed by green fields), as well as seaside resorts that have long been popular among Spaniards in the hot season. These resorts are perfect for visitors who find the intense mid-summer heat of Spain's Mediterranean *costas* overpowering. In addition, some of the north's beaches are exposed to strong Atlantic winds, making them ideal destinations for windsurfers.

Away from the coast, the area covered by this book also includes the northern reaches of the tablelands (meseta) of **Castilla y León**, which have a continental climate. If you are visiting **Burgos** and **León,** therefore, be prepared for extremely hot, dry summers and very cold winters. Burgos, in particular, is renowned for its icy winter winds. **La Rioja**, **Navarra**, **Aragón** and inland **Catalonia** all have very hot, sunny summers and cold, though often sunny, winters – especially in the upland villages. The only place in northern Spain with mild, pleasant winters is Catalonia's Costa Brava.

## Crime and safety

Northern Spain is as safe as most places in western Europe, which is to say that if you take sensible precautions you should have no trouble. In tourist areas watch out for pickpockets who sometimes work in pairs: while one person distracts you, the other dips into your bag. Lock valuables in a hotel safety deposit box, never take them to the beach. Keep a copy of your passport (separately). Don't leave anything visible in your car. Wear a bag that straps across you. Occasionally, on motorways you may see a motorist apparently in difficulty, or who indicates that you have a problem with your car, who flags you down and then robs you: take great care who you stop for.

Be very careful with fire in the countryside. Spain has a serious problem with forest fires in the summer months and it's a problem that is getting worse year on year. A carelessly discarded match, cigarette butt or even a bit of plastic can set off a blaze which quickly becomes out of control. Access to certain high risk fire areas can be closed during hot periods.

Spain has a bewildering number of police forces: away from the cities you will most often see the Guardia Civil. The *Policía Nacional* deal with urban crime, so report anything stolen to them. The *Policía Local* deal with minor urban crime and traffic control. The Basque Country and Catalunya have their own police forces. If you are in difficulty, you can approach any police officer in uniform or any police station and you will be told what to do.

In an **emergency**, if you can't find a police officer, dial **112**.

UK citizens can get up-to-date travel safety information from the **Foreign and Commonwealth Office** (www.gov.uk/foreign-travel-advice) and US citizens from the **State Department** (http://travel.state.gov).

## Customs regulations

EU nationals are not restricted in what they can import into their own countries of origin as long as it is for personal use. Moving products in commercial quantities will require appropriate licences. Gendarmes in France do carry out spot checks on cars returning from shopping trips to northern Spain.

For other countries, it is wise to check your personal duty-free allowance before heading for home. Note that now that the UK has left the EU much stricter rules apply on what can be taken to/from the UK and Spain (and neighbouring countries).

There are limits to what you can bring into Spain but as long as you exercise moderation you are unlikely to fall foul of the authorities. Visitors can bring the following items into the country duty-free: any personal effects, such as jewellery, camera, film, portable video and sound equipment, musical instruments, sports equipment, camping material, etc. If the item you are bringing with you is new and you do not have the purchase receipt, it would be advisable to ask a Customs official to certify that you brought it into the country with you.

Pets may be brought with you as long as you have a suitable Health Certificate for the animal which is signed by an officially recognised vet from the country of origin, which indicates the dates of the last vaccines and, in particular, that of an anti-rabies shot. Not all Spanish hotels admit pets so do check before making reservations. Animals are not allowed into restaurants, cafeterias and food shops. It is forbidden to bring animal food products into Spain, with the exception of baby milk in a sealed container.

## E

### Eating out

Except in the remotest areas of the countryside, you are likely to be spoilt for choice of places to eat. These range from highly rated Michelin-starred restaurants to the ordinary town bar on the main square where the presentation may be less glamorous but the food just as good. Most restaurants close one night of the week, usually Monday.

Every restaurant offers a three-course *menú del día* on weekday lunchtimes which is often extremely good value. A pitcher of house wine is usually included but sometimes it is an extra. A *menú de degustacion* is something entirely different: a sampler menu of the best the restaurant has to offer, usually at a price.

At any bar at any time outside meal times you can always order tapas, *raciones* (larger tapas) or a sandwich (*bocadillo*), which may be made specially for you to your requirements. Tapas are their richest and most varied in the bars of San Sebastián.

Eating hours in Spain are generally late for most people. Breakfast is generally a light affair and it is common for someone to have a substantial snack in a bar mid-morning. A normal time to have lunch is 2pm in the afternoon and dinner at 9pm. In places frequented by tourists you will be able to eat earlier. While restaurants open "late" they also close late and it is unheard of to turn a customer away if there is still someone working in the kitchen.

### Electricity

The electricity supply in Spain is 220 volts AC. Spanish plugs have two round pins. Travel adapters are available for the different types of plug are available in department stores and hypermarkets, but you should check that your appliance will work at this voltage.

It's not easy for vegetarians to eat out in Spain. Most dishes are either nothing but meat or at least contain meat. Few restaurants outside the largest cities put a vegetarian main course on the menu although this is gradually changing. On the plus side, there are some excellent vegetable dishes made in northern Spain including soups, stews and salads. If you can't see what you want on the menu, don't be afraid to ask. Restaurant staff will very often do they what they can for you: leaving out an ingredient you do not want or making whatever they can for you with what they have in stock. If you really can't find anything else to eat you can always order the great vegetarian standby, an omelette (*tortilla*) or some slices of local cheese. If you are in Bilbao, at least there you will find vegetarian, and even vegan, restaurants.

Coffee is a treat in Spain. There are various ways to order it: *café solo* is an expresso and *café con leche* is a coffee with hot, steamy milk. If you want a longer, weaker coffee, ask for an Americano.

### Embassies and consulates

**Australia** Embassy: Torre Espacio, Paseo de la Castellana, 259D – Level 24, Madrid.
Honorary Consulate: Avinguda Diagonal, 433 bis, Level 2, Barcelona; http://spain.embassy.gov.au

**Canada** Embassy: Torre Espacio Paseo de la Castellana 259D, Madrid.
Consulate: Plaça de Catalunya, 9, 1°, 2ª, Barcelona; tel: 93 270 3614.
http://canadainternational.gc.ca

**Ireland** Paseo de la Castellana 46-4, Madrid.
Honorary consulates in Bilbao, Barcelona and A Coruña.
www.irlanda.es

**US** Embassy: Calle de Serrano 75, Madrid.
Consulate: Paseo Reina Elisenda de Montcada 23, Barcelona.
http://es.usembassy.gov

**UK** Embassy: Torre Espacio, Paseo de la Castellana 259D, Madrid.
Consulate: Avda Diagonal 477-13, Barcelona.
www.gov.uk/world/organisations

### Emergencies

**General Emergencies** 112
**National Police** 091
**Municipal Police** 092
**Fire Department** 080
**Emergency Medical Care** 061
**Tourist Helpline** (English-speaking) 902-102112

### Etiquette

Spanish people set great store on human contact and common courtesy. Always say hello when entering a places where there are people (even a lift) and goodbye when you leave. *Gracias* (thank you) is used less frequently than in English but always appreciated.

## H

### Health and medical care

You don't need inoculations to visit Spain and there are no particular health issues to be aware of, but it is as well to take a few precautions. If you need prescription drugs it is best to bring them with you. Spanish medication may differ from your own and pharmacies (*farmacias*) in Spain do not honour foreign prescriptions. Make a note of the generic name of your medicine in case you need to find extra supplies locally.

Although the north is less sunny than the south, the summer sun can still be a potential hazard in the outdoors. Beware of sunburn, heat stroke and dehydration. Wear a hat, use sunscreen when necessary and choose shade rather than exposure when you can.

Spanish pharmacists are trained and knowledgeable and can advise you on minor ailments. If a city pharmacy is closed, details of one that is open will be displayed in the window.

EU citizens can get free treatment from doctors and hospitals (but not private ones) under the reciprocal agreements scheme by showing a European Health Insurance Card (EHIC). Since leaving the EU, UK citizens and residents no longer have the same rights to health care coverage and you should ensure that you have a valid travel health insurance policy before travelling. You can apply for a UK Global Health Insurance Card (GHIC) for some health care coverage.

Check online for the latest updates and requirements regarding the Covid-19 pandemic such as mask-wearing.

Generally all tap water across the north of Spain is safe and sanitary, although many people prefer to drink bottled water. Drinking from streams, no matter how clear they appear to be, is a risky business even in the upper reaches of the Picos de Europa and the Pyrenees. Plan to carry water and only re-supply from natural sources at springs or other sources clearly emerging directly from the earth – the higher the safer. If possible, ask the locals: they know where and where not to drink. Nowadays there are numerous excellent and reliable water filtration bottles (LifeStraw – www.lifestraw.com – is a good one) are cheaply available.

## L

### LGBTQ travellers

Gay men and lesbian women should have no particular problems when travelling in modern Spain. Bigger cities such as Bilbao have gay bars and clubs. www.gayiberia.com has listings and general information for major towns and cities throughout Spain.

### Maps

The best maps for general touring (by car or bicycle) in northern Spain are Michelin's 1/250 000 (1cm=2.5km) series with orange covers. You will need five maps to cover the whole of the north. For walking you will need to look for larger scale maps at your destination. Two useful websites for maps are https://tiendaverde.es and www.cnig.es.

### Media

There are two nationwide television channels in Spain, TVE 1 and TVE 2, and several private networks, including Antena 3, Tele 5 and Canal Plus. There are also local-language stations in the Basque Country and Catalunya. Satellite and cable TV are available in many hotels. Radio reception varies considerably across northern Spain, often depending on proximity to urban centres and whether or not there are mountains nearby. Radio stations include Radio Nacional (RNE 1: news and current affairs) and Radio 3 (contemporary music). The main Spanish national newspapers are *El País*, *ABC* and *El Mundo*.

International newspapers are available in the cities and at airports.

### Money

Spain uses the euro, which is divided into 100 *céntimos*. Although all prices are marked in euros, some older people occasionally talk in *pesetas*, or even "*duros*", an informal word for five *pesetas*. Credit cards are accepted everywhere except very small shops and market stalls – it is wise to have a least a little cash on you for smaller purchases.

Cash machines (**ATMs**) are located in every high street are all over urban areas centres. There is one at least in every large town. Look for the sign *Telebanco*. You can usually select your preferred language. Spanish banks don't charge a commission for using ATMs, but your own bank may charge a commission for the currency conversion.

There are money-changing facilities at the airport, but the best rates for travellers' cheques and foreign currency are obtained at banks. **Banking hours** vary slightly from one bank to another. Most are open 9am (although some open at 8.30am) to 2pm on weekdays and 9am–12.30pm or 1pm on Saturdays. All are closed on Sundays and holidays. Several banks keep their major branches in the business districts open all day.

**Tipping** is discretionary. Service is usually included in restaurants and hotels, but it is customary to leave the spare change in the dish when eating at a modest restaurant and a few coins at a bar. When dining at an averagely smart restaurant, 10 percent of the bill is appropriate. In other contexts, simply round up the bill to the nearest euro.

## O

### Opening hours

**Shops** and **offices** generally open Mon–Sat 9am–1pm and 4–8pm, although there are of course exceptions. Large supermarkets, out of town stores and shops in coastal resorts generally do not close for a lunch break. You will almost always find a shop or petrol station open on a Sunday.

### Postal services

Post offices (identified by a yellow sign saying *Correos*) are open Mon–Fri 9am–2pm and Sat 9am–1pm.

### Public holidays

Spain has ten public holidays a year, listed below. In addition, each region, town and village has its own holiday or holidays. If a major holiday falls on a Thursday or Tuesday, Spaniards will often take the intervening Friday or Monday off as a *puente* (bridge), so that they gain a long weekend. Banks, most shops and many museums are closed on major public holidays and fiesta days.

Dates marked † are not statutory national holidays, but are observed in many places.

1 January **New Year's Day** (*Año Nuevo*)
6 January **Epiphany** (*Día de los Reyes* – Three Kings Day, when children receive presents)
19 March **Saint Joseph** (*San José*) †
**Maundy Thursday** (*Jueves Santo*) variable †
**Good Friday** (*Viernes Santo*) variable
**Easter Monday** (*Día de Pascua*) variable †
1 May **Labour Day** (*Día del Trabajo*)
**Corpus Christi** (*Corpus*) 9th Thursday after Easter †
**Feast of St. John the Baptist** (*Fiesta de San Juan Bautista*) 24 June †
**Feast of St James the Apostle** (*Fiesta de Santiago Apóstol*) 25 July †
15 August **Assumption Day** (*Asunción*)
12 October **National Day** (*Día de la Hispanidad*)
1 November **All Saints' Day** (*Día de Todos los Santos*)
6 December **Constitution Day** (*Día de la Constitución*)
8 December **Immaculate Conception** (*Inmaculada Concepción*)
25 December **Christmas Day** (*Día de Navidad*)

Stamps can also be bought in an *estanco* or tobacconist's shop.

## R

### Religious services

Most cathedrals and churches hold their principal mass on Sunday morning but there may be services at other times of the week. You are welcome to attend but if you are just sightseeing, discreetly leave and come back when the service is over.

## T

### Tax

Non-EU citizens can claim back value-added tax (IVA in Spanish) on goods and services that cost over €90. To get a refund, you will need to present your passport in the shop and get a receipt which shows the IVA component. Present this at the airport or port before you leave.

### Telephones

Public pay phones are dwindling everywhere in the face of mobile phones, but there are still some around. To use one it is best to buy a phonecard from a tobacconist but you can also use coins: wait for the tone, deposit a coin and dial the number. Most bars have phones for public use. For an overseas call it is more convenient to go to a telephone shop (*locutorio*) where you can talk first and pay later. Calls from your hotel room will be expensive.

The international country code for dialling into Spain is 34. Area codes are incorporated into the country's standard nine-digit numbers. To call internationally from Spain you need to dial 00 followed by the country code (USA and Canada 1; UK 44), area code and local number.

For Yellow Pages (business search) see www.paginasamarillas.es. For white pages (people search) see: http://blancas.paginasamarillas.es.

Most foreign mobiles will work in Spain. Coverage for most networks is generally good. An alternative is to buy a pay-as-you go Spanish SIM card for the duration of your stay.

Many bars and cafés, and most hotels, now offer free Wi-fi.

### Time zone

Time in Spain is GMT +1 hour (winter); +2 hours (summer), equivalent to EST + 5 hours (winter); +6 hours (summer). Daylight Saving operates.

### Toilets

It is rare to find a municipal public toilet in Spain. You can often use a toilet in a monument you are visiting, but invariably the best bet is to have a drink in a bar and use the toilet there.

### Tourist information

#### Spanish Tourist Offices abroad

**UK** 6th floor, 64 North Row, London W1K 7DE
**Ireland** 1–3 Westmoreland Street, Dublin
**US** 60 East 42nd Street - Suite 5300 (53rd floor), New York
**Canada** 2 Bloor Street West 34th floor, M4W 3E2 Toronto
Spain's official tourism website is www.spain.info.

#### Local tourist offices

Spain is the most decentralised state in Europe. It is divided into 17 *Comunidades Autónomas* (Autonomous Communities), which are subdivided into provinces. The provinces are divided into towns and cities, each with its *ayuntamiento* (town council). The promotion of tourism is devolved along the same structure and this has the odd effect for tourists that you can get plenty of information about the place you are in but not usually about the place you are going to visit next – if it is over a provincial border.

These tourist offices (*oficinas de turismo)* are open all year:
**Catalonia** Plaça de l'Escorxador 2, Figueres; http://catalunya.com
**Aragón** Plaza López Allué, Huesca; www.turismodearagon.com
**Andorra** Plaza de la Rotonda, Andorra la Vella; http://visitandorra.com.
**Navarra** Navarrería 39, Pamplona; http://turismo.navarra.es
**Rioja** Escuelas Trevijano, Calle Portales, Logroño; www.lariojaturismo.com
**Basque Country** Plaza Circular, Bilbao Boulevard 8, San Sebastián https://tourism.euskadi.eus
**Asturias** Plaza de la Constitución, Oviedo; http://turismoasturias.es
**Cantabria** Hernán Cortés 4 (Mercado del Este), Santander; http://turismodecantabria.com
**Picos de Europa** Avenida de Covadonga, Cangas de Onís; www.picosdeeuropa.com
**Castilla y León** Plaza de San Marcelo, León; http://turismoleon.org. Calle Nuño Rasura 7, Burgos; http://turismoburgos.org.
**Galicia** 43 Rúa do Vilar, Santiago de Compostela; www.turismo.gal

### Tour operators and travel agents

Several holiday companies in the UK and the US operate organised, all-in tours of northern Spain. They include:
www.exodus.co.uk: walking holidays in the Picos de Europa.
www.responsiblevacation.com: walking in the Basque country, Picos and Pyrenees.
www.comtours.com: independent travel itineraries, including Las Sanfermines.
www.headwater.com: highlights of the Camino de Santiago.
www.naturetrek.co.uk: wolf, bear and bird watching throughout the north of Spain.
http://backroadstouring.com: small group and tailor-made tours of northern Spain.
www.pyreneanexperience.com: language holidays in Navarra.

## V

### Visas and passports

EU citizens can enter Spain with a valid ID card or passport. Citizens from countries such as the UK, USA, Canada, Australia and New Zealand don't need a visa for a stay of up to 90 days (renewable). Citizens of other countries should check with their nearest Spanish embassy to see if they require a visa.

## W

### Weights and measures

Spain uses the metric system: grams and kilograms for weights in shops and airport luggage scales; metres and kilometres for distances; metres for the heights of mountains and mountain passes; and litres for liquid measures.

# LANGUAGE

## IBERIAN BABEL

Across the north of Spain from Cabo Finisterre on the northwest corner to Cap de Creus on the northeast, all of Spain's four main language groups – Gallego (Galician), Euskara (Basque), Castilian (Spanish) and Catalan – are spoken.

**Galicia**, from the border with Portugal to the River Eo border with Asturias, speaks Gallego, a Portuguese-like Romance language.

**Asturias**, the next cultural and ethnic entity to the east, speaks Castilian and a dialect called Bable, taught in the schools as an elective.

**Cantabria** speaks only Castilian up to its eastern border with Vizcaya.

**The Basque provinces** of Vizcaya, Guipúzcoa and parts of Navarra as far east as the border with Aragón between Roncal and Ansó speak Euskara.

**Aragón** speaks Castilian (excepting several local dialects such as Chistavino and Grausin spoken in the Ara and Cinca Valleys) as far east as Benasque and the Noguera Ribagorçana Valley, the border with Catalunya.

**Catalonia**'s Vall d'Aran is where the people speak Aranés, which is closer to Gascon French than to Catalan. Catalan is spoken from the Vall d'Aran east to the Mediterranean (as far south as Alicante), including the Balearic islands.

**French** and **Langue d'Oc** (Occitanian) are the languages on the French side of the border.

So, how did so many languages develop and survive in such a small area? Ramón Menéndez Pidal, eminent Spanish historian and philologist, in his seminal work, *Orígenes del Español*, notes the existence of a horseshoe-like area that developed around the periphery of the Spanish meseta, the heart of which is Castilla.

Other philologists who have studied the Iberian languages agree that the peripheral romance languages – Gallego and Catalan – resemble each other more than either resembles Castilian. Both remain closer to the Vulgar Latin used in the Roman Empire, less Arabised than Castilian Spanish under seven centuries of Moorish domination.

**Gallego** is a Romance language similar to Portuguese, while **Catalan**, which is widely spoken within Catalonia, is similar to and derived from Provençal French. **Aranés** is a Gascon variant of Occitanian French.

**Euskara** is a non-Indoeuropean language, a linguistic missing link that has been falsely traced to Japanese, Finnish, Sanskrit, the language of the lost city of Atlantis and even Adam and Eve. The most widely accepted theory on Euskara, backed by toponyms throughout Spain and especially across the Pyrenees, is that this was an aboriginal Iberian language widely spoken on the Iberian Peninsula and best defended in the northern pocket of the Basque Country. Euskara is currently used by an estimated quarter of the people in the Basque Country.

**Catalan** and its dialects have prevailed on the eastern Mediterranean coast, while on the northwestern side the Galician-Portuguese languages have survived and have remained less affected by the Arabic influence of the Moorish occupation of the Iberian Peninsula between the 7th and 15th centuries.

In the area in the middle of the horseshoe, **Castilian** was developed. This early Romance language absorbed more Arabic, eventually developing into modern Castilian Spanish.

Fourteen languages and recognised dialects are still spoken across northern Spain. Apart from the four main language groups (Gallego, Euskara, Castilian and Catalan), they are: **Bable** (or Asturiano); Pyrenean dialects such as **Béarnais** and **Toy** on the French side of the border; Aragonese dialects such as **Belsetan**, **Cheso**, **Chistavino** and **Patues**; and **Occitanian**, **Gascon French** and **Aranés**.

These localised dialects seem to have a little of everything yet remain largely independent of the main language groups.

A guide to Spain's main language, **Castilian**, which everyone speaks, appears on the following pages.

### Basic Rules

As a general rule, the stress is on the second-to-last syllable, unless it is otherwise marked with an accent (´) or the word ends in *d*, *l*, *r* or *z*.

Vowels in Spanish are always pronounced the same way. The double *ll* is pronounced like the y in "yes", the double *rr* is rolled, as in Scots. The *h* is silent in Spanish, whereas *j* (and *g* when it precedes an *e* or *i*) is pronounced like a guttural *h* (as if you were clearing your throat). *V* is often pronounced as a b or somewhere in between the two sounds.

When addressing someone you are not familiar with, use the more formal *usted*. The informal *tu* is reserved for relatives and friends.

## SPANISH

Spanish – like French, Italian and Portuguese – is a Romance language, derived from the Latin spoken by the Romans who conquered the Iberian peninsula more than 2,000 years ago. Following the discovery of America by Europeans, Spaniards travelled all over the globe and took their language with them. Today, Spanish is spoken as a first language by over 400 million people in the world.

The Moors arrived in Spain in 711, and occupied parts of the peninsula for the next eight centuries. They left behind hundreds of Arabic words, many related to farming and crops, as well as place names including those of towns (often identified by the prefix *Al-*, meaning "the" or *Ben-*, meaning "son of") and rivers (the prefix *Guad-* means "river"). Some of these Arabic words passed on to other languages, including French, and from there into English. Among those present but usually altered in Spanish and English are: sugar *(azúcar)*, coffee *(café)*, apricot *(albaricoque)*, saffron *(azafrán)*, lemon *(limón)*, cotton *(algodón)*, alcohol *(alcohol)*, karat *(kilate)*, cipher *(cifra)*, elixir *(elixir)*, almanac *(almanaque)*, zenith *(cenit)*, and zero *(cero)*.

Unlike English, Spanish is a phonetic language: words are pronounced exactly as they are spelt, which is why it is somewhat harder for Spaniards to learn English than vice versa (although Spanish distinguishes between the two genders, masculine and feminine, and the subjunctive verb form is a source of headaches for students).

The English language is one of Britain's biggest exports to Spain. Spaniards spend millions on learning aids, language academies and sending their children to study English in the UK or Ireland, and are eager to practise their linguistic skills with foreign visitors. Even so, they will be flattered and delighted if you make the effort to communicate in Spanish or, across the north of Spain especially, in any of the local languages.

## WORDS AND PHRASES

**Hello** *Hola*
**How are you?** *¿Cómo está usted?*
**How much is it?** *¿Cuánto es?*
**What is your name?** *¿Cómo se llama usted?*
**My name is...** *Me llamo...*
**Do you speak English?** *¿Habla usted inglés?*
**I am British/American** *Soy británico/norteamericano*
**I don't understand** *No comprendo*
**Please speak more slowly** *Hable más despacio, por favor*
**Can you help me?** *¿Me puede ayudar?*
**I am looking for...** *Estoy buscando*
**Where is...?** *¿Dónde está...?*
**I'm sorry** *Lo siento*
**I don't know** *No lo sé*
**No problem** *No hay problema*
**Have a good day** *Que tenga un buen día*
**That's it** *Eso es/Ya está*
**Here it is** *Aquí está*
**There it is** *Allí está*
**Let's go** *Vámonos*
**See you tomorrow** *Hasta mañana*
**See you soon** *Hasta lluego, Hasta pronto*
**Show me the word in the book** *Muéstreme la palabra en el libro*
**At what time?** *¿A qué hora?*
**When?** *¿Cuándo?*
**What time is it?** *¿Qué hora es?*
**yes** *sí*
**no** *no*
**please** *por favor*
**thank you (very much)** *(muchas) gracias*
**you're welcome** *de nada*
**excuse me** *perdone*
**OK** *bien*
**goodbye** *adiós*
**good evening/night** *buenas tardes/noches*
**here** *aquí*
**there** *allí*
**today** *hoy*
**yesterday** *ayer*
**tomorrow** *mañana* (also means "morning")
**now** *ahora*
**later** *después*
**right away** *ahora mismo*
**this morning** *esta mañana*
**this afternoon** *esta tarde*
**this evening** *esta tarde*
**tonight** *esta noche*

## ON ARRIVAL

**I want to get off at...** *Quiero bajarme en...*
**Is there a bus to the museum?** *¿Hay un autobús al museo?*
**What street is this?** *¿Qué calle es ésta?*
**Which line do I take for...?** *¿Qué línea cojo para...?*
**How far is...?** *¿A qué distancia está...?*
**airport** *aeropuerto*
**customs** *aduana*
**train station** *estación de tren*
**bus station** *estación de autobuses*
**metro station** *estación de metro*
**bus** *autobús*
**bus stop** *parada de autobús*
**platform** *andén/via*
**ticket** billete
**return ticket** *billete de ida y vuelta*
**hitch-hiking** *auto-stop*
**toilets** *servicios*
**This is the hotel address** *Ésta es la dirección del hotel*
**I'd like a (single/double) room** *Quiero una habitación (sencilla/doble)*
**... with shower** *...con ducha*
**... with bath** *...con baño*
**... with a view** *...con vista*
**Does that include breakfast?** *¿Incluye desayuno?*
**May I see the room?** *¿Puedo ver la habitación?*
**washbasin** *lavabo*
**bed** *cama*
**key** *llave*
**lift** *ascensor*
**air conditioning** *aire acondicionado*

## ON THE ROAD

**Where is the spare wheel?** *¿Dónde está la rueda de repuesto?*
**Where is the nearest garage?** *¿Dónde está el taller más cerca?*
**Our car has broken down** *Nuestro coche se ha averiado*
**I want to have my car repaired** *Quiero que reparen mi coche*
**It's not your right of way** *Usted no tiene prioridad*
**I think I must have put diesel in my car by mistake** *Me parece que he echado gasoil por error*
**the road to...** *la carretera a...*
**left** *izquierda*
**right** *derecha*
**straight on** *derecho/todo recto*
**far** *lejos*
**near** *cerca*
**opposite** *frente a*
**beside** *al lado de*
**car park** *aparcamiento*
**over there** *allí*
**at the end** *al final*
**on foot** *a pie*
**by car** *en coche*
**town map** *plano de la ciudad*
**road map** *mapa de carreteras*
**street** *calle*

### The Alphabet

Learning the pronunciation of the Spanish alphabet is a good idea. In particular, learn how to spell out your own name. Spanish has three letters that don't exist in English: **ñ**, **ch** and **ll**.
**a** = ah, **b** = bay, **c** = thay (strong "th" as in "thought"), **ch** = chay, **d** = day, **e** = ay, **f** = effay, **g** = hay, **h** = ah-chay, **i** = ee, **j** = hotah, **k** = kah, **l** = ellay, **ll** = ellyay, **m** = emmay, **n** = ennay, **ñ** = enyay, **o** = oh, **p** = pay, **q** = koo, **r** = erray, **s** = essay, **t** = tay, **u** = oo, **v** = oovay, **w** = oovay doe-blay, **x** = eh-kiss, **y** = ee gree-ay-gah, **z** = thay-tah

**square** *plaza*
**give way** *ceda el paso*
**exit** *salida*
**dead end** *calle sin salida*
**wrong way** *dirección prohibida*
**no parking** *prohibido aparcar*
**motorway** *autovía*
**toll highway** *autopista*
**toll** *peaje*
**speed limit** *límite de velocidad*
**petrol station** *gasolinera*
**petrol** *gasolina*
**unleaded** *sin plomo*
**diesel** *gasoil*
**water/oil** *agua/aceite*
**air** *aire*
**puncture** *pinchazo*
**bulb** *bombilla*
**wipers** *limpia-parabrisas*

## ON THE TELEPHONE

**How do I make an outside call?** *¿Cómo hago una llamada exterior?*
**What is the area code?** *¿Cuál es el prefijo?*
**I want to make an international/local call** *Quiero hacer una llamada internacional/local*
**I'd like an alarm call for 8 tomorrow morning** *Quiero que me despierten a las ocho de la mañana*
**Hello?** *¿Dígame?*
**Who's calling?** *¿Quién llama?*
**Hold on, please** *Un momento, por favor*
**I can't hear you** *No le oigo*
**Can you hear me?** *¿Me oye?*
**He/she is not here** *No está aquí*
**The line is busy** *La línea está ocupada*
**I must have dialled the wrong number** *Debo haber marcado un número equivocado*

## SHOPPING

**Where is the nearest bank?** *¿Dónde está el banco más cerca?*
**I'd like to buy...** *Quiero comprar...*
**How much is it?** *¿Cuánto es?*
**Do you accept credit cards?** *¿Aceptan tarjetas?*
**I'm just looking** *Sólo estoy mirando*
**Have you got...?** *¿Tiene...?*
**I'll take it** *Me lo llevo*
**I'll take this one/that one** *Me llevo éste*
**What size is it?** *¿Que talla es?*
**Anything else?** *¿Otra cosa?*
**size (clothes)** *talla*
**small** *pequeño*
**large** *grande*
**cheap** *barato*
**expensive** *caro*
**enough** *suficiente*
**too much** *demasiado*
**a piece** *una pieza/un trozo*
**each** *cada una/la pieza/la unidad* (eg. *melones, 2 euros la unidad*)
**bill** *la factura* (shop), *la cuenta* (restaurant)
**bank** *banco*
**bookshop** *libería*
**chemist** *farmacia*
**hairdressers** *peluquería*
**jewellers** *joyería*
**post office** *correos*
**shoe shop** *zapatería*
**department store** *grandes almacenes*

### Market shopping

Supermarkets *(supermercados)* are self-service, but often the best and freshest produce is to be had at the town market *(mercado)* or at street markets *(mercadillo)*, where you place your order with the person in charge of each stand. Prices are usually by the kilo, sometimes by the gram *(gramo)* or the "piece" *(unidad)*.
**fresh** *fresco*
**frozen** *congelado*
**organic** *biológico*
**flavour** *sabor*
**basket** *cesta*
**bag** *bolsa*
**bakery** *panadería*
**butcher's** *carnicería*
**cake shop** *pastelería*
**fishmonger's** *pescadería*
**grocery** *verdulería*
**tobacconist** *estanco*
**market** *mercado*
**supermarket** *supermercado*
**junk shop** *tienda de segunda mano*

## SIGHTSEEING

**mountain** *montaña*
**hill** *colina*
**valley** *valle*
**river** *río*
**lake** *lago*
**lookout** *mirador*
**city** *ciudad*
**small town/village** *pueblo*
**old town** *casco antiguo/centro histórico*
**monastery** *monasterio*
**convent** *convento*
**cathedral** *catedral*
**church** *iglesia*
**palace** *palacio*
**hospital** *hospital*
**town hall** *ayuntamiento*
**nave** *nave*
**statue** *estátua*
**fountain** *fuente*
**staircase** *escalera*
**tower** *torre*
**castle** *castillo*
**Iberian** *ibérico*
**Phoenician** *fenicio*
**Roman** *romano*
**Moorish** *árabe*
**Romanesque** *románico*
**Gothic** *gótico*
**museum** *museo*
**art gallery** *galería de arte*
**exhibition** *exposición*
**tourist information office** *oficina de turismo*
**free** *gratis*
**open** *abierto*
**closed** *cerrado*
**every day** *diario/todos los días*
**all year** *todo el año*
**all day** *todo el día*
**swimming pool** *piscina*
**to book** *reservar*

## DINING OUT

In Spanish, *el menú* is not the main menu, but a fixed menu offered each day at a lower price. The main menu is *la carta*.
**breakfast** *desayuno*
**lunch** *almuerzo/comida*
**dinner** *cena*
**meal** *comida*
**first course** *primer plato*
**main course** *plato principal*
**dessert** *postre*
**made to order** *por encargo*
**drink included** *incluida consumición/bebida*
**wine list** *carta de vinos*
**the bill** *la cuenta*
**fork** *tenedor*
**knife** *cuchillo*
**spoon** *cuchara*
**plate** *plato*

### Emergencies

**Help!** *¡Socorro!*
**Stop!** *¡Pare!*
**Call a doctor** *Llame a un médico*
**Call an ambulance** *Llame a una ambulancia*
**Call the police** *Llame a la policía*
**Call the fire brigade** *Llame a los bomberos*
**Where is the nearest telephone?** *¿Dónde está el teléfono mas cercano?*
**Where is the nearest hospital?** *¿Dónde está el hospital más cercano?*
**I am sick** *Estoy enfermo*
**I have lost my passport/purse** *He perdido mi pasaporte/bolso*

**glass** *vaso*
**wine glass** *copa*
**napkin** *servilleta*
**ashtray** *cenicero*
**waiter, please!** *camarero, por favor*

### Desayuno/Aperitivos – Breakfast/Snacks

*pan* **bread**
*bollo* **bun/roll**
*mantequilla* **butter**
*mermelada/confitura* **jam**
*pimienta* **pepper**
*sal* **salt**
*azúcar* **sugar**
*huevos* **eggs**
*... cocidos* **boiled, cooked**
*... con beicon* **with bacon**
*... con jamón* **with ham**
*... fritos* **fried**
*... revueltos* **scrambled**
*yogúr* **yoghurt**
*tostada* **toast**
*sandwich* **sandwich in square slices of bread**
*bocadillo* **sandwich/filled baguette**

### First Course – Primer Plato

*ancas de rana* **frogs' legs**
*caldo gallego* **soup with white beans**
*entremeses* **mixed hors d'oeuvres**
*esqueixada* **raw cod with olives, tomato and onion**
*escabeche* **sauce of vinegar, oil, garlic**
*gazpacho* **cold soup**
*ensalada* **salad**
*sopa* **soup**
*pan con tomate* **bread rubbed with tomato, garlic and oil**

### Main Courses – Platos Principales

#### Carne – Meat

*poco hecho* **rare**
*en su punto* **medium**
*bien hecho* **well done**
*a la plancha* **grilled**
*estofado* **stew**
*en salsa* **in a sauce**
*parrillada* **mixed grill**
*asado/al horno* **roast**
*frito* **fried**
*a la brasa* **charcoal grilled**
*relleno* **stuffed**
*pinchito* **skewer**
*chuleta* **chop**
*costilla* **rib**
*filete* **steak**
*entrecot* **beef rib steak**
*solomillo* **fillet steak**
*lomo* **loin**
*pierna* **leg**
*carne picada* **minced meat**

### False Friends

"False friends" are words that look like English words but mean something different. Such as:
*Constipación* **a common cold**
*Simpático* **friendly**
*Tópico* **a cliché**
*Actualmente* **currently**
*Sensible* **sensitive**
*Disgustado* **angry**
*Embarazada* **pregnant**
*Suplir* **substitute**
*Informal* **unreliable (to describe a person)**
*Rape* **monkfish**
*Billón* **a million million**
*Soportar* **tolerate**
*Preservativo* **condom**

*ternera* **veal or young beef**
*buey* **beef**
*cordero* **lamb**
*chivo* **kid**
*cerdo* **pork**
*cochinillo* **suckling pig**
*jabalí* **wild boar**
*jamón* **ham**
*jamón cocido* **cooked ham**
*jamón serrano* **cured ham**
*salchichón* **sausage**
*chorizo* **sausage seasoned with paprika**
*morcilla* **black pudding**
*sesos* **brains**
*riñones* **kidneys**
*lengua* **tongue**
*conejo* **rabbit**
*liebre* **hare**
*pollo* **chicken**
*pintada* **guinea fowl**
*pavo* **turkey**
*pato* **duck**
*codorniz* **quail**
*perdiz* **partridge**
*faisán* **pheasant**
*pechuga* **breast**
*muslo* **leg**
*ala* **wing**

#### Pescado – Fish

*fritura* **mixed fry**
*anchoas* **anchovies**
*anguila* **eel**
*angula* **elver**
*atún* **tuna**
*bacalao* **cod**
*besugo* **red bream**
*boquerones* **fresh anchovies**
*caballa* **mackerel**
*cazón* **dogfish**
*dorada* **gilt head bream**
*lenguado* **sole**
*lubina* **sea bass**
*merluza* **hake**
*mero* **grouper**
*pescadilla* **small hake**
*pez espada* **swordfish**
*rape* **monkfish**
*rodaballo* **turbot**
*salmón* **salmon**
*salmonete* **red mullet**
*sardina* **sardine**
*trucha* **trout**

#### Mariscos – Shellfish

*mariscada* **mixed shellfish**
*almeja* **clam**
*bogavante/langosta* **lobster**
*calamar* **squid**
*caracola* **sea snail**
*cangrejo* **crab**
*centollo* **spider crab**
*chopito* **baby cuttlefish**
*cigala* **Dublin Bay prawn/scampi**
*concha fina* **venus shell clam**
*gamba* **shrimp/prawn**
*langosta* **spiny lobster**
*langostino* **large prawn**
*mejillón* **mussel**
*ostión* **Portuguese oyster**
*ostra* **oyster**
*percebe* **barnacle**
*peregrina* **scallop**
*pulpo* **octopus**
*sepia* **cuttlefish**
*vieira* **scallop**

#### Verduras – Vegetables

*crudo* **raw**
*ensalada* **salad**
*menestra* **cooked mixed vegetables**
*salteado* **sautéed**
*hervido* **boiled**
*ajo* **garlic**
*alcachofa* **artichoke**
*alcegas* **Swiss chard**
*alubia* **dried bean**
*apio* **celery**
*arroz* **rice**
*avellana* **hazelnut**
*berenjena* **aubergine/eggplant**
*cacahuete* **peanut**
*cebolla* **onion**
*champiñon* **mushroom**
*col* **cabbage**
*coliflor* **cauliflower**
*espárrago* **asparagus**
*espinaca* **spinach**
*garbanzo* **chickpea**
*guisante* **pea**
*haba* **broad bean**
*habichuela* **bean**
*judía* **green bean**
*lechuga* **lettuce**
*lenteja* **lentil**
*maíz* **corn/maize**
*nabo* **turnip**
*nuez* **walnut**

*patata* **potato**
*pepinillo* **gherkin**
*pepino* **cucumber**
*perejíl* **parsley**
*pimiento* **pepper**
*piñón* **pine nut**
*puerro* **leek**
*rábano* **radish**
*seta* **wild mushroom**
*tomate* **tomato**
*zanahoria* **carrot**

## FRUTA – FRUIT

*aguacate* **avocado**
*albaricoque* **apricot**
*cereza* **cherry**
*ciruela* **plum**
*frambuesa* **raspberry**
*fresa* **strawberry**
*granada* **pomegranate**
*higo* **fig**
*limón* **lemon**
*mandarina* **tangerine**
*manzana* **apple**
*melocotón* **peach**
*melón* **melon**
*naranja* **orange**
*pasa* **raisin**
*pera* **pear**
*piña* **pineapple**
*plátano* **banana**
*pomelo* **grapefruit**
*sandía* **watermelon**
*uva* **grape**

## POSTRE – DESSERT

*pastel* **cake**
*helado* **ice-cream**
*natilla* **custard**
*flan* **caramel custard**
*postre de músic* **mixed fruit and nuts**
*tocino de cielo* **milk pudding**
*bizcocho* **sponge cake**
*rosquillas* **doughnut**
*arroz con leche* **rice pudding**

### Table talk

**I am a vegetarian** *Soy vegetariano*
**I am on a diet** *Estoy a régimen*
**What do you recommend?** *¿Qué recomienda?*
**Do you have local specialities?** *¿Hay especialidades locales?*
**I'd like to order** *Quiero pedir*
**That is not what I ordered** *Ésto no es lo que he pedido*
**May I have more wine?** *¿Me da más vino?*
**Enjoy your meal** *Buen provecho*

## BEBIDAS – LIQUID REFRESHMENTS

**coffee** *café*
... **black** *sólo*
... **with milk** *con leche*
... **decaffeinated** *descafeinado*
**sugar** *azúcar*
**tea** *té*
... **with lemon** *con limón*
**herbal tea** *infusión*
**chocolate** *chocolate*
**milk** *leche*
**mineral water** *agua mineral*
... **fizzy** *con gas*
... **still** *sin gas*
**juice (fresh)** *zumo (natural)*
**cold** *fresco/frío*
**hot** *caliente*
**beer** *cerveza*
... **bottled** *en botella*
... **on tap** *de barril*
**soft drink** *refresco*
**diet drink** *bebida "light"*
**with ice** *con hielo*
**wine** *vino*
... **red** *tinto*
... **white** *blanco*
... **rosé** *rosado*
... **dry** *seco*
... **sweet** *dulce*
**house wine** *vino de la casa*
**sparkling wine** *vino espumoso*
**Where is this wine from?** *¿De dónde es este vino?*
**pitcher** *jarra*
**half litre** *medio litro*
**quarter litre** *cuarto de litro*
**cheers!** *¡salud!*

## NUMBERS, DAYS AND DATES

### Numbers

**0** *cero*
**1** *uno*
**2** *dos*
**3** *tres*
**4** *cuatro*
**5** *cinco*
**6** *seis*
**7** *siete*
**8** *ocho*
**9** *nueve*
**10** *diez*
**11** *once*
**12** *doce*
**13** *trece*
**14** *catorce*
**15** *quince*
**16** *dieciseis*
**17** *diecisiete*
**18** *dieciocho*
**19** *diecinueve*
**20** *veinte*
**21** *veintiuno*
**30** *treinta*
**40** *cuarenta*
**50** *cincuenta*
**60** *sesenta*
**70** *setenta*
**80** *ochenta*
**90** *noventa*
**100** *cien*
**200** *doscientos*
**1,000** *mil*
**10,000** *diez mil*
**1,000,000** *un millón*

### Saying the date

**12 August 2003**, *el doce de agosto de dos mil y tres* (no capital letters are used for days or months)

### Days of the week

**Monday** *lunes*
**Tuesday** *martes*
**Wednesday** *miércoles*
**Thursday** *jueves*
**Friday** *viernes*
**Saturday** *sábado*
**Sunday** *domingo*

### Seasons

**Spring** *primavera*
**Summer** *verano*
**Autumn** *otoño*
**Winter** *invierno*

### Months

**January** *enero*
**February** *febrero*
**March** *marzo*
**April** *abril*
**May** *mayo*
**June** *junio*
**July** *julio*
**August** *agosto*
**September** *septiembre*
**October** *octubre*
**November** *noviembre*
**December** *diciembre*

### Tapas (Pinchos)

One of Spain's great contributions to world cuisine, *tapas* (called *pinchos* in the Basque country) are small portions to be eaten with your drink at a bar. A *tapa* might be a plateful of olives (*aceitunas*), a spoonful of salad (*ensaladilla*), a cube of potato omelette (*tortilla de patatas*), a bit of cured ham (*jamón serrano*) or any of dozens of different treats. If you want a larger portion of a *tapa*, you can order a *ración*.

## ENGLISH LANGUAGE

***The Basque History of the World*** Mark Kurlansky (2000). Readable though rather ETA apologetic introduction to Basque history.

***Fiesta*** *(The Sun Also Rises)* Ernest Hemingway (1926). The one that told the world about Pamplona.

***Franco*** Paul Preston (1993). A full, reflective account of the dictator.

***Picos de Europa*** Teresa Farino (1996). The best guide in English to this great walking area.

***The Bible in Spain*** George Borrow (1843). Extraordinary accounts, especially in Galicia.

***The Iron Duke*** Lawrence James (1994). Gives a good, lively account of the Peninsular War.

***The New Spaniards*** John Hooper (second edition 2006). An imaginative and absorbing study of modern Spain.

***The Poem of El Cid*** The epic in English translation.

***Camino de Santiago*** John Brierley (2003 and with frequent updates). Compact guide to walking from St-Jean-Pied-de-Port to Santiago de Compostela.

***The Pyrenees*** Hilaire Belloc (1909). A classic, with helpful tips about using wineskins etc.

***Roads to Santiago*** Cees Nooteboom (1998). Travelogue peppered with thought-provoking observations on Spain.

***The Spanish Pyrenees*** Henry Myhill (1966). Perceptive visitor in the embryonic days of tourism.

### Send us your thoughts

We do our best to ensure the information in our books is as accurate and up-to-date as possible. The books are updated on a regular basis using destination experts, who painstakingly add, amend and correct as required. However, some details (such as opening times or travel pass costs) are particularly liable to change, and we are ultimately reliant on our readers to put us in the picture.

We welcome your feed back, especially your experience of using the book "on the road", and if you came across a great new attraction we missed.

We will acknowledge all contributions and offer an Insight Guide to the best messages received.

Please write to us at:
**Insight Guides**
**PO Box 7910**
**London SE1 1WE**

Or email us at:
**hello@insightguides.com**

# CREDITS

## PHOTO CREDITS

**Abel Alonso/Epa/REX/Shutterstock** 101
**Alvaro Barrientos/AP/REX/Shutterstock** 55
**AWL Images** 22, 195
**Christian Handl/imageBROKER/REX/Shutterstock** 147
**Corrie Wingate/Apa Publications** 6ML, 6MR, 6BL, 6MR, 7TL, 9BR, 11ML, 62, 87, 92, 179, 181, 183, 186, 187, 189, 190, 191, 196/197T, 196BL, 197ML, 197BR, 197BL, 198, 199, 201, 203, 204, 211, 214, 216, 226, 227, 229, 253BR, 254, 255, 256, 257, 266, 267, 272T, 274, 280
**Dreamstime** 196BR
**FLPA** 119, 122, 123, 125, 126, 127
**Getty Images** 10B, 14/15, 16/17, 20, 24, 26/27, 29, 30B, 35, 37, 38/39, 44, 45, 46, 47, 48, 49, 50, 51, 52/53, 54, 56, 57, 61, 63, 64, 65, 66, 67, 69, 70, 71, 72B, 74, 75, 76, 84, 85, 86, 91, 93, 94, 98, 102, 106, 107, 108, 109, 110, 124, 128/129, 130/131, 134, 145, 160, 168, 169, 171, 178, 185, 206, 207, 210, 217, 219, 230B, 246, 247, 252/253T, 253TR, 259, 261
**Gorka Estrada/Epa/REX/Shutterstock** 117ML
**hwo/imageBROKER/REX/Shutterstock** 270
**iStock** 7ML, 7MR, 8BL, 10TL, 10TR, 28, 34, 78, 112, 113, 135T, 135B, 139, 143, 146, 149, 150, 155, 159, 161, 165, 167, 175, 194, 221, 228, 232, 233, 236/237, 241, 252BR, 253BL, 262, 272B, 274/275
**Javier Etxezarreta/Epa/REX/Shutterstock** 21, 58, 103, 197TR
**Jesus Vecino/SIPA/REX/Shutterstock** 99
**Juan Carlos Munoz/Shutterstock** 25
**KeystoneUSA-ZUMA/REX/Shutterstock** 23
**Lavandeira Jr/EPA/REX/Shutterstock** 59
**Mark Baynes/REX/Shutterstock** 117BL
**Photoshot** 118
**Public domain** 30T, 36, 40, 43
**Raquel Manzanares/EPA-EFE/REX/**
**rui vale sousa/Shutterstock** 115
**Shutterstock** 7TR,7BR, 7BL, 8BR, 8MR, 9TL, 9TR, 11BR, 11TR, 19, 31, 32, 33, 68, 77, 79, 80, 81, 82, 83, 88, 89, 90, 95, 96, 97, 100, 104, 105, 111, 116/117T, 116B, 120, 142, 144, 148, 151, 152, 153, 156/157, 162, 163, 164, 172/173, 174, 176, 177, 184, 192, 193, 205, 213, 215, 222, 223, 224, 231BR, 231TR, 235, 239, 240, 242, 243, 245, 248, 249, 250, 251, 253ML, 260, 263, 265, 268, 269, 273
**SuperStock** 1, 4, 12/13, 18, 41, 42, 60, 72/73T, 73ML, 73BR, 73BL, 73TR, 114, 117BR, 117TR, 121, 132/133, 138, 154, 208/209, 218, 225, 230/231T, 231ML, 231BL, 252BL
**Villar Lopez/EPA/REX/Shutterstock** 166

## COVER CREDITS

**Front cover:** Cudillero village in Asturias *lunamarina/Shutterstock*
**Back cover:** Ordesa National Park *iStock*
**Front flap:** (from top) Old roman bridge in Navarre *Shutterstock*; Altamira cave museum *Shutterstock*; Torla-Ordesa *Shutterstock*; Bilbao *Shutterstock*
**Back flap:** San Sebastian *Shutterstock*

## INSIGHT GUIDE CREDITS

**Distribution**
**UK, Ireland and Europe**
Apa Publications (UK) Ltd;
sales@insightguides.com
**United States and Canada**
Ingram Publisher Services;
ips@ingramcontent.com
**Australia and New Zealand**
Booktopia;
retailer@booktopia.com.au
**Worldwide**
Apa Publications (UK) Ltd;
sales@insightguides.com
**Special Sales, Content Licensing and CoPublishing**
Insight Guides can be purchased in bulk quantities at discounted prices. We can create special editions, personalised jackets and corporate imprints tailored to your needs.
sales@insightguides.com
www.insightguides.biz

**Printed in China**



First Edition 1998
Fourth Edition 2023

This book was produced using **Typefi** automated publishing software.



**www.insightguides.com**

**Editors:** Zara Sekhavati and Annie Warren
**Author:** Nick Inman
**Picture Editor:** Tom Smyth
**Cartography:** original cartography Berndtson & Berndtson, updated by Carte
**Layout:** Greg Madejak
**Head of DTP and Pre-Press:** Katie Bennett
**Head of Publishing:** Kate Drynan

## CONTRIBUTORS

This new edition of Insight Guide Northern Spain was commissioned by Zara Sekhavati and comprehensively updated by travel writer **Stuart Butler**. It is based on the work of **Lyle Lawson**, **George Semler**, **Vicky Hayward**, **Patrick McConnell**, **Teresa Farino**, **Jeremy McClancy**, **Frank Smith**, **Rod Lee** and **Roger Williams**. The index was compiled by **Penny Phenix**.

## ABOUT INSIGHT GUIDES

**Insight Guides** have more than 45 years' experience of publishing high-quality, visual travel guides. We produce 400 full-colour titles, in both print and digital form, covering more than 200 destinations across the globe, in a variety of formats to meet your different needs.

**Insight Guides** are written by local authors, whose expertise is evident in the extensive historical and cultural background features. Each destination is carefully researched by regional experts to ensure our guides provide the very latest information. All the reviews in **Insight Guides** are independent; we strive to maintain an impartial view. Our reviews are carefully selected to guide you to the best places to eat, go out and shop, so you can be confident that when we say a place is special, we really mean it.

## Legend

### City maps

Freeway/Highway/Motorway
Divided Highway
Main Roads
Minor Roads
Pedestrian Roads
Steps
Footpath
Railway
Funicular Railway
Cable Car
Tunnel
City Wall
Important Building
Built Up Area
Other Land
Transport Hub
Park
Pedestrian Area
Bus Station
Tourist Information
Main Post Office
Cathedral/Church
Mosque
Synagogue
Statue/Monument
Beach
Airport

### Regional maps

Freeway/Highway/Motorway (with junction)
Freeway/Highway/Motorway (under construction)
Divided Highway
Main Road
Secondary Road
Minor Road
Track
Footpath
International Boundary
State/Province Boundary
National Park/Reserve
Marine Park
Ferry Route
Marshland/Swamp
Glacier
Salt Lake
Airport/Airfield
Ancient Site
Border Control
Cable Car
Castle/Castle Ruins
Cave
Chateau/Stately Home
Church/Church Ruins
Crater
Lighthouse
Mountain Peak
Place of Interest
Viewpoint

# INDEX

## D



## E

## H



## I



## J



## K



## L

## Q



## R



## S

## T



## U

ATLANTIC OCEA
Costa de Cantabria
Cabo Mayor
Cabo de Ajo
Santander
Ajo
Isla
Noja
Escalante
Santoña
Laredo
Cabo Machichaco
A8
Colindres
Solares
Castro-Urdiales
Plentzia
Bermeo
Mundaka
Bakio
Liérganes
Ampuero
Castillo de Butrón
Elantxobe
Lekeitio
Getxo
Las Arenas
Río Miera
Cantabria
El Puente
Santurtzi
Mungia
Arredondo
Portugalete
Gauteguiz de Arteaga
Ondarroa
Barakaldo
Bilbao/ Bilbo
Ramales de la Victoria
Gernika-Lumo
Puerto de Braguía 720
Markina-Xemein
Carrenza
Puerto de la Sía 1200
Zalla
Güeñes
Balmaseda
Galdakao
Elgoibar
Puerto de las Estacas de Trueba
Sodupe
Arrigorriaga
Amorebieta
Eibar
AP8
1154
Villasana de Mena
Artziniega
Llodio
Durango
Abadiño
S. Ignacio
Espinosa de los Monteros
Castillo y Elejabeitia
Elorrio
Embalse del Ebro
Villasante
Río Nervion
700
Alto de Baraza
Puerto Urquiola
Arrasate-Mondragon
1178
604
Cabanas de Virtus
Río Nela
Amurrio
Ciórraga
Peña Gorbea 1481
AP1
AP68
N240
Eskoriatza
A623
Quincoces de Yuso
Orduña
País Vasco
Legutiano
Villarcayo
Murguía
Arantzazu
617
Medina de Pomar
Puerto de Arlaban
Embalse de Urrúnaga
Embalse de Ullívarri
Valdenoceda
Castilla
Berberana
Ozaeta
Vitoria/ Vitoria-Gasteiz
Mendoza
Salvatierra
Agurain
Puerto de la Mazorra
1000
Trespaderne
Quintana Martín Galíndez
Subijana
Trespuentes
Estíbaliz
Puerto Azáceta 895
Alaiza
Sedano
Río Ebro
Salinas de Añana
Euskadi
Altotero 1176
Oña
Frias
Embalse de Sobrón
Treviño
Masa
Poza de la Sal
Busto de Bureba
Pancorbo
Miranda de Ebro
Zambrana
Puerto de Páramo de Masa 1050
y León
978
AP68
Briñas
Sta.
Lambastida
Briviesca
AP1
N232
Haro
Monasterio de Rodilla
Cerezo de Riotiron
Casalarreina
Abalos
Laguardia
N623
Briones
Viana
981
Oion
N232
Sotopalacios
Puerto de la Brújula
Río Oca
S. Domingo de la Calzada
Cenicero
Fuenmayor
Logroño
Rubena
Belorado
S. Asensio
Burgos
1078
Villafranca-Montes de Oca
A12
AP68
Nájera
N120
Río Oja
Navarrete
Arlanzón
Monasterio de Suso
A62
Berceo
Ezcaray
Pradoluengo
Monasterio de Yuso
S. Millán de la Cogolla
Leza de Río Leza
Valgañon
1491
MONTES DE OCA
Sarracín
Valdezcaray
Monasterio de Valvanera
Torrecilla en Cameros
S. Millán 2131
Río Iregua
Río Leza
Pineda de la Sierra
S. Lorenzo 2262
Anguiano
Cogollos
SIERRA DE LA DEMANDA
La Rio
Río Najerilla
SIERRA DE CAMERO NUEVO
Cuevas de S. Clemente
Riocavado de la Sierra
Ortigosa
S. Román de Cameros
A1
Canales de la Sierra
Villanueva de Cameros
Laguna de Cameros
S. Millán de Lara
Embalse de Mansilla
N234
Covarrubias
Villoslada del Cameros
Lumbreras
Yanguas
Lerma
Neila
Montenegro de Cameros
Ermita de Lomos de Orios
Río Arlanza
Barbadillo del Mercado
Salas de los Infantes
Laguna Negra de Urbion
Puerto de Piqueras 1710
Santo Domingo de Silos
2228
Quintanar de la Sierra
SIERRA DE URBIÓN
Cebollera 2142
Valdosa 1412
Castrillo de la Reina
N111
PEÑAS DE CERVERA
Palacios de la Sierra
Duruelo de la Sierra
Almarza
1484